W9-ADA-753

This is an authorized facsimile, made from the master copy of the original book.

Out-of-Print Books on Demand is a publishing service of UMI. The program offers xerographic reprints of more than 100,000 books that are no longer in print.

The primary focus is academic and professional resource materials originally published by university presses, academic societies and trade book publishers worldwide.

U·M·I Out-of-Print
Books on Demand

University Microfilms International
A Bell & Howell Information Company
300 N. Zeeb Road, Ann Arbor, Michigan 48106
800-521-0600 OR 313/761-4700

Printed in 1989 by xerographic process
on acid-free paper

The Development of an African Working Class:

Studies in Class Formation and Action

Edited by

RICHARD SANDBROOK
University of Toronto

ROBIN COHEN
University of Birmingham

University of Toronto Press
Toronto and Buffalo

Burgess
HD
8776.5
.D48
1975a

c · 1

© Longman Group Ltd 1975

First published 1975 in
Canada and the United States by
University of Toronto Press
Toronto and Buffalo

ISBN 0–8020–2221–9 (*cloth*)

ISBN 0–8020–6282–2 (*paper*)

All rights reserved. No part of this
publication may be reproduced, stored
in a retrieval system, or transmitted
in any form or by any means, electronic,
mechanical, photocopying, recording, or
otherwise, without the prior permission
of the Copyright owner.

Printed in Great Britain by
Western Printing Services Ltd, Bristol

Acknowledgements

The contributions to this book were, with two exceptions, originally presented to a conference on *Workers, Unions and Development* held at the University of Toronto from 6–8 April 1973. This was a truly international conference in that participants (union officials as well as academics) were drawn not only from Canada, but also from Tanzania, Kenya, Nigeria, South Africa, Holland, the United Kingdom and the United States. The attendance of such an array of expertise was possible only because of the generosity of a number of agencies: the University of Toronto, the Canada Council, the Canadian International Development Agency, the Canadian National Office of the United Steelworkers of America, and the International Studies Programme of the University of Toronto, who sponsored the conference. We wish to thank particularly Professor Harold Nelson, Chairman of the International Studies Programme, without whose encouragement and support this book would never have appeared. While gratefully acknowledging the financial assistance of all the organisations mentioned, we wish to emphasise that none of them bears any responsibility for any views expressed in this volume. The Editors wish to thank Peter Lloyd for his comments on the manuscript. Thanks are also due to the Tanzania Society, Dar es Salaam, for permission to reprint in revised form part of John Iliffe's article which appeared first in *Tanzania Notes and Records*, no. 71.

While this book was being prepared the Editors learnt of the South African Government's restriction and banning of David Hemson, one of our authors, for his activities amongst African workers. It is our fervent hope that this book will have some relevance to the struggle for workers' basic rights that Hemson was directly engaged in.

R.S. and R.C.

Notes
on the Contributors

Richard Sandbrook teaches in the Department of Political Economy in the University of Toronto. After research work in Kenya he published several articles and chapters concerned with Kenya's trade unions. He is author of a book, *Proletarians and African Capitalism: the Kenya Case 1962–70*.

Robin Cohen has taught at the University of Ibadan and now lectures in the Sociology of Development at the University of Birmingham. He has published a book, *Labour and Politics in Nigeria*, and has written mainly on the themes of class development in Africa and trade unions in Nigeria.

Sharon Stichter currently teaches in the Department of Sociology, University of Boston, Massachusetts. Her doctoral work was concerned with the evolution of a working class and trade unionism in Kenya, where she did her research. Her research interests are in the comparative sociology of labour and social stratification in Africa.

John Iliffe obtained his Ph.D. from Cambridge University in 1965 for a thesis on *Tanganyika under German Rule 1905–12*. He then taught history at the University of Dar es Salaam for six years and is now Assistant Director of Research in African History at Cambridge.

Arthur Turner studied at the University of Toronto and carried out his research work in Zambia. He is a doctoral candidate at the University of California (Los Angeles), and is writing a social and administrative history of Kabwe (Broken Hill).

Christopher Allen has held posts at the University of Sierra Leone and Ahmadu Bello University in Nigeria. He is now in the Department of Politics at Edinburgh University. While Research Fellow at Nuffield College, Oxford, he edited (with R. W. Johnson) a tribute to Thomas Hodgkin, *African Perspectives* (1970).

Paul Lubeck was a doctoral candidate at Northwestern University. He was involved in rural development work in Niger and has undertaken research in Ghana and Nigeria. He now teaches sociology at the University of California (Santa Cruz).

Dorothy Remy has recently obtained her doctorate in anthropology from the University of Michigan. She has researched in Kenya and Nigeria and is particularly interested in the experience of women in African societies. After teaching at Brunel University, England, she has taken a position in the Anthropology Department of the University of Maryland.

Ukandi Damachi did his doctoral work at Princeton University and taught at Lincoln University. He is a staff associate at the International Institute for Labor Studies in Geneva. He is author of *The Role of the Trade Unions in the Development Process: With a Case Study of Ghana*, and other forthcoming works.

L. Douwes Dekker is an executive member of an Urban Training Project and an industrial council official; **D. Hemson**, until his banning by the government, was research Officer of the Garment Workers' Union of South Africa; **J. Kane-Berman** is on the editorial staff of the *Financial Mail*, Johannesberg; **Jeffrey Lever** is a lecturer at the University of South Africa; **L. Schlemmer** is Director of the Institute for Social Research, University of Natal, Durban.

M. A. Bienefeld is the author of *Working Hours in British Industry: an Economic History*, a book based on his doctoral work at the London School of Economics. While Research Fellow at Dar es Salaam he has written reports on manpower, construction and housing problems. He is working on a labour force survey of Tanzanian urban areas, and is now attached to the Institute of Development Studies at the University of Sussex.

Richard Jeffries has studied at Cambridge and the University of London, where he has recently completed his doctoral thesis on Ghanaian labour politics. He is Research Fellow in the Department of Politics at the School of African and Oriental Studies.

Adrian Peace was Junior Research Fellow in the School of African and Asian Studies at the University of Sussex from 1969 to 1972. His research on industrial workers was conducted in Ikeja, Nigeria. He is currently lecturer in Anthropology at the University of Adelaide, South Australia.

John S. Saul taught for seven years at the University of Dar es Salaam, Tanzania. He now lives in Canada where he works for the Toronto Committee for the Liberation of Portugal's African Colonies. He is author (with G. Arrighi) of *Essays on the Political Economy of Africa* (1973), and co-editor of *Socialism in Politics and Policies* (1972–73, two volumes) and *Rural Cooperation in Tanzania* (1973).

Contents

Workers and Progressive Change in Underdeveloped Countries   I
  Richard Sandbrook and Robin Cohen

PART ONE Initial Stirrings of Working Class Consciousness

Introduction   *The Editors*   13

The Formation of a Working Class in Kenya   *Sharon Stichter*   21
The Creation of Group Consciousness: a History of the Dockworkers
  of Dar es Salaam   *John Iliffe*   49
The Growth of Railway Unionism in the Rhodesias, 1944–55
  Arthur Turner   73
Union-Party Relationships in Francophone West Africa: a Critique of
  'Téléguidage' Interpretations   *C. H. Allen·*   99

PART TWO Contemporary Working Class Organisation

Introduction   *The Editors*   129

Unions, Workers and Consciousness in Kano, Nigeria: a View from
  Below   *Paul Lubeck*   139
Economic Security and Industrial Unionism: a Nigerian Case Study
  Dorothy Remy   161
The Internal Dynamics of Trade Unions in Ghana   *Ukandi Damachi*   178

PART THREE Contemporary Working Class Action

Introduction   *The Editors*   195

Case Studies in African Labour Action in South Africa, and Namibia
  (South West Africa)   *L. Douwes Dekker, D. Hemson, J. S. Kane-*
  Berman, J. Lever and L. Schlemmer   207
Socialist Development and the Workers in Tanzania   *M. A. Bienefeld*   239
Populist Tendencies in the Ghanaian Trade Union Movement   *Richard*
  D. Jeffries   261
The Lagos Proletariat: Labour Aristocrats or Populist Militants   *Adrian*
  Peace   281
The 'Labour Aristocracy' Thesis Reconsidered   *John S. Saul*   303

CONCLUSION   *The Editors*   311

Select Bibliography   317
Index   325

Workers
and Progressive Change
in Underdeveloped Countries

RICHARD SANDBROOK and ROBIN COHEN

The historical role of the working class has recently been subject to reassessment. Frequently repudiated are the Marxist views that the proletariat constitutes either, as Marx's classic scheme would have it, *the* revolutionary class in capitalist societies, or, as Lenin maintained, the pre-eminent element in a revolutionary alliance with the poorest strata of the peasantry, or, finally, as Mao holds, the leadership cadres needed to mobilise the oppressed peasant masses into revolutionary action. Probably Frantz Fanon has been the most emphatic in dismissing the workers' progressive potential in Africa.[1] For Fanon it is the poor peasants, not the workers, who are the wretched of the earth. The native proletariat, enjoying a privileged and well-remunerated position under colonial (and, by implication, neo-colonial) rule, has everything to lose in a violent struggle for liberation. In contrast, the peasants, having nothing to lose but their impoverishment and retaining a 'stony pride' in the face of all indignities, represent the authentic revolutionary force. It is not only revolutionaries who have downgraded the historical role of the working class. Social scientists such as Clark Kerr and his associates expressed the same sort of scepticism towards the workers in their well-known *Industrialism and Industrial Man* a decade ago.[2] On the basis of a multiplicity of case studies carried out by a team of researchers around the world, they concluded that 'worker protest' is, contrary to their own expectations, a diminishing force as the 'evolution of industrialisation' unfolds. Class conflict involving the workers was on the decline, they argued, because the enlightened self-interest of employers made them amenable to compromise with trade unions, and, more ominously, because the elites have gained more experience in controlling worker protest.[3]

This volume, based mainly on the papers presented at a conference at the University of Toronto in April 1973, seeks to re-evaluate the societal role of

African workers in the light of views such as these. Controversy has long been associated with such reassessments and, true to form, the Toronto conference generated several disputes with distinguished historical antecedents. Once again at issue—but now in the context of African countries—were the efficacy of 'business' as opposed to radical unionism, the existence of a 'labour aristocracy', the proper relationship between leaders and led within the labour movements and the most desirable path toward socialism. Since participants were not selected on the basis of their adherence to any specific political perspective, the diversity of opinion made for lively discussion. Indeed, at times, the ghosts of Lenin, the Mensheviks and even the 'renegade Kautsky' seemed to stalk the hall! But good conferences do not necessarily lead to good books; too often edited volumes constitute merely an assemblage of articles with disparate themes and minimal coherence. What then holds the present collection together?

First, as we have mentioned, the contributors have reopened old debates in a different geographical context—a context where capitalism has either been nurtured in areas hitherto at the periphery of the world system, or, as in South Africa and Namibia, where a Herrenvolk democracy has been superimposed over the relations of capitalist production. So different an order of things requires a different analysis, and several of the contributors have risen to the challenge by providing substantial analytical extensions or modifications to traditional Eurocentric portrayals of the working class. Others again have been content to describe the situationally-specific features of their case studies.

Second, the authors of this volume, though their political convictions span the spectrum from Marxist to liberal, have produced analyses that can, with one or two exceptions, be classified as radical. This term is often taken to be synonymous with 'Marxist', but this is too narrow a denotation. A radical analysis, in general terms, is one which explicitly or implicitly rejects the existing social order and advocates active intervention into society in order to bring about progressive change. Most of the studies in this book are radical in that their authors accept the legitimacy of the interests of the working people they have intensively studied, believe that these interests have been systematically disregarded, and favour certain action by organised workers and others to create a more just society. Of course, once one queries the *nature* of the desirable changes and the *means* of bringing these about, contention emerges. There is the familiar division, for example, between those who maintain that progressive change can be achieved through reform, and those who hold that it can be attained only through revolution.

Our contributors were at least in agreement in identifying a crucial problem area: to what extent have workers in employment in the 'modern' sector been co-opted as partners, albeit junior partners, in the existing social order? The question of whether the better-off, more skilled segment of a working class has been 'bought off' by the existing order was debated even before Lenin railed against the 'narrow-minded, selfish, case-hardened, covetous, petty-bourgeois "labour aristocracy" ' of Western Europe.[4] This question is examined again in the African context in this book, especially in Part Three. While it would be superfluous to review the arguments at this point, we do need to anticipate the main conclusion in order to clarify the conception of the key problem informing most of our studies. Most of the participants at the conference were sceptical of the notion that either the unionised urban workers as a whole, or the skilled and semi-skilled segment of the wage-earning force, could appropriately be conceived as a privileged group *vis-à-vis* the urban sub-proletariat, unemployed, small-scale traders and peasantry. Although the income of the employed head of an urban household might be significantly higher than that of the head of a rural household, for example, this relative advantage is to a greater or lesser extent offset by the larger size of the dependent urban household, the higher cost of living in the towns, and the practice of transferring income from urban to rural households.[5] In addition, the more highly paid unionised workers are usually not separated from the underprivileged urban groups either residentially or socially.

Whatever the differences in living standards between 'modern'-sector workers and other poor groups, the gap in life-style between the workers and the ruling sectors of African societies is far more evident. Anyone who has walked or driven in a third-world city from the affluent suburbs of the business and civil service elites to the decrepit slums of the workers will know who are the real aristocrats. In some African countries, for instance, the ratio between the earnings of the highest-paid and lowest-paid (unskilled) employees of the central government is as much as 38 or 40 to 1.[6] In the Republic of South Africa, the exploitation of black workers is even more striking. Until the recent wage increases, brought about primarily by the pressure of workers themselves, the position of the black gold miners had worsened, relative both to their past real incomes and to the wages paid to white miners. Black cash earnings in 1969 were no higher and possibly even lower in real terms than they had been in 1911, whereas the real cash earnings of white miners increased by 70 per cent over the same period. Moreover, the earning gap ratio between white and black workers, during the same time, increased from 11.7:1 to 20.1:1.[7]

In sum, most of the authors of this book regard the term 'labour aristocracy' as misleading in the African situation. One should assume neither that the 'modern'-sector urban workers constitute a privileged group nor that they have been co-opted by the ruling sectors, thus acting as guarantors of the existing peripheral capitalist system. There are vast income disparities between the political and business classes on the one hand, and the unionised workers on the other, and this economic inequality clearly creates significant differences in life chances between these emergent classes. At the most basic level, the differences are often between being adequately fed or undernourished, between being adequately or inadequately housed and clothed, and between high or low quality medical treatment. Low income also plays an important part in determining the range of educational opportunities for one's children, and hence their job prospects. Since wealth is also a political resource, the better-off usually possess disproportionate political influence as well. Hence, income disparity, as is well known, is a leading factor in producing a range of other inequalities. What all this will mean in terms of political conflict is not yet clear. While grass-roots research indicates that significant numbers of workers perceive their relative deprivation, the extent to which they can adopt a strategy of political confrontation or forge alliances with less privileged groups remains an open question. Certainly in the studies of Sekondi-Takoradi and Lagos included in this book, the authors discovered the emergence of populist sentiments uniting 'modern'-sector workers with the urban sub-proletariat, small-scale traders and others of the urban poor against an elite regarded as corrupt, idle and supercilious. This sort of sporadic confrontation is surely an incipient form of class conflict.

If most of our contributors share a common view of the labour problem, what do they offer by way of a radical solution? Consider first the situation in an area characterised by 'internal colonialism'. One of our case studies is of African labour action in South Africa and Namibia: what role are African working people likely to play here in promoting change toward an egalitarian, non-racist society? As the authors of our study suggest, there are several ways of conceptualising the role of 'labour power' in fomenting progressive change in southern Africa. One of these is the economically deterministic view that advancing industrialisation, with the consequent enlargement of the productive and consumer power of black workers, will necessitate some accommodation to black aspirations on the part of the white ruling class. A second position rejects such a possibility of peaceful, undirected change; liberation for black workers can only come through their realisation of the necessity for revolutionary transformation. A third view, which is adopted by our South African authors, leaves open the question of whether progressive change will be achieved through reform or revolution. Their position, in short, is that, regardless of whether the struggle against apartheid is to be violent or non-violent, the level of black working-class solidarity and consciousness will be important in determining the outcome. Hence, their case studies of recent black strike activity are indispensable in estimating the present extent of such solidarity and consciousness.

Also in this book are several studies of workers' organisation and action in those countries of tropical Africa which have attained political independence. These countries may be distinguished on the basis of the development strategy their governments have adopted: obviously, the appropriate workers' programme for change will depend upon the type of development policy. Two models of such strategies may be discerned—the capitalist and the socialist. The generic features of a capitalist approach are the following: a conception of development as, at least in the short run, maximising production rather than ensuring social equality; a decision that development in this sense can best be stimulated by the prod of material incentives (especially the profit motive) and the associated institutions of private property and the market; a considerable reliance upon foreign capital and expertise to modernise the economy; and the official encouragement of indigenous entrepreneurship in both the rural and urban areas. Studies in this volume which relate to countries following this sort of strategy after independence include Nigeria, Ghana (except perhaps for the period 1961–66), Kenya, Zambia, and the former colonies of French West Africa. The polar, and rarer, type of development policy is the socialist one, characterised by: a conception of development whose prime goal is social equality; a decision that development in this sense as well as economic growth can best be achieved through the use of moral and collective incentives and the associated institutions of socialised property and comprehensive planning; and a tendency to rely less upon foreign capital and expertise and more upon indigenous resources. Among our case studies, Tanzania is the best example of a country pursuing a path close to this model.

How could a working class best enhance the workers' lot and that of other underprivileged strata within the two popular types of evolving political economies? It will come as no surprise to the reader to hear that the split on this question is the familiar one between the Marxists and those of an explicitly or vaguely social democratic orientation. The Marxist position, which is forcefully articulated in several papers, would accept Lenin's view that equality under capitalism can only be 'a fraud and hypocrisy', that 'the exploiters and exploited cannot be equal', and consequently that 'there can be no real equality until all possibility of the exploitation of one class by another has been destroyed'.[8] Since a structural transformation of peripheral capitalist societies is necessary before workers and peasants can liberate themselves, revolutionaries should enter and seek to lead trade unions in order to raise the workers' political consciousness and forge links with the peasantry. The proper role of radical labour leaders, therefore, is primarily to educate workers and build class solidarity rather than bargain with employers and government for incremental gains.

The implications of this position for studies of labour are clear. In countries whose governments are genuinely pursuing a socialist development path, the aim of analysis is to determine whether a working class has developed sufficient awareness of its interests to constitute a solid political base for the progressive leadership. This is basically the purpose of the study in this volume of workers and socialist development in Tanzania. In countries whose regimes have adopted a capitalist development strategy, a Marxist analysis probes the quality and strategy of radical labour leaders and the level of consciousness of organised workers. The aim here is to assess the revolutionary potential in the situation.

There is an obvious objection to this Marxist position at the level of strategy. Many would grant that a socialist revolution is desirable in some oppressive and exploitative societies—even, in a sense, historically 'necessary'—if institutional obstacles to progressive change are to be eliminated. But one should not, as a radical commentator has observed, confound the 'historically possible' with the 'historically necessary'.[9] Regardless of how historically necessary or desirable a socialist revolution may be in the politically independent peripheral capitalist countries of tropical Africa, one is unlikely to occur in the foreseeable future.[10] If such a revolution is a long way off, what should be the proper role of labour leaders and trade unions? Should not the appropriate strategy be to work *within* the existing system to win as many piecemeal reforms for working people as possible? The revolution may (or may not) occur in the future, but people have aspirations now. But if one accepts this point, then one has also to accept the legitimacy of research aimed at discovering how unions can more effectively bargain with employers and pressure governments within the existing political economy. Of course, as Lenin well knew, militant economism, to the extent that it succeeds in ameliorating the lot of workers, may have the unintended consequence of vitiating the workers' revolutionary impulse and propping up the capitalist system. This is the dilemma facing radical labour leaders in a situation where revolutionary conditions have not yet matured.

The social democrats at the conference were more willing to accept the capitalist political economy as given in the short run (though committed to socialism in the long run), and to inquire how workers could benefit more from this economic system. They advocated progressive labour policies, such as minimum wage laws, social security and supplementary benefits legislation, policies to restrain prices, low income housing policies, and less restrictive collective bargaining and trade union legislation. The problem then becomes: how can labour organise to apply pressure most effectively to recalcitrant governments and employers? The obvious objection to this perspective is that it is naïve to expect regimes with a vested interest in an inegalitarian *status quo* to accept and implement pro-labour policies—unless forced to do so. Policies aimed at rent control, for example, will often hurt a group—slum landlords—with a great deal of political influence. In any event, Marxists will rightly point out that any compromises worked out will have the effect of reinforcing the capitalist system by blunting the development of revolutionary consciousness. Hence, for these analysts, economism and co-operation with reactionary governments are to be avoided so that progressive change can later be brought about.

This attempt to draw out some of the critical assumptions underpinning the later studies has revealed a basic disagreement over strategy, a disagreement with long historical roots. Yet the various contributions do share enough common ground to warrant their inclusion in the same book. There is general agreement on the proposition that whatever distributive justice will be won by workers—whether through incremental or structural change, reform or revolution—will be a consequence of the collective action of the underprivileged *vis-à-vis* the ruling elite, external estate and property-owning classes. These studies place little faith in the benevolence of the ruling groups to develop their societies in the absence of organised pressure from below. Here once again we return to the characterisation of most of the contributors as radical in the generic sense. This viewpoint stands in contrast to the perspective inherent in most models of political development; these are generally conservative in that they adopt the point of view of the governing elites of 'developing countries', who are presumed to be genuinely committed to 'development'. There is, as one writer has argued, a tendency for some political development theorists to reformulate the first question of politics.

> Instead of 'what is the good society and how may it be achieved?' the question becomes, 'what is the stable society?' Order is not considered a prerequisite for achieving the highest political good, but itself becomes the highest political good.[11]

In this book, however, political order is only a secondary goal. While our contributors may disagree on the precise nature of the good society and the proper strategy for achieving it, they nonetheless agree that the working class and other underprivileged classes will play an active role in the process of creating it. This consensus is indeed the rationale for the book.

Our aim is to probe the extent to which a working class has formed in various parts of Africa. There are, as Marx, Lenin and others have noted, degrees of class cohesion. Teodor Shanin, in his excellent study of the peasantry as a political factor, has contended that the peasantry, for a number of well-known reasons, evinces a 'low classness'.[12] Urban workers, on the other hand, are in a better position to develop a 'high classness'—owing to their concentration in large numbers, the ease of communications, and the need to co-operate in production. It is perhaps useful to identify three levels of class consciousness. The most elementary form requires simply the acceptance by a group of workers of their common identity based on similar roles in the production process. A more developed consciousness includes a recognition that workers have common economic interests as a class which need to be protected through collective organisation against the opposing claims of other classes. Historically, workers have spontaneously attained this 'trade-union consciousness' without the leadership of outside intellectuals or socialist parties.[13] The highest level of consciousness, normally never attained, includes a further conviction that there is an irreconcilable antagonism between capital and labour, and that the interests of working people can only be achieved if the capitalist system is replaced by an alternative socialist system. While incremental change is associated with the first two levels of consciousness, the last form is obviously a thoroughly political consciousness often associated with sporadic or continual violence involving the workers.

This volume brings together studies on working-class formation and action by researchers who have recently conducted extensive field work. Unlike any previous volume on contemporary labour problems in Africa, the authors base their contributions either on a detailed consideration of primary historical sources, or on first-hand experience and observation of the contemporary scene. The studies in Part One examine the initial stirrings of working-class consciousness, and emphasise both that collective action on the part of workers predates the formal organisation of trade unions after the Second World War, and that unions in colonial Africa were seldom merely the appendages of nationalist parties. Part Two contains papers focusing upon the difficulties in organising and operating African unions in the contemporary period. To what extent do these unions express class solidarity and represent the aspirations of their memberships? The final part of the book is devoted to studies of the extent and nature of workers' protest in the present era, ending with a discussion of the potential of African workers as a revolutionary class. Each of the three Parts begins with a brief introduction by the Editors. The aim of these is not only to introduce and tie together the papers, but also to synthesise the available information and ideas on the various topics and to suggest hypotheses for further research in this curiously neglected field.

NOTES

1. F. Fanon, *The Wretched of the Earth*, Penguin, 1963, pp. 86, 101.
2. C. Kerr, J. T. Dunlop, F. H. Harbison and C. H. Myers, *Industrialism and Industrial Man: The Problems of Labour and Management in Economic Growth*, 2nd edn., Oxford University Press, 1964, pp. 187, 190.

3. For a more extended discussion of these ideas, see R. Sandbrook, 'The Working Class in the Future of the Third World', *World Politics*, 15 (3), 1973, pp. 448–50.

4. V. I. Lenin, ' "Left-Wing" Communism, an Infantile Disorder', in *Lenin on Politics and Revolution*, ed. James E. Connor, Pegasus, 1968, p. 295.

5. For an excellent survey of comparative incomes earned by workers and farmers in Black Africa, see C. Allen, 'Unions, Incomes and Development', in *Developmental Trends in Kenya*, Proceedings of a Seminar held in the Centre of African Studies, University of Edinburgh, 28–29 April, 1972, pp. 61–92.

6. See, for example, Kenya, *Report of the Commission of Inquiry (Public Service Structure and Remuneration Commission, 1970–71)*, Nairboi, Government Printer, 1971, para. 85; and Ghana, *Report of the Commission on the Structure, and Remuneration of the Public Services in Ghana*, Accra, Government Printer 1967, p. 41.

7. F. Wilson, *Labour in the South African Gold Mines, 1911–69*, Cambridge University Press, 1972, p. 46.

8. V. I. Lenin, *The Proletarian Revolution and Renegade Kautsky*, International Publishers, 1934, p. 34.

9. R. Murray, 'Second Thoughts on Ghana', *New Left Review*, 42, March–April 1967, p. 39.

10. See *ibid.* for a discussion of this theme in the Ghanaian context.

11. M. Kesselman, 'Order or Movement? The Literature of Political Development as Ideology', *World Politics*, 16 (1), 1973, p. 142.

12. T. Shanin, 'The Peasantry as a Political Factor', *Sociological Review*, 14, 1966, pp. 5–27.

13. See, for instance, E. P. Thompson, *The Making of the English Working Class*, Penguin, 1968, especially ch. 16 on class consciousness.

PART ONE

Initial Stirrings
of Working Class
Consciousness

Introduction

The creation of a wage-labour force in Africa is essentially a product of white settlement and the establishment of European colonial administrations. Yet, it is perhaps worth remembering that the expropriation of labour-power had also been widespread in indigenous societies. Various forms of chattel and domestic slavery existed in many pre-colonial states, customary family labour was common, while groups of workers, like the *aro* age groups of Yorubaland or the *ankofone* of Sierra Leone, engaged in house building or heavy farming on a basically contractual basis.[1] With the introduction of a stable and pervasive cash economy large movements of migrant labour took place in East Africa, among groundnut farmers in Senegal and the Gambia, and elsewhere. Piecework payments often applied to migrant labour of this kind, while in the Ivory Coast and Ghana a system of share-cropping (*abusa*) developed.[2] Within pre-colonial cities, craft traditions and guilds were well-established, most of which involved the use of apprentice labour. Lastly, in Liberia the Americo-Liberian settlers (often, ironically, agricultural labourers in origin themselves) used 'apprentices' as cheap farm labour. In 1887 it was estimated that every Americo-Liberian had 6–8 apprentices while the President of the Republic alone had 120 youths in service. Charges that forced labour and slavery continued to exist in Liberia persisted in the late 1920s when an International Commission of Enquiry found that this was indeed the case.[3]

Not that the Europeans had clean hands in this respect either. Forced labour was an accepted and widely practised part of the policies of the colonial powers, necessary, it was said, to 'persuade' Africans to accept the work ethic. Heinous labour policies were justified by reference to such a notion, probably the most brutal of which were put into effect in German South West Africa, in Oubangi-Shari and in the Congo Free State. According to King Leopold of Belgium, the policy of forcing Congolese to collect rubber for him would only be changed 'when the Negro has generally shaken off his idleness and becomes ready to work for the love of wages alone'. Similar statements were made by Lord Lugard and other bearers of the 'civilising mission'. The French for their part legalised and widely used forced labour until 1946 when *prestation*, a labour tax which allowed the Administration to compel all adult males to work for a number of days each year, was finally abolished.[4]

African labour was apparently not forthcoming in the numbers and with the qualities that the Europeans desired. Labour was needed in four main areas. Firstly, in South Africa, the Rhodesias and Kenya white settlers needed farm labourers. Dispossession and conquest had helped to create a landless group of labourers, who in exchange for squatting rights (themselves often precarious) could be used for heavy manual work. But the reserve army of labour was apparently not enough to satisfy the European demand, for Indian workers were imported on a large scale to work on the sugar plantations in Natal. Secondly, labour was needed in the extractive industries—to disembowel the earth of its tin, iron ore, gold and diamonds. Here the unappealing nature of this dangerous and enervating work resulted in the extensive use of contract labour. Thirdly, labour was required on public works programmes—to build roads and railways and improve or develop port facilities. Though public in name, such programmes were tied closely to the needs of the administration or of European industry, which may explain why pliant chiefs who connived with district officers to use traditional communal labour on government works are so frequently figures of abuse in African oral literature. Finally, governments needed substantial manpower to maintain the *pax colonica*—soldiers, policemen, junior clerks, court stenographers, sanitary inspectors, right down to messengers and grass cutters for the European quarters.

While many Africans aspired to jobs in the colonial civil service, other forms of wage labour were, not unsurprisingly, less popular. Early colonial reports were full of complaints about the unwillingness of Africans to engage in wage labour and several schemes were either contemplated or undertaken to introduce labour from outside the continent. The Indians were the largest group of imported workers, but Chinese constituted 27 per cent of the labour force in the South African gold mines in 1905 and small groups of workers from the Caribbean were also contracted, particularly for work on the railways. Neither forced labour nor recruitment from Asia could, however, meet the demand for labour in the long term. Africans therefore had to be 'induced' to sell their labourpower. The imposition of hut or poll taxes was the major method employed to this end. Despite the plea by some 'progressive' labour administrators that 'natural' motives like the desire for 'novelties' could be stimulated by better wages and conditions of service and that these provided a surer incentive to work,[5] wages remained low until the Second World War. Virtually from its inception, government unskilled labour in West Africa was remunerated at about 9d. a day, a situation that remained unchanged in Nigeria until 1937. In South Africa the cost of labour in agriculture and mining was notoriously low, a situation that changed little for eighty years.[6] Nonetheless the problems of labour recruitment all but disappeared in the 1930s. As Elliot Berg convincingly argues:

> The depression of the early 1930's marked the turning point. It radically changed conditions in the labor market; with the prices of primary products sinking to new lows, the volume of wage employment contracted sharply. Perhaps for the first time in most African countries, there were more men offering themselves for wage employment than there were jobs to be had.[7]

Through a combination, then, of the disruption of the indigenous economies, the forcing of Africans to pay taxes, the opening up of economic opportunities, and finally, changed conditions in the labour market, a relatively stable wage and salary-earning force emerged in nearly all colonial territories. But what was the consciousness of this new social category? This labour force was formed in conditions that were, of course, vastly different from those that obtained during the emergence of the European proletariat. One obvious difference in conditions was, as Sharon Stichter argues in her article, that African societies were incorporated into an international economy as peripheral appendages to industrialised societies. One would expect such differences to lead to a distinctive African working class identity and set of institutions, especially trade unions. Are any distinctive features discernible?

Most writers have been content to approach this issue by focusing on the conflict of loyalties between those forms of identity based on older forms of social organisation and those that were peculiar to the new occupations that the labour force engaged in. 'Migrants and Proletarians', 'Townsmen or Tribesmen', 'Modern Industry and the African'—the very titles of these studies suggest the subject of concern. The sociologists and social anthropologists working on the Copperbelt developed perhaps the most systematic and sensitive attempts to plot the conflicting pulls of tribe and class. In general terms these writers developed 'alternation models' of social change whereby a class or tribal identity was activated in appropriate circumstances. The workers' identity was thought to be situationally specific with selectivity taking place as various 'social fields' were encountered and different 'social networks' activated.[8] While there can be no doubt that studies of this kind provided a new vocabulary to comprehend the plurality of the social and cultural worlds through which urban Africans moved, alternation theories do tend towards an ahistorical position—that is, they do not demand a stance on such a fundamental question as 'When, and in what measure, has working class formation and proletarianisation occurred?'

Sharon Stichter ,whose article follows, agrees with the view that movement into and out of the working class category was at first quite common, but maintains that class crystallisation (and the related phenomena of class conscious-ness and class related collective action) takes place as working class membership becomes more nearly a life situation for the worker. In Kenya, at any rate, Stichter argues that class formation occurred in three stages. First, Africans resisted, on a 'communal' religious or individual basis, colonial labour policies and their incorporation into a colonial political economy. Secondly, 'societal' modes of protest by semi-proletarianised workers took place on an individual or collective basis *within* the capitalist economy. Finally, a more fully proletarianised urban group of African workers (the Indian segment of the working class re-mained separate) was able to initiate strike action or organise on a wider scale.

It is perhaps doubtful whether such an evolutionary pattern of increased class crystallisation can be sustained in all African countries and indeed Stichter recognises that even in her own case study of Kenya such solidarity as was achieved was based on *both* a racial and class consciousness. Analytically, how-ever, her argument does shift the locus of the problem from a discussion centred on the notion of competing social identities, to one which centres on the work force itself—the problems that it encountered and the attempts that workers have historically made to change their reality through organisation, strike action and other protests.

In fact we are only now beginning to write the labour history of Africa—not simply in terms of the self-interested concerns of white supremacists and colonial governments about labour supply, the cost of labour and the workers' productivity—but rather in terms of a worker-directed perspective of a social aggregate groping for group expression and class action. As new evidence comes to light, more and more cases appear of independent trade union organisa-tion and strike action undertaken without the help of external influences and flowing directly from the perceived injustices and inequalities of the work relationship. Several recent studies have documented the expressions of early discontent and strike action among African workers,[9] and the two studies included in this volume, by John Iliffe and Arthur Turner, make a substantial contribution to this area.

John Iliffe's discussion of group consciousness among Dar es Salaam dock-workers leads him to locate the history of the labour movement not in studies of organisation 'from the top' but in the history of work and its changing character. Industrialisation or a colonial economy, he argues, creates only *workers*. What he is concerned with is the process whereby workers become agents in the creation of group solidarity, consciousness and action in response to their common status. He cites with approval E. P. Thompson's view that 'The working class made itself as much as it was made', but strikes a cautious note in arguing that his study is concerned only with an earlier stage in the labour history of Tanganyika—the creation of group consciousness among dockers rather than a more generalised form of class consciousness.

Dockers and railwaymen were in fact often at the forefront of labour protest in the colonial period and it is with the second of these groups that Arthur Turner is concerned in his study of railway unionism in Northern Rhodesia (now Zambia) and Southern Rhodesia. The railwaymen's occupational bonds, social contiguity and easy lines of communications along the track provided a basis for an industrial union. In the major strikes that ensued the railwaymen successfully resisted the hostility of railway officials and the employers' attempt to sponsor a tame company union. At the same time the fact that Rhodesian railway workers did not interact closely with other urban Africans evidently meant that the union remained a cohesive force only when it concentrated on its industrial objectives. When external political pressures intervened, the major union was unable to contain factionalism and personal rivalry.

'External pressures' meant in this context the activity of nationalist parties, and Turner is categorical in maintaining that the development of the railway unions in the Rhodesias after the Second World War was not inspired by, used by, or directed by, African nationalist parties. Although the period John Iliffe is researching is much earlier, he too makes the point that the activity and organisation of dockers took place without the stimulus of nationalist politics. A description of the high degree of autonomous activity and protest undertaken by workers in most African countries is a theme that links all four contributions to Part One of this book.

Though obviously worker initiatives did not take place in a political vacuum, they did frequently occur independently of formal links to political parties and nationalist movements and without the benevolent guidance of French trade union centres or colonial labour advisers, which influences have sometimes been regarded as the precipitators or, even more invalidly, the creators of trade union activity. Christopher Allen's discussion of the 1947 railway strike in Senegal[10] and his more general description of labour organisation in French West Africa lead him to reject the manipulative view that unions were puppets or pupils of political parties. By paying close attention to primary data from contemporary observers and participants, Allen is able to portray the full extent of rank and

file initiatives and show how erroneous is the element of *téléguidage* in received
views.

As well as providing vital data for understanding how the process of class
formation begins, the emphasis our authors have laid on worker pressures
'from below' also contrasts strongly with the almost obsessive concern with
trade union/nationalist party relationships that pervaded much of the literature
on Africans unions and workers in the 1960s.[11] Christopher Allen directly
addresses himself to Berg and Butler's well-known and controversial survey of
the literature on unions and politics in Africa, which is centrally concerned with
the party/union relationship, but it may be worthwhile making a few general
points on this theme here. Berg and Butler operated at root with the assumption
that the political role of labour could only meaningfully be established once a
virtually umbilical link with a nationalist party was proved. To be fair, it should
be pointed out that Berg and Butler also acknowledged that the political impact
of a labour movement may be judged by other criteria, including the 'extent
and effectiveness of union participation in strikes, demonstrations and other
activities in support of political goals'.[12] Such criteria are, however, never convincingly employed in their presentation; they tend to make casual judgements
about the objectives of strike actions being 'essentially economic' and not
political 'in the proper sense of the word'. They dismiss also individual political
strikes as being 'not notably successful' whose political impact is still a matter
of controversy. Moreover, as Allen argues in this volume, Berg and Butler's
retrospective definitions of strikes being primarily 'economist' in motivation
are largely irrelevant, as they became 'political' in terms both of their long-run
effects and their interpretation by others.

However, within the limits imposed by Berg and Butler's aforementioned
assumption, their views on the colonial period carry a good deal of weight.
Only in Kenya and Guinea, so they argue, did an intimate union-party relationship exist. In Nigeria, the collaboration between the TUC and NCNC effectively ended in 1950; in the Gold Coast, after the strike called by the TUC in
1950 in support of the CPP's positive action campaign, a significant part of the
union movement tried to preserve trade union independence from the party.
In the French Cameroons, while 'highly ideological', the union movement was
hostile to the claims of the major nationalist party. In other parts of French West
Africa, despite a series of informal party-union pacts and in some cases an inter-
locking leadership, apparently '. . . the pattern of union-party relations failed
to develop along clear-cut lines of alliance and collaboration.' Let us ignore some
of the careful qualifications—like 'one segment of the labor movement threw
itself vigorously into political activity' (Nigeria), 'in the beginning informal ties
were close' (Zambia) or 'the growing labor movement and the growing nation-

alist movement at first entertained friendly relations with each other' (Southern Rhodesia)—and accept their major thesis: union-party relationships were often intermittent and sometimes non-existent before independence.

But this refutation of what they see as a well-worn orthodoxy, though essentially accurate, is itself of quite limited import. It is, firstly, by no means an obvious proposition that a lack of constant cooperation is evidence either of political apathy or political impotence; on the contrary, it may attest to a degree of political sophistication. For the unions to stand consistently shoulder to shoulder with parties deriving their power base from traditional rulers or from members of the aspirant political class was tantamount to giving up any claim to represent the working class. Many unionists were also conscious of the need to preserve a power base independent of the nationalist movement, even when they were in accord about common anti-colonialist objectives.

A second, and perhaps more far-reaching, objection to their analysis is that action undertaken by workers in defence of their class interests can have significant political implications even where nationalist parties are ineffective, proscribed, have ceased to exist or exist only in exile. Evidence for the assertion can be found, for instance, in the early years of the Emergency in Kenya where even the conservatively-led Kenya Federation of Labour gained some brief moments of political glory.

To look at overt links with nationalist parties and to confine labour's political role to that relationship expresses, in short, a very narrow outlook. In the later sections of this book, our authors show that the 'politics of labour' can include the opening up of a significant challenge to white supremacy (in South Africa) by black strikers in the absence of any nationalist party on the ground, the defence of local interests against the government, and the alliances that organised labour can forge with populist elements in the community at large. As far as the contributions in Part One are concerned, the authors have in general played down the issue of structural or institutional links between unions and political parties. Instead, they have sought to evaluate the social and political role of workers by placing a far greater emphasis on the day-to-day realities of African workers' lives, mapping out their social landscape, their relationship with other elements in the social structure and developments at the level of grass-roots unionism.

From the point of view of a theorist interested in the process of class formation, the precise character and possible long-range significance of the phenomenon of intermittent class action needs further explication. In particular, how valid would it be to regard the various instances of collective action by workers documented by our authors, as steps along a difficult road towards more complex, higher and more pervasive levels of class consciousness? To what extent, on the other hand, were these actions so contingent on particular historical circumstances, that their long-term effects on the development of a working-class identity are limited or negligible? Comparative research on other territories can no doubt illumine this issue. But the papers in this section represent, at the very least, a determined effort to open up the labour history of the continent, and to begin, from a non-elitist perspective, to draw the lines of social differentiation and political change in the colonial period.

NOTES

1. International Labour Office, *African Labour Survey*, Geneva, 1962, pp. 65–6.
2. P. Hill, *The Gold Coast Farmer*, Oxford University Press, 1956, pp. 8–24.
3. M. B. Akpan, *The African Policy of the Liberian Settlers 1841–1932: A Study in the Native Policy of a Non-Colonial Power in Africa*, Ph.D. thesis, Ibadan, 1968, pp. 158–9; and United States Government, *Report of the International Commission of Enquiry into the Existence of Slavery and Forced Labour in the Republic of Liberia*, Washington, Printing Office, 1931.
4. I. Davies, *African Trade Unions*, Penguin, 1966, pp. 33–5.
5. G. St. J. Orde Browne, *The African Labourer*, Frank Cass and Co., 1967, pp. 30–1.
6. S. Trapido, 'South Africa in a Comparative Study of Industrialisation', *Journal of Development Studies*, 7 (3), 1971, pp. 309–20.
7. E. J. Berg, 'The Development of a Labour Force in Sub-Saharan Africa', *Economic Development and Cultural Change*, 13, 1965, p. 412.
8. See most notably A. L. Epstein, *Politics in an Urban African Community*, Manchester University Press, 1958.
9. See A. G. Hopkins, 'The Lagos Strike of 1897: An Exploration in Nigerian Labour History', *Past and Present*, 35, 1966; H. F. Conway, 'Labour Protest Activity in Sierra Leone', *Labour History*, 15, 1968, pp. 49–63 and A. Hughes and R. Cohen, *Towards the Emergence of a Nigerian Working Class: The Social Identity of the Lagos Labour Force 1879–1939*, Occasional Paper, Faculty of Commerce and Social Science, University of Birmingham, Series D, 7, 1971.
10. For an evocative fictional recreation of the 1947 strike, see S. Ousmane, *God's Bits of Wood*, Heinemann Educational Books, 1970.
11. See for examples, I. Davies, *op. cit.*; J. Meynaud and A. Salah Bey, *Trade Unionism in Africa*, Methuen, 1967, and E. J. Berg and J. Butler, 'Trade Unions' in *Political Parties and National Integration in Tropical Africa*, eds. J. S. Coleman and C. G. Rosberg, University of California Press, 1964.
12. *Ibid.*, p. 361.

The
Formation of a
Working Class in Kenya

SHARON STICHTER

In the former colonial societies of the Third World a distinctive peripheral
capitalism was created between the fifteenth and nineteenth centuries by the
extension of market relationships from the industrialised centres. Peripheral
societies were incorporated into the international economy as exporters of raw
material and mineral commodities and became, essentially, dependent appendages to industrialised societies.[1] The extension of capitalism to Third World
political economies necessitated the creation of a Third World working class.
Whether the life situation and social context of this class is similar to or different
from that of the working class created in Western Europe during the early
nineteenth century is clearly a question of some interest.

In the case of Africa, three broad positions may be distinguished. First, there
are those who argue that it is as yet premature to apply a class terminology to
the wage-earner (or other social groups). It is thought that economic differentiation is not far enough advanced, and that status and prestige lines are frequently
based on factors extraneous to the relationship between capital and labour.[2]
Second, some authors maintain that principally because of his migrant character
and ties to the land, the African worker is so different from his equivalent in
industrialised societies that comparisons are misleading, if not impossible.[3]
Third, there are those, usually of an orthodox Marxist persuasion, who tend to see the
evolution of the African working class as similar to that of the proletariat in
other capitalist societies.[4] The first and second views, as I will argue, may easily
fail to appreciate some universal features of working class formation that have
already occurred, or which can be expected to take place, in response to capitalist
development anywhere.

The third view, however, must be qualified by taking note of the special
features which differentiate the working class in a peripheral society from that

in a metropolitan one. For example, the working class in African societies is still a relatively small part of the total population. A segment of the class remains migrant or semi-proletarianised, gaining part of its living from production on the land. Members of the working class usually maintain close social ties with the rural areas. What is equally important, however, is that the labour movement has evolved within a different class context in peripheral societies. In Africa the upper bourgeoisie and owners of capital have always been largely foreign, though the state, formerly controlled by foreign colonisers, is now in the hands of the local administrative bourgeoisie. Thus, in the colonial period, foreign-local conflicts (racial conflicts, the nationalist movement) were intrinsic to the working class struggle. In the post-colonial era, varying patterns of relationship between labour, the state, and foreign capital are only beginning to emerge.

These considerations suggest that capitalism on the periphery breeds a distinctive proletariat within a distinctive peripheral social context. The present essay provides an example of this process, in which African wage-earners, created by the growth of peripheral capitalism in Kenya in the first half of the twentieth century, evolved forms of class action that were in some ways similar to and in some ways different from those evolved by the Western European working class. The essay sketches the structural underpinnings of working class formation in Kenya between 1895 and 1947, the emergence of class consciousness as expressed in movements of political-economic protest, and the way in which these indigenously evolved forms of class protest were limited by the racial divisions in colonial society. It is in the slow pace and partial character of proletarianisation, and the effect of racial divisions, that the pattern of African labour evolution differed most from the pattern prevalent in Western Europe before the Industrial Revolution. It is in the forms of labour protest and the phases of their development that it is most similar.

Conceptually, the notion of class is used in both a structural sense, to refer to a social category defined by its relation to the various means of production or of administration, and in a social sense, to refer to class-related consciousness and action, especially political-economic action on the individual and collective levels. Structurally, the working class is defined as those who have no access to, or do not make use of their access to, productive means, but who instead sell their labour-power for a wage on the market. In Africa, individual movement into and out of the working class category was at first very great,[5] since workers were only partially proletarianised. Class formation in this situation centres on the process of class crystallisation, in which working class membership gradually becomes more nearly a life situation for the worker. This development provides the precondition for class formation in its fullest sense, the emergence over time of class consciousness and class related collective action.

Early class formation in Kenya may be divided into three stages, which result from structural changes in the largely African labour force arising from changes in the colonial political economy. The stages are defined by the resultant qualitative changes in the form of the African labour movement. First, tribal or religiously-based movements gave way to class-based movements, a change which was simultaneously a change from 'communal' to 'societal' movements.[6] Second, class-based movements themselves evolved from individual 'mass' movements to collective ones of various forms and increasingly larger size.[7] These changes were accompanied by changes in the content of protest from generalised protests against wage labour to within-system protests, which were initially specific but gradually became more general. Thus, there was a gradual rise in the militancy of protests.

In Stage I, 1895–1919, state-initiated labour creating policies provoked among Africans widespread negative reaction of a tribal, religious, or individual sort. In Stage II, 1920–39, a class of semi-proletarianised African workers evolved individual and collective modes of protest within the capitalist economy. In Stage III, 1939–47, a more fully proletarianised urban African working class escalated strike action and formed a general workers' union, while various groups of skilled workers formed occupational associations. These indigenous African developments remained largely separate from labour organising among the small but skilled and privileged Indian segment of the working class. The racial structure of colonial society thus posed a limitation to the emergence of a fully class-wide labour movement, a limitation which could not be overcome in the peripheral context.

Stage I: 1895–1919

Proletarianisation, or class formation in the structural sense, began in the first decades of colonial rule. Most fundamentally, proletarianisation refers to the increasingly 'necessary' character of African participation in the labour market, and hence to the closing off over time of available alternative means of getting a livelihood. Measures of proletarianisation in this sense include the extent to which Africans' traditional means of production (land) were expropriated, the extent to which state-initiated mechanisms such as forced labour and administrative pressure made wage-working mandatory for Africans, and the degree to which the income derivable from peasant production was in various ways reduced. 'Proletarianisation' may also refer simply to the increasing numbers of Africans taking up wage earning, the length of time spent in employment ('stabilisation'), and the percentage of total income derived from wages, without regard to whether such participation in the labour market is from 'choice' or from necessity. The degree and extent of proletarianisation in both senses in the settler territories of colonial Africa distinguishes these areas from non-settler ones. But such expropriation in Kenya at least was still not as complete or as widespread as that experienced by workers in metropolitan societies during industrial development. Nonetheless, it was a major social transformation.[8]

In developing a settler-type colonial political economy, the Kenya government undertook a number of direct and compulsory labour-creating measures. Taxation began in 1901 and gradually extended over the whole territory. It imposed an economic burden on Africans, payable in cash. Selling food for cash, instead of labour-power, was circumscribed by the partial expropriation of African lands by European settlers, and by legal restrictions on the growing of cash crops by Africans. To these regulations were added compulsory labour laws, used in particular to provide porters for government officials and labour for work on roads and railways, and—perhaps most important—indirect compulsory labour through administrative pressure.[9] Under the latter system, chiefs were usually simply informed that a certain number of labourers was needed, and were required to produce them. Considerable amounts of force, by both chiefs and by paid private labour recruiters, were used. The foregoing measures, together with the activities of labour recruiters plus some creation of new wants through the expansion of Asian and Arab mercantile capitalism, seem to have been the main factors accounting for African participation in the labour market before and during the First World War.

State intervention into the labour market was necessary because the demand for labour greatly exceeded the voluntary supply. The building of the railway to Uganda between 1895 and 1901 and afterwards, and the influx of white settlers beginning in 1903, engendered a large demand for labour, which, in the case of the railway, was met by the importation of Indian coolies. Such African voluntary supply as was available in these early years[10] is traceable to (1) some commercial penetration by Arabs and Swahili; (2) a small amount of seasonal under-employment in the subsistence economies of the Kikuyu, coastal, Nyanza and other tribes; and (3) periodic drought and famine in these tribes. To create a larger supply the free market solution of raising wages was not employed. Under colonial conditions forceful state intervention was the preferred solution.

Nor did taxation alone suffice to create an adequate supply, for, faced with demands for cash payments, most Africans preferred to sell traditional or newly introduced crops and livestock rather than work for wages. Hence, the additional labour-creating measures were required.

Forceful proletarianisation provoked widespread negative reaction among

Africans. In the circumstances, this reaction was bound up with reaction against the establishment of colonial rule *per se*. Tribal risings, early millenarian movements, and opposition to taxation and land expropriation, all expressed a rejection both of the imposed political-economic order, and of the African's status as a wage earner within it. Resistance to labour recruitment and high rates of desertion from employment are even more clearly rejections of wage labour and attempts to escape proletarianisation.

The link between opposition to colonial administration, to land expropriation, and to wage labour is well illustrated by the case of the Giriama Rising of 1913–1914. In the government's scheme of development for the coastal area of Kenya, the Giriama and other tribes were to provide labour for European and Arab sisal, cotton, rice and coconut plantations. Other local tribes, the Digo and Duruma, did provide such labour, partly in conformity with their traditional status as slaves or semi-slaves to Arabs. The Giriama, however, refused to be coerced into this pattern. The first D.C. of the area related that:

> In the latter part of 1912 there was considerable shortage of food in Giriama and it was thought that a vigorous collection of hut tax would result in an exodus of young men to the coast plantations in search of work . . . At the same time the elders were continually being exhorted to encourage their young men to seek money by work and the objects of labour and the terms offered were repeatedly explained to them. Tax money was however obtained by loans and sale of goats or payment was evaded by the simple process of temporarily absconding. So dilatory was the payment that the collection had to be continued after the expiration of the financial year. The scheme had failed signally.[11]

When, as a result, the Giriama were forcibly moved to a smaller land unit, they rose in revolt. The uprising was finally crushed in September 1914, after some 400 Giriama had been killed.

Among other tribes, initial opposition to taxation was less marked. But among the Kikuyu, the introduction of the Poll Tax in 1910, specifically designed to increase the labour supply by taxing young men without wives, was strongly opposed. The young men were reported to be on the verge of rebellion,[12] and the elders also opposed it, complaining that 'Europeans want our men to work for them for such long periods of time, they cannot help their families in the Reserve.'[13] Kikuyu opposition to land expropriation must also be seen in the context of reaction against increased proletarianisation, its inevitable result.

Tribal or communally based opposition to wage labour also took another, less direct form: millenarian religious movements. The most important such movement in Kenya is the Cult of Mumbo, which began its spread through

Nyanza Province during the time of widespread recruitment for the Carrier Corps in the First World War. Among the Gusii, where the cult was strongest, such recruiting was their first exposure to labour demands on a large scale.[14] Cult members believed that those who followed the God Mumbo would live forever in plenty; their crops would grow of themselves and there would be no more need to work. All Europeans would disappear from the country in a millennial cataclysm. In preparation for the millennium some Mumboites not only stopped cultivating farms and killed off their cattle, but also on occasion refused to do road work and other compulsory labour for the administration, and refused to pay more than Rs. 3/- tax.[15] A few refused to be recruited into the Carrier Corps.[16] By way of retaliation administrators in Gusii often punished Mumboites by sending them out to work.

Among the Kamba, there was a similar millenarian movement in 1912, put down by a military patrol. The religious 'unrest' was the climax of a period of direct opposition to labour recruitment. A semi-pastoral tribe, rich in cattle and goats but subject to periodic drought and famine, the Kamba initially refused to do agricultural work for nearby settlers, even during the food shortage of 1909. They also refused work on road building, or as porters. In the D.C.'s words, 'This labour can scarcely be called voluntary, and the most that can be done is to reduce coercion to a minimum.[17] Official and private recruiting among the Kamba had often to resort to force: for example, the women were 'in many cases brought into the recruiting camp to await substitution by their male relatives.'[18] In the years after the religious unrest, the Kamba were gradually drawn into the labour market, largely as skilled workmen and drivers.

Numerous instances, from each of the major tribes, of individual and small group resistance to labour recruitment could be cited. It is difficult, however, to estimate the extent of this kind of protest. Once recruited, the African's chief mode of protest was 'desertion'. Under the Masters and Servants Ordinance introduced in 1910, 'desertion' from employment, even from employment under the usual 30-day 'ticket' contract, was a criminal offence. Even so, high rates of desertion plagued employers throughout the early years. A 1907 report from Nyanza Province indicated that Baluhya from the Elgon District working on the railway were 'extremely apt to throw down their tools and run away on the smallest pretext.'[19] Another report from the Kikuyu area complained that 'no man can run a farm with monthly relays of raw natives: labour of this kind is always capricious and liable to desert'.[20] In 1909 the small Labour Office in Nairobi received 48 complaints from employers, 31 of them reports of desertions.[21]

The semi-proletarianisation of Kenya's Africans was well under way by the end of the First World War. By 1923 an official estimate put the number of

Africans in wage-earning employment at 134,500 on an average day.[22] Of these about 10 per cent were of non-Kenya origin, leaving some 120,000 Kenyans. Since each African is reported to have worked an average of only six months of the year, the total number who had engaged in wage-earning in that year may be estimated at 240,000. The total population of non-pastoral (non-Somali, Masai, Turkana, etc.) African males aged 15–40 at that time was estimated by the Native Affairs Department to have been about 420,000,[23] which, if correct, would mean that over half, about 55 per cent, of them had worked for wages at some time during the year. The Native Affairs Department also estimated that year that some 55 per cent of the adult male Kikuyu, Embu, and Meru population was at work on the census date, some 58 per cent of the adult male Teita population, 42 per cent of the Kavirondo (Luo and Baluhya) and 15 per cent of the Kamba.[24] On the whole, even as rough approximations, these estimates do indicate that the first two decades of colonial rule had imposed a rapid, widespread, and rather fundamental change in the social situation of a large number of Africans.

By this time, therefore, a semi-proletarianised stratum, a category of persons partly dependent on wage labour, may be said to have been created. Considering not individuals but an economically defined category, an African working class might be said to exist, but the movement of individual workers into and out of wage labour vitiated crystallisation, and the growth of class consciousness was hampered by the large and frequent fluctuations in class membership.

It is possible, moreover, to discern a steady increase in proletarianisation over this period. Railway reports from 1895–99 indicate that African workers were apt to run off at any time without warning. Nor would they work at any distance from their homes.[25] Carrier Corps recruiting during 1915–19 pressured more Africans into employment, for longer periods of time, since a job rendered one exempt from recruitment. In Kiambu, a main labour-supplying district, the average time spent in employment in 1916 increased from about four months *per annum* before recruiting began, to eight, and 'a large number of labourers were now working for the full twelve months in order to avoid recruitment.' After the war, the average months spent in employment fell back to six *per annum*, but did not fall to the prewar level.[26] By 1923, the Native Affairs Department estimated that on the average Africans from the main labour-supplying tribes (Kikuyu, Kamba, Luo and Baluhya) could be expected to work six months of the year.[27] Except in major urban areas, this pattern of part-time participation in wage-earning remained dominant through the 1930s until some time after 1939.

Stage II: 1919–1939

The growth of the African wage-earning population in the 'twenties[28] and 'thirties is shown in Table I.[29] Surprisingly, it took place despite a slow decline in the use of some of the main measures which had in the earlier period propelled Africans into the labour market. Two of the major methods of producing an African labour supply, direct compulsory labour and private labour recruiting, were less frequently used during this period. The number of Africans 'ordered out' under the compulsory labour ordinance fell steadily from 25,501 in 1923 and 19,323 in 1924 to 1,304 in 1938. The number employed on 'long contract' (since nearly all Africans recruited by agents were placed on these, they are an index to the activities of recruiters) fell from 27,490 in 1921 to 8,245 in 1939.[30] Increasingly, Africans began seeking employment independently of labour agents because, firstly, the labour registration system introduced in 1919 made it less easy to break a contract once recruited and, secondly, 'long contracts' generally involved arduous work for periods of up to two years. The third method of inducing Africans into employment, the policy of direct administrative pressure, also changed in 1922. Governor Northey's Labour Circular of 1919, urging officials to continue their 'encouragement' of the flow of African labour from the Reserves, provoked a burst of criticism from the British public and from, notably, the Bishops of East Africa. This criticism, together with other factors, resulted in a change in government policy to that of the encouragement of African labour in general, either on their own cash-crop enterprises, or as wage-earners outside the Reserves. The policy change may have had some effect in practice, though it was probably minimal until after the depression.

New factors, however, accounted for the growth in African employment in this period. The development of European agriculture caused pre-emption of the export market for agricultural produce by European producers, competition of European-grown produce on the domestic market, and a general stagnation in African agriculture throughout the 'twenties. In this decade, too, was introduced the compulsory registration scheme, applicable to all male Africans over 16 years of age, which probably made it less easy for an individual to evade administrative pressure to work for wages.

By the 1930s, population pressure and soil erosion in the Kikuyu, Kamba, and, to a lesser extent, Luo and Baluhya areas began to assume serious proportions, and to affect the African labour supply. Though African production of crops for the market also increased during the prosperity of the late 'thirties, so also did African consumption. Small-scale mercantile capitalism had increasingly instilled new wants in Africans, but the growth was accelerated in

TABLE I

Registered Adult Male Africans Reported in Employment

Monthly Labour Return Monthly Average		Special Labour Census	
1922	119,170	1941	208,008
1923	138,330	1942	247,401
1924	133,890	1943	248,426
1925	152,384	1944	249,708
1926		1945	259,211
1927	147,893	1946	252,244
1928	152,274	1947	265,514
1929	160,076		
1930	157,359		
1931	141,473		
1932	132,089		
1933	141,085		
1934	c. 145,000		
1935	c. 150,000		
1936	c. 162,000		
1937	est. 183,000		

Comment:

1922–25 Monthly Labour Returns were received from only 50–65 per cent of all known employers, and the number of known employers was rather less than the number of actual employers. Although coverage increased over time, official records show that the response rate diminished, so that the increases in employment shown are probably not due to increases in coverage.

For 1922–25 there was some confusion as to whether resident labourers were to be included. Beginning in 1927, resident labourers and daily-paid casual labourers were definitely excluded.

The figures should be used for comparative purposes only, and not as indications of the absolute number employed.

1936–47 Totals include 'sick', but exclude those on leave, absent, or absent without leave. Also excluded are male juveniles, female employees, resident labourers, daily paid 'casual' labour, and those in the armed services. In 1947 the total of monthly-paid adult and juvenile males and females, including sick, on leave, and absent, was 334,571.

Sources:

Native Affairs Department Annual Reports, 1923–38; Special Labour Censuses, 1936, 1941, 1942–45; Special Labour (Native) Census, 1946; Report on African Labour Census, 1947.

periods of rising incomes. By the end of the 1930s this combination of indirect pressures had largely superseded the more direct and compulsory methods, and the question of how to produce an African labour supply had ceased to be a major political issue in the colony.

At the beginning of Stage II, increasing proletarianisation led to an important change in the content of African labour protest. Whereas in the beginning the main response to the imposition of a new economic role was an attempt to escape from it or reject it, by the end of this period action within the new economic order, aimed at improving the workers' position *qua* worker, began of necessity to take precedence. Like the English workers of the previous century, 'From revolting against Capitalism, they passed to the task of organising their forces within it'.[31]

One of the most important and neglected aspects of early labour history in Africa is the extent to which even a migrant and semi-proletarianised work force is capable of individual and collective labour action. Intermittent wage-labour was a lifetime condition for these worker-peasants; since an increasingly significant part of their income derived from wages, they developed a strong interest in improving their work situation. The forms these attempts took included individual slowdowns and refusals to work, avoidance of bad employers, complaints to the Labour Department, small strikes, and political actions.

One of the first indications of change came at the close of the First World War, with the political protest movement in central Kenya led by Harry Thuku, and a similar political movement in Nyanza. Following upon the war came two years of economic depression, to which European employers reacted by cutting wages by one-third. In addition, the system of labour registration was introduced, requiring Africans to carry a *kipande*, or registration card. Hut and poll taxes were increased. These adverse measures precipitated the first African mass political movement, led by Harry Thuku. For present purposes, the important point about the Thuku movement is that two of its main grievances, the wages reduction and protest against the *kipande*, were clearly related to the wage labour system. Thuku also vigorously protested against the tax increase and the alienation of Kikuyu lands. His concerns reflected those of a semi-proletarianised stratum, with interests both on the land and in wage earning.[32]

Escape from wage earning became increasingly less possible in the 1920s. Reported desertions declined,[33] owing both to the introduction of the Registration Ordinance (which made it easier to trace 'deserters' and harder for a worker to find another job if not 'signed off' from the previous one) and to the decline in importance of private labour recruiting and of compulsory labour, from which desertion was the principal means of escape.

Moreover, the social significance of desertions underwent a change in this period. The evidence from the late 1920s suggests that by that time those who adopted this recourse in the face of poor conditions or binding 'long contracts' went elsewhere to work, for example, to Mombasa in search of high-wage casual employment, rather than back to the Reserves.[34]

As well, African workers would avoid, when they could, employers who meted out harsh treatment. At times when the labour supply was less than the demand for labour, these employers were the first ones to suffer shortages. Another channel of individual protest, in cases of non-receipt of wages or of beatings or lack of rations, was complaint to the Labour Department. During the 1920s and 1930s there was a marked long-run increase in the use of this channel by Africans, intensified during the depressions of 1922–23 and 1930–33. The number of African claimants for wages recovered by the department more than doubled between 1921 and 1923; the amounts recovered rose from £639 in 1921 to a high of £3,759 in 1932, to £2,821 in 1935.[35]

The change from permanent withdrawal of labour as a form of protest to withdrawal as a weapon of negotiation with the employer to improve conditions is a significant development in the evolution of working class movements.[36] In the 'twenties in Kenya, incidents of small-scale strikes, go-slows, and refusals to work became common. The transition from individual to collective action in this sphere also occurs at this time, resulting from the growing concentration of workers at work sites throughout the colony.

The first reported collective strike actions of any size occurred in the late 'twenties, in the large but isolated ballast-breaking camps and relaying gangs along the railway line. In these camps conditions were exceptionally bad—poor and insufficient food, malaria, scurvy, and enteritis epidemics, arduous and excessive work demands. Though wages were on a par with those for construction workers generally, Indian employers, operating on a small profit margin, often defaulted on payment. Workers were mostly Luo and Baluhya recruited on 'long contracts' for six to twelve months. Intolerable conditions led to the 'considerable trouble' in these camps in the late 'twenties—strikes of two or three hundred men in 1925, 1927 and 1928, large numbers of desertions, and 'constant agitations'. At times, compulsory labour had to be brought in for lack of voluntary labour.[37]

Crucial to the further development of collective action on the part of working Africans were the events of the depression in East Africa. As prices fell for Kenya's main exports, coffee, sisal, and maize, so did opportunities for Africans, the number in employment declining for the first time in 1930 and then again in both 1931 and 1932 (Table 1). And those who were employed in these years received 15 per cent to 50 per cent less in wages and salaries than those employed in 1929.[38]

During the depression, Africans who lost their jobs could not easily be reabsorbed into the agricultural sector, and those who were reabsorbed probably suffered a drop in their standard of living. Overcrowding was already becoming a problem in the Kikuyu areas in particular, and was aggravated by a reduction in 1931 of the number of squatters in most parts of the European settled areas. In addition prices of African local produce had fallen, and the produce trade had decreased or come to a standstill in most areas. Lack of cash from any source made it increasingly difficult for those in the reserves to pay their taxes. Because of the decline in the African produce trade, 'a far larger number than the normal were desirous of obtaining employment,'[39] even though opportunities for work were decreasing. In Nyanza, 'bands of labourers wandered from farm to farm looking for work and either failing to obtain it or doing so at a much reduced wage.'[40] In Central Province 'District Officers were besieged by natives inquiring for and hoping for work.'[41]

Instead of remaining in the reserves, therefore, Africans tended to migrate to the larger towns, in particular to Nairobi, in search of work.[42] In 1930 and 1932 there were large increases in the number of Africans committed to houses of detention for vagrancy, due directly to lack of employment.[43] Individual acts of rebellion increased in these years, even though the hardships—'hunger and even destitution'—did not provoke any organised protest. There were marked rises in the rates of crime and burglary in the towns. Most crimes were 'of a petty character, committed by workless vagabonds to procure such immediate necessities of life as food and clothes.'[44]

By 1934 there was a rise in employment, spurred by the discovery of gold in Nyanza. By 1935 the increase in employment opportunities was general. Wages, however, remained initially at the depression level. At the same time, prices for African local produce rose. These changes put some groups of labourers in a slightly better bargaining position. Coming after the previous period of hardship, they had the effect of stimulating collective labour action.

In the years immediately after the depression a rash of semi-organised African strikes erupted. In Kenya, a surge of collective protest movements occurred not during the period of greatest deprivation, but immediately afterwards, when there appeared an objective possibility for change.

Two examples come from the sisal plantations in the Thika area and the coffee farms in Kiambu. In Thika, with good rains and a rise in the world price of sisal in the last three months of 1935, the previously small demand for labour increased. At the same time 'frequent strikes and wholesale desertions' were reported. The District Commissioner concluded that unrest was due not only to a desire to work on their own *shambas*, to a normal dislike of sisal weeding, or to general dissatisfaction over the concurrent tax collection drive, but also that, 'naturally enough, when the sisal market began to rise, labourers began to agitate for increased pay.' Workers were clearly aware of the relation between improved market prospects and the chances for a pay increase.[45] In Kiambu in 1934, when good rains came and the demand for coffee pickers rose for the first time, 'an attempt was made by natives of the Kiambu District to force up the price of coffee picking on European farms, but on the conviction of the ringleader for illegally inducing coffee pickers to leave work, agitation ceased.'[46]

The post-depression period of prosperity brought a continued increase in the incidence of strike action by Africans, and somewhat greater success for these actions. An important early series of strikes occurred among a relatively large group of workers centred in Kisumu, the African fishermen working for Indian boat-owners. They struck for higher wages in 1935, and those in nearby Asembo Bay struck for the same reason in 1936. Both strikes were successful. Officials reported that

> ... Probably the main cause of the trouble was the growing realisation among the natives of Kavirondo that increasing prosperity in their own Reserve and the increased demand for their services as labourers is giving them a bargaining power that they have hitherto lacked.[47]

In the following years, an increasing number of strikes by farm workers is reported.

The earliest major urban strike occurred in July 1934 among Mombasa port workers. The dispute arose over a proposed reduction in wages; the strike lasted for three days. 'Strike gangs armed with sticks and knives picketed the approaches to the port ... police on one occasion were stoned and employees of the Oil Companies and Electric Light Works were also interfered with.'[48] The strike succeeded in preventing the wage reduction. At this time, there were some 600–700 employees of 'contractors, stevedoring and shipping companies' in Mombasa, the number having risen from about 500 in 1933.[49] Like dockworkers in other parts of Africa, including those described by John Iliffe in this volume, they were to become leaders in labour organising and protest.

In the period 1934–38 in Mombasa, more labour was steadily being employed, prices were rising, but wages lagged. This squeeze triggered several strikes: Kenya Landing and Shipping Company employees (1936), Shell Company employees (1937, 1938), and a number of smaller incidents. But discontent arising from the economic situation also led to tribal conflicts: hostility to upcountry labour which sometimes worked for lower wages showed itself in riots between the upcountry Luo or the Kikuyu and local tribesmen in Majengo, the African section of town (two in 1935, one in 1936, and the 'Majengo Riots' of 1937). The period culminated in the 1939 general strike, involving nearly all Mombasa workers.

In Nairobi there was also a tendency for prices of goods bought by Africans to rise during 1935 and 1937, and for wages to remain stationary or rise only slightly. Together with the increase of African consumption, these forces tended to predispose African workers to strike. In addition, the prolonged but successful strikes of Indian artisans in 1936 and 1937 provided an example to African workers. In May 1937 African stone masons, semi-skilled artisans employed by Indians in quarries near Nairobi, went on strike for ten days. Upon the intervention of the Labour Department, a settlement favourable to the strikers was reached. In the following few years, there were strikes of the African conductors employed by Kenya Bus Company in Nairobi, of 64 apprentices on the Kenya and Uganda Railway, and of the railway firemen.

A remark by the principal labour inspector in his annual report for 1936 may serve to sum up the change which had occurred in the second period of working-class evolution.

> There are signs that the more sophisticated natives are beginning to realise that they possess a powerful weapon in the strike. In the past the native has usually shown disapproval of real or imaginary grievances concerning conditions of his employment in two ways, viz. desertion or 'Ca'canny' (slow-down) methods in his work. The fact that he will eventually adopt more direct methods must be faced, and there is little doubt that the day of organised labour unions amongst Natives is not so very far distant . . .[50]

African workers were increasingly taking collective action deriving from their class position, revealing an incipient class consciousness. This consciousness was still limited to local groups of workers, and was not yet class-wide or industry-wide. It was also inhibited by the lack of full-time participation in wage-earning. Finally, class solidarity was limited by the 'new' tribal consciousness which was simultaneously emerging in urban areas and at work sites.

Stage III: 1939–1947

During the years surrounding the Second World War, the size of the African work force in Kenya greatly increased (Table 1). The growth of non-agricultural enterprise, in particular secondary industry, led to a shift in principal locus of African employment from rural to urban areas, and to increasing industrial and occupational differentiation in the work force. These two trends had differing effects on the character of working-class protest. The concentration of African workers in urban areas made possible city-wide strikes, and the emergence of organisations representing all or most of the workers in the urban area, while specialisation in the work force led to the formation of occupationally and industrially specific workers' associations.

Before the Second World War, working Africans were increasingly concentrated in the major urban centres. In Nairobi District the African population doubled between 1923 and 1931, and nearly doubled again by 1939.[51] Mombasa District also grew, though somewhat less spectacularly.[52] By 1947 over 40 per cent of the private non-agricultural work force was employed in the municipalities of Nairobi and Mombasa alone[53]. Urbanisation is also related to the growth of non-agricultural employment among Africans. Whereas in 1936 the ratio of agricultural to non-agricultural employees was 60:40, by 1944 these figures had been reversed.[54]

During the wartime years, and probably even earlier, the classic colonial pattern of part-time participation in the labour force began to change for the urban segment of African wage earners. For many workers in Mombasa and Nairobi, the pattern of a periodic one or two-year stint at wage-earning followed by an equally long return to the status of peasant or tribesman, was beginning to give way to one in which wage-earning occupied almost the whole of their working lives.

The Phillips Committee of 1945, for example, divided Mombasa's work force into two groups, those who had reached the state of 'temporary urbanisation' and those who had not. The former planned to stay in Mombasa for a large part of their working lives; of these, railway workers formed the largest group. On the railway in Mombasa, more than half of even the unskilled employees were men with over two years' continuous service; about 20 per cent had over five years' service and about 10 per cent more than ten years' service. At least 50 per cent of all railway workers in Mombasa were reported to be married, with their wives in town.[55] The percentage of 'temporarily urbanised' may have been rather less in Nairobi, given its proximity to the populous Kikuyu reserve from which workers could travel into town each day. Yet the Municipal Native Affairs Officer in Nairobi in 1941 was of the opinion that

> In Nairobi labour has passed from the migrant stage to that of temporary or permanent urbanisation. It is becoming less mobile and more stable and in fact the growing amount of industrial work proper, which much increased with the war, offers a field of employment where that desirable figure, the stable skilled or semi-skilled African worker, can emerge.[56]

Among the workers who inhabited Kariakor and Shauri Moyo, two housing

estates for municipal employees, it is reported in 1941 that from 22 per cent
(Shauri Moyo) to 58 per cent (Kariakor) were married and accompanied by their
wives in town.[57]

Hence by this time in urban areas, we are justified in speaking of an emerging
social aggregate, a small but gradually crystallising 'working class', with some
continuity of membership over time. This development was a pre-condition for
the emergence of the first African collective labour organisations. The degree
of commitment to, and length of time involved in, wage-earning undoubtedly
varied, however, among different occupations: white-collar workers seem to
have been the most committed, and unskilled workers the least so.

The larger context within which the African labour movement evolved was
a colonial social structure in which racial and economic divisions largely but not
completely coincided. Class categories, in particular the working class, might
encompass several racial groups, but within each class, occupational and status
specialisation according to race was marked. Besides the virtual exclusion of
some races from certain occupations (in the working class, for example, there
were no European manual workers; there were very few African skilled workers
or artisans, the majority of these being Asian), there persisted within those
occupations which were open to more than one race (e.g. clerks, artisans) a
racial hierarchy in the form of differential remuneration for the same job. On
the railway, for example, the ratio between African and Asian salaries for
corresponding posts was 50:100, and Asians made only 55 per cent of European
salaries for identical jobs.[58] Overall, average income differences between the
races were probably even wider. One study of the race-income structure
indicates that there were some income overlaps between races,[59] but income
equalities did not convey mutual social acceptance or prestige. Given this
structure, economic organisations in the colony, both of workers and of employers, were initially formed along racial lines. Thus there were separate
Indian and African labour movements.

In the period between 1939 and 1947, African consciousness of the larger
social structure grew. Demands for higher wages became linked, for the first
time, with demands for equality with Indian and European workers, and for
African equality with other races generally. Class consciousness became mixed
with race consciousness, and labour protest became linked with African nationalism.

Urbanisation, together with a rising cost of living and stagnating wages, had
led to the first major urban strike in Mombasa in 1934. Now the same forces led
to the first general strike in that city in 1939, marking a new development in the
use of the strike weapon. Urbanisation entailed concentration of workers,
facilitating communication, the realisation of common interests, and the

organisation of strikes. In the same way, concentration of workers at smaller work sites throughout the colony had facilitated earlier strikes. Thus urbanisation simply increased the scale of strike action. This effect may be illustrated by a comparison of Mombasa, where four general strikes took place in 1939, 1947, 1955 and 1957, with Nairobi, where only one, from more directly political causes in 1950, occurred.

What made Mombasa different was the concentration of its industry in the port area, and the fact that it was a place of predominantly long-range labour migration. Over half of Mombasa's work force were Kikuyu, Luo, Baluhya, Kamba and other long-range migrants from upcountry.[60] The time, effort, and money that had to be invested in transportation made long-distance migrants more dependent than short-distance ones on the wages they could make, and typically they stayed in employment for longer lengths of time. In Nairobi, on the other hand, places of employment were scattered throughout the city. The bulk of the work force were short-term Kikuyu, Embu, and Meru migrants from the nearby reserves.[61] The discontent over wages was therefore fused, throughout much of the colonial period, with the general Kikuyu agitation over the land question.

The strikes which began in Mombasa in July 1939 spread quickly throughout the city and into the port area. First to strike were the Public Works Department labourers, then the workers in the Municipal Conservancy Department and the municipal street sweepers. Later in the week African employees of private firms such as the Electric Light and Power Company, Texaco and other oil companies located in the port area, Mombasa aluminium works, Bata Shoe Company, building contractors, and Indian and Somali milk suppliers and vegetable growers went on strike. The following week, all the port labour, first the daily-paid labourers, then the few on monthly contracts, ceased work, and the operation of the port was brought to a standstill. Railway workers, also located in the port area, presented wage demands, but did not strike. Most domestic workers did not strike. The large 'reserve army' of un- or under-employed helped to swell the number of demonstrators.

Despite the Willan Commission's almost exclusive emphasis on failure of employers to provide proper housing facilities or payments in lieu, it is apparent from the report itself that the low level of wages relative to high living costs in general, and not only high rents, was the central issue.[62] This grievance was common to nearly all classes of workers, which helps to account for the strike's generality. Participants included artisans, skilled workers, some shop and office workers, and unskilled workers. But the hardship was in all likelihood greater for the lower-paid workers, which helps account for their propensity to strike first.

No formal organisation emerged during the 1939 strike. Though some groups of workers did send forward representatives, said to be mostly Kikuyu, to negotiate with employers, their leadership was limited to the duration of the strike. Most African strikers were reticent and suspicious, because of the not unfounded fear of reprisals from employers. The Willan Commission had to allow Arab and African workers to give evidence by groups, in order to overcome such fears.[63]

In addition to urbanisation, occupational differentiation, though limited in a colonial economy, also influenced the African labour movement. The occupational structure of the African work force at the high point of colonial society is briefly summarised in Tables II and III. This and other evidence suggests that by this time African higher-paid clerks and artisans had become a social category somewhat better off than the mass of African workers.

African clerks and salaried workers for government were a very small stratum, only 2–3 per cent of the employed African population in 1947. They were, however, the first to form occupational or staff associations. The Kenya African Civil Service Association was formed about 1930, the African Teachers' Union about 1934, the Railway African Staff Association (largely white collar) about 1940,[64] and the Municipal African Staff Association in Nairobi by 1941.[65] Not only were these African workers the most stabilised segment of the work force, and the most Western-educated, but they were also so placed as to experience directly the 'colour bar' which restricted African advancement and which was reinforced by the activities of the European and Asian staff associations. These European and Asian associations, however, provided models for the organisation of African staff associations. In addition, the government and the railway were in general favourably disposed towards the formation of these associations.

African artisans were also a proportionately small stratum, roughly 7 per cent of employed Africans in 1947.[66] With respect to incomes, they received substantially less than their Asian counterparts, but their wage was equal to or better than that of many African clerks. The first of these artisans to form craft associations were the journeymen in urban areas who lacked a fixed workplace and were employed by the job—masons, carpenters, house painters, barbers and cobblers. In addition, there was a growing number of taxi-cab drivers, a few self-employed, but most working on commission for Indian or European owners. The initial impetus to organisation among all these workers seems to have been actions by the government to license or otherwise to regulate them, especially during the 1940–45 wartime period. Barbers and taxi-cab drivers found themselves faced with attempts by the Nairobi City Council to introduce stringent licensing regulations,[67] while painters, masons and carpenters were hindered in their work by the pass regulations controlling the entry of Africans into Nairobi, and the laws against vagrancy.[68] Their organisations were thus as much political (concerned with government regulations) as economic (concerned with wages and conditions), and were much like trade protection societies. The

TABLE II

Adult Male African Employees by Occupation: 1947

Occupation	Number Employed
Private Employers	
Non-Agriculture	
Clerical staff	3,019
Shop, office and store boys	8,848
Domestic servants	21,917
Mechanics	1,097
Carpenters	716
Masons and stone dressers	2,834
Drivers (Motor Vehicle)	2,353
Other trained skilled workers	3,463
Factory skilled workers	3,414
Semi-skilled workers	6,297
Unskilled labourers	40,087
Agriculture	
Office staff	938
Domestic servants	5,603
Skilled workers	3,518
Labourers	96,492
Government Services	
Clerical staff	3,226
Office and store boys	2,752
Domestic servants	1,617
Artisans and mechanics	5,095
Other skilled workers	21,561
Labourers	47,010
	281,857

Source:

Kenya Colony and Protectorate, *African Labour Census, 1947*, Table 9.

Kikuyu Barbers' Association was very active in Nairobi in 1940, and was represented on the Municipal Native Affairs Council. By 1946 the Nairobi African Taxi Drivers' Union and the Thika Native Motor Drivers' Association

TABLE III

Average Monthly Basic Cash* Wages by Occupation
Adult Male African Employees: 1947

Occupation	Shillings
Clerical staff	62
Artisans	
Drivers	77
Carpenters	79
Masons	60
Mechanics	57
Skilled workers	61
Skilled factory workers	37
Domestic servants (indoor)	40
Shop, office and store boys	39
All semi-skilled workers	38
Domestic servants (Outdoor)	29
Labourers, not agricultural	25
Labourers, agricultural	
sisal	19
sugar	19
tea	16
coffee	16
pyrethrum	14
mixed	15

* Excluding all other advantages of employment.

Source:

East African High Commission, *East African Economic and Statistical Bulletin*, No. 3, March 1949, Table 6.

were formed to protest against the municipal licensing regulations. The Painters' Union was formed in 1944, as were similar associations of cobblers, masons, tailors, carpenters, and furniture polishers. These groups helped their members to get ration cards and residence permits. The painters attempted, apparently with some success, to use their association to raise their wages throughout

Nairobi.[69] As these associations expanded, they took in other skilled workers of the same trade, who were more permanent employees of small Asian-owned businesses. Other semi-skilled employees—shop-workers and messengers, nightwatchmen, and domestic employees—also began to form associations.

For all urban workers wartime meant rapid rises in the cost of living and few wage gains, so that real wages on the average declined. There was a moratorium on extending social services, such as badly needed housing for Africans, and there was a ban on strikes in essential industries. In addition to these grievances, there are clearly expressed in the wartime period, for the first time, grievances over racial discrimination with respect to wages, job opportunities, and advancement. Among the mass of urban workers not yet organised, it was the comparatively stabilised railway workers who took the lead in wartime strike protest, though unrest was always likely to spread throughout the urban area. Each year from 1940 to 1945 on the railway there were strikes or threats of strikes, the most important being the three strikes in 1942, involving about 3,300 men, and the threat of a general strike in 1945.

Wartime urban protest climaxed in the immediate post-war period. The failure of government to remedy even some of the African grievances led to another general strike in Mombasa in January 1947, lasting for 11 days. But whereas in the 1939 strike no labour organisation emerged, this time, with the legacy of war conditions and agitation, the African Workers' Federation was formed on the first day of the strike. On the Monday morning of January 13, all work stopped at the docks, on the railway, and in practically all hotels, offices, and banks in Mombasa. Private homes were without African servants. About 15,000 workers, nearly the whole of the Mombasa work force, eventually went on strike. A week and a half later, after the intervention of Eliud Mathu, the African representative in the Legislative Council, the strikers returned to work.

The African Workers' Federation (AWF), formed to represent all the workers on strike, proposed to unite all African workers in a single union, becoming a general workers' union encompassing all types of African workers and, indeed, the unemployed. AWF was thus the first organisation to attempt to represent the mass of African urban workers. Later, it also received substantial support from estate workers in rural areas near Nairobi and Mombasa. Nearly all sections of African workers supported the AWF except for the highest paid white-collar Africans, who were more sympathetic to their staff associations, leaving AWF to represent mainly non-clerical workers.[70] (Some clerks in lower-paid private employ, such as those in the Kenya Landing and Shipping African Staff Association, did support AWF. Chege Kibachia, the leader of AWF, had himself been a clerk and a salesman. In large measure, occupational divisions were minimised or muted within AWF by the combination of class and racial unity which it primarily expressed.)[71]

The main themes of AWF's protest were low wages and unjust discrimination against African workers. In a letter to the press, Chege Kibachia enumerated the specific grievances:

> (1) Indifference towards paying them [Africans] equally with the other workers of other races who performed identical or same duties. (2) Partiality and disrespect shown to African workers wherever they were employed. (3) Deliberative [deliberate] devices to keep the Africans poor that he may keep at his work all the time . . . indirect slavery camouflaged by sweet words and such salaries as would be taken for tips. (4) Not giving wives and children allowances. (5) Taking no notice of the present high cost of living.[72]

AWF's class-wide consciousness, its concern for all sections of African workers, was shown in its attack on the interim wages award which was announced in March by a government-appointed tribunal. The award applied only to employees of government and of large firms in the port, and did not apply to casual workers of these firms, to employees of smaller businesses in Mombasa, or to domestic servants, gardeners or shamba-workers. It was also much less than the strikers had asked for. AWF therefore boycotted the award; a huge AWF meeting, addressed by Kibachia, resolved:

> That the representation on the Tribunal was not impartial and the Africans involved in the strike were represented by a minority before the Tribunal. Moreover, the award which was confined to certain classes and sections of workers, is not impartial, and [is] therefore inconsistent with the democratic approach to the question of labour. In view of this great betrayal of responsibility. . . . the award should be boycotted altogether.[73]

Nearly all workers declined to accept the interim award. A larger award was subsequently given, and the minimum wage raised.

Other resolutions passed by AWF indicate that African racial solidarity extended even beyond the confines of the working class, to certain nearby social strata:

> That the removal of unemployed Africans from Mombasa, in view of the fact that there are many people of other races also unemployed on the island, is a serious betrayal of the principles of freedom and democracy and should be stopped immediately.
> That the shops recently nominated by Government for the supply of certain

commodities to Africans are being used also as a means to enforce the payment of poll tax, and the monopoly is in the hands of other races. These, therefore, should be boycotted and the Government asked to give Africans a chance to own such shops.[74]

Chege Kibachia travelled throughout the colony, to Nairobi, Nakuru, Nanyuki, Gilgil, Naivasha, and Uplands urging workers to join AWF. There was a rash of strikes in various parts of the colony, including a general strike in Kisumu on 14 April. In mid-1947 Mwangi Macharia of AWF arrived in Nairobi and began holding meetings with the various skilled and semi-skilled workers' associations there. By July 1947 several of the associations had decided to form a Nairobi branch of AWF, and in August Kibachia arrived to open it, naming its office, under a tree on open ground in Pumwani, the *Ofisi ya Maskini*, or Office of the Poor.

AWF viewed itself as closely allied with the Kenya African Union (KAU), the burgeoning post-war African nationalist movement, led by Jomo Kenyatta. AWF's support of KAU confirmed that African wage-carners, for the moment at least, saw their interests as compatible with those of the embryonic African petty bourgeoisie who led the nationalist movement. When, a few months after the Mombasa strike, Chege Kibachia was arrested and deported to a remote district, AWF threatened to call a general strike in Nairobi. KAU, however, called a mass meeting at which Kenyatta rejected this course of action, advising workers to strike only after proper notice had been given to employers.[75] This incident presaged the future conflicts between labour and the African national bourgeoisie in the post-independence era.

In the view of the colonial government, the potential power of AWF was too great to be permissible. Chege Kibachia, and eighteen other AWF leaders in Mombasa, were therefore arrested, an action which both removed existing leaders and inhibited potential ones from coming forth. The resulting lack of leadership, coupled with certain government initiatives, led to AWF's eventual decline.[76]

From this brief review of the beginnings of African labour organising in Kenya, it is apparent that both AWF and the smaller associations of African artisans evolved indigenously, in that, up to this point, no government officials or other Europeans had had a part in creating them. Instead, they were responses to incipient class-forming tendencies inherent in colonial capitalism.

The suppression of AWF marks, however, the beginning of a period of active government intervention in the African labour movement. In the years that followed, the government pursued a policy of promoting industrial and 'non-political' trade unions for Africans. At the same time, the government suppressed other militant labour organisations and exercised strong influence over the evolution of the occupational associations, so that eventually a colony-wide structure of industrially organised unions emerged.

The history of AWF reveals that strong impulses toward class-wide labour organisation among Africans had emerged by 1949. A general workers' union, representing all grades of labour, appeared to be the natural result of a particular combination of economic forces: increasing proletarianisation, urbanisation, a low level of skill differentiation in a peripheral labour force, and a predominance of unskilled labour. Potentially, the general workers' union was quite a powerful form of labour organisation.

In this case the class-wide consciousness of AWF was limited by racial homogeneity. AWF did not encompass Indian workers. The solidarity that held AWF members together was not only that they were all workers, but also that they were all Africans. AWF's combination of class and racial consciousness was the product of a racially divided social structure, common in peripheral colonised societies. In this situation, both the underdevelopment of the productive forces and the deep racial divisions limit the achievement of pure forms of class action.[77]

NOTES

1. André Gundar Frank, 'The Development of Underdevelopment', *Monthly Review*, 18(4), Sept. 1966, pp. 17–30.
2. For example, P. C. Lloyd, *The New Elites of Tropical Africa*, Oxford University Press, 1966, p. 56; J. C. Mitchell and A. L. Epstein, 'Occupational Prestige and Social Status', *Africa*, 29 (1959), pp. 35–6.
3. This position is implicit in much of the work on labour migration in Africa, especially W. Elkan, *Migrants and Proletarians*, Oxford University Press, 1960, and, excepting southern Africa, in G. Arrighi and J. Saul, 'Nationalism and Revolution in Sub-Saharan Africa', *The Socialist Register*, Monthly Review Press, 1969, pp. 158–9; and G. Arrighi, 'International Corporations, Labor Aristocracies, and Economic Development in Tropical Africa' in R. I. Rhodes (ed.), *Imperialism and Underdevelopment*, Monthly Review Press, 1970, pp. 234–5.
4. J. Woddis, *Africa: The Lion Awakes*, Lawrence and Wishart, 1959, R. Ledda, 'Social Classes and Political Struggle', *International Socialist Journal*, 4(22), 1967, and E. R. Braundi, 'Neo-Colonialism and Class Struggle, *Internationalist Journal*, 1 Jan. 1964, among others.
5. S. Chodak, 'Social Classes in Sub-Saharan Africa', *Africana Bulletin*, 4 (1966), p. 31.

6. These terms are used in their Weberian sense, to distinguish collective action based on emotional or traditional psychological bonds from that based primarily on instrumental or rational bonds. M. Weber, 'Class, Status, Party' in H. Gerth and C. W. Mills, (eds), *From Max Weber*, Oxford University Press, 1946, p. 183.

7. Weber also distinguished between individual actions, which if done by many he called 'mass' actions, and concerted or group actions, *ibid.*, p. 183; and *The Theory of Social and Economic Organisation*, The Free Press, 1964, pp. 138–9.

8. An excellent economic analysis of the proletarianisation of the Rhodesian peasantry is made by G. Arrighi, 'Labour Supplies in Historical Perspective: A Study of the Proletarianisation of the African Peasantry in Rhodesia', *Journal of Development Studies*, 6(3), April 1970, pp. 197–234.

9. As documentation of the widespread use of indirect administration pressure in Kenya, see, *inter alia*, *Report of the Native Labour Commission*, 1912–1913, *passim*.

10. 2,506 Africans were working for the railway in March 1901, as compared with 19,742 Indians. M. Hill, *The Permanent Way: Story of the Kenya and Uganda Railway*, vol. I, E.A.R. & H., Nairobi, 1949, p. 215.

11. *Malindi Political Record Book*, A. D. C. Arthur Champion, 'Labour Supply and the Wagiriama', 1914.

12. *Ukamba Province Annual Report*, 1910, p. 17.

13. M. Beech, 'The Kikuyu Point of View', 12 Dec. 1912, Dagoretti Political Record Book, 1908–1912.

14. A. Wipper makes this point in 'The Gusii Rebels' in R. Rotberg and A. Mazrui (eds), *Protest and Power in Black Africa*, Oxford University Press, 1970; this is based on her earlier 'The Cult of Mumbo', Proceedings of the E.A I.S.R., Jan. 1966, part D.

15. *Ibid.*, pp. 397–8, 423.

16. Kisii Political Record Book, letter to Mr W. Campbell, D.C. from D. Scheffer, Catholic Mission, Asumbi, 1 Dec. 1918.

17. Ukamba Province Annual Report, 1911, p. 29.

18. Ukamba Province Quarterly Report, Mar. 1912, p. 42.

19. Nyanza Province Annual Report, 1906–07.

20. Ukamba Province Annual Report, 1910, p. 10.

21. Labour Office, Nairobi, Report, 2 July 1909.

22. Native Affairs Department Annual Report (NAD AR), 1923, p. 35 and Appendices. This estimate does not include women, children, or resident labourers not 'at work' on the census date.

23. *Ibid.*, p. 35.

24. *Ibid.*, Appendix E, p. 41. The Report of the Labour Bureau Commission of 1921, however, had used a round figure of 50 per cent of adult males to estimate the labour supply from the main labour-supplying tribes. All of these rate-of-participation figures in all probability err on the high side because of underestimation of population figures, but there may also have been some underestimation of the numbers in employment.

25. M. Hill, *The Permanent Way*, p. 176.

26. Kiambu District Annual Report, 1916–1917.

27. NAD AR, 1923, 35. See also The Interim Report of the Economic and Finance Committee, 1925, Appendix B, which used a similar estimate.

28. Over the period 1923–30 there is an annual average increase in the wage-earning population of about 3.5 per cent which is higher than the annual rate of population increase, if we assume the latter to be between 1 and 2 per cent, as does J. E. Goldthorpe, 'The African Population of East Africa: A Summary of its Past and Present Trends', in *East Africa Royal Commission Report*, 1953–55, Appendix VII.

29. By 1938 an estimated 21 per cent of the total African able-bodied male population was reported to be in wage-earning employment. By 1954 this figure had risen to 27 per cent. The percentages compare to 7.8 per cent in 1938 and 16.2 per cent in 1954 in Uganda, where Africans were able to grow cash crops to a much greater extent than in Kenya. Jacques Denis, 'The Development of Wage-Earning Employment in Tropical Africa', *International Labor Review*, Sept. 1956, pp. 239–58.

30. NAD ARs, 1923–38.

31. G. D. H. Cole, *A Short History of the British Working Class Movement*, rev. edn., Allen and Unwin, 1948, p. 4.

32. On Thuku's movement, see K. King, 'The Nationalism of Harry Thuku: a Study in the beginnings of African politics in Kenya', *Transafrican Journal of History*, 1, Jan. 1971, pp. 39–59. Also the accounts in W. Ross, *Kenya From Within*, Frank Cass, 1968, pp. 217–29, C. Rosberg and J. Nottingham, *The Myth of Mau Mau*, Praeger, 1966, pp. 40–56, and J. Roelker, 'The Genesis of African Protest: Harry Thuku and the British Administration in Kenya, 1920–22', Syracuse University Occasional Paper No. 41, n.d.

33. NAD AR, 1923, 49, and 1928. See also 1924, p. 52.

34. NAD AR, Labour Section, 1928, 1929, 1931, p. 121.

35. NAD ARs, 1923–38.

36. Cf. E. Hobsbawm, *Primitive Rebels*, Manchester University Press, 1959.

37. NAD AR, Labour Section, 1925, 1926, 1927, 1928, n.p.

38. NAD AR, 1931, pp. 118, 144.

39. *Ibid.*, p. 96.

40. *Ibid.*, 97.
41. NAD AR, 1933, p. 9.
42. NAD AR, 1931, p. 6.
43. NAD AR, 1930, p. 74 and 1923, p. 120.
44. NAD AR, 1933, p. 97. See also 1934, p. 131.
45. Central Province Annual Report, 1935, n.p.
46. Central Province Annual Report, 1934, n.p.
47. NAD AR, Labour Section, 1936, p. 179.
48. NAD AR, 1934, 23.
49. Mombasa District Annual Report, 1933, 1934.
50. NAD AR, Labour Section, 1936, pp. 187–8.
51. NAD AR, 1924, 1925, 1931 and 1939–45.
52. NAD AR, 1924, 1931, 1939–45.
53. Calculated from *Report on African Labour Census*, 1947, Table 2.
54. M. Parker, *Political and Social Aspects of the Development of Municipal Government in Kenya*, London: Colonial Office, 1949, p. 9.
55. *Report of the Committee of Inquiry into Labour Unrest in Mombasa* (Phillips Report), 1945, pp. 53, 57.
56. Municipal Native Affairs Officer, Nairobi, Annual Report, 1941, n.p.
57. *Ibid.*, n.p.
58. C. H. Northcott, *African Labour Efficiency Survey*, Colonial Office, London, 1947, p. 66.
59. M. Parker, *Political and Social Aspects . . .*, pp. 9–11 and especially diagram pp. 23–4.
60. *Report on African Labour Census*, 1947, Table 13.
61. *Ibid.*, Table 13.
62. *Report of Commission of Inquiry to Examine Labour Conditions in Mombasa* (Willan Report), 1939, p. 39.
63. *Ibid.*, p. 2; see also p. 45.
64. M. Singh, *History of Kenya's Trade Union Movement to 1952*, East African Publishing House, Nairobi, 1969, pp. 44, 46, 83.
65. Municipal Native Affairs Officer, Nairobi, Annual Report, 1941, n.p.
66. Includes drivers, mechanics, carpenters, masons and stone dressers.
67. Municipal Affairs Officer, Nairobi, Annual Report, 1940; Singh, *History . . .*, pp. 131–2, 240–5.
68. Kenya National Archives (KNA) file 9/908/05.
69. KNA 9/908/07.
70. KNA 9/372/78, p. 80.
71. Except for the very early timing and racially specific character of AWF, there are suggestive parallels between its form and that of general labourers

unions in nineteenth-century Britain, described by E. J. Hobsbawm, 'General Labour Unions in Britain, 1889–1914' in *Labouring Men*, Doubleday, 1967, pp. 211–39.

72. *East African Standard*, 21 Jan. 1947.

73. *Ibid.*, 1 April 1947.

74. *Ibid.*, 1 April 1947.

75. Central Province Annual Report, 1947; Singh, *History* . . ., p. 158.

76. Because of the suppression of AWF, and the beginning of a 'go-slow' government policy towards African unionism, African workers' associations then moved into a period of alliance with the radical wing of the Indian trade union movement, led by Makhan Singh. But Singh's non-racial policy did not succeed in attracting the rest of the Asian trade unions, and eventually ended with the repression of the East African Trade Union Congress in 1950.

77. See also S. Stichter, 'Development and Labour Protest in Colonial Kenya' in *National Politics and the World Economy*, edited by T. K. Hopkins and I. Wallerstein, Routledge and Kegan Paul (forthcoming).

The Creation of Group Consciousness Among the Dockworkers of Dar es Salaam 1929–50

JOHN ILIFFE[1]

The concern with political nationalism which dominated the thinking of many social scientists working in Africa during the 1950s and 1960s has often distorted the writing of African labour history. It has led to an undue concern with the purely political behaviour of workers and their leaders, and it has encouraged observers to regard labour organisations as they have often regarded nationalist movements, as phenomena created from above through the initiative of small groups of educated activists. This is certainly the prevailing view of Tanzanian labour history, as expressed, for example, by Mr Tandau and Professor Friedland,[2] who are both concerned with the creation of a self-conscious labour movement in the 1950s by a group of young leaders who in 1955 formed the Tanganyika Federation of Labour (TFL), which subsequently stimulated organisation among a wide variety of workers and played an important role in political nationalism.

This article neither disputes the importance of the TFL nor denies that it was only in the 1950s that a large and militant trade union movement was created in Tanzania. Instead the article centres on three points. One is that the history of labour in Tanzania makes little sense unless it is taken back far beyond the semi-political trade unionism of the 1950s, back indeed to the attempts of the earliest groups of workers to act in solidarity. The second is that a labour movement has its roots not in politics but in work. It grows out of the nature of that work, the economic and social position of the worker, and his response to that position. To view it solely 'from the top' is to miss the dynamic which powers the movement. The history of a labour movement must therefore be based on a history of work, and the most profound source of change within it is the changing character of the work in which the men are engaged.

This leads to the third main point of the article. Organisation and group consciousness among workers are created by the workers themselves. It is often said that 'industrialisation creates a working class', or in Africa that the needs of a colonial economy create 'the embryonic proletariat of the towns'. Yet industrialisation or a colonial economy creates only *workers*. If these workers then come to feel solidarity among themselves, become conscious of forming a group with special common interests, and organise to advance these interests, then the workers are the agents in this process, creating their own group consciousness and organisation in response to their common status. Further, at all stages in the process there is an interplay between consciousness and action. Men work together, share common experiences, and realise that they have common interests. By acting together to advance these interests, they learn their need for unity. This growing consciousness enables them to act more effectively, and shared experience of successful action in turn intensifies group consciousness. This is how a nation creates itself, through common action by the people who form it. It is also how a working class creates itself. Marx stated this as follows:

> Economic conditions had first transformed the mass of the people of the country into workers. . . . This mass is thus already a class as against capital, but not yet for itself. *In the struggle* . . . this mass becomes united, and constitutes itself as a class for itself.[3]

Professor Thompson has analysed on these lines the process by which English workers formed themselves into a working class during the industrial revolution. He argues that as the workers acted in response to their experience of industrialisation they gradually learned—often from their defeats—to see themselves as a single group. 'In the struggle' they created their own class consciousness. 'The working class', Professor Thompson concludes, 'made itself as much as it was made.'[4]

A study of the Dar es Salaam dockers is not concerned with the creation of class consciousness but with an earlier stage in labour history: the creation by the dockers of their own group consciousness as dockers. Following Marx and Professor Thompson, this article will argue that the dockers first created this group consciousness through their actions during the 1930s and 1940s, then at the end of that period expressed their solidarity in trade union organisation. All of this took place without the stimulus of nationalist politics. All of it took place long before the TFL was conceived. All of it had its roots in work.

Work and workers in the 1930s

When the dockers of Dar es Salaam began to organise in the late 1930s, they faced five problems arising from the nature of their employment. First, they worked in a strategic industry whose operation was closely regulated by the colonial government. Second, their work was casual and irregular, which made permanent organisation difficult. Third, dock labour makes sharp distinctions between different grades of workers, which proved a serious obstacle to unity. Fourth, the dockers were working in a town where social conditions were appalling and there existed a large reserve of unemployed. Fifth, the dockers had few examples of labour organisation to guide them. These problems will be considered in turn.

Throughout this period, Dar es Salaam was a lighterage port. Ocean-going ships moored in the harbour and handled cargo by means of lighters. Port work was therefore divided into three stages: shore handling, lighterage work afloat and stevedoring on the ship itself. The distinction between the stevedore (who works on board a ship) and the dockworker (who works ashore) is traditional in port employment and by the 1930s had come to shape not only the organisation of labour but also the business structure of the port. Of the three stevedoring companies which worked on the ships, one was owned jointly by the two great shipping lines, Union-Castle and British-India, and another (the Tanganyika Boating Company) by the Holland-Afrika Lijn. Since 1929 the three companies had combined to operate a single shore-handling company. From 1941 all four companies operated under a cost-plus contract with the official Railway Administration, which had ultimate control of the port.[5] The companies were not subject to normal business competition and their main interest was not profit but the rapid turn-round of their ships.

This business structure shaped the development of organisation among the dockers in three ways. The unusually close cooperation among the employers stimulated united action among their workers. The close relationship with government gave any industrial action a political implication. And the cost-plus arrangement enabled the companies to absorb wage increases more easily than could other employers.

The second main feature of Dar es Salaam in the 1930s was that it was a small and unsophisticated port, where ships arrived irregularly. This meant that the demand for labour in the port fluctuated wildly, so that it did not have a stable labour force. The employers did not maintain a permanent force large enough to cope with the maximum number of ships which might be in the port at any time, since these men would normally be redundant. Nor was it in the workers' interest to specialise as dockers if they could obtain work only occasionally. On the other hand, certain skilled men had to be employed regularly if the port was to operate efficiently. Consequently, when the first evidence is available in 1928, a sharp distinction is made between permanent workers on monthly or fortnightly terms and a much larger body of casual labour employed by the day as occasion required. Permanent workers earned between Shs. 1.50 and Shs. 2.50 per day of nine hours. Casual labourers, usually called 'coolies' or *vibarua*, received Shs. 2.00 for a nine-hour day, their numbers depending on the ships in port. Although these wages now seem appallingly low, they were quite high by the standards of the time. Government departments paid casual labourers 77 cents a day.[6]

These conditions changed in two ways during the 1930s. First, the wages of casual labour were reduced in 1931, during the international depression, to Shs. 1.50 a day, although rough figures suggest that the cost of living fell still more sharply (see Table I). By 1939 casual wages were Shs. 1.50 a day. Second,

TABLE I

Cost of Living and Wage Indices: Dar es Salaam, 1928–50

(1 Sept. 1939 = 100)

Date	Cost of living index	Government daily rate, casual labour	Dock daily rate, casual labour	Est. dock take-home pay, casual labour
Jan. 1928	146[a]		133[a]	
1 Sept. 1939	100	100	100	100[d]
Feb.–Apr. 1940				154[e]
June 1940			120	
Oct. 1940		160		
Sept. 1942	122[b]			
1 Jan. 1943	155	200		
1 Jan. 1944	167	220		
1 Jan. 1945	177			
1 Jan. 1946	184	260		
1 Mar. 1947	187	260	153[c]	
10 Sept. 1948	247	320	260[c]	
Sept. 1949	287	320	260	
25 Oct. 1950	299	350	260	

Sources:

a D.O., Dar es Salaam, to P.C., Eastern, 10 Jan. 1928, TNA 61/295/27.
b 'Report of Enquiry into Wages and Cost of Living of Low Grade African Government Employees in Dar es Salaam' (Sept. 1942), TNA SMP 30598/15.
c Tabulation of Hatchell award, Sept. 1947, TNA SMP 16756/18.
d Molohan, 'Report on Conditions of Employment of Dock Labour in Dar es Salaam', 3 Jan. 1940, TNA SMP 25912/6A.
e Dickson (Labour Officer, Dar es Salaam) to Labour Commissioner, June 1940, TNA 61/14/22/I/2.
all other *Annual Reports of the Labour Department 1942–50, passim.*

during the mid-1930s[7] the employers tried to reduce their dependence on casual labour by establishing a registered pool of dockworkers, earmarking workers who would receive preference when casual labour was required, in order to stabilise and increase the skill of the labour force and augment the earnings of those who depended mainly on port employment. Given the sporadic arrival of ships, however, this was rather ineffective. As late as 1939 each of the gangs into which the registered labourers were divided worked only 12½ shifts a month, while each registered man worked on average only 8½ shifts. Employment in the port was too irregular to form the sole source of livelihood for most dockers. 'Port work is essentially spasmodic', it was observed in 1940, 'and in lean times the casual dock labourer is forced to get what credit he can or to avail himself of the services of the many Indian pawn-brokers.'[8]

Effective industrial action by the dockers, then, had to overcome the irregular and unprofessional nature of their employment and the rather sharp distinction between permanent and casual workers. A third problem was the great variety of occupations and terms of employment among the dockers themselves. In December 1939 the port employed 307 permanent workers on fortnightly or monthly terms, 360 registered casual labourers, and a fluctuating number of unregistered casual workers.[9] Among the permanent workers, the highest paid were 24 headmen, usually called *sarangs*, who controlled labour gangs under the supervision of European foremen. They could earn up to ninety shillings a month and were usually recruited from experienced stevedores. Below them came various specialists—winchmen, lightermen, tug and motor-boat crews—who earned from thirty to seventy-five shillings a month. About a hundred labourers were also on permanent terms at Shs. 25–36 a month, mainly experienced stevedores intended to stiffen the working gangs. The 360 registered casual labourers, who earned Shs. 1.50 for a nine-hour shift, were divided into eight gangs of 45 men. These gangs were employed in strict rotation. Each day the companies should estimate the number of gangs needed for the next day. The numbers of these gangs were posted on the wharf and in the African market. The day before a gang was required, its headman would go around the African town, accompanied by a bellringer, to warn his men. Gangs reported at 6.15 a.m. at the wharf, where their names were ticked off and vacancies were filled by picking suitable men from the crowd of unregistered casual workers who always assembled at the wharf gates at call-on time. When sufficient workers had been assembled, they were divided into working gangs of 17 to 24 men.

The permanent worker was guaranteed his wages whether work was available or not; he also earned 20–40 cents an hour overtime. The registered casual labourer was paid only when his gang was called on and he was present. During 1939 each gang worked on average 12½ shifts a month, and each registered casual labourer worked 8½ shifts. For each shift he received Shs. 15.0. Each shift also usually worked overtime to finish jobs in hand. For this the registered casual workers received 20 cents an hour. During 1939 the average earned was Shs. 1.75 per shift including overtime. The registered casual worker who attended most regularly could therefore earn up to Shs. 21.87 per month; the average was Shs. 14.87 per month. Unregistered casual labourers received the same pay for the days they worked.

Work in the port in the 1930s was tough and little mechanised, and discipline was harsh. The dockers were sharply divided into the three grades: the permanent staff (themselves divided on craft lines), the registered casuals summoned by the headman's bell, and the unregistered casuals who thronged the wharf gates at dawn. Most workers had little skill: as late as 1953, when figures are first available, the ratio of skilled to unskilled workers was only 1:4.02, compared with 1:1.53 on the railways and 1:1.98 in building.[10] To organise so unskilled, unstable and divided a work force was very difficult. It was made still more difficult by the fact that however harsh their own conditions the dockers were already a relatively favoured group. It is difficult to appreciate just how dreadful a place Dar es Salaam was in this period. An official survey made early in 1939 reckoned that the total African adult male labour force in the town was around 6,000.[11] Of these, some 25 per cent were thought to be unemployed at any time. Of those employed, 60 per cent probably earned less than fifteen shillings a month, the average for a registered casual docker. The social conditions of the town were equally dreadful. Some thousand children under the age of fourteen were thought to be employed, usually at a wage of Shs. 2–4 per month plus food. About 20,000–25,000 Africans were crowded into approximately 3,200 houses, many of them merely temporary shelters. Against this background, the crowds of casual workers thronging the wharf gates to earn Shs. 1.50 per day become comprehensible. For the docker, however, these crowds were a constant threat to his wage level. If he struck or otherwise challenged the discipline of the port, there were always a dozen hungry men fighting for his job. It is no wonder that throughout the dockers' history, both in Tanga and Dar es Salaam, the use of blackleg labour to break a strike was likely to lead to violence, and sometimes to death.

Besides these obstacles to organisation, the dockers had little experience of industrial action on which to draw. No important strike is recorded in Tanzania until 1937, when 250 wharf labourers in Tanga left work for two days.[12] Mombasa had experienced a fairly successful six-day strike in 1934, and doubtless the Dar es Salaam dockers knew of these earlier actions by their fellow-workers, for communication among the East African ports was always close. But in Dar es Salaam itself the only important actions prior to 1939 were three strikes in 1937 by skilled workers: Asian artisans, electricians, and winchmen employed by the African Wharfage Company.[13] The mass of casual workers had no other precedents to bring to their first major struggle in July 1939.

The docker was inexperienced not only in labour organisation but also in industrial discipline and urban life. Most dockers were men from agricultural societies moving for the first time into the insecurity of the town and the disciplined, large-scale employment of the port, so totally different from the work of a peasant. The docker needed a living wage and reasonable working conditions, but he also had needs which no strike or union bargaining could satisfy. He needed, first, some form of community to replace that which he had left behind. He usually found it among his fellow-tribesmen, but he could also find it among his fellow-workers. Second, he needed social security which he could not supply for himself, especially care if he were sick and burial if he died. Third, if he hoped ever to be anything but an unskilled labourer, he needed to become literate and gain some basic education. Finally, he had to adapt himself to the new conditions of industrial employment, with its clock-watching punctuality, its complex wage structures, and its unfamiliar patterns of discipline.

Throughout the world, these urban needs have led workers to combine for their own welfare. So it was among the Dar es Salaam dockers. They may have formed many such organisations, but the only one recorded is the African Labour Union, founded in 1937 by immigrant casual labourers in the port. It had 32 members in August 1937 and 40 by September. The idea had come from three members who had seen similar organisations in South Africa. The union's rules provide a picture of what work in the port and life in the town meant to the intelligent immigrant labourer.[14] First, the union was meant to be a community. It was to build a club house where the members could meet twice a month to discuss their affairs. The rules show that concern for proper procedure which has been so characteristic of early labour organisations elsewhere. 'Matters which have already been decided at a meeting should not be discussed again,' they insisted. 'Each member should talk by turn.' The subscription was Shs. 1.50 a month for committee members and Shs. 1.00 for ordinary members, relatively high figures because the union planned to provide benefits for its members. 'They say their union is for the purpose of helping one another when sick and for burial purposes,' it was reported,[15] and the rules promised that 'the union will assist any member in distress.' Each member was also exhorted to look after his own welfare and 'deposit a small sum in the Post Office Savings Bank for his needs in the event of being without work or against old age.'

Besides their desire for security, the members also sought advancement. 'Every member should learn to read and write', the rules stated, for which purpose 'the Union will employ a teacher to instruct members in reading and writing.' In the same improving vein was its attitude towards work discipline. 'Every member of the Union will implicitly obey his employer and also be submissive and courteous to everyone,' the rules insisted. Above all, the rules showed that intense concern for time and punctuality which is so obsessive for the new industrial worker:

> Every member will attend at his work before the prescribed time in order that he may not be late.
> No member should leave his work before the proper time or without his employer's permission.

Clearly the union had no intention of engaging in industrial disputes. 'If they have trouble with their employers,' it was reported, 'they will put up the matter to Government for settlement. They have no intention to try and influence the employment and control of labour.'

The African Labour Union disappears from the records in December 1937, and in terms of action it was clearly not an important body. But its rules show the aims of the ambitious docker of the late 1930s, his insecurity and his difficulties in adjusting to urban life and industrial work. They also show his anxiety to work steadily and quietly, to improve his skill and his standard of living. Only severe discontent could have forced such men into a strike. In July 1939 that discontent existed.

The growth of docker consciousness

Between 1939 and 1947 the dockers conducted three important strikes, from which they gained in three ways. First, they achieved a strong and self-conscious unity as dockers. Second, they won a privileged position as the best-paid workers in Tanzania. Third, they temporarily became the spearhead of anti-colonial activity throughout the territory. These developments show how the dockers created their own consciousness and organisation through their common actions, 'in the struggle'. The three strikes mark the stages in this process. The last, in 1947, approached the dimensions of a general strike, with the dockers as its leaders. The second, in 1943, was the first common action by all the workers in the port, and the first to pit them against the colonial government. The first strike, in July 1939, was less effective: the workers were divided and uncertain of their ability to challenge their employers successfully.

1939: The strike of the casual workers

The first large-scale strike among the dockers of Dar es Salaam began on 17 July 1939. Very little is known of it save the course of events.[16] On 17 July casual workers throughout the port stopped work. Permanent employees did not join them. On the first afternoon the District Officer addressed an orderly strike meeting. He thought that some strikers seemed ready to return immediately. He advised them to formulate their demands. This took some time, for the demands were not presented until two days later. Meanwhile, the dock gates were picketed, though some fifteen casual labourers returned to work as early as the second day. Unity was thus very quickly lost.

On the third day of the strike the District Officer received the workers' demands. They asked him to put their case sympathetically to the employers. They made five main demands: a daily wage of Shs. 2.00 instead of Shs. 1.50; a mid-day rest; a rate of Shs. 3.50 for night work; compensation for sickness and accidents such as permanent workers received; and better treatment on the job—'we do not like to be kicked and to be pushed or abused during working-time,' they complained. 'If our masters will accept the above statements,' they wrote, 'we shall be ready to do their work, provided that they will agree with what we have written above and sign the agreement before you, Sir.'[17] The petition is the only existing evidence as to the causes of the strike. It suggests three points. First, the demands are very clearly 'grass-roots' grievances emerging directly from daily work, as one would expect in the early stages of a labour movement. Second, the demand for sickness and accident compensation suggests that the casual workers desired to gain the benefits hitherto reserved for permanent workers; perhaps the refusal of the latter to support the strike is further evidence of this. Third, the demand for a standard daily wage of two shillings may have looked backwards to the conditions existing in the late 1920s, before the depression. The dockers were not alone in feeling that their employers had benefited from the revival of trade in the later 1930s while they had not. 'The Europeans of the Companies are treating the Africans unjustly,' the African-owned newspaper, *Kwetu*, had complained eight months before.

However, the Europeans of the Companies were in a powerful position. They refused to raise wages, stating that they could easily recruit a new labour force on the existing terms, and threatening to do so if the strike continued. They undertook to discuss other grievances once work was resumed. On 21 July the Provincial Commissioner met four of the workers' representatives—whose identity is unfortunately unknown—and advised them to return to work. The representatives then discussed the problem with the strikers. They knew that so long as only the casual workers were on strike the companies could replace them from among the town's abundant unemployed. There is no record of this meeting, but the representatives returned to tell the Provincial Commissioner that the men would not return to work but would remove their pickets, presumably meaning that the decision would be left to each individual worker. The pickets were withdrawn next day and gradually the strikers returned, until all were back on 25 July, eight days after the strike had started. Some victimisation by the employers followed.[18]

In material terms, the strike had failed completely. The only change that followed it was a reduction of the registered casual pool so that more work was available for each labourer. The workers' failure was clearly due principally to the refusal of the permanent workers to join them. There is no evidence of how the strike was organised or who led it, although leadership and solidarity seem to have been very weak. It was a spontaneous and loosely-organised action such as often occurs in the early history of a labour force. No organisation appears to have been created after the strike. Consequently, the next stage of industrial action, in 1943, was again a strike with little apparent organisation. This time, however, experience and economic pressure gave the workers the unity they had lacked in 1939.

1943: The strike of the dockers

The common grievance which brought the dockers together in 1943 was the impact of wartime inflation on their standard of living. As shown in Table 1, the cost of living for a man and his wife in Dar es Salaam is estimated to have risen by 55 per cent between September 1939 and January 1943. (It is necessary to stress the many uncertainties surrounding these figures.) As prices rose still faster in the inland trading centres, more and more Africans were forced into Dar es Salaam to seek wage employment. By September 1943 it was reckoned that the African population had grown by some 10,000—perhaps 40 per cent— since the outbreak of war.[19] In September 1942 an official enquiry discovered that 'some 87 per cent of Government employees in Dar es Salaam are in receipt of a wage on which they cannot possibly subsist without getting into debt and remaining in debt'.[20]

The port employers seem to have made one basic wage increase in this period, raising the casual daily rate in June 1940 from Shs. 1.50 to Shs. 1.80, with comparable increases for permanent staff. This 20 per cent rise fell short of the 55 per cent increase in the cost of living. For a time the actual take-home wages of registered casual workers kept pace with prices through a greater regularity of work, due to increased shipping and a reduction in the size of the casual pool. In July and August 1942 each gang worked twenty to thirty shifts a month, which, with overtime, gave the exceptionally regular worker the chance to earn up to eighty shillings a month. Work remained abundant during the first five months of 1943, but in June there was a sharp drop to fourteen shifts. This irregularity may have troubled the casual workers. Throughout this period, however, the permanent workers felt the impact of inflation most severely. Their loss of purchasing power was not compensated by a greater regularity of work. This may explain why they joined the strike which began on 23 August 1943.

The 1943 strike was important in two ways. First, the great majority of the dockers acted as a single group for the first time. With some exceptions the strike was solid among both permanent and casual workers. Second, the government responded sharply to the strike, and the dockers for the first time opposed the full weight of colonial authority.

The events leading up to the strike are most uncertain. There was growing discontent in the port as early as March 1943. Workers of the Tanganyika Boating Company complained to the chief secretary during May, but the issue is not recorded. The dockers may have been influenced by a short strike in Lindi earlier in the year, but there is no evidence of this. The immediate cause seems to have been a bonus granted early in August by the Tanganyika Boating Company to some of its skilled employees outside the port, to bring them into line with a cost of living bonus given to government employees. This put wages out of line throughout the port. The Boating Company's regular and casual workers struck for three days to bring their wages into line. When talk of a wider strike spread through the port, the District Commissioner advised the companies to standardise their rates.[21]

The companies decided to follow the District Commissioner's advice, which involved certain small increases. When these new rates were announced on 13 August the workers would not accept them. Two days later they presented their own demands. There the matter rested for a week, with the companies refusing to negotiate. On 22 August the men met and decided to strike the next day. Some 800 men came out: all the registered casual workers, 300 unregistered casuals, and about 170 of the 250 permanent workers. The main group not to join the strike were the headmen, although the four senior headmen signed the letter stating the workers' demands. Throughout the strike these headmen acted as the men's representatives while themselves still reporting for work each morning. The line between workers and management was not yet clearly drawn.

The strike almost immediately moved into an irreconcilable position. One reason was that on the first day the companies employed 62 convicts to clear a ship in port. Further, the companies felt they would receive strong backing from the government, for under a defence regulation, prepared for precisely this contingency early in the war, port work could be declared an essential service in which strikes were illegal. The District Commissioner believed that the strike had been incited by three 'agitators' previously dismissed by the companies and deported from Dar es Salaam. Nothing further is known of these men.

While the employers relied on wartime necessity, the workers clearly drew strength from the 'very complete' and 'most orderly' character of their action.[22] At no time did the employers threaten to recruit a new labour force: solidarity with the skilled permanent workers made that almost impossible. Indeed, the strike was probably led by skilled workers. The demands presented on the second day emphasised particularly the claims of permanent employees. They called for wage increases of around 25 per cent for most grades, a cost of living bonus, fourteen days' paid leave a year, retirement gratuities, a free mid-day meal, and improved sick pay and medical benefits. The casual workers made simpler demands: sick pay and medical treatment, a free mid-day meal and an increase in the basic casual daily rate from Shs. 1.80 to Shs.3.00.[23] The companies rejected these terms and demanded that the workers return on the rates existing before the revisions made by the Tanganyika Boating Company.

By now stronger considerations were pressing on the District Commissioner. Rapid movement of ships was essential in wartime, and he felt that the strikers were being misled by 'agitators'. On the morning of 25 August he advised the Provincial Commissioner to invoke defence regulations, and in the afternoon he told the strikers, 'You have left your work through obstinacy or because those who have been advising you have deceived you.' Warning them of defence regulations, he ordered them to return on the terms issued on 13 August. The men refused any terms but their own. Two days later the District Commissioner came to believe that some workers would return if guaranteed protection against intimidation. Hoping that the strike was breaking, he summoned the workers to a meeting. When none appeared he referred the matter to the Governor. Next day the port was declared an essential service in which, under defence regulations, strikes were illegal. The dispute was referred to a tribunal headed by Mr Justice Wilson.[24]

The dockers were now up against the law. On 28 August, 250–300 of them met and were addressed by the Yiwali of the town and his headmen, but these notables withdrew when the mood became dangerous. The men then unanimously resolved to stay out until their demands were met. At this point the District Commissioner became convinced that 'the strikers were bound by a religious oath—about which senior religious leaders were not sympathetic—not to return to work except on their own terms.' There is no other evidence of this.[25]

By 9 a.m. the next day no workers had returned and the Governor authorised the arrest of strikers. At least 142 were arrested during the next four days; most were given suspended sentences by the Resident Magistrate. Meanwhile the tribunal had begun its public hearings. It heard at least seventeen African witnesses, mostly dockers. No record of their evidence has been discovered.

Arrests began on 29 August, and they were effective. By 3 September, 205 permanent and 179 casual workers were back, although nobody had returned to the Tanganyika Boating Company. The next morning the port was working almost normally. After a total of twelve days, the strike was broken. The tribunal's award was published two days later. Casual workers gained little, certainly not enough to restore the real value of their daily rate to its 1939 level. The permanent workers gained more. The award generally followed the terms of the employers' offer of 13 August: to that extent the strike had failed.[26]

Although it was decided not to prosecute leaders or make those convicted serve their sentences, the Tanganyika Boating Company victimised those it considered 'trouble-makers'. At least five were dismissed without compensation, three of whom had given evidence before the tribunal. In the later stages of the strike the men had insisted on receiving assurances that there would be no victimisation. They were given such assurances. Now, lacking the power of a trade union and legally prohibited from striking, the workers could not prevent victimisation. Just as in 1939 they had learned that an effective strike required unity between permanent and casual workers, so now they learned that striking without union organisation was dangerous. Through their actions—'in the struggle'—the dockers of Dar es Salaam were learning the lesson of solidarity.

1947: The General Strike

'The African post-war freedom is only a mere joke,' a correspondent in *Kwetu* wrote on the day the 1943 strike began. 'The British victory is certain—we pray for that but we must not think that there will be any better change for the black.'[27] To the Africans of Dar es Salaam, that statement must have seemed bitterly true in the years following the war. This was probably the worst period in the town's history. The population roughly doubled during the war, while the number of African houses actually fell slightly between June 1939 and July 1944. At the latter date there were sixteen water kiosks in the African town to serve an estimated 40,000 people. Before 1943, the immigrant worker was spared the burden of rising rents. Now rents doubled between 1943 and 1947, although not a single African applied for redress to the Rent Restriction Board.[28] As Table 1 shows, the government's casual labour rate kept pace with the official cost of living. However, necessary goods were increasingly either sold on the black market or were simply not available. Public meetings to protest against rationing were held in the town during 1946. Of the 365 cases of stealing which the Resident Magistrate tried in the second half of that year, at least 60 were due to sheer hunger.[29]

This was the background to the Tanzanian strike of 1947. The strike was the high point in the dockers' history. They initiated it. They won impressive gains both in their working conditions and their own organisation and confidence. Briefly they led the most widespread protest in Tanzanian history between the end of the Maji Maji rising and the formation of TANU.

The major grievance of the dockers who began the strike was the failure of their wages to keep pace with rising prices. While the Dar es Salaam price index (even at 'controlled' prices) rose between 1939 and March 1947 by 87 per cent, the basic wage of the registered casual docker rose only 53 per cent. There are no data to show whether this was balanced by more regular work. It may have been, for in December 1946 a record tonnage passed over the wharf. However, the dockers shared the general grievances of Tanzanians. 'If you don't riot you won't get your right,' the eminently respectable secretary of the African Association urged during a meeting in September 1946.[30] Eight strikes were threatened in Dar es Salaam early in 1947. All the disputes were resolved without strike action, but some protest was bound to come. That it came from the dockers was due mainly to their superior striking power.

On 22 August 1949, the dockers warned their employers that unless they received substantial improvements in wages and conditions they would strike at the end of the month. After a fortnight's delay, the employers made an offer on 5 September. By this time, however, the dockers had reached a point of no return, and the Labour Department hastened to replace the emergency regulations in force since 1943 by a new ordinance providing for compulsory arbitration. The next evening the dockers met to decide whether to strike. It seems that the leaders were overruled by their followers. The next morning the strike was almost complete.[31]

Attitudes soon hardened. The men refused to work or negotiate. They demanded a rise in the casual daily rate from Shs. 2.30 to Shs. 5.00 and a general rate of Shs. 100.00 per month for skilled permanent employees—including headmen, who probably first joined a strike on this occasion. The employers had offered permanent workers increases of a few shillings a month and casual workers 20 cents more a day. On the second day the strike began to spread to other casual workers and some violence and intimidation began, probably not so much from the dockers as from the town's unemployed. The next day, after the Labour Officer had failed to persuade a meeting of 700 dockers to return, the strike began to spread in earnest. The first organised group to join were the railway workers, who walked out unanimously at lunchtime on 10 September. Better organised than the dockers—since 1945 their Railway African Association had been nearly 2,000 strong—they had also the advantage · of a network stretching throughout the country, through which the strike was to spread.[32]

Dar es Salaam on the morning of 11 September was dead. The strike was general and pickets were out throughout the town. 'I managed to outwit the mobs and pickets till I reached the New Palace Hotel,' a worker later excused himself, 'but there I found pickets were stationed everywhere. I tried to pass through but I was threatened by the pickets with sticks. I was therefore forced to return home.'[33] Forty-five men were arrested during the day, and in the evening three hundred special constables patrolled the town.

The dockers still dominated the situation. The next afternoon they heard speeches by the Labour Commissioner and the Provincial Commissioner promising to appoint a tribunal if they returned to work. They decided to continue the strike, but the government detected 'some indication of better understanding by actual wharf leaders.'[34]

Meanwhile the strike had begun to spread up-country along the railway line. Railway workers in Morogoro, Dodoma, and Tabora walked out on 11 September. The next day they were joined by their colleagues at Kilosa and by sisal workers at Morogoro, while on the thirteenth the strike in Tabora became general and was joined even by the African teachers at the two government schools.

On the morning of the thirteenth the general strike in Dar es Salaam began to break. Lorries with police protection moved into the African town to transport those who were prepared to work, and that evening the government warned African civil servants—among whom the strike was widespread—that anyone who did not return to work on the morning of Monday, 15 September, would be dismissed. A mass meeting of dockers on Sunday morning was reported to be equally divided between continuing the strike and returning to work, but in the afternoon the pickets were removed and leaders announced that they would return to work next day. Seventy per cent of the dockers reported for work on Monday, and gradually during the day Dar es Salaam returned to normal. The dock workers went back more quickly than the stevedores, and casual workers more quickly than those on permanent terms. A tribunal under the chairmanship of G. W. Hatchell was appointed on 15 September.

The general strike in the capital was over, but up-country it was only just beginning. Kigoma and Mwanza struck on 15 September. The Kigoma strike was headed by railway clerks, while in Mwanza the dockers struck first and then moved through the town calling out other workers and stoning Barclay's Bank. The strike then spread to trading settlements in Bakumbi and Masungwe. Two days later the situation was normal again in both Kigoma and Mwanza. Workers on the Kongwa Groundnut Scheme struck on 15 September for ten days. There was a brief stoppage in Arusha on 17 September, while saltworkers at Uvinza remained out until 22 September. The final incident took place on 6 October at Uruwira lead mines in Mpanda. The strike had taken precisely a month to spread from Dar es Salaam to Mpanda.

The astonishing success of the strike and the seething discontent it demonstrated undoubtedly influenced the tribunal which sat from 17 to 23 September. The employers' and workers' representatives failed to reach agreement, so Hatchell imposed his own award. He was well known to be critical of the obscurantism of the port employers, an attitude he had expressed as far back as the 1939 strike in Tanga. His award, which was published on 26 September, was designed to stimulate the conversion of port employment from irregular casual labour to a regular profession. He urged the introduction of a shift system to end excessive overtime and create 'a professional class of waterfront workmen'. He introduced a five-shilling bonus for attendance on twenty days in any month, regular free meals, and free hospital treatment for workers. Perhaps more important to the dockers, he awarded wage increases variously estimated at 40–50 per cent of existing pay, raising the casual daily wage from Shs. 2.30 to Shs. 3.90 and finally pushing the dockers' wages well above the price increases since 1939. The government and many private employers brought their rates into line in the following months. The dockers had won a substantial economic advance for Tanganyikan workers as a whole.[35]

The dockers were delighted, and with reason. They had maintained their solidarity throughout the strike: there is no indication on this occasion of any permanent workers remaining outside it. With the help of the railway workers they had paralysed the town for two days and spread their strike throughout the country. They had defeated their employers before the hitherto hostile machinery of government. It was noted that during the tribunal the dockers recognised that their real negotiating partner was not the employers but the government.[36] Given the experience of 1943, the fact that the tribunal was officially appointed, and the cost-plus contract existing between the companies and government, this attitude was realistic.

The 1947 award made the dockers a privileged group among Tanzanian workers, the best paid, most formidable labour force in the country. It was won by the first real exercise of African power in Tanzania since the end of Maji Maji —an exhilarating and enlightening experience for those who participated.[37] But the award had to be implemented. Hatchell himself had recognised this by insisting that 'the workmen shall appoint accredited representatives of each category of workmen who shall be allowed to represent the workmen and to discuss with the employers any matters arising out of the employment'.[38] Thus encouraged, and with the experience of victimisation in 1943 to guide them, the dockers now formed their first permanent organisation. Action had created consciousness; now consciousness was institutionalised in a trade union.

The emergence of a trade union

The Dockworkers' and Stevedores' Union was formed by the dockers themselves soon after the publication of the Hatchell Award in September 1947. By the end of the year it claimed some 1,500 members, probably very nearly all the men regularly employed in the port. Led mainly by the headmen, the union was registered on 9 December, without the assistance or knowledge of the Labour Department.[39]

The attitude of the British authorities to trade unions was ambivalent. A few unions had already been registered under an ordinance of 1932: first Asian unions in the 1930s, then in 1946 a small union of African domestic servants. Two more powerful organisations, the Tanganyika African Government Servants Association and the Railway African Association, were both regarded as staff associations, although the distinction was not very precise. Presented now with a much more powerful body which it feared might come under communist influence, the government decided to try to direct it into 'constructive' channels. On 21 January 1948, Hamilton, a Labour Department official, met the Union Executive and worked out with it the basic essentials of a permanent organisation. The Executive decided to equip an office, buy the necessary registers and stationery, print a rule book, and appoint a paid full-time general secretary. The sources of its funds are not clear, but Hamilton reckoned it would have an annual income of £2,000.[40] In February the union chose as its first general secretary, Abdul Wahid Sykes, a well-educated ex-soldier from a family prominent in Dar es Salaam for fifty years.

The present evidence allows one to see the union only through the eyes of the Labour Department. Hamilton clearly saw it as a means of introducing enlightened labour relations and a more professional form of employment into the port. By March 1948 he had persuaded it to take initial steps in these directions.

First, both sides agreed to participate in a joint committee, which met informally on 1 March. A negotiated voluntary agreement on wages and conditions of work—the first in the territory—came into force on 1 November. The second and more complicated issue was to professionalise the work of the dockers. Early in 1948 the port was still worked mainly by casual labour. At least 1,500 casual workers sought intermittent employment alongside the specialised, permanent workers in an industry whose normal labour needs did not exceed 1,000. Consequently the mass of workers were unskilled and undisciplined. To remedy this situation, Hamilton proposed a three-stage programme. First, all men working in the port should be registered. Second, they should receive some form of identification. Finally, 'at the appropriate moment and after propaganda amongst Dock Workers', a system of control should be introduced by which a port registration committee, made up of workers' and employers' representatives, would control all recruitment, registration, training, allocation, conditions, welfare, and discharge of dockers. This would stabilise the labour force, make it more flexible, provide more regular work, and break down the authoritarian disciplinary system. The employers welcomed this but were unwilling to initiate it, perhaps fearing the workers' reactions.[41]

Hamilton next sought to persuade the workers to accept the registration scheme. Their reaction cannot be documented, but logically, and by analogy with later responses to decasualisation, the workers would have been ambivalent towards it. On the one hand, the Hatchell award had made them a relatively privileged group and encouraged them to exclude outsiders from their occupation. Consequently, as Hamilton reported, 'the Union is desirous that steps be taken to introduce some measure of control over the labour force'.[42] On the other hand, the full implementation of a registration scheme would reduce the number of dockers, threatening both to make some existing workers redundant and to reduce the numerical and financial strength of the union. There is evidence of some conflict between the union executive and its members in the middle of 1948. Dissatisfied with the short-sightedness of the members and the indiscipline of the leaders, Sykes resigned his post in July; but a meeting of some 500 dockers on 13 August accepted registration and decasualisation so long as compensation was paid to redundant long-service workers. The negotiated agreement which came into force on 1 November gave final approval to the scheme.

The scheme was intended to be operated by a joint committee of workers and employers, but participation by the workers in control of labour was vetoed by the port authority, and the scheme was implemented by the Labour Department during 1949. This may have been the key to later events. The workers were prepared to accept registration controlled by the government or jointly by themselves, and by May 1949 Hamilton had registered 1,800 dockers and nearly completed this stage of the operation. He then went on leave, and in his absence the operation of the scheme was handed over to the Landing and Shipping Company. Now began the most difficult part, for the company had to establish the rule that any registered worker who was absent for more than six days in any month would lose his registration card and his right to work in the port. A scheme originally designed to achieve greater regularity of work for the dockers and give them a degree of control over their labour had become a means of discipline. There was increasing discontent in the port. A go-slow began at the end of the year, although the Labour Department thought other reasons also lay behind this.

At the same time, in December 1949, the government became dissatisfied with the union. It was indeed a remarkable body, the first powerful organisation created by the largely illiterate casual workers of Dar es Salaam. Abdul Sykes later recalled the horror with which his dignified, respectable father used to witness meetings of the executive in his house, often while union members danced an *ngoma* outside. When Sykes resigned, the post of secretary passed— against the government's wishes—to a still more remarkable man, Erika Fiah, the editor of *Kwetu*. A Muganda who had come to Tanzania with the British forces during the First World War, Fiah had been the storm centre of Dar es Salaam politics for fifteen years. A disciple of the American negro leader Marcus Garvey, Fiah had already tried to organise the shopkeepers of the town and the farmers of the suburbs. He was eventually ousted through government intrigue, but under his leadership the union asserted its presence by building a two-storey headquarters. One storey had been completed at a cost of Shs. 15,000 when the organisation was banned. Membership grew steadily through 1949, from 1,000 to 2,259 paid-up members. At the height of its success, the union possessed cash and property said to be worth Shs. 65,000. There is evidence of considerable solidarity among the members. A general meeting in August 1948 was prepared to reprimand nine winchmen and two headmen who had worked during a stoppage, and there was to be much evidence of unity during the 1950 strike.[43] Nevertheless, the union's organisation did not satisfy the government. Many allegations of extortion and corruption were made. High salaries were paid to union officers and it is said that every worker, as he went off shift, had to pay fifty cents from his wages to ensure future employment. However, these allegations were never proved.

Exactly what led the union to strike on 1 February 1950 is now very difficult to discover. On that day a new gate and call-on stance were to be used for the first time. It is not clear whether these were designed to prevent the corruption which the government believed to exist. As in 1947, it seems, the men's leaders first opposed a strike, but on 31 January the union executive instructed its members not to enter the port through the new gate. Next morning the strike was complete save for a few permanent workers. The port was guarded by steel-helmeted police, whose unusually rapid and determined intervention supports the view, which some of those involved still hold, that the government believed the strike had been fomented by left-wing elements in the town.

The three previous dock strikes in Dar es Salaam had been disciplined and orderly. That of 1950, although again very solid, soon degenerated into the worst violence the town experienced before independence. The reasons were almost certainly the attitude of the authorities and the use of blackleg labour on the first day, which provoked the dockers to fury. Violence that began with intimidation to prevent strike-breaking quickly turned against the police who protected the blacklegs. When no dockers reported on 1 February the employers announced that work was available for any applicant. By 9 a.m. 300 volunteers had been found, and next day some 600 were working.[44] The dockers' leaders tried at first to preserve discipline. Pickets were out on the first day, but there was no interference with the strike-breakers. That evening the leaders told a meeting of 400–500 dockers to remain calm; the meeting ended with prayers. By lunchtime the second day the dockers' mood was changing. In the afternoon the executive told the employers that there would be trouble if any union member was employed in the docks. Violence began on the third morning, Friday, 3 February. At 7 a.m. union members picketing the dock gate clashed with police guarding the docks. A police officer was injured and 16 dockers were arrested. Later, another 41 dockers were arrested when they sought to release their fellows from the police lines. Meanwhile a much more serious riot took place in the 'open space' separating the African town from the commercial zone. A police riot squad was surrounded, stoned, and threatened by a crowd of 500–600 people. The police were cut off and their officers opened fire with revolvers, killing one African, fatally wounding another and injuring six more. The infuriated crowd rushed the police and one European and one Asian police officer were critically injured. That afternoon armed police patrolled the town, the KAR were called in, and many arrests were made, including all members of the union executive.[45]

Altogether 145 men were charged with offences arising from the strike and the ensuing violence. Eight members of the union executive charged with unlawful assembly and conspiring to prevent casual labourers from exercising their occupation were released for lack of evidence. Of those charged with offences arising from the riot, one was sentenced to ten years for attempted murder and nine others—including one described as a union official—were imprisoned for lesser crimes. Another 77 were convicted of offences in other incidents. Only one reported statement by a prisoner sheds any light on the reasons for violence. This arose from the incident at the dock gates:

> The only accused to make a statement said that he was a member of the Union which had decided to strike because of oppression.
>
> 'After starting the strike,' he declared, 'we heard that some of our members were still working . . . and we went to see whether this was true. . .
>
> 'Our intention was to go and prevent our workers going there, but when the police found our weapons they thought we were going to create a disturbance.'[46]

The riot had taken place on 3 February. By 5 February the port was again working normally with volunteer labour. Many of the casual workers who had struck soon filtered cautiously back. Many of the skilled permanent workers never returned, and the employers began to train winchmen and headmen from scratch. Officially, the strike was never called off by the union before it was dissolved by High Court order on 2 June 1950. Its property—the half-completed building and Shs. 24,000 in cash—was transferred to the public trustee.

Thus ended not only the first attempt at permanent organisation among the dockers but also a whole period of labour history in Tanzania. The government's relatively liberal attitude towards trade unionism changed abruptly. 'Government were of the opinion that the African was at the present time quite unable to accept responsibility in a Trades Union sense,' Hamilton told employers in Tanga in April 1950, 'and were doing absolutely nothing to encourage Trade Unionism at this time.'[47] This negative attitude, which so angered trade union organisers in the mid-1950s, largely resulted from the 1950 dock strike.

The dockers themselves lost something still more important. The almost complete turnover of senior workers destroyed the traditions and experience they had built up during the previous eleven years. The pioneers of labour organisation in Tanganyika, they now lost the initiative to other workers. They took little part in the creation of the TFL in 1955, and when they again became a powerful, self-conscious group at the end of the decade, it was in the different environment of nationalism.

NOTES

1. This article is based on a longer paper, 'A History of the Dockworkers of Dar es Salaam', *Tanzania Notes and Records*, 71, 1970, pp. 119–48. For access to records in their keeping I must thank the Director of the Tanzania National Archives (TNA), the Principal Secretary to the Tanzania Ministry of Labour (LD), and the Administrative Secretary of the Tanganyika African National

Union (TANU). For further information I am grateful to Mr M. T. Barkart, Mrs Daisy Sykes Buruku, Mr B. Mpangala, and Mr M. L. Willers.

2. A. C. A. Tandau, *Historia ya Kuundwa kwa T.F.L. (1955–62) na Kuanzishwa kwa NUTA (1964)*, Dar es Salaam, n.d.; W. H. Friedland, *Vuta Kamba: the Development of Trade Unions in Tanganyika*, Stanford, 1969.

3. Karl Marx, *The Poverty of Philosophy*, Moscow edn, n.d., p. 195 (italics not in original).

4. E. P. Thompson, *The Making of the English Working Class*, Gollancz, 1963, p. 194.

5. G. Maxwell, 'Railway Enquiry into the Dar es Salaam Lighterage and Wharfage Charges', Mar. 1934, TNA SMP 25312/1/2.

6. Manager, Lighterage and Stevedoring Company, to D.O., Dar es Salaam, 10 Jan. 1928, TNA 61/295/32; T. P. S. Dawkins (D.O., Dar es Salaam) to P.C., Eastern, 10 Jan. 1928, TNA 61/295/27.

7. The date is given as approximately 1934 by M. J. B. Molohan, 'Report on Conditions of Employment of Dock Labour in Dar es Salaam', 3 Jan. 1940, TNA SMP 25912/6a.

8. J. Dickson (L.O., Dar es Salaam) to Labour Commissioner, June 1940, TNA 61/14/22/I/2.

9. This account is based on Molohan's report cited in note 7 above.

10. *Labour Department Annual Report (Labour Report)*, 1953, p. 46.

11. A. H. Pike, 'Report on Native Affairs in Dar es Salaam Township', 5 June 1939, TNA 61/207/2/220.

12. *Annual Reports of the Provincial Commissioners*, 1937, 73. The Superintendent of Police told the Commission of Enquiry into the Tanga strike of 1939 that there had been a major strike in Tanga in 1929, but it is not mentioned in any other source. There is also a reference to a dock strike in Dar es Salaam in 1936, again without corroboration. See Molohan (L.O., Dar es Salaam) to P.C., Eastern, 23 Aug. 1943, TNA 61/679/12.

13. See the correspondence in TNA SMP 24829; P.M. (Huggins ?), 12 Aug. 1937, on Mrisho Sultani to Chief Secretary, 7 Aug. 1937, TMA SMP 25201/2.

14. 'The African Labour Union: Mroja wa Wenyeji Watumishi wa Kazi, etc. Sheria na Kanuni za Chama', enclosed in Mrisho Sultani to Chief Secretary, 7 Aug. 1937, TNA 61/14/14/1–2.

15. H. M. T. Kayamba, minute, 26 Aug. 1937, TNA SMP 25201/10.

16. This account is drawn from unsigned notes in TNA 61/679/1, virtually the only source of information on the strike yet discovered.

17. 'All Coolies, Dar es Salaam' to D.O., Dar es Salaam, 19 July 1939, TNA 61/679/5.

18. Molohan, 'Report on Conditions of Employment', 3 Jan. 1940, TNA SMP 25912/6a.
19. *Tanganyika Standard* (2 Sept. 1943).
20. 'Report of Enquiry into Wages and Cost of Living of Low Grade African Government Employees in Dar es Salaam' (Sept. 1942), TNA SMP 30598/15.
21. Dickson (L.O., Eastern), to Labour Commissioner (April 1943), TNA 61/14/22/I/57; *Tanganyika Standard* (3 Sept. 1943); *Labour Report 1943*, 7; Molohan (D.C., Uzaramo) to P.C., Eastern, 23 Aug. 1943, TNA 61/679/12.
22. *Tanganyika Standard* (28 Aug. 1943).
23. Molohan (D.C., Uzaramo) to P.C., Eastern, 25 Aug. 1943, TNA 61/679/16; *Labour Report, 1943*, p. 8.
24. Notes by Molohan, 25 Aug. 1943, TNA 61/679/23; note dated 27 Aug. 1943, TNA 61/679/28; *Gazette Supplement*, 28 Aug. 1943.
25. Notes by P. C. Baker (P.C., Eastern), 28 Aug. 1943, TNA 61/679/32; *Tanganyika Standard* (2 Sept. 1943).
26. Award in TNA 61/679/47.
27. *Kwetu* (22 Sept. 1943).
28. *Labour Report 1948*, pp. 72–3; *Tanganyika Standard* (20 Sept. 1947); minutes in TNA 61/750/2.
29. *Tanganyika Standard* (27 Sept. and 30 Aug. 1947); O. Flynn (P.C., Eastern) to Chief Secretary, 10 Dec. 1946, TNA SMP 20217/2/74.
30. Dennis Mkande, 'General Meeting on 5/9/46', TANU 7.
31. Ordinance No. 11 of 1947 (5 Sept. 1947); *Labour Report 1947*, 21; *Tanganyika Standard* (9 and 13 Sept. 1947).
32. *Tanganyika Standard* (13 Sept. 1947).
33. Ali Omar to Director of Public Works, 26 Sept. 1947, TNA SMP 36490/6a.
34. TBC broadcast script, 12 Sept. 1947, 6.30 p.m., TNA SMP 27271/7; Chief Secretary to Provincial Commissioners, telegram, 12 Sept. 1947, TNA 63/L/1/4/65.
35. The Hatchell award is printed in full in *Labour Report 1947*, pp. 44–7.
36. R. A. Maguire to Governor, minute, 24 Sept. 1947, TNA SMP 16795.
37. See, for example, Mwinjuma (Hon. Sec., African Association, Morogoro) to Hon. Sec., A.A., Dar es Salaam, 14 Sept. 1947, TANU 7.
38. *Labour Report 1947*, p. 47.
39. *Ibid.*, 22; R. M. Bell (for Labour Commissioner) to Labour Commissioner, Nairobi, 23 Aug. 1948. LD 126/3/7; *Labour Report 1945*, p. 119.
40. G. Hamilton, report for quarter ended 31 Mar. 1948, LD 126/3/3.
41. Hamilton, report for quarter ended 31 Mar. 1948, LD 126/3/3; Labour Commissioner to Member for Education, Labour and Social Welfare, 1 June 1948, LD 126/9/5; memorandum enclosed in Hamilton to P. C.

Jerrard, 6 Mar. 1948, LL 126/3/1a; R. W. Bart (L.D., Dar es Salaam) to Hamilton, 24 Mar. 1948, LD 126/3/3a.

42. Hamilton, report for quarter ended 31 Mar. 1948, LD 126/3/3.

43. Minutes of a meeting, Tanga, 28 April 1950, LD 126/4/3; *Labour Report 1948*, 119; *ibid.*, 1949, 29; *ibid.*, 1950, 18; Barkart, report, 14 Aug. 1948, LD 126/3/6a.

44. *Labour Report 1950*, p. 19; *Tanganyika Standard* (2 Feb. 1950).

45. *Tanganyika Standard* (4 Feb. and 18–24 Mar. 1950); *Labour Report 1950*, p. 20.

46. *Tanganyika Standard* (4 Feb. 1950).

47. Minutes of a meeting, Tanga, 28 April 1950, LD 126/4/3.

The Growth of Railway Unionism in the Rhodesias, 1944–1955

ARTHUR TURNER

The events leading up to the formation of the Railway African Workers' Union in Northern and Southern Rhodesia have been almost totally ignored.[1] As a result of the previous tendency by historians to examine the industrial history of Central Africa on a territorial basis, the interterritorial development of the RAWU and its importance to the development of Central African trade unionism has been missed. The history of the RAWU must be seen within the context of two politically distinct systems bound together by a line of rail. The RAWU was the product of the complex interaction of two African labour organisations, two governments and Rhodesia Railways.

The nascent African railway labour movement was more highly developed in Southern Rhodesia than in Northern Rhodesia when, in 1945, a strike spreading from Bulawayo to the Copperbelt was organised. The strike was successful, but Rhodesia Railways, backed by the Southern Rhodesian Government, was able to maintain strict control over African labour organisation and prevented the foundation of an African railway union in Southern Rhodesia. In contrast, Northern Rhodesia was prompted by the post-war British Labour Government to actively encourage the formation of African trade unions in an effort to defuse a potentially explosive industrial situation. The two governments' opposed approaches to labour relations resulted in a political environment which encouraged African railway unions to pursue short-term material advances within their own industry.

The development of the Rhodesian railway unions was not inspired by, directed by, or used by African nationalist parties. Nor were they forces behind parties. Although there was considerable contact between the Northern Rhodesian union and the African National Congress between 1950 and 1955, actual concerted action was minimal. In Southern Rhodesia the formation of the

Rhodesia Railways African Employees' Association in 1944 preceded the development of a nationalist party by thirteen years. In Northern Rhodesia the creation of the African Railway Workers' Trade Union in 1950 was one year later than, but not dependent upon, the development of the African National Congress. The Northern Rhodesian Government's refusal to tolerate union political activity discouraged the union rank and file from involvement in political issues which might endanger short-range economic goals. The evidence concerning railway union development in the Rhodesias supports E. J. Berg's and J. Butler's general thesis that colonial tropical African trade union involvement with nationalist parties was limited.[2]

Railway union members' parochial attitude was not simply the result of government coercion but was a reflection of the social divisions in Rhodesian towns. Unlike the Francophone West African and Sierra Leonean railway workers and Lagosian workers described by C. H. Allen, H. E. Conway and A. Peace, Rhodesian railway workers did not interact closely with other urban Africans even during strikes.[3] When Rhodesian railway workers went on strike they continued to live in their isolated railways compound housing and to receive railways rations. They were not dependent upon the general populace for sustenance during their trials of strength with railway management.[4] Conversely, the general urban African populace was not badly hurt by strikes, for the vast majority of urban entrepreneurial activity was in the hands of Europeans and Asians. African hawkers were itinerant, marketeers few and mostly concerned with supplementing the wage earner's income. There was relatively little contact between workers of different industries at the rank and file level. The workers' attention was focused on their own industrial employer. Along the railway line, workers stationed at small depots could not have contact with other industrial workers, although they had closer contacts with villagers. Some rural Africans made a small income selling produce to these workers, and villagers generally looked forward to the remittances of working relatives. But these people were too far removed from the scenes of industrial action, and too dispersed to influence the short-range course of industrial events. While the urban-rural turnover of African labour undoubtedly had long-range political consequences, the growing number of long-term workers' concern for protecting their gratuities, pensions and paid holiday benefits had a more immediate effect on the union's conduct of industrial relations.

The 1945 strike

In March 1944 the Rhodesian Railways African Employees' Association was formed in Bulawayo to protect the rapidly declining value of African workers' meagre wages. While costs of manufactured goods had soared by 100 per cent to 200 per cent and food by 50 per cent to 100 per cent their wages had remained at depression levels.[5] Government officials counselled patience and exhorted them to contribute to the war effort, but European unions flexed their muscles and forced industry to pay unprecedented wage increases in order to keep the strategic supplies of copper moving along the line of rail. The new organisation set up branches in Southern Rhodesia and even a few in Northern Rhodesia, though membership was smaller there.[6] The railways ignored the Association and refused to recognise the importance of its complaints. All along the line railway officials discouraged Africans from voicing grievances. Communications between labour and management were negligible when the railways introduced a new system of overtime payments 'which benefited lower-paid workers but penalised the small number of better-off and more politically conscious workmen'.[7] On 25 October 1945, the anger of these men found a ready audience among the mass of frustrated African railway workers and the strike began.

As the last trains made their runs, word of the strike passed up the line from Bulawayo. Because African train crews changed trains at mid-points between major depots, they returned home each day and it was easy for them to spread the word in their compound. In Broken Hill, organisers, at least one of whom was an association member, went up and down the rows of African barracks informing workers of the strike in different languages.[8] The workers' response to the organisers' appeal was immediate and whole-hearted—so much so that today every railway worker remembers the strike as being spontaneous. The strike easily cut across ethnic lines and every depot except Livingstone took part.[9]

One by one the depots from Bulawayo to Ndola ground to a halt and European Rhodesians found themselves gripped in a crisis of major proportions. The railways were far and away the most important transportation system in Central Africa. Both Southern and Northern Rhodesia were dependent upon the railways for the transportation of crops, material goods, coal for power, and income-producing minerals, including Northern Rhodesia's great export: copper. Farmers feared their crops would rot, manufacturers feared their production would cease, mine managers that their mines would flood, and government officials, particularly in Northern Rhodesia, feared that the strike would become general. In Broken Hill African mineworkers did strike and commercial and domestic workers threatened to do so. Northern Rhodesian officials feared European control was endangered; Southern Rhodesian employers feared a general increase in labour costs.[10]

The strike was peacefully conducted at all depots, both workers and officials showing restraint. Both parties remembered the violence of the 1935 and 1940

Copperbelt strikes and were determined to avoid a repetition. Upon being promised an impartial commission of inquiry the Bulawayo railwaymen went back to work on 29 October 1945. The railways' promise to abide by the commission's recommendations was crucial in persuading the labourers to end the strike. However, the Broken Hill railwaymen remained out for an additional seven days until they were convinced that this arrangement was the best that could be obtained.[11] The mineworkers' strike started and ended later than the railway workers' strike and seems to have been independently conducted. Suffering from many of the same problems as the railwaymen, the mineworkers followed their example. However, it is significant that today many Broken Hill mineworkers clearly remember the 1935 and 1940 Copperbelt strikes, which they did not witness, but have indistinct memories of the railway workers' strike in Broken Hill. Virtually all the mineworkers I interviewed believed that they were the first to go on strike and that the strike was directed from the Copperbelt. Some did not remember any railway strike at all. The railway workers have more accurate memories concerning their own role, although some of them also believe Copperbelt workers headed the strike. Obviously, the events in the Copperbelt have had a powerful influence upon the memories of Broken Hill industrial labourers. But it is also clear that their identity has become industry oriented and that they do not primarily identify themselves as part of a class cutting across the whole labouring strata of Broken Hill society. The growth of Northern Rhodesian trade unions bound workers of the same industry together irrespective of city. This pattern of union development had the effect of keeping different labour organisations in the same city apart. The resulting divisions were reinforced by the fact that African labour resided in isolated company compounds. As a result, Broken Hill workers are more concerned with matters in their own industry or enterprise, regardless of geographical location, than with the affairs of another industry in their own town.[12]

After the strike, the railwaymen's representatives poured forth their grievances concerning inedible or inadequate food rations, cramped housing, filthy sanitation, inadequate water supplies, unfair dismissals, and the arbitrary loss of health, leave and gratuity benefits to the Commission of Inquiry.[13]

The commission recommended wage increases (5s. per month), promotion according to merit, improved food rations (but not money in lieu of food), sick-leave pay, immediate payment of injury compensation, one month's paid leave after three years of service and a guaranteed gratuity after 20 years' service, more closely calculated overtime pay, better housing, more protective clothing and better welfare and recreation provisions. A reorganisation of the railways' personnel department was recommended so that African grievances could be more quickly, effectively and peacefully handled. The commission also suggested that the system of compound elders and tribal representatives be extended so that worker complaints could be more effectively voiced before feelings reached a crisis point. The commission failed to differentiate between the system of tribal elders which had been established for half a dozen years and the workers' councils which had formed during (or slightly before) the strike. This was a crucial error, for in neither mine nor railway compounds were compound elders regarded as effective worker representatives in industrial affairs.[14] The workers regarded the compound elders as effective social arbitrators but not as industrial leaders. As a result, no real progress was made in improving management-labour relations. The evidence from Broken Hill labour officers' reports (1940–1945) and from interviews with African workers confirms A. L. Epstein's first observation of this division of social and industrial roles within the Luanshya mine compound.[15]

In many ways the 1945 strike was a success. The inquiry deemed some action necessary on almost every African complaint, although recommended measures were often inadequate. African railwaymen had proved their ability to organise a peaceful, cohesive strike for an effective period of time to Bulawayo, Lusaka, London and to themselves. However, the workers had serious difficulty in effectively and accurately formulating and presenting their living costs and wage demands. They had no coherent argument to back their demand for 5s. a day, although they were better able to articulate their ration, housing and working condition needs.

In one important respect the strike failed. African workers never met management officials at the bargaining table and they did not gain first-hand negotiating experience. Government and corporation officials refused to recognise African workers as negotiating partners. Africans were still to be lectured to, not negotiated with. They were to remain the objects of paternalism until they succeeded in forming their own independent, organised power base.

Post-war labour organisation: the rise of the ARWTU

The Labour Government in London observed the strike with an anxious eye. It could not view labour unrest in a colony with equanimity. The House of Commons exerted pressure on the Secretary of State for the colonies who in turn requested the colonial government to inform him closely and confidentially about the implementation of the commission's recommendations during 1946. Further, London informed the Northern Rhodesian Government that the question of forming African trade unions was under active consideration. The strike of 1945 spurred the Labour Government to encourage union formation in

Northern Rhodesia as the Forster Report had recommended after the Copperbelt strike of 1940.[16] A British trade unionist, William Comrie, was sent to Northern Rhodesia to aid and guide African workers in the formation of trade unions in 1947. By 1950 the railway workers in Broken Hill were prepared to follow the example of the Copperbelt miners and formed a trade union.

Labour organisers in Southern Rhodesia had a much more difficult time. The Rhodesian Railways African Employees' Association was ready to transform itself into a union immediately after the strike, but dared not do so. Because the association's existence was possible only with the toleration of the railways and the Southern Rhodesian Government, it approached the problem of expanding its powers with extreme caution. European prosperity in Southern Rhodesia was dependent upon cheap African agricultural and industrial labour. Neither the government nor its railway was going to permit the existence of any organisation which threatened to make African labour more expensive. No help would be forthcoming from the European railwaymen's union either. It was concerned with preserving European jobs against the threat of cheaper African labour and with maintaining European workers' right to discipline African workers.

In such circumstances the association's progress was minimal. Its frustration was clearly evident when it testified in 1947 before the National Native Labour Board, itself a product of the strike.

> In view of the fact that before the strike the management refused to have anything to do with the Association, and in view of the terms of the Strike Commission Report on this matter, the Association felt that if it approached the Administration direct it might receive the same reception as before. . . . In regard to further approach for recognition, we were specifically advised . . . not to broach the matter directly at once but to wait for legislation as recommended by the Strike Commission and the establishment of this machinery. It was expected that this would be a matter of a few months. As time went on and the law was still not passed we were advised to continue to be patient as we were always prepared to be. Now, after nearly two years, we are acting accordingly in putting the issue before this Board.[17]

The association did everything possible to convince Rhodesia Railways that it was a moderate, reasonable body. It took part in the railways' new programme of compound committees and avoided compromising situations. When the association secretary became involved in an industrial dispute he withdrew from the leadership of the compound committee. Having assured the Labour Board that it was not a group of 'agitators' and was not funded by Europeans or outsiders, the association won the right to survive, and was formally recognised by the railways in February 1948. Its constitution was a long elaborate document which the European union helped formulate, but its status was that of a 'consultative body'.[18] It was not difficult for the railways to control the association. 'Difficult' workers could be moved from place to place along the line, or dismissed and replaced by migrants from other Central African territories. In 1947 the railways threatened to deport uncooperative Northern Rhodesian workers from Southern Rhodesia.[19] The railways' active disapproval of the association would frighten insecure workers from associating with it, thus crippling it.

The Rhodesia Railways Act of 1949 included a section called the 'Special Industrial Council' which prohibited the formation of an African union and strike action by any African organisation. African grievances were to be dealt with by management or by the final arbitration of Southern Rhodesian Government Ministers in irreconcilable cases. When the Southern Rhodesian Government bought Rhodesia Railways in 1947 it began playing three roles simultaneously: (1) as the government it was answerable to a white settler electorate; (2) as the owner of Rhodesia Railways, it was concerned with profits; (3) as the final arbitrator it judged management-labour disputes. The government's first two roles precluded impartiality in the third. In a land split in every sphere of life by racial considerations, African labour could not regard the government as an impartial arbitrator.

Rhodesia Railways' chief officer in charge of African affairs, Dr E. M. B. West, did not perceive much of a threat in the new Northern Rhodesian African Railway Workers' Trade Union formed in June 1950. The new union had even fewer educated personnel than the association whose books were in an 'unholy mess'. The union's general secretary, John Sichalwe, a railway messenger/interpreter, was the only literate man willing to risk his job when the prospective union's rank and file looked for help. West thought it would be easy to destroy the union by telling Sichalwe he would have to choose between his job and the union. He assumed Sichalwe would contritely renounce the union in the timid manner used by association members.[20] However, there was a great difference between the association and the union; the union was openly supported by the Northern Rhodesian Government. West assumed the union was illegal, but was bluntly informed that it was not only legal but supported.[21] As for Sichalwe, he assured West that he was not leaving his position as general secretary of the ARWTU and went on building the new union.[22]

Very shortly the railways found the 'so-called union' to be a nuisance. It challenged management's right to transfer African workers without their consent. The district engineer ordered the 'boys to be dismissed', but the union prompted second thoughts among management and the order was rescinded, a reprimand and loss of increment being substituted as punishment. Five

European workers resigned because they did not feel the punishment was sufficient. The chief engineer claimed that they feared they would lose control of their African subordinates if they were allowed to successfully resist the dismissal order. Unwilling to allow the resignations to take place, the general manager asked Roy Welensky, union leader and politician, to explain the need for caution to the European union. The European union feared that organised African workers would become unmanageable, and repeatedly put pressure on the railways to retain their previous harsh disciplinary measures. Far from aiding the African unionist, the evidence of the railway records shows that the individual European unionist harassed him whenever he could during the early years.

The railways gave Sichalwe an ultimatum to discontinue his union activities only to find that their action was illegal.[23] Victimisation was illegal in Northern Rhodesia and the railways were forced to offer Sichalwe other positions of equal status with the face-saving explanation that his current position as interpreter was too sensitive to be held by a union official.[24] Sichalwe decided to test the railways' resolve, refused to be transferred, and eventually left the railways to become a full-time general secretary paid by the union.[25] Soon afterwards the union complained that branch general secretaries were quitting their union positions because they were afraid of dismissal. Since they were all messenger/interpreters, the best educated African workers, union growth suffered a temporary setback.[26]

Throughout the early years of the union, dues collection was a problem and Sichalwe's source of pay uncertain. During the early years, union members could not see much return for their dues, and they suspected that union funds were being misused by their leaders, or simply felt dues took too large a bite out of their pockets and they refused to pay. As a result union organisers sometimes went hungry and were tempted to take a little extra for themselves when the possibility arose. In addition, they simply were not good bookkeepers. During the annual union meeting in September 1952, Union President Dixon Konkola, a railway welfare assistant, accused Sichalwe of mishandling union funds and forced him to resign. Although an accounting firm exonerated Sichalwe, he did not return to the union and Konkola became the union chief.[27] In 1952 the railways allowed union officials to collect dues at the pay lines but consistently refused to operate a check-off system for the union in the persistent hope that the union would fail financially.[28]

By the end of 1950, the railways realised that the union was not going to disintegrate of its own accord, and they set about considering how it might be destroyed. A campaign of alternately ignoring and intimidating Sichalwe failed. Sichalwe took his duties as general secretary seriously and peppered the African

Affairs Department with complaints about working conditions, arbitrary discipline, unfair dismissals, and victimisation. His letters showed an ignorance of English grammar and British politeness, but the railways' replies were belittling and unnecessarily harsh. Sichalwe and later union leaders found such replies frustrating and discouraging but they remained undaunted and continued to press their demands.

The railways also tried to set up a rival organisation in Northern Rhodesia. In Bulawayo the railways established compound committees through which they could hear grievances and enunciate their own policy. They sought to do this in Broken Hill and other Northern Rhodesian railway centres as well, but encountered union suspicion and hostility. For two years the railways attempted 'to create from the ranks of [their] own employees a solid and responsible body of men who, by contact with the Regional Controllers and Area Controllers learn[ed] to appreciate the Railway point of view and, therefore, in time to come, [could] be relied upon to counter any irresponsible element.' This idea failed to recognise the degree of African dissatisfaction with wages and working conditions. The scheme was finally abandoned because the Regional Controller feared that Konkola would pack the compound committee with his own followers and make it another instrument of union organisation.[29]

In a more serious effort, the railways started a long programme aimed at emasculating the union. The railways' objective was to persuade the union to join the association whose range of action was severely circumscribed by the laws of Southern Rhodesia. The railways would thus effectively control both organisations. The assistant chief officer, E. A. Cordell, explained to Sichalwe and his union executive that under the Rhodesia Railways Ordinance only one union could be registered in Southern Rhodesia as a statutory union with the right to declare grievances and ultimately to strike if arbitration failed. He pointed out how a single union would be beneficial for both African employees and the railway administration. He described the railways' excellent relations with the association. The railways offered 'all possible assistance' to the association, and the new union 'might be able to learn something from the experience of the RRAEA and possibly, avoid mistakes which had, in the past, been made by that body.' Of course the railways did not intend to allow a statutory union to come into being. They were simply using this ploy in an attempt to cripple the union. Sichalwe was not decieved. He replied that if there could only be one union then the RRAEA had better join his union.[30]

The refusal of the union to put itself under the wing of the association left Rhodesia Railways in a much more serious position than it had anticipated, especially since Northern Rhodesian Government officials were being quite unsympathetic to the approach of the railways. Since the early 1940s, Northern

Rhodesian labour officers had constantly battled with the railways in an attempt to get better housing and living conditions for African employees. The labour officers' worst fears were realised when the strike of 1945 took place. It looked as if Northern Rhodesian industrial agitation might get out of hand. Although labour officers publicly deplored the African strike action, privately they were displeased with the railways' attitude towards African employees before, during and after the strike.

The railway management was very angry with the Northern Rhodesian Government for giving such full support to the union. The railways explained how the association and the union might engage in a battle to gain adherents by 'making extravagant demands' of the railways. This would result in ruinous strikes which would paralyse the system and severely damage the economy. Northern Rhodesian officials agreed with the railways but suggested that they deal with both unions jointly. This was not the solution the railways were looking for. They feared that under such an arrangement the union would dominate the emasculated association.[31] However, the necessity for some sort of co-ordinated conciliation procedure was clear. But the different approach of each territory to industrial relations made the establishment of such a procedure difficult. In Southern Rhodesia the government ministers controlled the conciliation process through the Special Industrial Council. In Northern Rhodesia disputes were handled by an independent conciliation body appointed by the Governor or by direct negotiations between interested parties. In each case the outcome would be valid only in the territory concerned. Thus, the railways were faced with the possibility that settlements in one territory might be unsatisfactory or contradictory in the other.

The fight for recognition

The railways did not recognise the union and recognised the association only as a 'consultative' body with no legal power to strike. Railway management was determined to avoid any future formal recognition of these bodies as unions. However, realising that the Northern Rhodesian Government would insist that it negotiate with the union if the union declared a dispute,[32] the railways decided to construct a negotiation procedure that would satisfy the Northern Rhodesian Government without recognising the African labour organisations as legal unions. The Governor of Northern Rhodesia was asked to nominate a conciliation board whose members might be included in the Special Industrial Council which would handle disputes of interterritorial significance. Management and African representation would be 'equal'. There would be four railway officials and four Africans *appointed by Southern Rhodesian ministers* to represent African interests.[33] Thus, with the cooperation of the Southern Rhodesian Government, the railways would be able to control the nomination of the African representatives and be able to direct the 'conciliation' process. The Northern Rhodesian Government agreed with the railways' suggestion to create a standing conciliation board. But its conversations with the union revealed that the union would demand to be directly represented on any conciliation body, and the government sympathised with that demand.[34]

The union was determined to force the railway to recognise it. It put pressure on the railways by contesting every railway disciplinary action or dismissal concerning African labour.[35] In August 1951 the union declared a dispute with the railways according to Northern Rhodesian law. The general manager of Rhodesia Railways, Sir Arthur Griffin, bitterly resented the government's acceptance of the union's claim of a dispute. He feared that Northern Rhodesia was forcing him to adopt the conciliation process used by the Copperbelt mining companies, a process he believed would be ruinous to the railways and Southern Rhodesia. Griffin believed the Broken Hill labour officer was acting as a union agent. He thought that the railways had been patient and fair in the face of the provocative activities of the 'so-called union', and mistakenly believed that the issue was a local one which could be brought to a head and defeated because it did not concern most African railway employees.[36] However, constant union harassment and the threat of a strike persuaded Griffin to accept direct union representation on a conciliation board while association members would be represented by a European spokesman.[37]

The composition of African representation on an interterritorial board was hammered out in a series of conferences and consultations involving Rhodesia Railways, Northern and Southern Rhodesian Government officials, and the union leadership. Railway management wanted a small, manageable board with a pliable labour representation. The Southern Rhodesian Government was anxious to have African labour represented by Europeans who would supposedly consider African interests together with European industrial interests. The union wanted at least eight of their own representatives on the board so that a significant number of union leaders would have the chance to gain experience in negotiating with European management, and so there would be more men to report the proceedings back to the scattered rank and file. The Northern Rhodesian Government supported the union's position in a conference with railway management and Southern Rhodesian officials. At first the railways and the Southern Rhodesian Government insisted that a European represent unorganised African labourers in an effort to deny the association's right to represent all Africans. But upon further consideration the railways board decided against this idea. There was no reason to expand the consciousness of African labour by intimating that non-association African labour had a right to be represented at all.

It was finally agreed that four railways representatives would meet two African union and association representatives each, plus two alternates each, a total of eight. Local matters would be handled by the Northern or Southern Rhodesian African labour representatives as needed. The two governments could not agree on the procedure to be followed should negotiations fail. The Southern Rhodesian Government could not allow the possibility of a legal strike. The negotiations on procedure were deadlocked and it was decided simply to wait and observe what would happen if management-labour negotiations actually failed. Backed by the Northern Rhodesian Government, the union obtained largely what it wanted. The railways were as content as could be expected but the Southern Rhodesian Government was unhappy that its plan that Europeans should represent Africans was quashed.

In late November 1951 the Interterritorial Conciliation Board was hastily set up and convened to allay union unrest and suspicion. The Railways Board was now confident that the board could be used as an instrument 'to bring the Trades Union and the Association closer together, and draw the Trade Union away from the influence of the Copperbelt.'[38] The union decided to limit its demands to the question of wages. It noted that the cost of soap, African taxes, transportation, material goods and school fees were all up. Their requests and arguments were treated with incredulous ridicule by the chief officer, West. Railway negotiating tactics were to belittle African demands and intimidate African negotiators at every turn. The African leaders were in fact cowed in this first 'conciliation meeting' and most of the African arguments were presented by Percy Ibbotson, a liberal clergyman who was one of the association's representatives, not by the African representatives. The association was even more timid than the union. It would not state its demands at all but only go so far as to say that it agreed with the union. Although the labour leaders did poorly in the meetings with management, they did gain some valuable experience in conducting formal negotiations. Moreover, they were pleased to have brought the railways administration to the bargaining table at all.

The railways agreed to increase wages in the upper grades by 2s. 6d. per month for employees of three years' experience or less, and 5s. on the fourth year. However, the fourth year increase would not be automatic for efficiency barriers were introduced to the fourth, eighth and twelfth years of service. The general manager was very satisfied with the agreement; it 'exceeded my expectations', he noted happily.[39]

Railways management believed it had outmanoeuvred the union and had

African labour well under control. It did not understand the depth of African labour's grievances in both Southern and Northern Rhodesia. The docile fashion in which the association put forward its requests and the crude way that the union managed its bookkeeping and made its demands led management to underestimate the union leaders' iniative and strategic expertise. Completely lacking viable political support, Joshua Nkomo was unable to press his association's demands lest the railways further circumscribe the association's power. In retrospect, he may have underestimated his organisation's potential but it must be remembered that his opponents' power was great and unforgiving.[40]

The failure of the association to win any real gains resulted in the disaffection of Shona-speaking branches in Umtali and Salisbury. Unable to see any benefit from the dues they were paying the workers assumed that their money was simply lining Ndebele pockets in Bulawayo, and they rebelled and broke away. Early in 1952 Sichalwe and Konkola seized this opportunity to expand the strength of the union and sent emissaries to the disaffected association branches. In contrast to the association, the union could proudly point to its militant demands on, and denunciations of, Rhodesia Railways.[41]

The union leaders may have contemplated proving their militancy by joining the African Mineworkers' Union in a strike on 9 April 1952, on behalf of Simon ber Zukas, a white socialist who was about to be deported by the Northern Rhodesian Government for his active role in the African National Congress and his advocacy of African strike action in opposition to the proposed federation of the Rhodesias.[42] However, the mineworkers' union was split into radical and conservative factions and the leader of the conservative faction, Lawrence Katilungu, succeeded in stifling the radical faction's strike plans.[43] Only about 200 workers actually struck and the railway leaders had dropped the idea. But Sichalwe and Konkola were determined to prove that their union had muscle. A month later, after attempts to negotiate with management had failed, they led the railway workers on a strike in protest against the mistreatment and dismissal of a worker. The strike was poorly conceived, the union leaders inexperienced. They failed to get the worker reinstated, and after a few days were persuaded by a Northern Rhodesian labour officer to call off the strike.[44]

Railway management was galvanised by the information that the union was taking branches away from the association, especially when the union threatened to strike.[45] The railways' plan to destroy the union by persuading it to join the association was in critical danger. Only one union could become the statutory union with legally recognised independent negotiating powers. Instead of the association becoming the statutory union, it was the union that threatened to do so. To avoid this eventuality the railways were forced to boost the prestige of the association by allowing it to become a registered union. This necessitated the amendment of Southern Rhodesian labour laws to permit the recognition and registration of two African railway unions. Thus, the ARWTU, by successfully expanding its branches and powers, forced the railways to recognise the association as a union so that it would be able to compete with the 'more extreme' union in the north. The railway management assumed that even as a union the association would be a more moderate, more controllable body.[46]

With the proposed elevation of the association to union status, previous ARWTU objections to the formation of a joint industrial council for the whole railway system fell away. A joint industrial council would have much the same composition as the earlier interterritorial council with the crucial difference that now both Northern and Southern Rhodesian African labour organisations would be able to negotiate without restrictions and would presumably be able to call a legal strike if all efforts at conciliation failed.[47]

In September 1952 the union and the association agreed to the formation of the joint industrial council and met to discuss the demands to be presented to the first meeting in January 1953. At this meeting the association leaders' greater familiarity with industrial relations procedures became evident. The Northern Rhodesian delegates' ideas concerning the formulation of the demands to be put forward were a little hazy and Joshua Nkomo, now full-time general secretary of the association, dominated the meeting.[48]

The two labour organisations presented the railways with a comprehensive agenda covering many aspects of working and living conditions. The railways carefully considered every point and drew up their position on them.[49] The stage was set for a dramatic test of strength between management and labour but the meeting was aborted because the Southern Rhodesian Government would not permit Dixon Konkola, the union's president, to enter the territory.[50]

Amalgamation and its aftermath

In November 1952 the union and the association quietly met in Broken Hill and agreed to amalgamate. The proposed union applied for recognition as the statutory union and informed the railways that it would not take any disputes to the Special Industrial Council Conciliation Board. Rather it would declare its disputes to the Northern Rhodesian Government until Southern Rhodesian conciliation procedures were amended to be like those in Northern Rhodesia. If conciliation failed, the union would strike, an action legal in Northern Rhodesia but not in Southern Rhodesia. The fact that the strike would be legal in Northern Rhodesia would strengthen Nkomo's union in Southern Rhodesia. Rhodesia Railways would not be able to crack down on the southern branch of the proposed union without incurring great difficulties with the northern branch and with the Northern Rhodesian Government.[51] The railways realised the problem, dropped the plan to recognise two unions and prepared to recognise the proposed almalgamated union. The railways were losing the battle to subordinate the northern union to the southern one. Rather, the northern union had lifted the association to its own level of power despite the railways' constant scheming to prevent this occurrence. However, the railways still found plenty of union weaknesses to exploit.

During a one-day meeting in the Easter of 1953 the two unions held a three-hour discussion on amalgamation. The two unions were in conflict over matters of precedence. Would headquarters be in Broken Hill or Bulawayo? Would the top man be Konkola or Nkomo? The southern union, now called the Rhodesia Railways African Workers' Union, heavily weighted its delegation in favour of Bulawayo and reduced the representation of Umtali and other eastern centres which had had close ties with Broken Hill. For its part, the ARWTU was not willing to relinquish the dominant position it had held since 1950. The unions agreed to put off the amalgamation issue until the year's end. In the meantime the ARWTU would continue to push the railways for settlement of its grievances.[52]

During the year 1953 railway management and the unions battled inconclusively. The railways harassed the unions whenever possible. They refused to answer or recognise union mail; to give union leaders leave of absence to attend union meetings; to give rail passes unless the unions handed over minutes of meetings; to recognise the unions.[53] All of these measures would appear to be petty but in fact they caused the unions considerable trouble. The railways prepared themselves for an impending clash over wages by conferring with the Chambers of Commerce and Industry, and of Mines in both Rhodesias to determine what support would be available in the event the railways had 'to resist extravagant increased demands of rates of pay . . . arising from the arbitration award on the Copperbelt in January 1953.'[54]

The ARWTU also prepared for a confrontation. Frustrated by the railways' unwillingness to cooperate, the ARWTU submitted a dispute to the Northern Rhodesian Government demanding the deduction of union subscriptions from railway pay sheets, a closed shop, and the introduction of a procedure agreement. The union was persuaded to withdraw the dispute and the issues were debated in a series of joint industrial councils during 1953–54.[55]

However, during this period Konkola extended his political activities to the point where his ability to maintain union effectiveness was weakened. He considered committing the ARWTU to a general strike which the African National Congress was planning in Northern Rhodesia as a protest against the establishment of the federation of the Rhodesias. He was also spending a lot of time organising congress activities in Broken Hill, and was arrested and sentenced to six months in jail in June 1953 for leading a boycott against the colour bar in the post office and local shops.[56] By this action the Northern Rhodesian Government made it clear to the union that, while it would support African labour's right to negotiate freely with the railways, it would not tolerate any political agitation by union members. Konkola had impaired his ability to conduct union activity in two ways. First, he could not effectively conduct union business in jail and his absence weakened the union's organisation and sense of direction. Second, his close connections with Copperbelt, Bemba-speaking union and political leaders had made Lozi and Nyasa members concentrated in Livingstone suspicious of Konkola's political ambitions. The Lozi and the Nyasa represented a large proportion of the skilled and educated workmen in Northern Rhodesia and were in conflict with the less well educated Bemba-speaking workers on the Copperbelt.[57] As a result they feared that, if Konkola became politically important, his ties with the Bemba-speaking community would leave them at a disadvantage both within the union and the general political situation in Northern Rhodesia. They attempted to circumscribe Konkola's power by supporting his rival, the union's General Secretary, T. M. Mtonga, a man with close connections with Joshua Nkomo, the General Secretary of the Southern Rhodesian union.[58] Nkomo was using the Livingstone branch's disaffection with Konkola to offset Konkola's continuing influence with the Southern Rhodesian Umtali branch in their personal battle for supremacy in the future amalgamated union. Nkomo was also pursuing his own political goals in Southern Rhodesia where in 1953 he attempted to become an African representative in the Federal Assembly.

In November 1953 the ARWTU's wage contract with the railways expired. No agreement was reached in the negotiations for a new contract. Instead the railways unilaterally gave the workers a small wage increase in an attempt to drive a wedge between the rank and file and the union leadership.[59] Konkola sounded out the union's branches to determine their attitude towards strike action. Although the Copperbelt and Umtali railway workers were strike-minded, the Broken Hill and Livingstone workers both favoured arbitration over strike action. Moreover, the Livingstone members questioned Konkola's use of union dues and asserted that they would no longer remit their dues to Broken Hill but would keep them in Livingstone.[60] Thus, when Konkola declared a dispute with the Northern Rhodesian Government, he implied acceptance of the government's desire to settle the dispute through arbitration. In April 1954, after lengthy negotiations, the Northern and Southern Rhodesian Governments agreed to a formula whereby an arbitration tribunal was set up under Judge H. J. Hoffman to operate under the different laws of each territory.[61]

Unknown to the unions, Judge Hoffman agreed to cooperate with the Southern Rhodesian Government in an effort to keep the wage award down. If Judge Hoffman found that the unions would not accept the sort of wage increase the Southern Rhodesian Government had in mind he would delay the award in an attempt to break the unions' unity and resolve.[62] This was precisely what happened. The unions demanded much more than the railways were prepared to offer and Judge Hoffman dragged out the arbitration proceedings for six months. During this period union members became very unhappy with the delay and stopped paying their union dues. Unaccountably Konkola took this arbitration period to go to England to take a summer course.

Railway officials hoped that an unfavourable award would cause angry and disappointed African railwaymen to desert the unions, causing them to collapse. At the very least, the militant Northern Rhodesian union leaders might be forced to collaborate with a chastened, moderate Joshua Nkomo.[63]

During October 1954 neither railwaymen nor Copperbelt miners joined the Northern Rhodesia General Workers' Union strike despite the urging of the African National Congress because they did not want to jeopardise the arbitration decisions that both awaited in their respective industries. Just before the award was announced, Konkola came back from Britain to find the union riven with strife and in a financial shambles. Moreover, an educated group of railway workers, probably with the support of the Livingstone branch and under the leadership of ARWTU general secretary T. M. Mtonga, had attempted to 'rescind' Konkola's election to the union presidency earlier that year.[64] Konkola refused to accept this situation and was able to ignore it because of the support he had from the majority of the workers.

The Hoffman Award was finally announced on 3 November 1954. It was a bitter disappointment to both unions. Only those with five years of experience or more who had passed efficiency barriers were to get rises. The mass of the rank and file would get nothing. Konkola effectively used the issue to revive the union. He held mass union meetings at depots all along the railway line in Northern Rhodesia. The railways, he declared, were trying to split the older skilled workers from the rest in an attempt to destroy the union. And, indeed, the regional controller did attempt to foment distrust of union headquarters among Livingstone's Lozi and Nyasa workers.[65] He was aware that these people were distrustful of Konkola's use of union funds and of his involvement in Bemba-area politics. But so deep was the railwaymen's anger at the awards that even in Livingstone many wanted to join hands with Konkola.

If it were not for the fact that the tribal leaders in Livingstone deeply mistrust and possibly despise Konkola and Company, I would guess that the

Livingstone section would throw in their lot with Broken Hill. I am quite certain that Konkola has now quite a following in Livingstone and the powerful tribal influences must be working overtime in order to maintain control. [66]

In Southern Rhodesia, Nkomo had great difficulty with the rank and file. He pleaded with the general manager, H. B. Everard, for a rise for these men but was brusquely reminded that it was his responsibility to keep the workers under control. Everard warned Nkomo that a strike was illegal in Southern Rhodesia and threatened to dismiss all the workers if they went on strike. This meant they would lose any seniority benefits they had thus far accrued. Nkomo was left in a desperate position. His union was disintegrating because the membership was unhappy with the results of the arbitration. Yet, unlike Konkola, he could take no decisive action, for the railways could deprive all the workers of their hard-won seniority if he did so, and that would make a mockery of his union. [87]

Two years after their initial announcement of amalgamation, the ARWTU and the RRAWU still had not come together. During those two years they had failed to build an effective labour organisation. The power of their opponent was immense and it was clear that if they did not cooperate with each other they would not be effective. Both union leaders made attempts to get added support from organisations within their own territories. Nkomo looked briefly to the European Rhodesia Railway Workers' Union but was quickly disillusioned. [68] Konkola constantly strove to tighten ties between Northern Rhodesian African labour organisations and in 1955 became president of the Trade Union Congress. [69] But past events had shown that different African unions were preoccupied with their own struggles and could not be counted on to aid others. Congress' efforts to gather active labour support behind its campaign against federation or behind the General Workers' Union strike had failed. Members of both railway unions refused to pay dues unless they could see some immediate and concrete result. They were concerned lest their money be used for the personal aggrandisement of the leadership or, in the case of the Livingstone workers (and possibly the Umtali workers), the political aggrandisement of some other ethnic group. Money contributed was to be spent for the workers' industrial well-being or it would not be forthcoming. In these circumstances, it was not advisable for the union leadership to look for aid outside their own organisation. The surest way for the two African railway unions to gain the power they needed was to submerge their differences and unite.

On 30 July 1955, at a joint conference of the African Railway Workers' Trade Union and the Rhodesia Railways African Workers' Union in Broken

Hill, the two unions amalgamated to become the Railway African Workers' Union, headquartered in Bulawayo. The establishment of the new union's headquarters in Bulawayo indicated that the ARWTU now believed that amalgamation had become imperative and was willing to give the RRAWU the advantage of having the headquarters in Southern Rhodesia. The spirit of unity was emphasised by the fact that the leadership of the new union was shared by the two leaders of the old unions. Dixon Konkola was president and Joshua Nkomo general secretary. The relative importance of the two positions had not yet been determined.

Conclusions

During the period 1944–55 African railwaymen learned that they could successfully confront a European-controlled industry provided they had some political support. The support of the Northern Rhodesian Government was crucial in the ARWTU's formation and struggle to survive. With a firm base of political support and encouragement the union leadership was able to develop the organisational and negotiating expertise necessary to withstand successfully the railways' assaults on its existence. Management's unremittingly hostile attitude to all aspects of union activity engendered a thorough and enduring suspicion of management in the union. However, in order to be able to negotiate effectively with management the unions had to learn how to (a) accurately calculate and articulate their needs, (b) carefully plan their strategy, and (c) maintain a financially solvent, united union. But union development was complicated by the fact that the unions were not only a vehicle for the amelioration of industrial conditions but also a means of political change.

The Northern Rhodesian Government's support of African union organisation was crucial but conditional. It would not tolerate union activities which challenged its political control of the territory. The government's prompt repression of union involvement in political agitation impressed upon Konkola and the rank and file the risk that active union involvement in politics entailed. The practical consequence of this realisation was the union leadership's unwillingness to risk possible industrial improvements for more remote political goals. As a result the union's active organisational identification with the general African populace was truncated.

The Northern Rhodesian Government's pressure against union political activity distorted the union's relationship with the congress. Union members were able to press for industrial change. The government's refusal to permit the open cooperation of unions and political parties forced African politicians to negotiate with union executives covertly. Because congress did not have open, regular organisational channels of communication with the ARWTU, there was no comprehensive representation of the union's different economic and ethnic interests to the congress. The dominant Lozi and Nyasa groups of the Livingstone branch felt unconfident of their ability to direct Konkola's political activities within the Congress Party. They feared that Konkola would represent Bemba-speaking interests in the political arena and that this would ultimately hurt their ability to protect their position in the industrial sphere. Nor did Konkola have the complete confidence of other branches. Everywhere the union membership feared that his involvement in politics would hinder his ability to negotiate effectively with the railways for their material benefit. Because of their relative isolation from the other residents in the towns along the line of rail, the railwaymen did not actively identify with other sections of the African population, and were not prepared to sacrifice their own well-being for the industrial and political goals of others employed outside the railway system. The Northern Rhodesian Government's policy of encouraging African industrial organisation, but discouraging union political activity had the effect of making the ARWTU parochial in its interests and of preventing the development of regular responsive union-congress ties.

Both Dixon Konkola and Joshua Nkomo saw union leadership as one of the few means of acquiring a personal political power base and an entrée into territorial politics at a time when Europeans controlled modern Rhodesian society. Union leaders had the education and developed the expertise to negotiate with the railways which the rank and file lacked. Because there was a severe shortage of men who were capable of leading the unions and the new political movements, the union leaders found themselves in a strong position. They appeared to have a ready-made constituency, which, if not compact and completely stable, was at least relatively easy to reach and influence. However, the leadership could not dictatorially command the union to follow its policies, but found itself in a rough state of equilibrium with the rank and file. Through their ability to withhold dues and choose between rival labour organisations, the rank and file were able to regulate the activities of the leadership. The leadership could not persist in following industrial and political policies without referring to the rank and file unless it was prepared to see the membership split along occupational, ethnic and territorial lines.

With Northern Rhodesian support, the ARWTU was able to present an aggressive stance and expand its influence into Southern Rhodesia. Fearful of losing control of Southern Rhodesian labour to the ARWTU, the railways were forced to loosen their rigid control of the association so that it would still be able to compete for labour membership on a more equal footing with the union. The railways believed that they would always be better able to control a southern based organisation than a northern one. However, once recognised, the Southern Rhodesia union was able to collaborate openly with the aggressive northern union and together they proceeded to press wage demands which threatened the Southern Rhodesian Government's wage-price structure. In an effort to prevent this eventuality the Southern Rhodesian Government conspired with the railways and the arbitrator to break the union's power. This attempt was so nearly successful that it backfired by forcing the unions to discipline their energies and amalgamate. It had become very clear to the union leaders that a broad base of support was essential if they were to successfully withstand the pressures of Southern Rhodesia's unscrupulous European industrial power structure.

The formation of the Railway African Workers' Union represented the end of an era of Rhodesian history when African workers were men without power. They had been unable effectively to change their living and working conditions. They had had virtually no hope of promotion, their colour had barred all occupational, economic and social advance. They had been a working caste. After the strike of 1945 the workers became conscious of themselves as a pressure group. The struggle to develop an effective union created a craft consciousness among the railway workers of two territories. But external and internal pressures combined to prevent the railway workers from becoming integrated into a wider class organisation. Rather, the development of the union denoted the creation of a class organisation with an occupational rather than a geographical focus. The members of the RAWU were only a cohesive force when they were concentrating on their own industrial objectives. However, they did sympathise with other labour movements and with the nationalist movement in Northern Rhodesia. The cumulative effect was to provide a climate of opinion that was increasingly class-conscious and nationalist.

NOTES

1. I wish to thank Professor T. O. Ranger, my thesis supervisor, for having read this paper and made suggestions, and for the intellectual stimulation he has given me in the past. I gratefully acknowledge the support of the Canada Council for the research on which this paper is based.

    Much of the data is from the Rhodesia Railways Industrial Relations files now on deposit in the National Archives of Zambia. All references are to these files unless otherwise noted.

2. Elliot J. Berg and Jeffrey Butler, 'Trade Unions' in James S. Coleman and

C. G. Rosberg (eds), *Political Parties and National Integration in Tropical Africa*, Berkeley: University of California Press, 1964, pp. 340, 380. It is pertinent to note Butler's research experience was in Southern Africa.

3. H. E. Conway, 'Labour Protest Activity in Sierra Leone During the Early Part of the Twentieth Century', *Labour History*, 15, Nov. 1968, p. 57; and C. H. Allen, 'Union-Party Relationships in Francophone West Africa: A Critique of "Téléguidage" Interpretations', and A. Peace, 'The Lagos Proletariat: Labour Aristocrats or Populist Militants?', both in this volume.

4. From the 1945 strike onwards railways management and the Northern and Southern Rhodesian Government agreed to continue the supply of rations in order to avoid violence and the spread of discontent in the general populace.

5. Tredgold Commission, Railway Strike Evidence 1945, National Archives of Zambia (NAZ), SEC/LAB/80, p. 87.

6. National Native Labour Board, *Investigations into Conditions of Employment of Railway African Employees*, 1947.

7. L. H. Gann and M. Gelfand, *Huggins of Rhodesia*, Allen and Unwin, 1964, p. 186.

8. Interview with Limited Sakala, Kabwe (Broken Hill), 12 May 1972.

9. W. F. Stubbs, the Northern Rhodesia Labour Commissioner believed that the Livingstone workers did not go on strike because of the Livingstone Compound Manager's particularly good relations with the workers.

10. H. L. Brigham, Provincial Commissioner, Broken Hill, to Chief Secretary, N.R., N.D., NAZ, Sec/LAB/144/44. The following short forms will be used henceforth. Area Controller (A.C.); Regional Controller (R.C.); Acting Chief Officer (A.C.O.); Chief Officer (C.O.); General Manager (G.M.); Broken Hill (B.H.); Rhodesian Railways (R.R.); Northern Rhodesian Government (N.R.G.); Southern Rhodesian Government (S.R.G.); Chief Secretary (C.S.); General Secretary (G.S.).

11. The authorities brought up two representatives of the Bulawayo strikers to assure the Broken Hill men that they had indeed gone back to work but the Broken Hill strikers were determined at the time to remain on strike until they had received a firm wage increase. They stayed on strike until 5 November, when a combination of threats and cajoling by government and railway officials plus reassurances by Stewart Gore-Browne persuaded them to return to work without a definite wage increase. Strike Diary, 26 Oct. to 5 Nov. 1945 SEC/LMB/81/7–38.

12. This information is based on interviewing 16 African miners and 14 African railwaymen, most of whom had been working in Kabwe at least 27 years.

13. *Evidence of Railway Strike Commission*, 30 Nov. 1945, NAZ, SEC/LAB/80.

14. Northern Rhodesia Government, *Report of Investigation into the Grievances which gave rise to the Strike Amongst the African Employees of the Rhodesia Railways and the Conditions of Employment Incidental to such Grievances and to make Recommendations for the Elimination of any Grievance Proved to be well founded*, 1945 (Tredgold Report), NAZ, SEC/LAB/144/74/1.

The Report for Southern Rhodesia was very similar to that for Northern Rhodesia. It recommended that the Southern Rhodesian Government be more forceful in demanding employers build suitable African housing.

Southern Rhodesian Government, *Report of the Commission*, NAZ, SEC/LAB/144/125/1.

15. A. L. Epstein, *Politics in an African Urban Community*, Manchester University Press, 1958, p. 235.

16. Telegrams between the Governor of Northern Rhodesia and the Secretary of State for the Colonies, Spring 1946, NAZ, SEC/LAB/144/126.

17. National Native Labour Board, *Investigation into Conditions of Employment of Railway African Employees*, 1947. Testimony of Nayeza Simon, Chairman of the R.R.A.E.A. The association collected over £1,000 to pay for legal representation before the National Native Labour Board. R. Gray, *The Two Nations*, Oxford University Press, 1960, p. 317.

18. E. A. Cordell, Acting Chief Officer, African Affairs Department, Rhodesia Railways, to General Manager, 30 Mar. 1949.

19. Meeting between C.O. and C.S., N.R. and Labour Commissioner in Lusaka, N.D. (1947).

20. C.O., notes, Northern Tour: September 1950, 12 Sept. 1950; Interview with John Sichalwe, Liteta, 23 Aug. 1972.

21. West to C.S., N.R.G., 11 Nov. 1950.

22. Interview with Sichalwe; C.O., note, 30 Aug. 1950.

23. West, note on John Sichalwe, 30 Aug. 1950; West to Sichalwe, 29 Jan. 1951.

24. Cordell, notes of a meeting with N.R.G. officials in Lusaka, 10 Feb. 1951.

25. Sichalwe to West, 29 Jan. 1951. N.R.G. support made a difference in Sichalwe's attitude. He told West how Comrie 'told the people present . . . that there was nothing to stop any African from being Secretary to the Union if he was a member of that nation.'

26. A.A.D., note, N.D.

27. C.O. note, Tour of Northern Rhodesia, 13–23 Sept. 1952. Interview with Sichalwe.

28. Notes of Meeting of Joint Industrial Committee in Bulawayo, 8–9 Sept. 1952.

29. Notes of a meeting of railway officials with Union executive, 10 Feb. 1951. R.C. to C.O., 23 Nov. 1953.

30. Notes of a meeting of railway officials with Union executive, 10 Feb. 1951.
31. A.C.O., Cordell, note on meeting with C.S. and labour officials in Lusaka, 9 Feb. 1951.
32. Rhodesia Railway Board, Notes, 30 Mar. 1951.
33. C.O., notes, 24 Feb. 1951.
34. C.S., N.R. to Secretary, R.R. Higher Authority, 17 July 1951.
35. R.C., Broken Hill, memorandum on ARWTU, 2 Apr. 1951. The R.C. found himself in a very difficult position. Told to handle the union with 'sympathy, understanding and tact,' he was nevertheless unable to recognise the union formally or to negotiate with it. He urged the C.O. to institute some mode of procedure for handling an increasingly explosive situation and relieving union officials of their increasing frustration and bitterness. This advice was repeated by the Chief Secretary of N.R. to the Secretary of the R.R. Higher Authority, 9 Aug. 1951.
36. Sir Arthur Griffin, note, N.D.; G.M. to C.S., N.R. 4 Aug. 1951; R.R. Board, memorandum, 16 Aug. 1951.
37. Griffin to C.O., 11 Oct. 1951.
38. Minutes of a meeting attended by R.R., S.R.G. officials, N.R. Commissioner for Labour and Mines, Salisbury, 3 Oct. 1951; minutes of a meeting between the full executive council of the ARWTU and the Acting Labour Commissioner, N.R., 23 Oct. 1951. The union feared the combined board initially. It feared that the railways would use the association to overwhelm its negotiating power.

   Chief Engineer, R.R., note, 1 Nov. 1951; notes of a meeting attended by R.R. officials in the C.S.'s office, Lusaka, 28 Oct. 1951; minutes of a meeting between R.R. Board and S.R. ministers, Salisbury, 2 Nov. 1951. The ministers were against the recognition of the union and did not want any African labour representatives in Southern Rhodesia. They were afraid that this would be a step towards recognising the association as a union.
39. Notes, author unstated, but probably C.O. West, 20 Nov. 1951, 23 Nov. 1951, 30 Nov. 1951; and G.M. to Secretary R.R. Board, 28 Nov. 1951. West wrote: 'The demands as put forward are as we know grotesque, but the arguments in support of them were still more childish, and it is quite clear that the Northern Rhodesian Union had never done anything to think out what they were doing and asking. . . I am more than ever convinced now that this type of African who is representing Northern Rhodesia is altogether unfit for such negotiation work and Trade Union principles.' West was originally supposed to be the railways' senior African welfare officer but he had clearly no sympathy for, and little knowledge of, Africans and their needs.

40. Notes of a meeting between West and RRAEA, 25 Jan. 1951; notes of a meeting between AAD and RRAEA, 29 May 1952. The railways refused to make any concessions which cost money and refused to collect association dues.

41. C.O. to G.M., 29 Feb. 1951; A.C. to C.O., 21 Mar. 1951.

42. *Central African Post*, 3 Apr. 1952.

43. Shimshon Zelnicker, 'Changing Patterns of Trade Unionism: The Zambian Case: 1948–1964', unpublished Ph.D. dissertation, University of California, 1970, p. 205.

44. Interview with John Sichalwe, 23 Aug. 1972.

45. AAD, notes, 19 Apr. 1952.

46. G.M. to R.R. Board, 20 Apr. 1953.

47. C.O. to Commissioner for Labour and Mines, N.R., 1 Aug. 1952.

48. C.O., Tour of Northern Rhodesia, notes, 13–23 Sept. 1952.

49. C.O. to G.M., 30 Dec. 1952; AAD, Notes on Items of Agenda, 9 Jan. 1953, 12 Jan. 1953. Again the railways were prepared to acquiesce to demands that would not cost money and to argue vociferously that it could not afford those that did.

50. Railway Administrator, note, 29 Jan. 1953. The African labour delegates requested a postponement of the meeting. Railway representative argued that the meeting should continue. They claimed Konkola's absence was not their fault and that the railways had sponsored his entry into Southern Rhodesia. After inconclusive wrangling, the labour representatives walked out.

51. A.C.O. to G.M., 15 Apr. 1953.

52. R.C., B.H. to C.O., 10 Apr. 1953.

53. AAD, note, 28 Jan. 1953; Commissioner for Labour and Mines, N.R. to Railway Representative, N.R., 10 Mar. 1953, C.O. to S.G., ARWTU, 19 Feb. 1953; A.C. Livingstone to R.C., B.H., 25 Feb. 1953, 26 Feb. 1953.

54. C.O., notes, 22 May 1953.

55. G.S., ARWTU to Commissioner for Labour and Mines, N.R., 9 Apr. 1953; R.C., B.H. to C.O. 10 Nov. 1953. The N.R.G. persuaded the S.R.G. to allow Konkola to attend J.I.C. meetings in Bulawayo, and in turn the union withdrew the dispute. R.C., N.R., memorandum, 15 Apr. 1953; C.O., notes, 22 May 1953.

56. R.C., B.H. to C.O., 20 May 1953; extract from Monthly Letter, N.R. Region, May, 1953; R.C. to C.O., 24 June 1953, 26 June 1953.

57. Epstein, *Politics*, p.236.

58. R.C., B.H. to C.O., 23 Nov. 1953; extract from letter received from A.C., Livingstone, 4 Apr. 1954.

59. C.O. to all R.C., 23 Feb. 1954.

60. R.C., N.R. to C.O., 24 Feb. 1954; minutes of meeting in C.O.'s office, 17 Mar. 1954; extract from letter received from A.C., Livingstone, 4 Apr. 1954.

61. C.O. to R.C., B.H., 23 Apr. 1954.

62. Notes of a meeting held in the office of the Prime Minister, Garfield Todd, Salisbury, 26 Apr. 1954.

63. R.C., B.H. to C.O., 8 Oct. 1954.

64. R.C., B.H. to C.O., 18 Oct. 1954. The R.C. noted that Konkola blamed the attempt to dismiss him on 'the Union intellectual (?) group Messenger Interpreters, Welfare Assistants etc., as being the culprits who wish him harm and who pulled the wool over the eyes of the ignoramus group.'

65. R.C., B.H. to C.O., 11 Dec. 1954.

66. R.C., B.H. to C.O., 15 Nov. 1954.

67. C.O. to R.C., B.H., 26 Nov. 1954.
   The railways also came under pressure at this time. On November 4 1954, the Rhodesian Selection Trust, one of the two Copperbelt mining companies, announced that it would no longer deny African advancement on grounds of colour. European workers' faith in the future of the federation was shaken and European pressure on publicly owned R.R. against following the R.S.T. example was bound to result. *Northern News*, 5 Nov. 1954; R.C., B.H. to C.O., 4 Nov. 1954.

68. Memorandum of meeting held in G.M.'s office, 8 Sept. 1953.

69. R.C., B.H., to C.O., 10 May 1955.

Union-Party Relationships in Francophone West Africa: A Critique of 'Téléguidage' Interpretations[*]

C. H. ALLEN

This paper has two objects: it is firstly an exercise in labour history, focusing on two episodes in post-war union activity in francophone West Africa (henceforth AOF), for which published information or analysis is inadequate or misleading; and secondly it argues against a view of the interaction of unions and parties in Africa which was widely accepted by politicians, administrators and scholars, and which is still influential, mainly in default of a substantial rival.

The most common interpretation of the episodes I have chosen is that the unions' actions were controlled (*téléguidé*) by certain political parties; this in a more general and sophisticated form is the view that I wish to undermine. The structure of the paper is straightforward; after a brief survey of AOF union history up to 1956, the received (or modal) view of the two episodes is presented. I then attempt a critique of the received view, and finish by generalising this to produce a critique of representative studies of union-party relationships, notably the influential survey by Berg and Butler.[1]

Background

Membership of trade unions in AOF was open to the bulk of Africans only during 1937–40, and again after 1944 as part of the package of reforms stemming from the Brazzaville Conference. Thus although unions were formed in the 1920s, and several existed among public employees during 1937–40, it was only

* I have received a great deal of help in studying francophone African unions, so that a full list of those to whom I would like to give thanks would be too long for this paper. I should, however, mention at least Thomas Hodgkin, Jean Suret-Canale, Bill Johnson and Paul Beckett, all of whom helped to eliminate errors of fact and foolish interpretations; that some remain is my fault.

after the war that there was any sustained growth in membership and activity. The resulting trade union movement was strongly influenced in its formal structure and overt ideology by the two main metropolitan centres, the *Confédération Générale du Travail* (CGT), and the *Confédération Française des Travailleurs Chrétiens* (CFTC), to which the majority of unions were affiliated. Until the 1950s, the CFTC had few African supporters, even in Dakar and Douala (where the French Catholic deputy Dr Aujoulat encouraged CFTC affiliation), in part because of the hostility of the mission staffs.[2]

The CGT, which corresponded roughly in political composition to that of the French 'United Front' government was the centre to which the bulk of African trade unionists were formally affiliated throughout the post-war decade. The reasons for this predominance are principally two; (a) almost all experienced European or African trade unionists in AOF were, or had been, CGT members, and (b) the CGT alone built up and preserved a reputation for both militancy and success.

The overall structure of trade unionism corresponded to that in France: all members were organised initially in sections based on a particular trade or locality, which were grouped in *syndicats de base*, units comparable to union branches, chapels, or locals, but not identical to any of them. The *syndicats* were in turn organised into *unions des syndicats*, both horizontally by industry, and vertically by geographical units (urban centre, region, territory and federation). Only some of the industrial unions were important, notably the railwaymen (whose federal body was not affiliated to any metropolitan centre), teachers and civil servants (notably postal workers). In the private sector they were inactive, although bodies of related composition, such as the *Intersyndicale Ouvrière* headed by Abbas Guèye (a deputy, and client of Senghor) existed in Dakar. Of the vertical unions, the most important were the territorial bodies; the federal bodies varied in importance with the nature of their links with the metropolitan centre (these links being the subject of much conflict), while the urban unions were important primarily in Senegal. Here Dakar was given territorial status, and it and other towns, notably St Louis and Thies, formed the fiefs for which the various union clan leaders competed.[3]

The growing hostility between the French Communist Party (PCF) and the other parties in the United Front led to the expulsion from this government of the PCF ministers, to a split within the metropolitan CGT, and in AOF, to repression of the major federal party, the *Rassemblement Démocratique Africain* (RDA), and the CGT. The repression was excused by the formal links then existing between these bodies and the PCF, but was probably due more to their political or syndical activity. There resulted a decline in membership and activity for the CGT and the trade union movement overall during 1949–51, and greater support for the CFTC and the social-democratic *Force Ouvrière* (FO). This latter, a splinter group from the metropolitan CGT, had inherited the great majority of the white CGT members in AOF (the bulk of whom had refused to form racially integrated branches in any case), and then acquired the more timorous of the public sector affiliates of the African CGT. Never less than half whites, FO was always small and played a minor role, despite administrative support. The CFTC, however, had considerable support in many Catholic areas, and its relationships with the CGT are an important part of trade union history in the early 1950s.

CGT membership recovered after 1951, and there followed several years of fairly intense industrial activity and political lobbying. In 1955 it became involved in division over the issue of affiliation to metropolitan and international unions. Sekou Touré, by then secretary-general of the Guinean territorial union, and one of the three federal CGT secretaries, called for the creation of autonomous unions without such affiliations at the RDA Co-ordinating Committee meeting in July. A few months later the Senegal-Mauritania union split, and an autonomous centre was formed, headed by Bassirou Guèye, the second of the federal CGT secretaries. In February 1956, the CGT's federal co-ordinating committee met, only to split on the issue, with the three secretaries (Touré, Guèye, and the Malian, Seydou Diallo), announcing the formation of a new federal body, the CGT 'Africaine' (CGTA). Heavy defections to this body followed in the next six months, including some from the CFTC and FO, and the remaining CGT loyalists (with the major exception of Jacques N'Gom in the Cameroun) realised the necessity of abandoning their opposition. With the railway union leaders mediating, the rival leaderships met to re-unite the CGT and CGTA. at the price of the former replacing its formal external links with informal ones. The re-unified body, UGTAN (*Union Générale des Travailleurs d'Afrique Noire*), survived but two years. Its Guinean and Malian sections came quickly to share the policies and often the personnel of the ruling party (in each case, a section of the RDA). Elsewhere, the UGTAN sections were gradually weakened by splits, banned or dissolved, and new union centres created by governmental threat or edict, headed by compliant leaders, often originally from FO unions, and subordinate—as far as policy and leadership were concerned—to party and government.

Two episodes in union history

The episodes I have chosen are the 1947-48 rail strike, and the formation of the CGTA in 1955-56. The former is the longest strike in African union history, and illustrates many features of AOF industrial activity in this period; yet it has received no extended scholarly treatment (as far as I know), provided one excepts Sembene Ousmane's long and moving commentary in his novel of the strike, *God's Bits of Wood*.

The formation of the CGTA involved a marked change in the structural focus of AOF trade unionism, and allowed the process of elimination of the formal disunity of the trade union movement, itself an expression of metropolitan rather than African rivalries (though the latter became attached to the former, as might be expected). I shall also argue that it was the outcome of long-term processes within the separate union movements, arising from the changing demands and political consciousness of the rank-and-file, and mediated by the various levels of leadership within the movements.

The two episodes are thus of intrinsic importance, making worthwhile the correction of factual error and reinterpretation of the significance of the events. My own reinterpretation will centre on the causes of the events, which have frequently (though not universally) been presented as stemming from the aims and intervention of political parties, either in France or AOF.

The rail strike

Late in 1947, soon after the expulsion of the Communist ministers from the French government and the beginnings of a series of massive strikes called in France by the CGT, the workers of the four railways networks in AOF went on strike. Although the Ivorian network returned to work after three months, the others stayed out for 160 days. At the time, the strike was presented in the settler press, and that of the missions, as a communist plot, locally directed by the RDA in order to embarrass the SFIO (*Section Française de l'Internationale Ouvrière*), which was a partner in the new French governing coalition, and provided much of the opposition to the RDA within AOF.

This interpretation has been carried over into academic analyses. Franz Ansprenger simply states that the CGT at the instance of the PCF deliberately extended the strike for higher ends than the workers' interests, though he admits that he has no direct evidence. Others are less cautious: 'When a general "insurrectional" strike against the (French) government was called by the CGT in October 1947, the African unions affiliated to the CGT were ordered to take part. For five months the railwaymen on the Dakar–Bamako line were out on strike—yet there was no immediate interest of theirs at stake', says Mortimore. For Pfefferman the strike was an 'episode in the fight between the Communist Party and the French Government', and similar remarks can be found in Andras

November's book.[4] As a result of the exploitation of the strike, the same sources assert, the Federal Railway Union disaffiliated from the CGT.

The formation of the CGTA

This episode has been dealt with more frequently and far more thoroughly than the rail strike, and there exist contemporary or near-contemporary accounts by participants, administrators and academics. Some of these make only passing or oblique references to the formation of the CGTA, so that to talk of a 'received' view is somewhat tendentious. Nonetheless, there is a consensus that three factors were important causally; the pressure from parties (the RDA, and in Senegal, the BDS of Senghor) for union autonomy; the active support of the colonial administration; and the growth of nationalist sentiment. While some authors, perhaps for lack of space, do not mention the second factor, the account that emerges from secondary sources is the following. The RDA and BDS had both publicly declared in favour of union autonomy, and the RDA in particular had several trade union leaders among its supporters and officials. Union leaders had become increasingly resentful of subordination to the French CGT in matters of policy and status, and were thus receptive to the call for autonomy. 'Autonomy' was itself increasingly popular as a general political slogan, while the administration, notably Bernard Cornut-Gentille (the Governor-General), wished for their own reasons to encourage disaffiliation. Thus Berg, for example, says that:

> The leading African political parties, especially the RDA, played a role; they sought an autonomous African union movement in which they could exercise greater influence. The administration, too, encouraged the break. It was anxious to end the relationship between the metropolitan CGT and the African unions. Probably the most basic factor, however, was the desire of African unionists themselves for greater independence. The leaders of the CGTA were sensitive to dictation from Paris, and therefore sought to eliminate the interference of metropolitan unionists in African union affairs.

Pfefferman, again less cautious, asserts that:

> In the first instance the movement was directed against the influence not of metropolitan France, but of the PCF; it was actively encouraged by the administration. . . The CGTA could not have been created without the full support of the RDA and the French colonial administration.[5]

That this version is still current is well, if abruptly, illustrated by Zuccarelli:

> From 1953, the *Indépendants d'Outre-Mer* called for union autonomy and

unification. They had little influence on the leaders of the largest centre, the CGT. When, however, the RDA Co-ordinating Committee met at Conakry in 1955, and added its support to the demands, Sekou Touré was able to carry out this policy, as were the Senegalese CGT members, who were mostly members of the RDA territorial section. This explains the birth of the CGTA and everything that followed.[6]

Critique

The interpretations outlined above embody a simple model of the origins of union action: a policy decision by a party or its leadership is conveyed to party militants within the union organisation(s) who are then able to make the party decision into union policy. Evidence for the validity of such a model is thus of two types, (a) evidence that the organisations involved did have the policies, or performed the actions mentioned, and that their membership overlapped with the union other than at the base (in order that it may be feasible for a party to influence the union); and (b) evidence that such a process of policy transmission did in fact occur, whether openly or not. It is not enough to produce only evidence of type (a) above, since this does not by itself establish that the party or its leadership initiated the policy or action referred to. As I have presented them, the interpretations of the episodes described rely on type (a) evidence alone, and are therefore invalid. In this section, I shall argue that in addition to this formal—and weak—point, it is possible to produce evidence for contrary interpretations, though this is somewhat limited as I have not yet finished collecting the necessary data. Thus my critique is partly empirical, and partly in terms of hypotheses that are more defensible, and of greater explanatory power, than those they replace.[7]

The strike

What is argued in the quoted sources is that the strike was opportunistically ordered and/or prolonged by the PCF; that it was not in the interest of the strikers; and that therefore the federal railway union disaffiliated from the CGT after the strike. Not one statement is true, although it is true that the metropolitan CGT, through overlapping membership and related ideology, was strongly influenced by the PCF, especially after 1947; and it is also true that a very small group of French communists, including a handful among the railwaymen, were active in AOF unions. These tenuous links may have provided a catalyst or kernel for the quoted accounts.

The strike in fact originated in demands made in August 1946 by the federal committee of the railwaymen, led by Ibrahima Sarr, for several items, the most important of which was that for a '*cadre unique*'. Their basic aim was clear: 'They wished that everybody, European or African, should be within a single hierarchy (*cadre*), governed by the same agreements and statutes, with the same chance of success.'[8]

This type of demand was both widespread among, and characteristic of, public sector employees of middle and higher grades in AOF, during the late colonial period—being, for example, the major demand of those involved in the general strikes of 1945–46 in Dakar and was tactically the best way of gaining increases in pay or benefits for established employees (i.e. those with a monthly or yearly contract of employment).[9] These were, of course, a minority of the African work force: of the 18,000 railway workers, only 1,700 fell into this category, though the union also demanded that a significant number of experienced but unestablished workers (*personnel auxiliaires*) should be taken onto the permanent staff, implying greater pay and security for them.[10] The small white labour force (440 men), all in the senior grades from which Africans were excluded, were opposed to both demands, with the exception of the tiny group of workers at Abidjan. Their opposition helped to undermine the initial negotiations, which began in December under the chairmanship of the AOF *Directeur des Chemins de Fers et Transports*, Bosc, a social-democrat unpopular with the white employees.

By January 1947, both the unions representing the whites were demanding that the negotiations cease, essentially because the *cadre unique* might threaten their privileges, an attitude much resented by the African union leaders, who saw it as 'prompted by open racism and rampant egoism'.[11] The railway management were faced with heavy operating losses, despite frequent increases in charges, and were reluctant to make concessions. The colonial administration's position was complicated by the fact that many of its senior officials were among the negotiators, making mediation difficult (the whites also distrusted the Governor-General Barthes, which had the same effect). The reluctance of the management to give way was increased by the transformation of the railway in December 1946 into a public corporation, with its own independent Board of Directors and financial autonomy; previously it had been the responsibility of the Department of Rails and Transport.

This change had several repercussions on the strike. The management negotiators were now headed by Nicholas, who was both head of the Board and AOF Colonial Secretary (*Secrétaire-Général du Gouvernement Général de l'AOF*); he seems to have had little sympathy for African employees, unlike Bosc.[12] The new Board included representatives of the major commercial firms, who were anxious to avoid further increases in freight charges, and were perhaps more sympathetic to the racism of white workers; thus the management side became more stubborn. The new status of the railway implied that its employees would cease to be civil servants—with a statutory right to equal treatment regardless of race—and would have to negotiate new collective agreements. This the African unions feared would impede acceptance of the *cadre unique*. Finally the new management began laying off African workers to reduce costs; within a few months over 3,000 had been sacked, generating a new set of union demands over the extent of dismissals and the manner in which they should be done.

By April 1947, the African union had lost confidence in negotiation, and decided to strike in protest, choosing to begin on the day of the arrival in Dakar of the President of the (French) Republic. To end this embarrassing action, the administration asked several African politicians, including Lamine Guèye and Senghor, to mediate with the union leaders, and end the strike. To get this, they had to agree to the *cadre unique* and certain other demands, including the resumption of detailed negotiations in June. The new negotiations, which lasted until early August, reached agreement on new conditions of employment. The Board, however, despite Nicholas having signed the protocol ending the April strike, refused to accept the new conditions, only the four African members voting in favour.

The union could now only resort to a full-scale strike, of which they gave notice early in September; just before it was due to begin, Governor-General Barthes denounced it as illegal, his sole response to the union's demands. The union retorted:

> Open your prisons, make ready your machine-guns and cannons; nevertheless, at midnight on October the tenth, if our demands are not met, we declare the general strike.[13]

Such apparent grandiloquence was justified; earlier railway strikes had prepared them for violence by the state, as Ousmane's novel suggests, and during the strike there were numerous arrests of strikers and union officials, including Sarr, Fiankan (Secretary of the Abidjan-Niger section), and the entire executive of the Benin-Niger section.[14]

Whatever their fears, the railwaymen's solidarity was enormous; of the 19,000 Africans employed on the railway and docks, only 858 had returned after 82 days on strike, and only 4,500 (plus those in the Ivory Coast) after 160 days, when the strike ended (the dates were 11 November 1947 to 19 March 1948). For two months not a train ran to or from Bobo-Dioulasso; during the same period, according to a reporter sympathetic to the strike, Conakry 'was wrapped in a deathly silence'. While commercial firms lost profits, and the export of the groundnut crop was delayed although not prevented, the main sufferers must have been the strikers and their dependants, including the numerous petty traders who provided them with food and services. Little emerges from contemporary sources of their plight, though we may gain some sympathy for it from *God's Bits of Wood*, and from this brief report from a small town on the line of rail:

> At Toukoto, since the strike began, the African railwaymen have lived like beasts trapped in their lairs . . . The normal flow of food from the villages and by truck from the towns has been hindered. In the village, military control grows daily without relaxation: access to the station is forbidden. . . . Troops fill the town.[15]

How then did the strikers survive? Solidarity donations came from a wide variety of sources: CGT unions in AOF gave hundreds of thousands of CFA francs and the RDA provided 350,000 francs for the Abidjan–Niger section; local notables gave quite large sums, as did individual traders and their organisations (e.g. the *Syndicat des Petits Commerçants du Soudan*, 50,000 CFA frs). The largest single donation came, however, from the metropolitan CGT's strike fund (then under some domestic pressure); at 500,000 CFA francs, it made up 25 per cent of the total donated.[16] With the minimum wage then standing at a little over 300 francs a week, however, this amount would only have provided the strikers' needs for a week at most. Much more important was credit from the railwaymen's co-operative, which gave out goods worth 25 million francs, enough perhaps for 90 days of austere consumption. Other sources must therefore have provided the equivalent of 15–20 million further francs. We can readily guess what these must have been: savings, casual labour and trading in the larger towns, gifts and food from rural kin and neighbours and credit from traders. Thus in some sense the strike was a popular movement against aspects of colonial rule, though not perhaps to the extent of the 1953 strike in Guinea, or (in its own context) the 1961 Sekondi–Takoradi strike.[17]

The immediate response of the colonial administration to the strike was to appoint an Arbitration Board, which failed to reach agreement. They then appointed as Final Arbitrator Maître André Ferrey, President of the *Tribunal de Première Instance*. His sentence, handed down on 20 October, incorporated the principle of the *cadre unique* (which he treated as an existing management decision), but refused any concession on other demands. Had the union accepted his ruling, the bulk of its membership would have gained nothing from the year's activity, while those who stood to gain in the abstract would have received far less than they considered their due. Thus the strike concerned more the details of the way in which employees should be integrated into the new *cadre*, rather than the principle of the *cadre unique* itself. During the strike demands for pay increases were added, reflecting the increasing cost of living in AOF.

As the strike continued, the administration tried to undermine solidarity by the use of trade union and political leaders. Dumas, a metropolitan CFTC leader with African experience, was summoned officially to persuade the unions to give in, particularly the Benin-Niger section, which was a CFTC affiliate. His support for the government position, and the indifference of the metropolitan CFTC to the strikers (in marked contrast to the CGT), prevented his visit from having any success. The politicians were perhaps more effective, at least in the Ivory Coast, where, as in most of AOF, the parties opposing the RDA, opposed the strike also. Thus, for example, it was denounced early on by Fily Dabe Cissoko (*Parti Progressiste Soudanais*), Yacine Diallo (*Amicale Gilbert Vieillard*, Guinea), and the leadership of the Parti Progressiste in the Ivory Coast. In their analysis of the premature ending of the strike on the Abidjan-Niger section, the senior officials of the executive blamed the intervention of PPCI and other notables, but there is at present little corroborative evidence.[18] In Senegal, however, where the RDA had very little support even in the towns, the SFIO leadership were sympathetic to the strikers, in part, perhaps, because trade unionists were then a significant proportion of the electorate. As in April, but this time at the request of the AOF *Grand Conseil*, Senghor and Lamine Guèye tried to resolve the dispute. They and the RDA deputies met the railway leaders on 19 December and then on Christmas Eve, the Governor-General Barthes, who refused any concessions. The deputies' activity then shifted to Paris.

In Paris, the National Assembly took no position, but in the Assembly of the *Union Française* the African representatives, with PCF support, obtained a vote in favour of ending the strike through compromise, early in February. Within the French context, the Assembly was powerless, but this demonstration of the unanimity of African representatives may well have created additional pressure on the AOF government. A fortnight later (but not for that reason), Governor-General Barthes was replaced by an SFIO deputy, Paul Béchard, and within three weeks the strike had been resolved, at Béchard's insistence. The new agreement made several important concessions absent from Ferrey's arbitration decision, including backdating of many changes, collective promotions, re-employment of the bulk of the strikers (in contrast to the Ivory Coast), and a 20 per cent increase in all pay and allowances.[19] There were, of course, losses; the strikers got no pay for the strike period, but had heavy debts; some lost their jobs, often to scabs taken on during the strike; and aspects of racial discrimination in allowances and privileges remained. Overall, however, the strike was a success, and a remarkable demonstration of both worker solidarity and general popular support.

More specifically, it had been a demonstration of CGT support, especially at the local level where the various *unions* organised numerous collections, meetings and demonstrations in support of the strike and the strikers. This had a profound effect on the railwaymen's attitude to the CGT. At the beginning of the strike, the Benin-Niger section was affiliated to the CFTC, while the rest, and the federal union, were autonomous. The white workers, as elsewhere in AOF in 1947, were CGT affiliates, although the most senior grades had created a new and autonomous union early in the year. Since, therefore, the only CGT members among railwaymen opposed the strike, the African union was sceptical of the value of the CGT affiliation, as Sarr pointed out to the CGT 27th Congress. A month after the strike, however, the federal executive of the union wrote to the CGT commenting on the opening of the FO campaign to split the CGT:

> The great bulk of the supporters of the *Union des Syndicats Confédérés d'AOF* are confirming their confidence in the CGT. This does not surprise us at all, since the CGT has always been on the side of those who suffer and who fight to shake the foundations of imperialism. As for ourselves, we cannot sit on sidelines and watch the manoeuvres of rival organisations . . .[20]

This position was reiterated several times during 1948, and in 1949, despite the beginnings of administrative repression of the CGT, two sections decided to affiliate to it (Dakar-Niger, Abidjan-Niger). Conakry-Niger remained autonomous, while Benin-Niger dropped its long-standing CFTC affiliation; the federal union also remained autonomous but decided to attend meetings of the CGT's Co-ordinating Committee.

I can now return briefly to the 'received' view. It is clearly wrong, and the PCF was at best marginally involved in the strike (indeed it is very difficult to imagine by what means it could have played the role assigned to it). That the strike occurred can be seen to be the outcome of fundamental demands by the workers and a refusal to compromise by the management, itself explicable in economic terms. The timing of the strike can be fully explained in terms of the progress of negotiations, which began several months before the Communist ministers were dropped from the government (in May 1947). The duration of the strike was determined not by expedient calculations in Paris, but by the solidarity of the railwaymen and the obduracy of the management and the colonial government; even the donations from Paris would not have kept the strikers alive for more than a few days—local gifts and credit were what mattered. Finally, there were always important African interests involved, and major gains were secured by the strike, which created not disillusionment with the CGT, but its opposite.

The formation of the CGTA

Here the received view is partly correct: the parties and the changing consciousness of the politically active were important contributory causes to the formation of the CGTA. Whether the administration did more than simply 'not discourage the formation of CGTA', as Morgenthau suggests,[21] I am still uncertain. Professor Morgenthau was a contemporary observer of the main union events of 1955–56, and there is no evidence of any administrative help for CGTA—such as money,[22] or the expulsion of the CGT from the *Bourses du Travail* (union offices provided by government) in favour of the CGTA. Johnson, who has studied PDG politics in this period, mentions that 'the concessions and compromises made by the PDG had all been made at leadership level—even, it appears likely, between Touré and . . . Cornut-Gentille personally'.[23] One of his sources, and the one claiming eye-witness acquaintance with such deals is, however, Touré's old opponent David Soumah, now in exile in Dakar, and I have found that other material from him needs careful evaluation.[24] Thus the evidence is partially contradictory, and not always reliable.

What is missing in the received view, however, is explanatory power. The factors offered are either processes which themselves require explanation (such as the growth of nationalist sentiment), or institutions whose influence on, and relationship with, union activity require both elaboration and proof. In such a situation it is possible that the explanation is itself false, misleading or partial, as I shall try to prove.

It is quite clear that the BDS and RDA supported disaffiliation from the metropolitan CGT. Speeches by Mamadou Dia at the BDS conferences in 1952 and 1956 called for disaffiliation and unification of the unions, and corresponding motions were passed. In 1955 and 1956, speeches and resolutions urged BDS trade unionists to seek greater influence in the unions (and significantly, not to regard following the BDS line as an attack on their own independence). It is clear from BDS and trade union papers that at least some of the BDS members followed the conference decisions. The RDA, or rather those sections of it most influenced by Houphouët-Boigny, had supported or encouraged disaffiliation on opportunist grounds since the RDA's ending of its parliamentary alliance in Paris with the PCF (1950–51). Touré's speech to the 1955 co-ordinating committee meeting was, however, the first statement of principle regarding disaffiliation. Thereafter, RDA leaders (especially those who were also trade unionists) were active protagonists of 'autonomy'.[25]

Several questions can immediately be raised: did the parties initiate the demand for autonomy, or were they simply channels for it? Why did the parties demand that unions should sever their metropolitan links when they were not willing to demand independence, a politically parallel action? Why did the union members and leaders support the demand?

What followed on disaffiliation was the unification of the two CGT factions, together with substantial parts of FO and CFTC. In the party arena, the campaign for trade union unity coincided in Senegal with attempts to unify the major political parties—the BDS of Senghor, the social-democratic SFIO of Lamine Guèye, and the small but influential UDS, once an RDA section (until 1955), but opposed to its Houphouëtiste line; it was also the party of the bulk of union leaders in Dakar. It was this campaign for unity among parties and among unions that gave rise to the campaign for union autonomy, for the major barrier to trade union unification was the affiliation of unions to rival French and international centres.

That there should be simultaneous campaigns for party and union unity was no coincidence, for the same factors underlay both campaigns. In Senegal (the territory with most trade unionists), unity and autonomy were the demands of a new educated elite, influential in both parties and unions. In Guinea (with the second largest group of union members), and in other RDA sections, they were the demands of an older, less-educated trade union elite which had become influential within the party, often as an outcome of the repression of 1949–51. I shall discuss the situation in Senegal and Guinea only, since these territories had the greater part of trade union supporters, and are the best documented. Furthermore, although there were separate campaigns in Mali and the Ivory Coast, and while each territory had its own specificity, the key arenas for rival union tendencies were Senegal and Guinea; once the CGTA had gained majority support there, the result of the AOF-wide campaign was no longer in doubt.

During the whole pre-independence period in AOF, civil servants were unusually important in trade unionism. The combination of the necessity of literacy in French for union officials and of legal provisions whereby civil servants might continue to receive their salaries when they became full-time union officials, made their predominance a matter of practical necessity. The personal discrimination suffered by civil servants (in comparison with Frenchmen in AOF), and the lack of alternative means to wealth or status[26] attracted even the more senior civil servants into union activity. Even private sector unions were led by men who were or had been civil servants. The first group of such men very largely left the CGT during 1949–51, driven out by fear of the repression of the RDA and CGT, or drawn out—in Senegal at least—by the rival attractions of the re-organised co-operative organisations,[27] or by the expansion of the BDS.

In Senegal they were partially replaced in the CGT, once it began to recover, by returning graduates from French universities. This group suffered the same barriers to socio-economic advancement as the earlier elite, and found themselves excluded from the parties by this elite; they were thus found principally outside the main parties, or as union leaders.[28] Their views were more radical than those of the older elite, and several of them were strongly influenced by French Marxism; 'they saw Senegal's main problem to be self-government and economic development and continued the Pan-Africanist orientation of their student days'.[29] Their allies in Senegal were two: the union leadership (which overlapped with them in any case), and the younger BDS members.

This second group, though not graduates, were also restricted to middle and low level posts, and—like the CGT leaders—found themselves increasingly exposed to job competition from French immigrants. This was particularly true in Dakar whose French population had tripled in the post-war decade, and made up a tenth of the urban population. For these groups there was nothing to be gained from continued colonial rule; it is doubtful, indeed, whether they ever thought there was.[30]

Within and without the BDS, these groups increasingly pressed for independence, aided by the growing autonomy of other French colonies, notably in the Maghreb.[31] The BDS itself, or rather the more influential part of its leadership, was seeking to increase its support in urban areas—especially Dakar and St Louis—and to improve the intellectual quality of its intermediate leadership. As a result, BDS policy became more radical, and the party leadership began to make overtures to the graduates, to the UDS (to which many graduates belonged), and to the SFIO. The graduates and UDS were attracted by the new BDS policy, and its position as the sole mass party, and returned the overtures. At the same time as the campaign for the CGTA began in Dakar, so the negotiations began between the BDS and UDS. The same non-trade unionists were involved in both movements;[32] the trade union leaders—like the lawyer Abdoulaye Thiaw and teacher Abdoulaye Guèye—seem to have been completely absorbed in union activity.

In Guinea the group common to unions and party consisted of trade union leaders and 'the new products of the elementary and upper primary schools who also found little scope in the existing system.'[33] These men had no personal or cultural stake in continued colonial rule (unlike Senghor or Houphouët-Boigny), and the RDA section (the *Parti Démocratique du Guinée*, PDG) had been saved from cooptation of the type that occurred in the Ivory Coast by the continuation of repression into the early 1950s. From the experience of its members during 1945–55 came the PDG's stress on unity and its radical, nationalist programme. Within the unions whose leadership and membership overlapped that of the PDG to a considerable—but not complete—extent, this programme became the slogan of 'unity and autonomy'.

The creation of the CGTA was thus the outcome (among other factors) of widespread urban sentiment in favour of the ending of French rule and of African unity, in part generated by trade union middle-level leadership and the graduate elite. This elite and the union leadership channelled these demands into the RDA and BDS where, as far as the union autonomy was concerned, they coincided with more opportunistic calculations by the party leaderships. The role of the parties was therefore one of mediation and amplification of the demands for autonomy and unity, and not one of initiation.

I have now answered the greater part of two of my three questions—the role of the parties and the role of nationalism, though the latter has been dealt with mainly by a combination of assertion and assumption. A question and a sub-question remain; why did trade unionists accept autonomy (indeed, *did* they all accept it?); and why was the political programme of union autonomy not mirrored in demands for national independence? An answer to the first will help relieve the faults I have just mentioned in my discussion of nationalism, in that the unions formed the main arena, until 1957, for nationalist expression, diffuse though it was, and trade unionists formed an important part of the parties' urban constituency. The subquestion requires more discussion than this paper will allow, though I shall sketch in a possible part-answer at the end of this section, which will also consider the related question of why the parties' 'moderacy' was not reflected in the trade union movement.

'Trade unionists' is a rather vague term, and needs refining. The rank and file should be distinguished from the leadership (above the branch level), and the leadership divided at least into those holding federal or territorial posts, and those with lesser positions (e.g. the officials of the union of a town or district). Of middle-level leadership very little is known (less even than of the same group in Anglophone Africa), so that I shall have to concentrate on the other groups. To understand their response I shall discuss certain features of union history in 1945–55.

There was already in the CGT (and perhaps CFTC) and among the autonomous unions, a long-standing dislike of trade union activity by Europeans in AOF and of European interference in African unionism. This had two main sources—the presence of French employees in AOF (affecting all grades of trade unionist), and the influence of the French CGT through the officials who dealt with African questions (affecting only senior leadership). Both are most important in the period up to 1951, by which time the African CGT had more autonomy, and French employees were mainly in FO or autonomous white unions.

The bulk of French trade unionists in AOF in 1944 were CGT members (the

CGT still having a politically broad spectrum of membership). With only a few exceptions, they refused to join African *syndicats*, or to admit Africans to existing *syndicats*; while in the unions, they demanded a disproportionate share of official posts. This led to racial tension, to shunning of the CGT and to splits within the unions. The 1947 Dakar CGT union conference called for the amalgamation of segregated *syndicats*, but the bulk of the white *syndicats* responded by joining FO. This in itself transformed racial into factional hostility, while in the CGT— especially after the deportation of many white communist unionists in 1948— Africans quickly filled all the leadership positions. Given, however, the social and economic position of most trade unionists (especially those who remained loyal during the repression), and the growth of French employment in major capitals (Dakar, Conakry, Douala, etc.), it seems very likely that unionists' dislike of Europeans persisted though most of the earlier cause had disappeared.

The direct influence of the French CGT through its officials responsible for African unions is hard to assess. The officials concerned either deny they imposed decisions or decline to discuss the issue. The CGT archives, even if open to the researcher, would I fear, tell little, as large parts were destroyed as a precaution during the OAS period. A few points can be made, however. Until 1948, there were a number of European CGT members in leading positions in the unions, which would have made imposition of policy easier and sharpened African resentment at such imposition. I know, however, of no such case, except (perhaps) the curious attempt to achieve biracial leadership in the unions in 1946–47, by having one secretary from each race. This was unpopular and short-lived, and may well have been a French CGT imposition.[34] The structure of AOF trade unionism would also have aided French CGT influence, for while a federal body was created in 1945, it was staffed entirely by Dakar unionists, and lost importance as the various territorial *unions* expanded. Thus the French CGT's early relationships with African centres were largely at the territorial and not federal level, which would have allowed greater pressure to be exerted (through personal contact, by use of local French CGT members, or withdrawal of subsidies and exclusion from benefits such as visits to Europe). Finally, in addition to the trend towards autonomy created by the repression of 1948–51, there was within the African CGT strong support for *greater* (if not total) autonomy, which suggests that French influence was both felt and resented.

Thus in 1951, the French CGT organised a conference at Bamako of trade unionists from AOF, AEF, Togo and Cameroun (intended originally as a second Pan-African conference, an aim thwarted by the French Government). Much of its time was spent on the question of relations with the metropole, and Sekou Touré, with the connivance but not support of the administration,[35] attempted to create an autonomous body. This failed, in part, because potential supporters did not attend the conference. There was enough support for greater autonomy, however, for the French CGT to agree to a relatively strong federal organisation being set up, which would in future mediate relations between Paris and the territories; subsidies were also agreed upon. After 1951, the metropolitan link was present partly on sufferance, and was maintained more by subsidies, and by benefits given to individual loyalists, as far as the senior leadership was concerned, than by conviction of its rightness (although commitment to the CGT's ideology was important for some trade unionists).

By 1951, therefore, both leadership and rank and file had come to dislike and distrust European involvement in their affairs; among the leadership the metropolitan link had been questioned, and had become increasingly a matter of convenience; and one leader at least, Sekou Touré, was committed to autonomy.[36] The next four years see two key changes which quicken this latent autonomism; among rank and file there arises strong pressure for a unified trade union movement; and it becomes clear that unification under a CGT banner was not feasible.

A characteristic feature of trade unionism in 1952–55 was unity of action between the four groups of unions: CGT, CFTC, FO and the autonomous unions. Its origin was in the campaign to have a new and more liberal Labour Code enacted in Paris. The code, in one form or another, had been under consideration from 1947. The lethargy of its progress, the inability of the unions to achieve any major economic advance save by such legislation,[37] and the sudden increase of bargaining power for the African deputies after the RDA broke with the PCF, all dictated to the African unions a campaign of parliamentary pressure in Paris through sympathetic deputies, backed by campaigns of industrial action and pressure group activity in AOF itself.

The latter began in 1950, and for various reasons, took the form of united action first in Guinea. Not until after the 1951 and 1952 elections, however, were the two Guinean union leaders, Sekou Touré and David Soumah (of the CFTC), able to extend unity of action beyond Guinea. A conference was called in October, with broad participation, and a campaign of strikes decided on to force enactment of the code (which, *inter alia*, implied a 20 per cent wage increase). The campaign was successful, and each succeeding year had its particular focus for joint activity: application of the code in 1953; the application and extension of the principle of racial equality in the public sector in 1954; both of these aims, and structural unity, in 1955.

The pressure for joint action came from the rank and file, who stood to gain considerably from its success, and had less attachment to their centres' particularity than their leaders. That the CGT had the support of most workers was due more to its early lead in organisation, and to its consistent reputation for militancy and success, than to its apparent ideology. Support for the CFTC seems to have derived from two sources—mission influence, and the training in bargaining and negotiation that it gave, which made individual CFTC members prominent at plant level. Thus in both cases, affiliation was based more on expediency than on conviction, and as with the leadership, the metropolitan connection had to prove its value for it to avoid a challenge and retain support.

The various campaigns were successful during 1952–54. As a result Sekou Touré became the most respected and popular trade union leader in AOF, helped by the famous two-month strike in Guinea for application of the code. His prestige gave him also the leadership of the PDG (of which he was not the most senior member, or even the one who had suffered most); and it gave the PDG far greater overt support.[38] Thus within the CGT, the balance between commitment to autonomy and expedient affiliation shifted to the former: Touré and two supporters became the secretaries of the AOF Co-ordinating Committee in 1954. They used their position, however, to press not so much for autonomy, as for structural unity.

Pressure for such unity had been increasing among rank and file members, as a result of their expedient view of affiliation and the success of joint actions. It was amplified by increasing defections to the CGT and perhaps by the influence of the newly returned radical graduates. Defection to the CGT provided a form of *de facto* unification; it was, however, slow, and left behind it a still divided leadership. Short of removing the leaders, therefore, the only solution was to break the affiliations. Only a few leaders (of whom Abdoulaye Diallo is the best known) were eventually removed, and the move to disaffiliation might have been much slower if the value of affiliation had not simultaneously decreased. The campaigns of 1951–53 had depended for success on both the French CGT's influence within the National Assembly, and the funds and materials it made available. During 1954–55, however, the focus of industrial activity was mainly within the AOF; joint activity was less successful; and the African CGT both made less effort to secure unity of action, and spent more time on internal and factional disputes. For the rank and file, and for a substantial group of leaders, the metropolitan connection had therefore lost its value, and autonomy had become politically feasible.

The situation was different, however, for the parties, since the crucial locus of decision-making remained in Paris until after 1956. Furthermore, although anti-French, anti-administration, or anti-colonial sentiment was widespread at every level of trade unionism, within the parties the nationalists formed but one urban faction, opposing powerful urban and rural patrons and notables more interested in maintaining their personal followings or ethnic political machines than in such 'ideological' issues. Thus not only was the metropolitan link more obviously useful for the party leadership, but the pressure for nationalist policies acting on them was only one of many contradictory forces to which they were exposed.[39]

The creation of the CGTA was not therefore the work of the RDA and administration supported by a diffuse nationalist sentiment. It was rather the outcome of several forces acting at different levels of union membership, and including: long-standing dislike of European interference in trade unionism, most prominent in 1945–51, but present thereafter, especially among rank and file, and key leaders; the growing demand for trade union unity which grew out of the 1952–55 experience; the decline in the means whereby the metropolitan connection might be represented as valuable; and the overt mass repugnance, personal as well as political, for French rule, supported and fed by the newer elite, especially those with trade union office or contacts. The parties, affected by similar or related forces, appear principally as a means for achieving autonomy and unity, rather than as forces in themselves. And the administration features less as a clandestine manipulator than as interested onlooker.

Commentary

All this may seem but one halfpennyworth of analysis to an intolerable deal o fact; there is, however, a little more general significance in the paper than mere rival narrative and interpretation. The points I shall make in this section are simple, hardly controversial, and not original; they are implicit in much recent work on micropolitics, and in the work on unions of Richard Sandbrook and Adrian Peace, among others. They are worth mentioning, however, since the analyses of union–party relationships on which they would throw doubt are still influential and continue to appear in new studies,[40] while studies which avoid these forms of analysis are mostly still to be published, or only recently published.

On the surface, I have criticised the 'received views' of the two episodes in different ways—one as simply wrong in all details, the other as mistaking a mechanism for a determinant force. In both cases, however, I have been discussing the relationship between a union and other organisations, usually parties. What I object to, in both cases, is the element of *téléguidage* in the received views, so that the unions are seen only as pupils or puppets of parties. This in turn derives from the personification of the organisations concerned, both by their identification with individuals (Touré, Houphouët-Boigny, etc.) and by their treatment as monolithic, homogeneous bodies, as a political counterpart to the 'legal individual'. In this fashion, union–party relationships become virtually sexual relationships: 'there existed a spectrum of pre-independence relationships from mutual hostility to extensive inter-penetration of union and party'.[41] Berg and Butler, while suggesting that the relationships are not as they appear in the earlier literature (essentially brother and sister against colonialism), do not free themselves from the overall 'sexual' pattern, suggesting for some unions a more marital version (courtship, honeymoon, and 'seven year itch').

Berg and Butler's account will bear a slightly more detailed examination.[42] It has two basic faults. Firstly, it treats unions as 'political individuals', and identifies them with their leaders (usually the secretary or president). The various short case studies in the article contain several statements such as, 'the CPP could not simply impose itself on the labor movement'; or 'the labor movement, if not completely subordinate to the party, is at least pliable and responsive to party pressures'; or 'these rewards (to union leaders) . . . frequently suffice to bring understanding between trade unions and governing parties'; or even,'in French Camerouns . . . organised labor was highly ideological'. Often, of course, this is no more than metaphor or shorthand, to avoid the repetition of the same clumsy formulations in every paragraph. The relative absence, however, of references to factions, the separate interests of leaders, or the interests and actions of the rank and file, who appear only in order to explain union 'weaknesses', means that the metaphor becomes the model, there being no alternative offered. The potential for misinterpretation that this creates is, I hope, illustrated by my discussion of the formation of the CGTA.

Secondly, the criteria used to identify 'the nature and intensity of the commitment of unions to politics and parties' are unduly narrow, and tend to equate 'politics' with 'party activities'. Thus Berg and Butler define 'a political work stoppage' as 'one whose main objectives are not directly related to the short-run occupational interests of the wage earners concerned'. There have, of course, been attempts at strikes that very clearly have fitted this definition, such as those in Nigeria in December 1964 (called against electoral fraud) and in Sierra Leone in 1963 (called to force action on a report alleging ministerial corruption). Like these examples, they have usually been abortive, which would tend to confirm the Berg and Butler thesis that 'to the extent that they (unions) entered the political arena their role was usually negligible'. Other means exist, however, of entry into the political arena. Unions may, by withdrawing their supporters' labour and organising demonstrations, prove the extent of governmental incapacity, as has occurred in the Sudan, Congo–Brazzaville, etc., and thus contribute to a change in government. More importantly for this discussion, strikes which clearly stem from 'short-run occupational interests' of wage earners have frequently had both an immediate and long-term political impact unintended by the strikers. They have, for example, forced governments to abandon or modify policies of wage restraint, which in turn has forced further changes in economic policy. They have also undermined, even if only temporarily, the security of governments which have responded by such overtly political actions as seeking or consolidating support from other sources; an example is Senegal after the May 1968 strikes.[43]

It is this latter feature of certain major strikes that accounts for the older interpretation of African trade unionism as 'political unionism'. That it occurs is due, in general, to a combination of four factors:

1. The grievances of wage earners—essentially that real incomes were declining —had common origins with those of other urban (and on occasions, rural) social groups.
2. Responsibility for the existence of these grievances was attributed by all the groups to the same agency, such as colonial maladministration or malice, and elite indifference and corruption.
3. Urban social groups have close daily contact with each other, and are in frequent touch with rural kin.
4. The various groups of urban poor are economically interdependent, in that, for example, the spending of wage earners supports not merely their families and other dependants, but an array of traders, artisans and others working in the informal sector.[44]

Through these links and the mechanisms they imply, strikes have become a general symbol of the discontent of the entire urban poor, and developed into broad protests against colonial or independent governments, the transformation being aided in turn by the authorities' interpretation and denunciation of the strike as a political intervention. Thus what was essentially 'economist' in motivation became 'political', both in terms of its longer-run effects and of its interpretation by others; this can be easily seen in the case of the 1947–48 AOF rail strike.

Berg and Butler also define too narrowly the sources of union 'political impact', restricting them to provision of organisational services (leaders, money, union 'machines') and to 'activities in support of political goals'. Again, 'politics' is too little distinguished from 'parties', and there is no mention of the influence of the political ideas developed within the trade union movement by union supporters, as a result of taking part in successive industrial actions against metropolitan employers, and colonial or independent governments (as employers). This seems, however, to have been the most significant political impact of AOF trade unions, at least up to 1958. Such influence is diffuse, hard to trace or prove, and has often been assumed present as part of the romanticisation of the union role, against which Berg and Butler quite correctly have argued; nonetheless, it ought not to be simply ignored.

These basic faults lead in combination to others, which I shall only summarise. There is firstly a reluctance to admit that unions can play a politically determinant role, that they can be other than politically neutral or subordinate. Secondly, Berg and Butler mistake the co-optation of union leaders, and the coercion of both leaders and rank and file, by post-independence governments, for take-overs of trade union organisations by parties; this makes subsequent resistance to government by union members (and sometimes leaders) difficult to explain. Thirdly, they tend to explain the activities and fates of individual leaders (e.g. Lawrence Katilungu) by reference to their apparent ideological positions, without considering whether these might be dependent variables.

To continue picking holes in Berg and Butler's account would be self-indulgent,[45] particularly as my objection to it is not so much to its occasional falseness (it is, after all, based on material at least ten years old), as to its mystifying function. Their formulations do not help us to explain the phenomena with which they deal, instead encouraging misleading, partial or even false explanations, which are in turn difficult to incorporate within general theories of political activity and organisation in modern Africa. It is improper to think of unions as monolithic and homogeneous organisations, which can be treated analytically as individual political actors, and represented by a single leader or small leadership group. Rather, they are organisations which are divided in at least three ways: sociologically by status, grade and occupational differences among members; and politically by, on the one hand, the members' relative position within the union and extra-union hierachies, and on the other, by factional alignments, which may or may not coincide with alignment by ethnicity, militancy, etc. What happens within unions, during union activities (such as industrial actions, conferences and elections), and the ways in which unions interact with other institutions, are influenced by all these divisions and the differing and opposed interests associated with them. They must therefore be considered, to the extent that the relevant empirical data can be found, in one's analyses of episodes and periods in union history.[46] A related, though not wholly derivative, point is that one's analyses should proceed from relatively independent and objective variables, such as economic interest, differences of status and grade, rather than from consideration of imprecise and usually dependent variables, such as ethnicity or militancy, or from the relative ideological positions of the actors involved. Thus, for example, even where factions within a union or union branch have different ideological positions, this should not be assumed to be the primary reason for the existence, maintenance, or activity of the factions.[47]

NOTES

1. E. Berg and J. Butler, 'Trade Unions', in J. S. Coleman and C. G. Rosberg (eds), *Political Parties and National Integration in Tropical Africa*, University of California Press, 1964, pp. 340–81.

2. See e.g. P. A. Martel, 'Le syndicalisme au Cameroun', *Bulletin des Missions*, 22(3), 1948, p. 135.

3. A *clan* is no more than a patron plus his clients, or a set of such patron-client clusters. For discussion of them in Senegal see: François Zuccarelli, *Un Parti Politique Africain: L'U.P.S.*, Librairie Générale de Droit et de Jurisprudence, 1970, pp. 165–89; Clement Cottingham, *Clan Politics and Rural Modernisation in Senegal*, Ph.D. thesis, Berkeley, 1969; W. J. Foltz, 'Social structure and political behaviour of Senegalese elites', *Behaviour Science Notes*, 4(2), 1969, pp. 145–63; Guy Pfefferman, *Industrial Labor in the Republic of Senagal*, Praeger, 1968, p. 85.

4. Quotations from: Franz Ansprenger, *Politik im Schwarzen Afrika*, Koln, 1961, p. 85; Edward Mortimer, *France and the Africans*, Faber, 1969, p. 118; Andras November, *L'Evolution du mouvement syndicale en Afrique occidentale*, Mouton, 1965, pp. 81, 93; Guy Pfefferman, 'Trade unions and politics in French West Africa during the Fourth Republic', *African Affairs*, 66 1967, p. 217. These sources are, of course, interdependent, and in some cases merely survey works; other readily available sources treat the strike as being without political significance, e.g. Ioan Davies, *African Trade Unions*, Penguin, 1966, pp. 85–6, or ignore it (c.f. Jean Meynaud and Anisse Salah-Bey, *Le syndicalisme africaine*, Payot, 1963).

5. The quotations are from Elliot Berg, 'French West Africa', in Walter Galenson (ed.), *Labor and Economic Development*, Wiley, 1959, p. 213; and Pfefferman, 'Trade unions and politics', pp. 218–20. For other secondary treatments, see: Davies, *African Trade Unions*, pp. 86–90, 198; Meynaud and Salah-Bey, *Le Syndicalisme*, pp. 72–5; Berg and Butler, 'Trade Unions', p. 359; Ansprenger, *Schwarzen Afrika*, p. 222; November, *Evolution*, p. 93; R. F. Gonidec, 'The development of trade unionism in black Africa', *Bulletin of the Inter-African Labor Institute*, 10, 2 1962, p. 136; Jean Lacouture, *Cinq hommes et la France*, Seuil, 1961, p. 332. The best secondary accounts are by Ruth Schachter Morgenthau, in: *Political Parties in French Speaking West Africa*, Oxford University Press, 1964, p. 159; 'Trade unions seek autonomy', *West Africa*, 19 and 26 Jan. 1957; *Trade unions and politics in French West Africa*, Oxford (mimeo), 1957; and by R. W. Johnson, 'Politics

in Guinée to the Emergence of the PDG, 1945–53', B.Phil. thesis, Oxford, 1967, pp. 100–4.

6. Zuccarelli, *L'U.P.S.*, p. 297. All translations are by the author.

7. To indicate the source for every assertion that follows would require too many footnotes; I have restricted these, therefore, to quotations or further points. The primary sources used consist of trade union documents, interviews, and newspapers, especially *Le Réveil*, *L'AOF* and *L'Unité*, all published in Dakar.

8. Speech by Sarr to the 27th metropolitan CGT Congress, in *Compte-rendu du congrès*, CGT, 1948, p. 180.

9. See Berg, 'French West Africa', pp. 232–7.

10. For the full demands, see *Paris–Dakar*, 9 Oct. 1947 and Inspection Générale du Travail de l'AOF, *Rapport Annuel* (1947), pp. 60–2. For a general discussion, see P. Morlet, 'La grève des cheminots africains d'AOF,' *Servir la France*, May 1948, pp. 36–42. Morlet was a French communist active in Malian trade unionism, and acted as liaison between the railwaymen and the CGT; his is the only contemporary commentary on the strike.

11. Bureau of the federal railway union to the chairman of the *Commission paritaire*, 30 Jan. 1947. I return to the importance of white racism later in the paper.

12. Thus, in January 1948, speaking to the Abidjan railway workers after they had decided to end the strike, he is reported as saying: 'Tomorrow, Monday . . . work starts again; those who get back their old jobs will be lucky; as for those who don't, so much the worse for them.' (Report on the return to work to the federal executive by the Abidjan executive, 24 Feb. 1948.)

13. Sarr to 27th CGT Congress, p. 181.

14. See Morlet, 'Grève des cheminots', p. 40. For earlier strikes, see Jean Suret-Canale, *L'Afrique Noire; l'ère coloniale*, Editions Sociales, 1964, pp. 556–8; there is also an account of the 1938 strike at Thies, in which six strikers were killed and forty injured, by M. S. M'Bengue, including long quotations from the strike leader, Cheikh Diack. Though I have seen his article, it had unfortunately been removed from the magazine containing it, so that I cannot give the precise reference.

15. Material from *Paris–Dakar*, 12 Dec. 1947; *L'AOF*, 19 Dec. 1947; *L'AOF*, 12 Dec. 1947; the stations were guarded by troops in other towns also.

16. *L'AOF*, Dec. 1947 to Mar. 1948; Morlet, 'Grève des cheminots'.

17. See Johnson, *Politics in Guinée*, pp. 153–78. For the Ghanaian strike see Richard Jeffries' paper in this volume.

18. In any case, it seems more likely to me that divisions within the union were both more important and allowed what political intervention did occur.

19. *Marchés Coloniaux*, 124 (27 Mar. 1948), pp. 491–3.

20. Sarr to Comité de Co-ordination des Unions des Syndicats Confédérées de l'AOF, 22 Apr. 1948.

21. Morgenthau, 'Trade Unions and Politics', p. 32.

22. Touré in fact contacted the ICFTU, the main rival of the international centre to which the French CGT was affiliated. This may not, however, have been in search of funds, but simply exploring possible support in the future. See 'Notes on conversation with Sekou Touré', in J. B. Krane to Albert Hammerton, 3 Feb. 1956, in ICFTU *West Africa* file, Brussels. The lack of funds of the CGTA is mentioned by Morgenthau, *ibid.*, p. 50.

23. R. W. Johnson; 'The PDG and the "Mamou" Deviation', in *African Perspectives*, eds. C. H. Allen and R. W. Johnson, Cambridge University Press, 1970, p. 348.

24. Pfefferman's article, for example, is based to a large extent on interviews with Sonmah.

25. See Morgenthau, 'Trade unions and politics', pp. 37–49.

26. Opportunities in the parties were slight, for they had few posts and these were often monopolised by pre-war citizens or ethnic representatives; there were also very few elective positions until the 1950s. Opportunities in trade were much less than in anglophone West Africa, and only in the Ivory Coast was there any major agricultural outlet for the ambitious educated elite; for business opportunities, see S. Amin, *Le Monde des Affaires Sénégalais*, Minuit, 1969.

27. See Pfefferman, 'Trade unions and politics', pp. 224–6; Henri de Decker, *Nation et Développement communitaire*, Mouton, 1967, pp. 349–50.

28. See especially Paul Mercier, 'Evolution of Senegalese elites', *International Social Science Bulletin*, 8 (1956), 441–51; and his 'La vie politique dans les centres urbains du Sénégal', *Cahiers internationaux du sociologie*, 26, 1959, pp. 55–84.

29. Morgenthau, *Political Parties*, p. 156.

30. Pfefferman argues that 'the assimilationist spirit of the CGT leaders was clear' at the time of the formation of CGTA ('Trade unions and politics', p. 219) and that they 'admitted . . . that higher real wages and more favourable social legislation could be obtained only within (the French) colonial system', (p. 229). The first of these mistakes tactical use of the economic implications of assimilation (equal pay) with attachment to assimilation itself; and for the second I can find no evidence.

31. Growing trade union autonomy in the Maghreb was also an important propaganda point used in the campaign for the CGTA. For nationalism among trade unionists in the early 1950s see P. Richard, *Aperçu général et*

social du centre-ouest du Sénégal, unpublished memoir, Ecole Nationale du Formation d'Outre Mer, 1953/4, 67 (this memoir was given 18 marks out of 20 by Senghor as *correcteur*); Mercier, *op. cit.*, and 29th CGT Congress, Jan. 1951, *Compte-rendu*, 158 for the interesting remark from a delegate that 'in Tchad . . . we wish to run the country ourselves'.

32. Abdoulaye Ly, Naguib Accar, Falilou Diop, Amadou Moctar, M'Bow etc. See Morgenthau, 'Trade unions and politics', p. 32, n.2 and *Political Parties*, pp. 158–9; P. H. Siriex, *Une Nouvelle Afrique*, Paris, 1957, p. 255. Unification did not, however, produce a new party firmly committed to independence, and this group (with losses from self-interest) finally left Senghor's party in 1958.

33. Morgenthau, *Political Parties*, p. 251.

34. A rather different case is provided by the support given to the Malian Abdoulaye Diallo by the French CGT, which resulted in his gaining certain federal positions despite his minority support in Bamako itself, and in his becoming a vice-president of WFTU. Even this declined after 1951 (or its effectiveness did).

35. The evidence for this statement is too long to quote; it is supported by references to Touré's past in CGT papers at the time of the split, by a contemporary French intelligence report, and by a Deuxième Bureau report.

36. The reasons for this, I suspect, lie in Touré's own social position (as a clerk) with its attendant racial discrimination, resulting in contempt for the French CGT's essentially 'left assimilationist' position. The repression of both the PDG and CGT in Guinea, which had a highly destructive effect, made him fear that continued affiliation might mean continued repression. Furthermore, he (and the Guinea CGT) had not had much aid from the French centre after the middle 1940s. With the lessening of repression against the Guinean CGT and the increase in aid after 1951, Touré's pressure for autonomy may well have slackened.

37. See Berg, 'French West Africa', pp. 227–9; major wage increases were won by simple strike action in 1945–46, but this was a result of the war as well as the power of the unions; from 1948 onwards there are complaints by union leaders of the failure to gain local increases.

38. For the strike and its effects see M. Rezeau, *Un exemple de la mise en application du Code du Travail Outre-Mer*, memoir, ENFOM, 1951; Johnson, *Politics in Guinée*, pp. 153–78.

39. See also Mercier, 'La vie politique', pp. 68–77; Michael Crowder, 'Independence as a goal in French West African politics' in W. Lewis (ed.), *French-speaking Africa*, Walker and Company, 1965, pp. 15–41; Elliot Berg, 'The

economic basis of political choice in French West Africa', *American Political Science Review*, 54, 1960, pp. 391–405.

40. See e.g. Shimshon Zelnicker, 'Changing Patterns of Trade Unionism: the Zambian Case, 1948–64', Ph.D. thesis, UCLA, 1970; R. H. Bates, *Unions, Parties and Political Development*, Yale University Press, 1971.

41. Christopher Allen, 'African trade unionism in microcosm: the Gambian labor movement, 1939–67', in Allen and Johnson, *African Perspectives*, p. 393.

42. Individual references to each quotation will not be given. I have benefited from reading Robin Cohen's critique of Berg and Butler in his 'The Role of Organised Labour in the Nigerian Political Process', Ph.D. thesis, Birmingham, 1971, ch. 3.

43. Clement Cottingham, 'Political consolidation and local-central relations in Senegal', *Canadian Journal of African Studies*, 4(1) 1970, pp. 101–20.

44. I have expanded this argument in my 'Unions, incomes and development', in *Development Trends in Kenya*, Centre of African Studies, Edinburgh, 1972, pp. 61–92.

45. So also would be a similar and repetitive exercise with such accounts as Davies, *African Trade Unions*, chs 4, 7 and 8; Meynaud and Salah-Bey, *Le syndicalisme*, Part 2; G. Lynd (pseud.), *The Politics of African Trade Unionism*, Praeger, 1968, chs 1–3; Michael Lofchie and Carl Rosberg, 'The political status of African trade unions', in W. A. Beling (ed.), *The Role of Labor in African Nation Building*, Praeger, 1968; R. D. Scott, 'Are trade unions still necessary in Africa?', *Transition*, 35, 1967, pp. 27–31; S. H. Goodman, 'Trade unions and political parties: the case of East Africa', *Economic Development and Cultural Change*, 17, 3 1969, pp. 338–45, etc.

46. I am well aware that my own case studies fail the tests implied by this statement: I must plead absence of data, and the intention of making further attempts to collect them. A study that does not fail the tests is that by Richard Sandbrook, 'Politics in Emergent Trade Unions: Kenya 1952–70', Ph.D. thesis, Sussex, 1970.

47. See e.g. Ralph Grillo, 'The tribal factor in an East African trade union', in P. H. Gulliver (ed.), *Tradition and Transition in East Africa*, Routledge and Kegan Paul, 1969.

PART TWO

Contemporary Working Class
Organisation

Introduction

The most concrete manifestation of emerging working-class consciousness is the workers' adherence to, or creation of, institutions dedicated to fostering their distinctive interests. Since institutions such as trade unions or radical political parties usually arise in the context of struggle, the connection between organisation and action is obviously an intimate one. This interconnection is well illustrated by the first three studies of the previous section. We now know that working people in various parts of Africa developed their own organisation during confrontations with employers and the colonial state, long before the right to form unions was officially approved. A clear-cut distinction between organisation and action is thus artificial; yet the treatment of contemporary organisation in a separate section can be justified on analytical grounds. While formal class organisations grow out of collective action, their establishment increases the likelihood of better planned and coordinated—in short, more conscious—action in the future. Hence, the student of working-class formation needs to understand the obstacles in the way of creating responsive class institutions and the dynamics of their internal operation.

Before turning to these facets of working-class life, however, we should provide a rough idea of the size of the African wage-earning category for which workers' organisations could theoretically cater. Reliable information on this subject is difficult to garner owing to the varying quality and coverage of national statistics; some estimates of wage-employment includes that in small-scale urban and rural enterprises, for example, whereas others exclude this sector. Nonetheless, one thorough effort to glean information from the available statistical sources arrived at the following estimates for 1960.[1] The African labour force apparently numbered about 100 million in that year out of a total population of over 250 million—an activity rate of under 40 per cent. Of this labour force, about one-fifth, or a little under 20 million, were wage-earners. But these aggregate figures mask immense variations between countries and regions. Among the countries referred to in this book, the Republic of South Africa had the highest proportion of its labour force in wage-employment (67 per cent), whereas the small countries formerly comprising French West Africa had the lowest proportion (about 4 per cent). In Zambia, Kenya and Ghana, around 20 per cent of the work force were employed by others, while Tanzania registered only about 10 per cent and Nigeria 5 per cent. Since, however, Nigeria's population of about 50 million in 1960 was seven or eight times that of Ghana and five or six times that of Kenya or Tanzania, Nigeria recorded the highest absolute number of wage-earners in Black Africa, about 900,000. Only a small proportion of the wage-earners in any of these countries, except South Africa, were employed in manufacturing.

What sort of institutions have emerged to cater for the interests of these wage-earners? In contemporary Africa, as in much of the rest of the world, the trade union appears to be the pre-eminent workers' organisation. Worker-oriented political parties (such as the Sudanese Communist Party and the Socialist Workers' and Farmers' Party in pre-coup Nigeria) have emerged, but they have seldom been very successful in eliciting broad support—even from the workers themselves. Several governing parties have, at one time or another, ordered the establishment of party branches at places of work, though again these experiments do not seem to have aroused much enthusiasm among workers, the ostensible beneficiaries. Even in the case of as relatively dynamic a governing party as the Tanganyika African National Union, its industrial branches, according to a recent study, are more or less moribund, possessing no definite function.[2] Tribal unions, many of whose urban members are wage-earners, remain important as social clubs with certain social welfare functions; however, these are hardly workers' organisations *per se* as their membership is defined in terms of place of origin, not of economic role. Councils designed to involve employees' representatives in management constitute another potentially, but not actually, effective workers' institution in Africa. One is thus left with the trade union as the main institution for advancing the interests of the working class. The alternative—as examined in the contributions by Paul Lubeck and Dorothy Remy in the Nigerian context and by Douwes Dekker *et al.* in the South African milieu—is the absence, banning or failure of formally organised labour bodies, and their replacement in certain circumstances by informal, *ad hoc* workers' committees to direct protest activities.

Where unions function, do they in fact generally operate to advance the interests of workers? This is a theme pursued in each of the articles in this section. How can one conceive of unions as workers' institutions when, according to most reports, the top and even middle-level union leaders in Africa, partially excepting Nigeria and the Sudan, are drawn predominantly from white-collar employees rather than from the manual workers who comprise the bulk of the membership?[3] Such a situation was probably inevitable, given the widespread illiteracy among manual workers and the necessity for union leaders to communicate with management and sometimes government in English or French. Nevertheless, the predominance of upwardly mobile, white collar employees in union government forcefully raises a question about the unions' internal power relations: are ordinary union members in a position to hold their leaders accountable for their actions?

Since this question is not one that receives much attention in the contributions to this book (except in Ukandi Damachi's piece), it deserves some discussion here. Leadership responsiveness is, in fact, a difficult question to deal with in the African context, owing partly to the paucity of studies of internal union dynamics and partly to wide variations in the structure of unionism, especially between the Anglophone and Francophone areas. Some unions are organised on a craft or occupational basis ('craft unions'), others on the basis of the enterprise or establishment employing the members ('house unions'), others on the basis of the industry or service ('industrial unions'), and still others on a general basis, embracing all or a substantial portion of a country's workers ('general unions'). Even within Anglophone Africa the variation is immense: in Nigeria, for example, there were, in 1971, 873 unions, many of them 'house' unions, whereas in Tanzania there is only one official general union. Given this diversity, a sociological analysis of African unionism can only suggest some tentative hypotheses about the kinds of pressures upon union leaders from below. But even this level of knowledge, we submit, is crucial for understanding why unions act as they do.

Do rank and file members possess any resources which provide them with leverage over their leaders? To answer this question, one must begin by distinguishing three levels of union leaders: the 'lower-level leaders' (shop stewards, shop delegates), 'middle-level leaders' (branch officials in industrial or general unions; the heads of house unions; the full-time *sécrétaires de syndicat*), and 'top leaders' (executive committee members of national unions and union federations). The lower-level leaders do not generally differ from the rank and file in terms of education, skill and income or of interests and orientation. The question of responsiveness therefore relates mainly to the full-time top leaders and those among the middle leaders who are full-time union officials; these are the people who carry out the important negotiations with employers and the government. What power ordinary members have over these full-time leaders depends largely on their ability to affect adversely two sorts of goals shared by permanent officials but not shared by the rank and file.[4] One such goal is, of course, a leader's desire to further his own personal ambitions: after all, if a union leader is ousted from office, he may have no alternative employment, at least at the level of remuneration and prestige to which he has become accustomed. In principle, therefore, the rank and file's primary resource is the vote in union elections. The other personal goal of a top union leader is to advance the institutional interests of his union by safeguarding its security against internal and external enemies, and by providing a basis for growth in membership cohesion and power. A union leader's power and prestige is very closely linked to that of the organisation he heads. Hence, another resource ordinary members often enjoy is the ability to undermine their institution's strength, either by ignoring the directives of unpopular leaders or by withdrawing from membership (if a compulsory 'check-off' system does not operate), thus ceasing to contribute financially to the union.

Consider first the electoral power of the unions' membership. The right of members to vote in union elections has rarely constituted a significant resource anywhere in the world; most studies of internal union politics have simply rediscovered or confirmed Robert Michels' famous 'iron law of oligarchy'.[5] In the African context, the few available studies on this topic (including Damachi's study of Ghana below) tend to support the view that full-time union leaders do not, in practice, hold their offices at the pleasure of the majority of their members.[6] While the forms of democracy—elections at the various levels, annual reports, the convening of various committees—persist in most unions, the reality is often central control of information and decision-making, an oligarchical situation at variance with constitutional provisions. The specific stratagems employed by full-time union leaders in an attempt to consolidate their positions cannot detain us here; suffice it to say that these include such popular tactics as the monopolisation of a union's communication channels and the construction of a personal machine within the union through the distribution of patronage.

To say that full-time union leaders do not generally hold office at the pleasure of the rank and file is not to assert that a member's voting right counts for nothing or that leaders do not seek popularity. In the first place, there are obviously degrees of accountability: the ordinary members of a dockworkers' union or other house union who directly elect their highly visible top officials may have much more control over their leaders' actions than, say, the members of a widely dispersed agricultural union who vote only for their branch officials. In the second place, where trade unionists have been legally deprived of their right to elect some of their top union officials—as in Tanzania since 1964—members have complained bitterly about this situation.[7] We would not argue, therefore, that the right of members to vote is simply or always a facade behind which an oligarchy manipulates the membership. But given the facility with which leaders can circumvent constitutional proprieties, we submit that the leaders' responsiveness to members, to the extent this exists, must be dependent upon mechanisms other than the electoral process.

Although the evidence is scanty and further research is required, one such mechanism may well be the factionalism which is endemic to many African unions. The available studies indicate that the tendency toward oligarchy has not yet reached the point where top leaders are stable and irremovable.[8] As long as incumbent officials remain vulnerable to the manoeuvres of ambitious contenders, they live with a pervasive sense of personal insecurity whose effect is normally to push them towards militantly espousing traditional union aims. Insecurity breeds militancy as top leaders try to ensure that they are not outflanked by aspirants to their highly-prized positions. Note, however, that factionalism is not simply another form of union democracy because such conflict is not conducted according to any rules of fair play, is not regarded as legitimate activity by the other side, and usually involves only the various levels of union leaders, not the rank and file. Nonetheless, factionalism may be a rather unseemly surrogate for union democracy to the extent that such conflict impels top leaders to respond to the aspirations of their members.

Why has it been so difficult for established union leaders in Africa to consolidate their positions by eliminating all actual or potential opposition, in the way that, for instance, their American counterparts have usually done? This is, of course, a very large topic which requires far more research. We have only space here to mention briefly several likely causes suggested by the literature. One factor is undoubtedly the existence of certain sharply defined cleavages within many African unions. Two cleavages stand out in studies of African unionism: occupational status and ethnicity. Occupational status may become a salient principle of solidarity if union members and lower level leaders believe that top and middle leaders are advancing the interests of a particular occupational category at the expense of others.[9] Given the fact that the higher union officials are usually predominantly from technical and clerical occupations while the ordinary members are largely manual workers (at least in most industrial and general unions), we should not be surprised that occupation has sometimes represented a significant line of cleavage. The latent hostility of manual workers towards their 'white-collar' leaders based on a belief that the latter are concentrating on winning benefits for their own group, is often a resource waiting to be tapped by an aspirant to union power.

Another potential line of cleavage is represented by ethnicity. Ethnicity may become the salient principle of solidarity, within unions as within societies as a whole, if workers and their leaders perceive that one ethnic group is seeking to monopolise jobs and power at the expense of others.[10] To avoid misunderstanding, one must immediately emphasise that 'tribalism' is not here conceived as a regressive and unthinking loyalty irremediably infecting African workers and undermining their organisational efforts. On the contrary, the tribal heterogeneity of union memberships seldom vitiates employee solidarity *vis-à-vis* employers.[11] Moreover, in conflict within trade unions, tribal appeals are not automatically effective, as tribal affiliation does not morally bind a person in conflict situations. In fact, blatant public attempts to manipulate tribal loyalty are liable to prove counter-productive, owing to the opprobrium attached to such attempts. Challengers will usually only succeed in temporarily activating ethnic identity for internal union struggles when a differential distribution of power, prestige or material benefits exist among the various ethnic groups comprising the membership. Needless to add, occupational and ethnic lines will sometimes overlap, exacerbating the conflict situation.

Political strife may also create or exacerbate intra-union factionalism. Studies conducted in various parts of Africa have noted a tendency for high union officials, especially those in a national union federation, to involve themselves in politics, sometimes by attaching themselves to a powerful patron. It is not surprising, therefore, that conflicts in national or local political arenas have 'spilled over' into trade union arenas. This occurs when either politicians or contenders for control of a national union federation channel money and organisation resources to challengers within unions led by individuals the patron opposes.[12] Hence, political involvement on the part of union leaders may augment their personal insecurity by creating new enemies.

While factionalism may operate inadequately and sporadically to prod union leaders into action, ordinary members often possess another, more potent, means of ensuring leadership responsiveness. We would contend that, from the point of view of the rank and file, the absence of union democracy is unimportant so long as members have the right to withdraw from their unions without suffering reprisals. If a leadership disregards the interests of workers, present members can withdraw their financial contribution by terminating their membership while potential members will refuse to join. Since any diminution of the membership and influence of a union diminishes the prestige and power of its leaders, the self-interest of office-holders dictates their attention to the individual and collective grievances of workers. In short, as V. L. Allen has argued in a much different context, the ultimate dependence of the unions' economic power upon the consent of members is crucial for the operation of the unions in the workers' interests.[13]

Paradoxically, then, a compulsory 'check-off' system may prove detrimental to the development of a strong union movement. In principle, the financial viability accruing to unions from either the 'union' or 'closed shop' variety of compulsory unionism should augment their effectiveness in pressing workers' claims. But, in practice, these schemes tend to undermine the members' power *vis-à-vis* their leaders, reducing the incentive for the latter to respond to the aspirations of the rank and file. Top leaders need not fear membership alienation if members cannot voluntarily withdraw their financial contributions, and if the swelling union coffers permit incumbent officials to construct ever more formidable personal machines. In Tanzania, for instance, the persistent demands by workers for the abolition of the National Union of Tanganyika Workers (NUTA) are a consequence of its aloofness from the concerns of the rank-and-file, an aloofness that is facilitated by a compulsory 'check-off' system and governmental appointment of its top officials. Strike action in Tanzania today generally bypasses the union structure entirely as workers follow their own informal leaders.

Since the union officials who attended the Toronto conference challenged the validity of the thesis just presented, we should carefully consider the basis of their objections.[14] These officials rightly drew attention to the immense difficulties which arose when unions were denied a reliable and secure income, such as that provided by a compulsory 'check-off' system. In the first place, workers were unable to sustain the expense of a prolonged strike (should one be permitted) unless their unions had the requisite financial base to establish a strike fund. In the second place, the union leaders pointed out that African unions were often at a disadvantage *vis-à-vis* large employers and the government in collective bargaining or arbitration proceedings, as the latter could afford experts (especially economists) to research their cases whereas unions could not. A secure income would thus permit unions to hire the expertise and bargain more effectively. Finally, the trade unionists noted that a paucity of funds in the coffers of a union makes its affiliation with an aid-dispensing international labour federation all the more tempting to its insecure and harassed leadership. Such affiliation, however, may be detrimental to a union's interests; it creates a dependency relationship that may introduce irrelevant 'cold war' quarrels into the labour movement of a poor country and perhaps deflect the movement from an indigenous pattern of development.

While the first objection is rather unpersuasive in that extended strikes are generally rare and illegal, the force of the last two points cannot be gainsaid. African unions do require large and reliable incomes to operate effectively and autonomously. At the same time, there is a need for an institutional mechanism to ensure that union officials retain the will to operate effectively in their members' interests. Both goals of financial viability and responsiveness can be achieved through a *voluntary* or revocable 'check-off 'agreement (plus amalgamations of small unions), whereas only the former goal is guaranteed through compulsory unionism.

In sum, we have suggested that the top and/or middle level leaders of many African unions, regardless of their own personal occupational backgrounds and governmental blandishments, are still sensitive to their members' desires and take these into account when making decisions. This can be the case even when a clique at the top centralises control of a union's activities into its own hands, by influencing the elections of middle-level officials and packing the union with its own supporters. In the absence of union democracy, pervasive factionalism may ensure that leaders remain personally insecure, and hence militant in the defence of workers' rights. But the rank and file's most effective weapon in holding leaders responsible for their actions is the right to withdraw from the union by revoking their 'check-off' agreement. Where voluntary membership exists, unions can be very strong and popular at the 'grass-roots'.[15] Of the three studies in this section, however, only the one by Damachi on Ghanaian unions presents a portrait of reasonably responsive unions. The contributions by Lubeck and Remy on Nigerian situations illustrate mainly the obstacles to the institutionalisation of genuine workers' organisations. Indeed it is notable that both authors argue that the long-established central labour organisations in Nigeria (damaged, to be sure, by the effects of the civil war), were unable to make their presence felt outside their traditional areas of strength, or where an immediate situation of crisis at the workplace occurred. Yet Lubeck's study is encouraging in that it shows how, even in the absence of functioning trade unions, illiterate workers with little industrial experience were able to create informal but responsive workers' committees that were highly effective in coping with the grievances of the moment.

NOTES

1. K. C. Doctor and H. Gallis, 'Size and Characteristics of Wage Employment in Africa', *International Labour Review*, 93, 1966, pp. 159–69.
2. H. Mapolu, 'The Organization and Participation of Workers in Tanzania', Economic Research Bureau Paper 72.1, University of Dar es Salaam, 1972.
3. See, in addition to the studies in this section, I. Davies, *African Trade Unions*, Penguin Books, 1966, p. 93. While Damachi does not classify the occupational backgrounds of the top seventeen Ghanaian union leaders, their relatively high educational level suggests that the usual gap between leaders and led obtains in Ghanaian unions too.
4. See A. M. Ross, *Trade Union Wage Policy*, University of California Press,

1948, p. 27; and J. Seidman, 'The Labour Union as an Organization', in *Industrial Conflict*, eds. A. Kornhauser *et al.*, McGraw-Hill, 1954.

5. See, for instance, C. P. Magrath, 'Democracy in Overalls: The Futile Quest for Union Democracy', *Industrial and Labour Relations Review*, 12, 1959; S. M. Lipset, 'The Political Process in Trade Unions: A Theoretical Statement', in *Freedom and Control in Modern Society*, eds. M. Berger, C. Page, T. Abel and Van Nostrand, 1954; J. Goldstein, *The Government of British Trade Unions*, Allen and Unwin, 1952; J. Barbash, *American Unions: Structure, Government and Politics*, Random House, 1967, pp. 134–5 and *passim*.

6. See W. Ananaba, *The Trade Union Movement in Nigeria*, C. Hurst, 1969, pp. 281–6; R. Cohen, *Labour and Politics in Nigeria*, Heinemann, 1974, ch. 4; R. Sandbrook, *Proletarians and African Capitalism: The Kenyan Case*, Cambridge University Press, 1975, chs 3 and 4; R. Scott, *The Development of Trade Unions in Uganda*, East African Publishing House, 1966, pp. 24–5; D. R. Smock, *Conflict and Control in an African Trade Union*, Hoover Institution Press, 1969; W. A. Warmington, *A West African Trade Union*, Oxford University Press, 1960, pp. 132–7. For a slightly divergent view, see R. H. Bates, *Unions, Parties, and Political Development: A Study of Mineworkers in Zambia*, Yale University Press, 1971, pp. 83–103.

7. See Republic of Tanzania, *Report of the Presidential Commission on the National Union of Tanganyika Workers*, Government Printer, Dar es Salaam, 1967, pp. 6–7.

8. See Ananaba, *Trade Union Movement in Nigeria*, pp. 261–75; G. Pfefferman, *Industrial Labor in the Republic of the Senegal*, Praeger, 1968, p. 85; Sandbrook, *Proletarians and African Capitalism*, ch. 4; Smock, *Conflict and Control*, p. 126.

9. See Sandbrook, *Proletarians and Capitalism*, ch. 5; Smock, *Conflict and Control*, pp. 43–4, 13, 84.

10. See R. D. Grillo, 'The Tribal Factor in an East African Trades Union', in *Tradition and Transition in East Africa*, ed. P. H. Gulliver, University of California Press, 1969, pp. 306, 307, 328; Sandbrook, *Proletarians and African Capitalism*, ch. 5; R. D. Scott, 'Trade Unions and Ethnicity in Uganda', *Mawazo*, 1 (3), 1968, pp. 42–52; Smock, *Conflict and Control*, p. 13.

11. See A. L. Epstein, *Politics in an Urban African Community*, Manchester University Press, 1958, pp. 127–8.

12. See R. Gerritsen, 'The Evolution of the Ghana Trade Union Congress under the Convention Peoples' Party: Towards a Reinterpretation', *Transactions of the Ghana Historical Society*, 1972; Pfefferman, *Industrial Labor*, p. 85; R. Sandbrook, 'Patrons, Clients and Unions: The Labour Movement and Political Conflict in Kenya', *Journal of Commonwealth Political Studies*, 16 (1), 1972.

13. V. L. Allen, *Power in Trade Unions: A Study of their Organization in Great Britain*, Longman, 1954, pp. 63–4.

14. This thesis was most vigorously rejected by Jacob Ochino, General Secretary of the Kenya Petroleum Oil Workers' Union, and Sylvester Ejiofoh, Assistant Secretary-General of the Nigerian Trade Union Congress, who were present at the conference.

15. See, for example, Epstein, *Politics in an Urban African Community*, p. 121; A. J. Peace, 'Industrial Protest at Ikeja, Nigeria', in *Sociology and Development*, eds. Emanuel de Kadt and G. P. Williams, Tavistock Publications, 1974; Sandbrook, *Proletarians and African Capitalism*, *passim*; A.-R. Taha, *The Sudanese Labor Movement: A Study of Labor Unionism in a Developing Society*, Ph.D. dissertation, University of California, 1970, pp. 782–3.

Unions, Workers and Consciousness in Kano, Nigeria: A View from Below[*]

PAUL M. LUBECK

As the title suggests, the objective of this paper is to analyse the crucial relationship between leaders and members of factory trade unions from the perspective of the inarticulate yet experienced unskilled factory worker. Though the material presented below concerns only Kano, an area second only to Lagos in industrial development in Nigeria, the embracing theoretical question focuses on the problematic relationship between the 'organisers' and the 'organised'; an issue, it goes without saying, that has both intrigued and plagued political sociologists and trade unions from their inceptions. However, while this case study concentrates on this theoretical issue, the trust of the presentation will be on documenting and empirically describing the experience of an emerging social category as it struggles to deal with the new inequalities associated with urban industrial labour.

Discussions of this 'problematic relationship' in Africa generally but not always have stressed ignorance, intransigent traditional values, and apathy on the part of the first generation factory workers.[1] Yet despite the popularity of this interpretation in explaining trade union problems, little research has described, or more importantly, attempted to understand, the perspective of the often illiterate and usually unskilled worker, and how he views his situation. A view from below, irrespective of its alleged ignorance, surely merits the serious consideration of scholars concerned with the labour movement in Africa. A secondary objective of this paper is to argue that the industrial workers, though burdened with few skills and an understandable ignorance of complex industrial organisations,

[*] The data presented in this paper was gathered during twenty months of field work in Kano, Nigeria. Both observational and survey data were collected while the author was resident in a workers' ward adjacent to the industrial estate, where three factories, identified simply as A, B and C, were researched.

respond to their very limited choices with rational action towards situations of structured social inequality; and furthermore, that in these situations they are not significantly influenced by primordial traditional values. Therefore, in contrast to the orientation stressing apathy and traditionalism in explaining the workers' erratic relationship to formal trade union organisations, this paper will argue that in the case of Kano, at least, manipulations by the political elite, careerism on the part of union officials, rampant corruption at all levels of union activity and the workers' experience of profound economic and social insecurity are at least equally responsible for the demise of trade unions in Kano and in Nigeria generally.

Given Kano's status as an industrial centre, why, in the second largest industrial area in the most populous nation of Africa, was there not at least one active factory trade union during 1970–72? The official records of the United Labour Congress (ULC) list no factory union in Kano, nor were any representatives of factory unions unofficially represented at the bi-annual ULC conference in 1972. Though one assumes that the total absence of any union organisation at the factory level is only temporary, the body of this paper is concerned with explaining how such a situation developed and how, in the absence of professional trade unionists, rank-and-file workers responded with admittedly ephemeral, yet largely effective, strike committees in order to deal with conflict over payment of the Adebo wage recommendations of 1971.

Thus, with these objectives and questions in mind, the following topics will be covered:

(1) The structure of manufacturing industries in Kano with reference to Arrighi's theory of dependency.[2]
(2) The role of formal union organisation and national congresses in Kano.
(3) Rank-and-file organisations with emphasis on strike committees.

The structure of manufacturing industries in Kano

The most striking feature of industrial structure in Kano is the minor, if not insignificant, role played by multinational corporate capitalism in manufacturing though, one might add, it is dominant in wholesale and modern commercial services. Instead, the overwhelming majority of industries are owned and managed by alien and indigenous Hausa entrepreneurs who traded initially in export commodities such as groundnuts and leather, but have now made the transition from commerce into light manufacturing. Existing industrial development neatly fits into early industrialisation's traditional production categories: the processing of agricultural raw materials such as groundnuts and leather, textiles using imported yarns, and various import substitution industries whose products are destined for consumption in northern Nigeria.[3]

The absence of significant investment by multinational corporations contrasts sharply with industrial development in Lagos and, according to Arrighi, with the modal patterns of industrial development elsewhere in Africa.[4] Explanations for this probably temporary anomaly need not excessively detain us, but its origins can be found in the role of alien and Hausa traders in the groundnut trade, the versatility of Hausa capitalists who were able to rotate adroitly from the precolonial trans-Saharan and Asante trade to the Atlantic trade, and the political conflict between Kano and Kaduna over location of industries during the political party period. Capital accumulation necessary for existing industries also derived from profits made on the groundnut trade, either through the direct participation of the entrepeneur as a licensed buying agent, or indirectly through investments of regional marketing board surpluses in local industries (often selected by political criteria). Note that investment of the marketing boards' surpluses by state development corporations immensely benefited both alien and indigenous entrepreneurs, as investments were made in industries partially owned, but completely managed, by alien entrepreneurs. However, despite this rather anomalous industrialisation by entrepreneurial capitalists, the overall features of Arrighi's 'theory of dependency' still apply. Not only is there no industrial investment in capital goods or any risk investment, but both indigenous entrepreneurs and alien capitalists are totally dependent on foreign, but not necessarily western, sources of capital equipment, highly skilled technicians, many basic raw materials and increasingly on multinational corporations for necessary patents and local licensing agreements.

Now the question arises as to how such a pattern of entrepreneurial capitalism affects individual labourers and, in particular, their ability to develop workers' organisations such as trade unions. First, in comparison with multinational corporations, whose capital resources encourage capital intensive machinery, entrepreneurial industries in Kano tend to be more labour-intensive, and tend to exploit inefficiently the unlimited supplies of available labour. Secondly, whereas multinational corporate enterprises are usually integrated vertically, from extraction of raw materials to distribution to consumers where at each stage a profit is exacted, entrepreneurs enjoy no such latitude as they can neither significantly influence prices of raw materials or capital goods, nor can they control the often mercurial fluctuations in local market demand for their products. Thus, in contrast to Arrighi's somewhat deterministic analysis of corporate labour policy, the exploitation of labour in Kano by methods traditionally associated with entrepreneurial capitalism becomes a major means of profit and capital accumulation.[5] Thirdly, because the managers have often recently disengaged from commerce, or in many cases, still engage in wholesale or even retail sales, their attitude towards labour and labour unions differs radically from managers employed by multinational corporations, who usually are at least familiar with modern industrial relations ideologies. For example, the Nigerian Employers' Consultative Association (NECA), an acknowledged spokesman for corporate management in Nigeria, advocates both collective bargaining and 'house unions'. Needless to say, entrepreneurial management neither advocates rationalised industrial relations nor usually tolerates union activity at any level.

Continuing then, with the structural relationship of entrepreneurial capitalism in Kano, the potential squeeze on labour for reasons of capital accumulation is most apparent among indigenous Hausa-owned industries most of whom, during the 1970 and 1971 Adebo wage revisions, conspicuously refused to pay either arrears in full or maintain the recommended Adebo level of 8s. 9d. for an eight-hour day.* With the promulgation of the recent Indigenisation of Industries Decree the probable net effect will be to increase the proportion of indigenous ownership and thus intensify the squeeze on labour resulting in wage rates well below Federal Military Government recommendations. Finally, with regard to Arrighi's theory of labour aristocracy and his hypothesis of cleavage between semi-skilled and semi-proletarianised labour, the empirical situation in Kano suggests the opposite: increased deprivation of the urban industrial labourers and considerably less differentiation between those employed in modern industries and those in more diffuse wage employment.[6]

The menacing potential of indigenous entrepreneurs' policy of refusing to pay Adebo recommendations was recognised by experienced workers (though less apparent to inexperienced workers), as the following statement by an experienced, urban-born worker indicates:

> Everyone paid but them. You know he (managing director) is a Hausa and comes from the same ward as us, but he closed the factory when the workers went on strike [for their Adebo]. The workers had families, but they were forced to return to work. He has no mercy for his brothers.

Thus the situation presented by entrepreneurial capitalist management policy constitutes a dilemma for trade unionists. Moreover, the situation is likely to become more difficult for unions owing to increasing investment in manufacturing industries by the local political elite whose investments previously have been marginal. Though the organisation of unions is occasionally attempted, usually

* A fuller description of the labour agitation after the Nigerian civil war, and in particular the deliberation of the Adebo wage commission, is provided in the Editors' introduction to Part Three of this volume. Readers of this chapter, the following chapter by Dorothy Remy, and the contribution by Adrian Peace in Part Three may wish to refer to the Introduction to Part Three for background information. R.S. and R.C.

without success, by rank and file workers, the hostility of the management results either in the demise of the union or the dismissal of the worker. On the other hand, the absence of active industrial unions confirms that organisation by professional organisers, though required for strong unions, has not been successful. An explanation of this requires mention of the social characteristics of Kano's industrial labour force.

The role of formal union organisation

In researching union histories at individual factories and the policies of the Nigerian labour congresses in Kano, I discovered that the 'crisis' and resulting civil war had a profound effect on both the patterns of industrial labour recruitment and the organisation of trade unions at all levels.[7] Informants who were employed previous to 1966 stated that a significant number of Ibos were employed before the crisis and that they played a prominent role in union organisation at the shop level. Since then, labour in factories has become increasingly Hausa–Fulani, with significant numbers migrating from Northeastern State, especially from Biu where the Babur-Bura people reside.[8] Moreover, as the war economy opened opportunities for import substitution industries, since 1966 the absolute number of industrial workers increased several times.

Besides altering the ethnic characteristics of the work force, the crisis brought a ban on all political activity and political parties by the Federal Military Government (FMG). Since many of the existing union organisations were either affiliated or associated with a political party, these unions were dissolved by order of the state government. While loyalties fluctuated according to fashion and instrumental alliances, the Northern People's Congress (NPC), the ruling party at the time of the 1966 coup, was associated with the Western-oriented United Labour Congress (ULC) while the opposition party, Nigerian Elements Progressive Union (NEPU) was associated with both the Socialist-oriented Nigerian Trade Union Congress (NTUC) and the Christian Trade Union-affiliated Nigerian Workers' Council. Since many of the political party-sponsored unions had been thrust upon the workers, there was often constant confusion in their minds between union membership and membership in a political party. In discussing the experience of being organised, workers projected the feeling of overt political manipulation by what was, to many of them, an invidious occupation—the urban professional politician. For example, an experienced, rural-born Hausa worker recounted: 'I was forced to join when a big politician came and said that I must join. And if we were found without a card, we would be sacked . . . and we had to pay two shillings for the card.' Another worker who later became a prominent member of a strike committee commented similarly: 'They took our money and did not even work in our factory. Our heads were in darkness [i.e. ignorant] as they took our money but never told us how they were selected as our leaders or when the elections would take place.' In short, the net result of such attempts at union organisation during the political party period was negative in that such unions, in the minds of many workers, are now associated with a corrupt political class who extracted union dues but contributed little to the worker.

At best, then, workers who are reasonably familiar with unions view such externally initiated unions as 'brokers' to whom workers must relate in a 'fee for service' relationship as one would deal with legal services. In most cases the union organiser is assumed to be corrupt, or generally suspected of being corrupt, so that any questionable action or suggestion by an honest organiser, even if well motivated, would probably be interpreted as evidence of accepting bribes (*haunchi*) from the management. Nevertheless, among some experienced and more articulate workers, a notable exception was made for an (Ibo) organiser associated with the NTUC.

To understand the failure of professional organisers' attempts to organise industrial unions in the private sector, one must also point out the differences in the backgrounds and career patterns of professional organisers and rank-and-file workers. Simply stated, the overwhelming mass of unskilled and semi-skilled workers are illiterate, rural-born migrants who have almost never participated in formal organisations or state bureaucracy or attended primary school.[9] They are predominantly Muslim and are rarely able to speak English, but almost all speak Hausa as the *lingua franca*. Survey data illustrate that few of Kano's urban-born work in factories because both the local entrepreneurial ethic and relatively higher urban status orient the urban-born to trading and commerce of all varieties. Note also that the occupational aspiration of the migrants is to leave factory labour, which they regard as insecure, poorly paid and restrictive, in order to enter commerce.

On the other hand, the background and careers of three officials, representing the Kano branch of the United Labour Congress, contrast sharply with those of the rank-and-file workers. Representing Kano State for the ULC is an employee of a statutory corporation, whose main entrepreneurial activity, apart from his official post in the Kano State ULC, is as pilgrims' agent for the Hajj to Mecca. Readers unfamiliar with Nigerian Islamic culture should note that this appointed and quite lucrative franchise enables the agent to receive a substantial fee for each pilgrim making the pilgrimage under his franchise. In short, he is engaged in commercial services and would be labelled a wealthy trader by workers.

Two other official organisers merit special attention. Each has completed some secondary schooling and both are Hausa–Fulani. Neither has ever actually worked at manual wage labour. Further, given the relationship between the ULC and ICFTU and the Afro-American Labor Center, each anxiously awaits an opportunity to receive advanced training in industrial relations at institutes in Israel, Western Europe or the United States. At the conclusion of my research the first had already received his appointment for school in Western Europe, while the second was patiently awaiting his opportunity. There are thus obvious disparities between officials and workers in terms of education, life style, and career aspirations.

The inimical effects of glamorous training programmes on the development of trade unions also merits discussion. Although detailed data are unavailable, observation and informal discussions with administrators of these training programmes suggest that many trainees, upon their return to Nigeria, leave the labour movement for positions in government, politics or even multinational corporations. Leaving aside the obvious 'dependency' relationships between national trade union congresses and their benefactors in international trade union organisation, it is clear that such arrangements are inimical to the development of an effective labour movement. The net result of these programmes is to siphon off local leaders into positions outside the labour movement; and secondly, the 'foreign aid' nature of international trade union organisations vitiates the accountability of union leadership to the demands of the rank and file.

Rank-and-file organisations

Space does not permit discussion of the multitude of organisational efforts attempted by novice organisers in their factories. Brief mention will be made of two internally generated unions, one of which originated during the political party period while the other is of more recent origin.

The first example took place in a textile firm that was owned and managed by indigenous Hausa entrepreneurs, which we will call factory C. As one of the first such ventures it enjoyed a considerable level of trust from the workers because, as one of them remarked, 'Our relatives had money in the firm.' Although the upper echelon of management was Hausa, the technical direction was conducted by a British engineer. Initially, the workers' conflict with the technical manager concerned allocation of time for prayer. Some time during 1961 a worker was caught praying without permission and was penalised by a seven-day suspension from work. He was able to arouse support for his position among fellow workers, so that an appeal was made to the Emir resulting in the worker's reinstatement along with a provision for proper prayer breaks. According to this informant, who was learned in Muslim scholarship and is now a full-time Koranic teacher, a meeting was initiated by him to consider further action.

> I told them that we should not agree to this ruining of our religion by this company, we must do something about it. I told them the Koran and the *Hadith* of Bukari instructed us to come together in order to help each other.

The informant was elected secretary, and a popular worker, active in the NPC, was elected president. The union apparently persisted until the 1966 coup and was instrumental in gaining Morgan payments and wage increases in 1964.[10] Throughout the union's existence there was a tension between the president, owing to his formal political allegiance to the NPC, and a large number of workers who were affiliated with the opposition party, the Nigerian Element's Progressive Union (NEPU). When the coup and crisis period began, the union, apparently labelled as a political appendage of the NPC, was banned despite the wide support it enjoyed amongst the workers.

Stress must be placed upon the significance of Muslim culture among workers in northern Nigeria. Although the grievances might be identical to those in non-Muslim situations, they are likely to be interpreted as violations of Muslim practice. In the above case, the informant, in discussing the origins of the union, commented in detail on the alienating aspects of industrial discipline such as the relative lack of freedom, but chose to dwell upon one aspect for ideological reasons, the prayer issue, in order for him to develop support for an organisation amongst less militant workers.

The second example takes place in a large textile firm which I will call factory B. The firm is capitalised both by state development corporations and alien entrepreneurs, but managed exclusively by the latter. The informant-organiser, M.B.L., in this case was a Kano-born, former petty trader who was active in both the Nigerian Youth Congress and NEPU ward organisations. Owing partly to the relative economic stagnation in Nigeria during 1966, he took a factory job in a large textile firm. Previously, efforts to organise this firm by textile union organisers from Kaduna had failed largely because unionised workers were threatened with dismissals. After working there for one year, M.B.L. initiated his organisational effort by starting a friendly society whose chief function was to collect money for workers' expenses encountered during ceremonial occasions, such as those associated with marriage and birth. Next, he discreetly informed the Local Government Authority that the management refused to allow workers an opportunity to pray at the appropriate time, and thus brought an investigation which eventually resulted in recognition of prayer time. His success created some rank-and-file support, as the prayer issue irritates and continues to offend Muslims in all social categories. Despite his discreet organising activities little progress was made until a prominent civilian commissioner of the Federal Military Government, while touring centres of industrial development, made a visit to the firm and inquired about the union. (It appears that the commissioner began his political career in the labour movement.) In any event, after being informed of the situation the commissioner ordered that a union be organised, and M.B.L. was delegated to carry out this task.

While this example may appear bizarre, the subsequent deterioration of the union is illustrative of a repetitive, almost a structural quality of unions in Kano, that is, their domination by supervisors. When the informant called a meeting the only workers willing to attend were supervisors as all the others were threatened with dismissal if they dared to attend. Finally the supervisors and foremen met and elected each other to the proper offices and began operating a 'union'. Within a few months the informant was dismissed because of a 're-organisation of the factory'. Meanwhile, the union deteriorated into a management-sanctioned extortion agency whereby supervisors forced workers, especially recent rural origin migrants, to pay initiation fees and monthly dues. Understandably, when interviewed almost all workers denounced the union as useless, corrupt and exploitive, though a majority still recognised the need for a fair and useful union.

Here one must pause to understand why the supervisors are an obstacle to organising trade unions in Kano. Recruitment of labour in the larger, more impersonal firms is often left to the supervisors' discretion and, because of the surplus of unskilled labourers as well as the traditional Hausa practice of paying 'office money' (*kudin sarauta*), a large number of positions are sold by supervisors. Note that in such a situation it is to the distinct advantage of supervisors as opposed to the management to have a high turnover in workers, because each time the position changes, payments of some kind accrue to the supervisor. Obviously then, a union organisation promising rationalisation of dismissal practices and increased job security is a threat to such entrepreneurial supervisors. Yet, from the worker's point of view, it is apparently not that simple. For example, many of the workers in factory B where the supervisors took over the union, assumed that the 'union dues' were merely a bribe that must be paid in order to maintain their jobs. Understandably, this interpretation was confined almost exclusively to inexperienced, recently urbanised or 'commuter' workers. The urban-born, experienced workers were able to distinguish between the authority and interest of the supervisor and that of a union official, as this worker in factory B indicates:

We want a labourer like me to become the head of the union. I do not want a headman or a foreman to do it. If we have a labourer, I can talk to him, and tell him what bothers me; but with the foremen I am afraid of them because if I tell them anything it becomes a mistake in their eyes.

Another urban-born and experienced worker similarly commented: 'If you talk to the foreman and ask him to go to the manager he will not do anything. He will say it is a strike, but we are afraid to go ourselves.' This last statement is suggestive of the complexity of the issue of supervisor domination of unions; for, in addition to the influence and authority supervisors wield, which appears to be especially impressive for the rural resident commuters and recent urban migrants, the supervisors are the highest placed Africans in what are often racially stratified organisations. For some workers, therefore, in the absence of unions and in situations of conflict with non-African managers, the supervisors are often the only source of leadership that the masses of workers will recognise. Hence, while supervisors are often opposed to initiating unions, when unions are established they are often able to dominate them easily and so maintain their privileges.

Workers' evaluations of trade unions

In order to test the reliability of informants' accounts of unions in the three firms included in my sample, Hausa-Fulani workers were interviewed and asked: first, if they knew what a union's purpose was; and secondly, among those workers familiar with a union, whether they felt unions, as they had experienced them, were useful to workers like them or not. Table I summarises the results of these interviews.

Generally, we see that the informants' accounts are validated by the formal interviews. Despite the claims of national congresses to represent or at least to be actively organising industrial workers in Kano we see that 38 per cent of the workers interviewed were unfamiliar with unions. The variation in familiarity with unions across factories should be noted when interpreting the overall 38 per cent unfamiliarity figure. Although factory A has not experienced any union organisational drive since 1966, the high proportion of rural resident or 'commuter' workers, who have less involvement with industrial workers at their place of residence, appears to be a contributing factor to the higher 'unfamiliarity' response. Among those workers who were familiar with unions, approximately 61 per cent were unfavourably disposed towards unions. In factory A where political organisers were active, 77 per cent were either unfamiliar with unions or unfavourably disposed towards unions. In factory B, representing the case study where the union was appropriated by the supervisors, a larger number of workers were familiar with unions (62 per cent), while the quality of their experience was reflected in that only 16 per cent of those familiar with unions were still favourable toward unions. With reference to factories A and B therefore, both the informants' criticism and the researcher's observations are validated by the survey interviews.

TABLE I

Workers' Attitudes to Trade Unions

	Factory A	Factory B	Factory C	Totals A, B, C
Unfamiliar with unions	50% (15)	38% (32)	26% (7)	38% (54)
Familiar and favourable towards unions	27% (8)	10% (8)	63% (17)	24% (33)
Familiar and unfavourable towards unions	23% (7)	52% (43)	11% (3)	38% (53)
Totals	100% (30)	100% (83)	100% (27)	100% (140)

In the case of factory C, in contrast to cases A and B, the union was initiated by a worker *cum mallam* and was said to enjoy the support of the workers. Only 26 per cent were unfamiliar with unions, and of those familiar with unions 85 per cent were favourably disposed towards unions. Here the evidence is clear in illustrating the importance of having rank-and-file-led unions and that, contrary to arguments proposing traditional values as outstanding obstacles to union support, in this case Islamic values appear to have increased the legitimacy and thus the support for the union. Most important, however, is the evidence that workers respond positively to legitimate organisations that pursue workers' interests.

Strike committees: class consciousness in a conflict situation
Inflation and the Adebo Commission

In the previous sections we examined problems associated with formal union organisations and workers' evaluations of these. However important these formal organisations may be in the development of Kano's wage-earning class, our next topic is perhaps vastly more significant, for it concerns the nature of emergent class consciousness and workers' efforts to mould this consciousness into an organisation capable of altering the power relations controlling their means of livelihood. Because the strike actions and strike committees generated by conflict over Adebo recommendations did not involve professional union organisers, the consciousness and the organisations involved in this strike can be viewed as a purer reproduction of actual rank-and-file normative orientations and organisational capabilities. That is, in the absence of formal education and professional expertise, the workers' ideology and tactics derive precisely from inequalities experienced daily and repetitively in the labour process of capitalist production.

Before discussing these events in detail, we should first understand the post-war situation in Nigeria which led to the appointment of the Adebo Wage and Salary Review Commission; and secondly, we should also seek to isolate factors explaining the impact of the Adebo Commission's First Report on Kano's industrial workers. Though exacerbated by inflationary pressures present in the world economy, the principal cause of inflation in Nigeria derived from the immediate cost of the civil war and the stimulus to demand for goods and services that a war economy normally generates. Given a situation where the lower income wage-labour groups had not received a general wage increase since 1964 (and then only after a general strike), and further a situation where any attempt to employ industrial actions such as strikes for wage increases was banned by Decree Number 53, it is not an exaggeration to say that workers' real incomes were being literally ravaged by runaway inflation. Below, Table II indicates the degree of inflation as recorded by the Federal Office of Statistics in their urban cost of living index.[11]

In response to the inflationary spiral and workers' agitation, the FMG appointed a commission, the Adebo Commission, to review wages and investigate increases in the cost of living. After several months of investigation and heavy pressure from representatives of labour for an interim cost of living award (COLA), the Adebo Commission issued an interim report in December 1970, known as the First Adebo Commission Report. Apart from reviewing the inflationary trends in Nigeria as a whole, the commission's report made some

TABLE II

Cost of Living Indices in Three Nigerian Cities[a]

Years	Lagos		Kaduna		Kano	
	Food	All items	Food	All items	Food	All items
Annual average for 1968	117	124	113	120	112	115
January 1969	128	129	120	125	117	119
June 1969	145	139	136	136	130	129
January 1970	158	147	141	136	111	116
June 1970	166	154	164	150	152	143
January 1971	186	165	153	147	146	141
March 1971	191	168	165	155	162	149
April 1971	193	169	171	159	n.d.	n.d.
Difference[b]	65	40	51	34	45[c]	30[c]

a 1960 equals 100.
b Points difference from January 1969 to April 1971.
c Kano's difference is based on prices until March 1971 rather than April 1971; however, if the trend of the indices is taken into consideration the actual difference should be even greater.

Source:

Federal Office of Statistics, Nigeria.

explicit criticisms both of the national income distribution, and of the problem of widespread corruption. In discussing the plight of the lower income groups during the recent political crisis, the report makes some pointed accusations:

Such sacrifices [of the lower income groups] would be easier to bear, however, if it was seen to fall equitably on all sections of the population, such that the least sacrifice was made by the lowest income group. From some of the representations made to us it is clear not only that there is intolerable suffering at the bottom of the income scale, because of the rise in the cost of living, but also that *the suffering is made even more intolerable by manifestations of affluence and wasteful expenditure which cannot be explained on the basis of visible and legitimate means of income.* [their italics][12]

The report emphasises the perception of inequity by the lower strata, for it was the visibility of recent affluence which pervaded the social atmosphere in Kano on the eve of the report's publication.

The publication of the report helped to crystallise class antagonisms between workers and managers. The Adebo Report, in recommending a daily wage increase of 1s. 7d. per worker retroactive to the nine previous months, created a situation where an unskilled worker was to receive up to N £18 in one lump sum. Bearing in mind the fact that the minimum daily wage at that time was 5s. 4d. per eight-hour day, the arrears payment meant that a worker was to receive a sum equal to ten or eleven times his normal weekly salary. Such a substantial sum would enable a worker to alter his status either by purchasing luxury goods, or by capitalising a second occupation like tailoring or petty trading, or even by enabling him to pay marriage expenses for a new wife. Thus, once the size of the payment was announced, what might be termed a subdued conflict relationship between worker and manager quickly accelerated into a high conflict situation.

Besides the sheer size of the payment, the realisation among the private sector workers that the public sector workers were virtually assured of payment increased the private sector workers' suspicion of management's explanations and procrastinations over immediate payment. For as January progressed without payment and the Muslim festival of *Id el Fitr* approached, workers' anxieties and suspicions accelerated and were further inflated by great economic pressures placed upon workers by their dependants, all of whom expected gifts and a reasonable celebration of this major Muslim event. Therefore, in this instance traditional Islamic customs interacted with industrial conflict so as to buttress the class solidarity of the workers in their demands for the Adebo payment. Moreover, data from interviews indicate that at least some workers, who normally would not have supported the strike, were moved closer to a pro-strike orientation precisely because of the pressures that the festival placed upon them. For example, an otherwise conservative *mallam*-store worker described the situation like this:

> The company said it needed time to figure up Adebo, but the workers said that they must have the money before the festival. If there were no festival there would not have been any strike ... Me, I agree [with the strike] but it was a lack of patience that brought it. I wanted the money like everyone else.

His ambivalence is obvious, but at the same time the desire for consumer goods as well as the demands for gifts that such a sum would satisfy appear to be a deciding factor. With these factors in mind, let us examine the organisational response when finally workers' patience was exhausted and strike actions were called.

The question of spontaneity

Our first example takes place in factory B, the firm in which the supervisors appropriated the union. While the strike committee formed was ephemeral, lasting only for two days, the remarkable memory of the participants requires emphasis. Apparently, during the 1964 general strike over payment of the Morgan arrears, the management deceived the national congresses by paying arrears only to supervisors and then dispatched the supervisors to announce to the trade union congresses that the factory workforce had been paid. Now, once the Adebo arrears pay announcement was made, the experienced workers, quickly drawing the analogy to events of the Morgan payment, informed the less experienced workers of the company's tactic in 1964. Hence, when the company attempted to postpone payment and then to retrench a shift, wildcat strikes broke out first among those being retrenched and soon afterwards among the remaining two shifts. The following account by the strike committee chairman illustrates the long-term perspective and the fact that as a concrete social category, an industrial working class has a collective memory, which enables the participants to consider proper actions:

> We were inside the factory watching those workers being paid outside [retrenched workers]. We thought about the last time, during the time of Morgan (1964), we were patient then; but now we feared that we would not be paid, just like before. And after that, where would we carry our cries? When we saw the other shift being paid, we thought that we did not agree with this.

While these industrial actions may have employed relatively low levels of organisation and while few strike committees endured beyond the Adebo payment, the actions were clearly not spontaneous in the minds of the participants, but rather reflected the daily inequality experiences and often exploitive relationships in which workers found themselves. Not surprisingly, then, the propensity to strike was highly correlated with the reputation of each factory for fair or unfair treatment of its workers. Furthermore, once the strike occurred, though initially concerning Adebo payments, workers' demands immediately escalated into calls for improvements in working conditions, safety devices, health programmes and improved job security; that is to say, once the break with authority occurred grievances unrelated to Adebo, but germane to the work process and their class situation, were put forward. To term a strike-response spontaneous in this context merely mystifies the problem of class formation in a situation of weakly institutionalised organisations so often characteristic of early industrialisation. In retrospect the participants, rather than reacting 'spontaneously' (an image that brings to mind the 'unwashed urban mob') were both aware and quite fearful of the risks involved in striking; for they, better than either union organisers or impartial observers, realised that swift and arbitrary dismissals were a highly probable outcome. Hence, the image emerging from this situation is that of a cautious group of workers, who, considering past experiences and the failure of negotiations, enter into conflict with management, but with a realistic understanding of both the possible gains and risks involved.

Strike committees and problems of leadership

Whereas the strike committee organised at factory B did not endure beyond the specific demands of Adebo, factories A and C generated strike committees which lasted several months. But before discussing the remaining factory committees, let us first consider some general attributes of these more permanent committees.

First, leadership was recruited from older, experienced workers who, more often than not, were assistant headmen or even headmen. As distinct from supervisors or foremen, headmen are leaders of a work group and are involved in the labour process; they thus generally perform the same tasks as an unskilled labourer and experience the same risks from safety hazards, tedious and repetitive tasks and other alienating aspects of unskilled factory labour. Not only were the headmen able to command the respect and trust of their workers, but because of their seniority and relatively higher skill levels, they were also strategic and necessary for the process of production. Moreover, once the headmen of a section decided to support the strike, their authority was used to coax timid and even recalcitrant workers into supporting the strike.

Secondly, and understandably, certain factory sections were more likely than others to be militant and to generate leadership for strike committee positions. For example, those sections where the work process was accompanied by high risk of personal injury, or continuous and repetitive exposure to heat, dust or painful noise, both support for the strike and strike leadership were much more likely to occur. In one case mentioned previously, that of factory A, the productive process required that workers feed several open furnaces without protective clothing and at the same time the work process also involved high interdependence between workers as they passed products to each other. Moreover, communication was further facilitated by several rest breaks granted from the searing heat, during which time conversation and close primary relationships were able to develop. In addition to these factors, those sections in which a greater hierarchy of supervisors existed—hence relatively greater degrees of inequality, such as a weaving shed—provided both support for the strike and recruitment of strike leaders. For example, the strike leader quoted above in factory B as well as the strike committee leader of factory C, whose role will be discussed below, were both from weaving sections.

Thirdly, once a strike committee emerged, it usually vigorously attempted to suppress violent tactics on the part of workers: in several cases, the violence-oriented factions were threatened with physical reprisals if they did not desist. However, in the case of factory A, during the initial hours of conflict with the management over payment of Adebo, the committee members co-operated with a younger violent faction by allowing them to threaten and stone the management until the police arrived. Once the police arrived, by prior agreement between the committee members and the violent faction, the latter fled and the committee remained to negotiate the arrears payment.

Fourthly, with obvious fear of future reprisals in mind, committee members sought to avoid overt leadership roles in preference to a collective front.

Fifthly, and relating to the previous point, strike committee members, while negotiating with management, were fully conscious of potential accusations of bribe-taking, so that all agreements pertaining to timing and amount of Adebo payments were ratified in open meetings. In the case of factory B, the chairman of the committee returned to the assembled workers with each offer from the management (three times in all) before the workers gave their final approval. Again, problems of rank-and-file distrust of leadership, stemming partially from disastrous experiences with manipulative union organisers, were always present.

Finally, an outstanding characteristic of these committees was the absence of communal, ethnic or religious rivalry in either recruitment of leaders or decisions taken. Interviews with leaders indicate that when a decision was made to go out on strike, the leaders chose to call out workers, not on the basis of religious or ethnic affiliation, but rather by the role each worker played in the process of production. For example, after several weeks of one-day walk-outs and management's subsequent promise to pay the award in the forthcoming week, the workers secured a written promise from the management through the representations of an educated worker of a southern ethnic group. Because communal conflict between northerners and this particular ethnic group was widespread at the time of the research, an informant, who was also a strike committee member, was asked why such high trust was given by Hausa workers to this non-Hausa worker. His response was: 'Well, we do not have trust with them, but only at work do we agree to trust him.' Here, the example illustrates that at the place of work, organisational pressures tend to homogenise differential ethnic statuses into a common class identity that derives from common inequality relationships and common class interests. This is not to deny the reality of communal conflict in Nigeria, but only to illustrate how, during early industrialisation, communal loyalties begin to erode, at least in work situations, in favour of class-based loyalties.

Whereas few strike committees survived beyond the successful payment of Adebo, the members of one particular committee (that of factory A) attempted to transform itself into an organisation representing workers in other areas of disagreement with the management. Initially, at least, they enjoyed the support of a majority of the workers mostly because of the factory's unusually exploitative working conditions, high risk of personal injury, frequent use of underpaid day labourers, and verbal abuse of workers by alien supervisors. A long list of grievances was composed and an open meeting between all employees and managerial personnel was held where management made promises to reform certain conditions. The committee sought to gain the management's acknowledgement as mediators of disputes, especially dismissals, between labourers and alien supervisors. However, after about five months, while workers were discussing and enjoying the new powers of the committee, the management created a new level of supervisory personnel in between headmen and alien supervisors and announced that several of the most articulate members of the strike committee were to hold these new positions at approximately three times the wage of a common labourer. With this announcement, and the acceptance of the positions by the new appointees, those remaining members of the committee refused to continue an involvement with the strike committee. The committee had endured less than six months and was responsible for some minor reforms in working conditions which were discontinued when the committee was dissolved.

The following dialogue concerning the committee's dissolution between two friends, one an active strike supporter, Y.B., and the other a committee member *cum* new supervisor, S.H., illustrates the monumental desire for security and upward mobility on the part of low-status workers. It was related to me by Y.B.:

Y.B. We chose you to be one of our leaders and now you have become a big man, but not with our agreement nor with our advice. Now you must be a friend of the manager but you must go and tell the manager that you represent and are a friend of the labourers. How can you do this?

S.H. No! Allah has given us our new position. I want the new job and it is a victory [advancement] so I want it.

Y.B. Since you have achieved victory do you think we small labourers will tell you what is bothering us now that you are friends with the manager and will tell him?

s.h. No, no, it is not like that. Do not tell the other labourers what I told you. Whatever bothers you small labourers I will go and tell the manager, but the manager has not done anything about them. I will not tell the manager anything labourers tell me secretly.

Though S.H. was ambivalent about his new position, the benefits and mobility were too lucrative to ignore; thus, the strike committee collapsed and the factory returned to pre-Adebo circumstances. Again, bearing in mind cynical fears of rank and file workers concerning the reliability of their leadership, the central issue here is the question of upward mobility. As long as the mass of workers believe that mobility is possible either outside the firm in the commercial sector or within the factory organisation, as in this case, it will be difficult to maintain class-based, rank and file workers' committees. In such situations of profound economic insecurity and with the high visibility of new affluence surrounding each worker, it is not surprising that management was able to co-opt the committee. However, it should be born in mind that, just as management's tactics employed in factory B during the Morgan strike of 1964 were understood and were influential in actions taken during the Adebo strike of 1971, the events associated with the collapse of this strike committee will serve as an important reference for workers in their future efforts at organisation.

Although the workers in factory C went out on strike and formed a strike committee in similar fashion, their situation differs radically from the previous case studies in that, despite their efforts, the management refused to pay any arrears, or further, to pay the Adebo recommended daily wage rate of at least 8s. 9d. per day. While the two previous cases were alien-owned and alien-managed, this final example was both owned and managed by indigenous Hausa entrepreneurs, several of whom held prominent political positions within the state government. Whereas this firm's management style and reward practices had been comparatively more paternalistic and more particularistic, during the past few years once-generous labour policies were being discarded in favour of more rationalised and more economical policies.

After learning of the successful strikes of the above firms they too called a strike, yet no violence occurred during the two weeks that they remained away from the factory. Here workers voiced great concern that no violence was allowed as the firm was owned by indigenous entrepreneurs and the workers did not wish to appear as hooligans in the eyes of the local community. Accordingly, the committee met and negotiated with both the local labour office officials and representatives of the manager until, after two weeks without work, the workers returned. Upon resuming work some militant workers sabotaged several weaving machines, a move which brought swift retribution from the management in the form of a two-week lockout which caused great suffering among workers already spent financially by the two-week strike. Understandably, such a failure had a negative effect on the workers' morale and sense of efficacy, as the following account illustrates:

> I agreed with it then, as it was fair to receive our Adebo just as everyone else did. But now we lost over two weeks pay and still no increase [in wages]. I do not think strikes have any value . . . The next strike if three men return to work, I will be the fourth.

An outstanding feature of this strike committee was the prominent role played by the factory's *Imam*, or leader in prayer, who though a weaver was literate in English, Arabic and Hausa. Thus, in the minds of many workers, 'he had mastered both western and Islamic scholarship.' During the political period he had been active in the ward organisation of the opposition party, NEPU, and even held an office in the defunct union which had been banned by the authorities in 1966. His influence on the strike might be termed tactically conservative, as he believed, quite correctly, that if the workers struck the management could and would continue to refuse to pay Adebo arrears. However, once the workers went out on strike he agreed to be a representative on their committee. Despite a sustained effort on the *Imam*'s part he was unable to form a union, for after two weeks without work the majority of workers were exhausted financially and morally and only wished to return for fear of losing their positions to strike breakers. Thus, at the end of the conflict the committee was unable to transform itself into a permanent organisation as most workers felt it would be a useless endeavour.

Some concluding remarks

Questions posed earlier concerning the role and perception of formal union organisations require little discussion here, but questions relating to the nature of rank-and-file consciousness and the problems of leadership do require some comment. First, in the case of Kano as well as in most Islamic contexts, both class-based deprivation and criteria for leadership are likely to be mediated through an Islamic ideology, less because of deep religiosity, but more because, for uneducated workers, it is the only known and accepted standard of legitimacy. By reaching back into pre-industrial ideologies with its emphasis on rights and duties, Islam provides a basis for demanding greater equity in an industrialising context. What E. P. Thompson terms 'the tradition of the free-born Englishman' is analogous to Islamic definitions of fairness and dignity, both of which serve to provide an ideological basis for newly proletarianised workers in their demands for a more equitable position within society.[13]

A second point is the role played by the character of factory ownership and organisation in determining leadership, tactics and consciousness of the emergent urban working class in Africa. The issue of irrationality and spontaneity needs to be seriously reconsidered. The evidence presented here indicates that just as the organisation of the factory tends to define leadership roles, the rationality involved in industrial labour as well as the repetitive and cumulative experiences of inequality produce an effective, if loosely organised, plan of strike tactics, which can hardly be characterised as spontaneous.

Returning to our original question, as to why there are no active factory unions in Kano, we realise that there is certainly no shortage of factors either structural or normative to explain why past attempts to organise have failed. Unfortunately the reasons for the demise of unions are legion and the outlook for a rapid development of responsible factory unions in Kano is certainly not promising. Yet it is obvious from the above description that several reliable professional organisers are not only required, but could probably achieve substantial success if they are sensitive to the particular problems and orientations of northern workers. It is clear from my research that the single most salient issue in the consciousness of workers interviewed is job security. Any union organisation that is able demonstrably to diminish the profound insecurity of unskilled labourers in Kano will have little difficulty in recruiting and maintaining loyal members.

NOTES

1. See e.g., T. Yesufu, *An Introduction to Industrial Relations in Nigeria*, Oxford University Press, 1962.
2. See J. Saul and G. Arrighi, 'Socialism and Economic Development in Tropical Africa', *Journal of Modern African Studies*, 6(2), 1968. G. Arrighi, 'International Corporations, Labor Aristocracies and Economic Development in Tropical Africa', in R. Rhodes (ed.), *Imperialism and Underdevelopment*, Monthly Review Press, 1970.
3. Official statistics estimate the number of industrial workers in Kano at 25,000. However, this figure includes workers in automotive repairing shops.

4. For Lagos, see A. Peace, 'Industrial Protest at Ikeja, Nigeria', in Emanuel de Kadt and G. P. Williams (eds), *Sociology and Development*, Tavistock Publications, 1974. For Africa see Arrighi, in Rhodes, *Imperialism and Underdevelopment*.

5. Arrighi states, 'For the companies in question the exploitation of natural resources or of market opportunities in the periphery with capital intensive techniques is far more important than the exploitation of cheap labor.' *Imperialism and Underdevelopment*, p. 237.

6. Space does not permit a critique of Arrighi's theory of 'labour aristocracy', but it should be pointed out that he imputes a cleavage between semi-skilled and semi-proletarianised workers that simply does not exist in Kano; rather the evidence suggests a high degree of mutual aid and support between these groups. An analysis of factory workers' careers, for example, indicates that, in a monocrop economy like northern Nigeria, instability of demand and thus production are experienced at the workers' level by repetitive fluctuations between semi-skilled and casual labour categories, so that a privileged labour aristocracy can hardly be said to exist.

7. See Morris Zukerman, 'Crisis in Nigeria: The Economic Impact of the North', *Journal of Modern African Studies*, 8(2), April 1970.

8. Author's survey.

9. Note that access to education is still very limited in Kano. Official statistics estimate the number of primary school age children who are actually in primary school at 9 per cent.

10. On the 1964 general strike in Nigeria, see R. Melson, 'Nigerian Politics and the General Strike of 1964', in R. Rotberg *et al.*, *Protest and Power in Black Africa*, Oxford University Press, 1971.

11. 'Retail Prices and Consumer Price Indices for Selected Urban Centres for April 1971', (FOS/1971/PU4) Table 14, 'Consumer Price Indices for Lower Income Groups in Urban Centres', Federal Office of Statistics, Lagos, undated.

12. See the official reports of the Adebo Commission: *First Report of the Wages and Salaries Review Commission*, Federal Ministry of Information, Lagos, 1971, p. 9. *Second and Final Report of the Wages and Salary Review Commission*, Federal Ministry of Information, Lagos, 1971.

13. E. P. Thompson, *The Making of the English Working Class*, Penguin, 1968.

Economic Security
and Industrial Unionism:
A Nigerian Case Study

DOROTHY REMY

Recent research on African trade union movements has focused mainly on the influence of unions on national wage policy and on historical analysis of the interaction between national politicians and union leaders. Such attention to variations in union effectiveness and roles over time and between countries has proved a valuable corrective to more sweeping continental generalisations.[1] However, even generalisations restricted to one country, based as they are on aggregate data supplemented with interviews with national union officials, have inadequately considered variation in trade union effectiveness in relation to the industrial structure of the country and its pattern of urban development. It is the argument of this paper that the behaviour of industrial workers is strongly influenced by the type of industry in which they are employed and by the nature of the wider urban environment in which they live.

Workers do not face a monolithic enemy. Subsidiaries of multinational corporations, foreign-owned single-product industries and Nigerian-owned processing industries occupy structurally different positions in the national political economy. Source of capital and technology, degree of product differentiation within the corporate structure, proportion of local intermediate goods and the relationship of wages to total costs all shape the specific environment in which workers struggle. Similarly, the urban environment of the industrial proletariat is not uniform. The presence or absence of a supportive proletarian community and of alternatives to industrial employment shape both the relation of individual workers to their employer and the amount of community support workers can expect during industrial disputes.

Nigerian industries can be placed on a continuum with regard to the proportion of wages in total costs and of local intermediate goods in the final product. These two variables are closely associated with ownership, capital intensity and management attitude towards workers. *Subsidiaries of multinational corporations* are part of a protected enclave in the national political economy in that the investment capital is wholly foreign and there is little or no product competition. The technology used is imported, but there is extensive use of local intermediate goods. The industries are capital intensive at prevailing market prices and the wage bill constitutes a relatively small portion of total costs. Wages are often above the government minimum, working conditions are comparable with those of the parent factories and workers enjoy a range of amenities including pension plans, medical care and allowances for transportation. The companies foster 'good labour-management relations', which include establishment of house unions through which there is a degree of consultation with workers.

A second category of industrial employers consists of *international corporations* which produce and market a *single product* in several countries. The technology used, like that of the subsidiaries of multi-product corporations, is imported, although there is less use of domestic intermediate goods, as some raw products, such as synthetic fibre used in textile production, are imported. The goods produced compete with products manufactured in Nigeria and with imports. Although wages tend to conform to the government minimum, the wage bill forms a significant proportion of total costs, and the companies provide few amenities to their workers.

For companies in the third category, *Nigerian-owned processing industries*, wages constitute a large proportion of total costs. The capital for these industries derives from local sources, from a pooling of resources of Nigerian entrepreneurs and from government loans. Largely as a result of their much lower level of capital investment, wages are often below the government minimum, there are few amenities provided for workers, and working conditions reflect efforts to cut production costs. The economic environment for such companies is more competitive than for either of the two other categories. They compete for government support and with other companies producing similar products.

The distinction between the three categories of industrial employers is significant from the point of view of effective industrial strategy. Employers in Nigerian-owned companies are often hostile to any form of union activity among their employees. Workers, then, must fight for union recognition. The relatively low level of capital investment and the high proportion of total costs represented by the wage bill make owners resistant to any pressure to increase wages or improve working conditions. Workers in the foreign-owned corporations may have to contend with a paternalistic attitude on the management's part, but do not face issues of union organisation and recognition. The arena for wage negotiations is, however, different for the two categories of foreign-owned companies. Single-product companies tend to pay workers the government minimum wage. It is in the interest of workers, therefore, to combine with government employees to exert pressure for government wage reviews. An increase in the minimum wage benefits employees in multinational corporations; however, such companies often increase wages without reference to government guidelines. Employees therefore may direct their efforts to improve wages and working conditions on the single corporation of which they are a part.

The contrast between the behaviour of workers in Kano and Lagos on the one hand and Ibadan and Zaria on the other at the time of the 1971 Adebo wage award[2] reflects these differences while at the same time draws attention to the importance of the urban environment as an influence on worker behaviour. The size and concentration of the industrial proletariat and the relative importance of formal and informal economic activities[3] in the city shape the external parameters of industrial action. In Kano and Lagos factories are concentrated on large industrial estates built by the government as part of its policy of encouraging industrial development. Such concentrations, in turn, have stimulated the growth of proletarian dormitories—Tudun Wada in Kano and Agege in Lagos. In Zaria and Ibadan, on the other hand, there are fewer industries, each of which has an individual site. Workers live in occupationally heterogeneous neighbourhoods scattered throughout the city.

The high concentration of industrial employees in Tudun Wada and Agege has opened economic opportunities in the informal sector of the economy for the 'stranger' population. In Zaria and Ibadan, on the other hand, the informal economy is dominated by the host populations. Here strangers find it more difficult to establish sufficiently large networks of customers, the basis of successful entrepreneurial activity.[4] In 1970 over half of the owners of small-scale manufacturing enterprises in the Zaria Sabon Gari, where the proportion of strangers is highest, were Zaria-born Hausa.[5]

Successful entrepreneurs in the dormitory communities of Tudun Wada and Agege earn a relatively high income and maintain a level of personal independence not possible for the wage employed. The visible economic success of local entrepreneurs provides a stimulus for the wage earner to accumulate sufficient capital to become established in business. At the same time, the concentration of workers serves to increase the level of proletarian consciousness and to facilitate collective industrial action. Adrian Peace has discussed the paradox which this situation generates: the desire of workers to leave industrial employment and enter the informal economy *increases* the pressure for higher wages and thereby workers' willingness to engage in collective action.[6] The close links between the formal and the informal economy in turn increase community support of industrial action.

A different set of economic and social conditions is found in Ibadan and Zaria. Here the informal economy has closer links to agriculture than to industry.[7] The tenuous links between industrial workers and the informal economy reduces the economic interest of local entrepreneurs in industrial disputes and thereby the amount of support industrial workers could expect from their host community. Further, the absence of economic alternatives, either in the formal economy, in which in each case the Nigerian Tobacco Company plays a large part, or the informal economy, dominated by the host community, increases the desirability of and competition for NTC employment. This situation has encouraged the emergence of a system of sponsorship or patronship through which workers in the factory exert influence on the personnel manager in order to obtain employment for co-ethnics. At the same time, the scarcity of alternative sources of income places pressure on those who have jobs to keep them. The close ties maintained between industrial workers and their ethnic communities, in the absence of a large industrial work force, reduces proletarian consciousness and the effectiveness of sustained collective action.

The economic and social setting of industrial unions in Nigeria thus varies along two axes—type of industry and urban context. More empirical work exploring the relationship between workers and their environment is needed to give precision to what can only be outlined here. That such variation exists suggests that a typology of unions can be made. Such a typology is beyond the scope of this paper. To the extent that such a typology and the present analysis are empirically sound they transcend academic exercises and are relevant to the practical work of organising Nigerian workers.

The case material which follows was obtained from a subsidiary of a multi-national corporation in a non-industrial city: the Nigerian Tobacco Company in Zaria.[8] The analysis focuses on the interaction between the specific industrial environment in its urban context and worker response to three situations in which effective union action failed to materialise in 1971.

The workers' environment

Zaria continues to be an economic centre for its surrounding agricultural hinterland. The informal economy based on trade in agricultural surplus and the manufacture and distribution of locally-made products flourishes in interaction with an expanding formal economy oriented toward the advanced industrial countries. The two economic systems intersect in the Nigerian Tobacco Company (NTC), the only major manufacturing firm in the city. The tobacco used in the manufacture of cigarettes is grown by peasant farmers in rural Northern Nigeria. The tobacco is processed and made into cigarettes in a factory employing European production methods and technology. Agents franchised by the company distribute the cigarettes through the indigenous market system.

The Zaria economy as a whole has a labour surplus and there is strong competition for industrial employment. NTC, in particular, is regarded as a desirable place to work as its wages are above the government minimum, working conditions are generally favourable and its fringe benefits are attractive. Informal mechanisms for allocating jobs have developed, one of which is the use of patronage.

A patron–client relationship is asymmetrical, for the patron provides economic aid and protection to a client, who repays with demonstrations of esteem, information of value to the patron, and political support. The ties between the two are multifaceted and extend beyond the immediate needs of the moment Demostrations of trust underwrite the promise of future mutual support. Eric Wolf comments that such ties are 'especially functional in situations where the formal institutional structure of society is weak and unable to deliver a sufficiently steady supply of goods and services, especially to the terminal levels of the social order.'[9] Later in the same discussion he suggests that, in comparison with such situations, 'patron–client relations would operate in markedly different ways in situations in which the institutional framework is strong and ramifying.[10] In the second situation, which the NTC industrial arena exemplifies, 'patronage takes the form of sponsorship, in which the patron provides the connections . . . with the institutional order.'[11] In the Zaria case, the sponsor uses his influence within NTC to obtain employment for men unable or unlikely to secure jobs directly. Still following Wolf's analysis, the ethnic heterogeneity among the NTC labour force[12] suggests a situation 'sufficiently open for each seeker after support and each person capable of extending support to enter into independent dyadic contracts.'[13] At this point our data make it clear that such dyadic relations vary in their duration from 'contacts' to 'contracts'. Thus, ethnic ties within the migrant community are strong and provide the contacts which are the basis for sponsorship relations between more established residents and newcomers. The relationship in a sponsorship dyad has continuity only in that as co-ethnics the men continue to participate in the activities of their ethnic group. However, these dyadic contracts are based on a generalised reciprocity by which strangers in Zaria provide assistance to each other without a mutual expectation of continuing personal obligation.

In contrast to the above situation, in a few of Zaria's ethnic groups the generalised recipocity of sponsorship has been developed into a formal sort of patronage embedded in a corporate group, which in the Zaria context is an ethnic association. A limited number of men with influence in the institutional structure of NTC act as patrons for carefully selected clients from such associations. The patrons and clients have daily personal contact with each other and the obligation of the client to provide political support to his patron within the corporate group is articulated. Patronage is thus distinguished from sponsorship by the patron's continuing interest and ability in influencing his client's occupational welfare and by the client's continuing obligation to provide political support for the patron in the ethnic association and in the NTC industrial union. By contrast, a sponsor is likely to intervene on the behalf of a friend or acquaintance only once during his employment at NTC, and do so out of a sense of general responsibility for a co-ethnic rather than in the expectation of reciprocal assistance. Sponsorship may, of course, develop into patronage, or may depend upon a patron of the sponsor. Thus, both sponsors and patrons become obligated to the personnel manager who actually hires the new employees.

Such considerations are particularly germane to NTC hiring practices which are analysed from two perspectives. The first is the manner in which the worker initially obtained his job. The second is the manner in which the worker has assisted others in securing NTC employment. As might be expected, there is an important distinction to be made between stated company hiring policies and what actually happens. Officially, hiring works in the following manner: job seekers pick up application forms in the company offices and return them completed. When a vacancy occurs, NTC advertises the post and considers both standing and new applications. A small number of applicants are called in for interview and are asked to take an aptitude test. The person with the highest score is offered the job.

Contrary to the official version of hiring practices, I found that most of the unskilled workers at NTC had apparently obtained their jobs through the intervention of another person. Of twenty-four workers interviewed (sixteen of whom were unskilled while eight were skilled) fifteen made reference to a specific person who had helped him get a job. Two of the remaining workers had attended technical college from which they were hired directly as skilled workers. Three others received assistance from co-ethnics in completing their application forms, but were hired without influence being exerted on their behalf. Only four of those interviewed indicated that they had simply applied for the job and were hired. Almost all of the instances of intervention fall into the 'sponsorship' category. Of the men's sponsors, two were friends of the personnel manager, but eleven were supervisors, foremen or managers of the company.

The concentration of helping hands in the higher levels of the company hierarchy is a functional prerequisite of patronage or sponsorship, but we should know which is involved. One of the contributions a client may make to a patron, as Wolf suggests, is 'offered in the form of information on the machinations of others'.[14] My informal discussion with workers about their relations with the personnel manager revealed a general belief in his widespread use of 'spies' among the workers to keep himself informed about their attitudes. Although the personnel manager is said to obtain some information directly, it is obvious that through a well-developed system of collection of gossip he could keep informed on many aspects of factory life.

With only two exceptions, none of the twenty-four men who discussed hiring practices with me had sufficient influence with the personnel manager to obtain employment for friends who sought work at NTC. A few of those hired through the formal procedure had assisted others in completing their application forms, and one man had sent his cousin to the same senior clerk who had helped him get a job, and the cousin was also hired.

The two men who had been able to place friends in the factory provide examples of patron-client relations operating within both a corporate ethnic group and an industrial structure. One of the men was an Igala with a Middle School Certificate who worked in a skilled position. The other was a Tiv who had exerted influence to obtain employment for a co-ethnic. The Tiv patronage system is discussed in detail below. Although my evidence is impressionistic, the Igala patronage system appears to be similar in its general features. There are over thirty Igala in the factory; Igala men served as foremen and manager of one shift and both were members of an active Igala Youth Association. The Tiv and the Igala within the patronage system benefited from the symbiotic relationship which had been cultivated. The patrons selected their clients with care and supervised them on the job. NTC was thus assured of conscientious and reliable workers, while the patrons, in a context of scarcity of well-paid jobs for those without technical qualifications, were ensured loyal clients who could be expected to provide support within their ethnic associations.

Two Tiv men, whom we shall call David Gundu and Paul Makere, acted as patrons. Both were skilled workers who had been with NTC for over eight years. They had a year or two of secondary schooling, but had increased their qualifications by attending night school and completing correspondence courses. In this respect, David Gundu had the higher qualifications. Paul Makere had started work at NTC as a seasonal worker and secured a permanent post through the intervention of a tribal 'brother'. Paul Makere had been promoted from seasonal work in the Re-drying Plant to acting supervisor, but a disagreement with a European manager led to his demotion and subsequent bitterness towards all European managers. David Gundu was more reticent about his initial employment, but like Paul Makere had risen from an unskilled position to a skilled one. His ambition was to move into the marketing division of NTC in order to acquire additional skills which could be of use to him when he established himself in business in Tiv Division of Benue Plateau State to the south. While working together to promote Tiv interests within NTC the two men were competitors in the Tiv community and their ethnic association. To a large degree they obtained status among the Tiv through their ability to secure NTC employment for younger migrants to Zaria.

In their role as patrons, they helped Tiv migrants looking for work by advising them where to apply for jobs and assisting in filling out applications. They often gave guidance regarding technical schooling. While providing assistance generally, the patrons gave some men special consideration. Only these few men became clients in the sense of having a defined reciprocal relationship with a patron. In his role as patron, Paul Makere had talked with the personnel manager on behalf of a 'carefully selected' Tiv 'brother' on at least two occasions during the previous year. The personnel manager followed his recommendation in both cases. During the field study, the personnel manager took a two-month leave of absence and an acting personnel manager assumed responsibility for hiring. Paul Makere waited to recommend another 'brother' until the regular manager returned from leave.

Those who secured positions maintained close ties with their patrons. While a client was applying for his job he was provided with free room and board by his patron. David Gundu owned and managed a farm on the edge of town which provided food to supplement that which he purchased for his many guests and boarders. The support did not end when the client began work; he continued to receive his food and shelter without charge for several months until he could furnish his room 'decently' and send some money home. Only when he was in a secure financial position did the direct aid end. During this period, the clients were supervised on the job, and immediately reported even minor problems to their patron.

The patronage system links NTC to the wider community as social ties developed outside the industrial context are mobilised by those seeking industrial positions. Increasingly, however, NTC relies on school qualifications in allocating jobs, especially as mechanics and clerks.

Before 1966 NTC relied on a policy of interval promotion and on-the-job training. Both Nigerian and European supervisory staff regarded such training as the best means of developing and maintaining an efficient labour force. Its function does not appear to be to prepare men for promotion to skilled workers, however, but to ensure a reserve supply of trained labour able to relieve the skilled workers when necessary. Normally, this relief is for a short period only—

while a skilled worker is on break, ill or on annual leave. An indication of the extent of the true skill reserve at NTC is shown in the discussion of the third shift below.

The policy of internal promotion to mechanic has given way to exclusive reliance on technical college graduates. The policy brought about a discontinuity in internal promotions. In the period from the opening of the factory in 1957 to 1965 over half of the men hired as unskilled workers had been promoted into a higher skill category. Over half of the unskilled workers employed in 1970 were hired between 1966 and 1969 yet only one of them had been promoted to skilled, clerical or supervisory positions by February 1970 when the sample was drawn. During the same period eleven men were hired directly from secondary school or technical college.

All of the interviewed workers had a very clear perception of the status hierarchy within the factory and recognised that schooling was the prerequisite for the higher paying jobs. No one, for example, thought it unfair that those in management should receive an annual income as much as four times as great as their own. The fact that the managers had attended university appeared to justify the income differential in the eyes of the workers. On the other hand, it is becoming increasingly unlikely that a person hired as an unskilled labourer will ever be promoted to a position higher than that of machine minder. A division has thus emerged between those who have schooling and can expect some promotion and certainly a high income, and those without schooling who have no alternative within the system but to accept their second class status. One young unskilled worker articulated the position of his class: 'There is no hope for us workers. I live for the day, for tomorrow I may be dead.'

He and other unskilled workers nonetheless indicated an overwhelming preference for continuing to work at NTC until retirement. The desire to remain at NTC cut across ethnic lines and indicated a shared awareness of their inability 'to obtain an adequate income from informal economic activities.

The skilled workers, on the other hand, had both more capital and greater skills to call upon in pursuing alternative or supplementary income opportunities. Three of the skilled workers interviewed had businesses which they ran while not on duty at NTC, while another helped with a family business. A young Yoruba man had made careful plans for a future clothing store and was already saving towards the N £400 he considered to be adequate initial capital. An Idoma man wanted to learn a skill such as photography or mechanics, which he could use outside factory hours, but had not yet done so. Two of the skilled workers had no plans for future self-employment. One had applied for advanced technical college training and had also applied for a job as a mechanic in a new factory. A Tiv said he would become a trader if he did not continue to be promoted at NTC, but had no definite plans for self-employment.

Two points emerged from the earlier discussion of the economic structure of Zaria which are relevant here. The first is that income from the informal economy is relatively low, certainly in comparison with industrial wages. The second is that it requires initial capital and/or a network of personal contacts to become established as an independent entrepreneur in the informal economy. Skilled workers, whose income is over N £400 a year, can afford both to meet their family obligations and to save in order to make such investments.

The union's ineffectiveness

Patronage, reduced upward mobility for unskilled workers and investment in the informal economy by skilled workers diffuse worker solidarity. Patronage creates vertical links between unskilled workers and supervisory and managerial staff which vitiates any collective solution to their common concerns as workers. Union-management consultations are conducted in English. With very few exceptions, only workers who have post-primary school training are sufficiently 'articulate' from the point of view of management. An obvious consequence is the concentration of skilled workers, who have been to secondary school, in leadership positions in the union. To a large extent, therefore, workers who have less schooling are dependent on the goodwill of the 'articulate' leaders they elect to represent them. In this context, the concern with investment in the informal economy or in developing a patronage network, often manifested by skilled workers, is directly relevant to consideration of union effectiveness. The relevance of these observations emerges more clearly in the context of two specific issues and a concluding discussion of union leadership during the field work period.

The Adebo award

Since the 1930s the most important mechanism for wage determination in Nigeria has been government wage awards.[15] The legalisation of workers' organisations in the same decade and the rapid growth of nominal trade union membership in the late 1940s altered the institutional context in which the wage awards were applied, but in no way reduced their predominant role in wage determination in both the state and private sectors.[16] Since the first award in 1934, through colonial and independent governments, the wage award system had changed little. In response to organised or unorganised worker unrest, a board of 'impartial' dignitaries is appointed (in some cases it has been only one man) to hold hearings, deliberate and issue a report. In only one case out of seven since 1934 has the government of the day blatantly rejected the submitted report (the Morgan Award of 1964). In all cases the revised wage rates applied to the state sector only, in all cases it appears that most of the large expatriate and Nigerian firms followed. The Adebo Commission, which met in 1970–71, was the latest wage commission to be appointed and this section examines the response of NTC workers and management to it.

The Adebo award stimulated, and was the focus of, industrial protest throughout Nigeria.[17] In most cases conflict raged on two levels: specific grievances generated at plant level and at the national level between management head offices and union secretariats. In the NTC's plant at Zaria the entire conflict was played out in the external arena with no organised local action taken.

As in all towns of Nigeria, food prices and rents in Zaria increased steadily during and immediately after the civil war. However, whereas industrial workers in Kano and Lagos protested to the Federal Military Government commission on wages and prices, calling for an interim award, the wage employees in Zaria remained quiet. In December 1970, the Adebo Commission granted an interim cost of living allowance (COLA) of two pounds per month for workers earning less than N £500 per year. In January 1971 the government qualified the award, excluding those companies which had granted wage increases based on the cost of living since the Morgan Commission awards of 1964. NTC, like most other multi-national firms, had granted wage increases, the last in 1969, but had not explicitly tied them to increases in the cost of living. Following the Nigerian Employers' Consultative Association's lead, NTC resisted giving COLA increases to its employees. In Kano and Lagos workers faced with similar reluctance engaged in what often became violent protest. National union leadership attempted initially to direct the protest, and subsequently negotiated with management over the terms of the settlement.

At NTC in Zaria, however, there was virtually no industrial action taken over the issue. For about a week during the period when workers elsewhere were protesting, 'Adebo' and 'Adebo must be paid' appeared written in chalk on the walls, sidewalks and even doors of the administration block. However, production remained constant, and while Adebo was a constant topic of conversation, there were no union meetings called to discuss possible action. The union executive arranged a meeting with management to discuss the award, but before the meeting was held the plant manager had gone to Lagos to discuss with the national NTC management its position on Adebo. The union executive sent a telegram to the plant manager urging acceptance of Adebo and agreed to stop union members from such action as writing 'Adebo' on the factory walls and floor. In the event, NTC granted the interim award to its employees.

A former union branch president, 'Christopher Ogbadu', remarked that the union let NTC off lightly by accepting Adebo, rather than pressing for a larger wages claim at the upcoming March wage negotiations. He pointed out that the excise tax revenue from cigarettes, which is public information, rose substantially since the last wage settlement in 1969. Since the tax paid is an indicator of sales, profits must have risen as well. A strong president, he felt, would have called a general meeting and explained to the workers the advantage of not asking for Adebo, but, instead, pressing for a larger wage increase based on profits at the scheduled negotiations. The management, incidentally, covered itself by announcing that the COLA would be granted in lieu of any additional wage increase.

The ineffectual union activity in this case reflects the cumulative inertia built over a year of weak leadership under a president whose full brother held a prominent position in the Federal Military Government. It was thought that because of this link it would be highly unlikely for the union to engage in any action which might be interpreted as a violation of Decree 53 which prohibited strike action during the war and reconstruction state of emergency.

The third shift

A second issue which affected workers directly, and again was not challenged by the union, was the introduction of a third production shift in the factory. Workers were arbitrarily reassigned to the new shift. Over one hundred temporary workers, who could be dismissed without notice or cause given, were hired. Virtually all unskilled workers were placed on 'acting' status in higher positions. The third shift was announced to last only six months, but, in fact, lasted almost a year. Workers sought confirmation in their new posts, both because of the internal status implications, but more especially because they did not receive full pay for their new positions as long as they were only 'acting'. They felt they were being cheated—doing more skilled work, but being paid at a less skilled rate. Perhaps more importantly, workers felt powerless during the year of the third shift to obtain confirmation either through their patrons or through the union. Undoubtedly the union's lack of success influenced the widespread belief that it could not help with promotions generally.

Leadership and worker solidarity

Both the Adebo award and the third shift issue indicate the extent to which workers were unable to utilise the union to advance their interests and the extent to which the union executive neither responded to workers' grievances nor took initiative in promoting their interests. The two issues are discussed separately, beginning with the lack of organised pressure from workers.

A reason for the ineffectual pressure from below may lie in the structural position of the articulate unskilled workers themselves. Men with schooling, but without technical qualifications, who are most capable of articulating the grievances of the workers through union activism, are also the men most likely to be promoted. At the same time, they are constrained in their activities by the desire not to jeopardise their chances by being labelled a 'trouble-maker'. This generalisation may be clarified by the following incidents.

Workers in the NTC Re-drying Plant (RDP), where farm-cured tobacco is processed before being used in the manufacture of cigarettes, were not members of the union. Although many of them were engaged in this seasonal employment only to provide supplementary income, men who had been to school were likely to view RDP as a stepping stone to permanent NTC employment. The following account of RDP protest in 1971 illustrates both the vulnerability of the seasonal workers and the successful use of political activism as a strategy for upward mobility within the NTC hierarchy. In January 1971 seasonal workers organised a protest against the failure of management to hire workers from RDP on a permanent basis. A Yoruba secondary school graduate wrote a petition to management, expressing the grievances of his fellow workers. Within a few days after the presentation of the petition, its author was called for a meeting with the personnel manager and the union president. There he was threatened with dismissal for 'inciting' the workers, was accused of being a 'trouble-maker', and ordered back to work. Nothing came of the petition; 'outsiders' continued to be hired for permanent positions in the factory. However, the author of the petition was immediately promoted to a clerical position on the permanent staff. While this ultimately alienated him from the seasonal workers, he sought to justify himself to his erstwhile peers on the grounds that he was working on the inside to aid them in their fight against the management. In the meantime he urged a 'wait and see' attitude for the seasonal workers.

About a month later RDP workers stopped work because they had no protective masks against the intense dust in the plant. A group arrived at the desk of the recently promoted clerk. He told them to see him during his work break or outside the factory. The RDP workers returned to work and nothing further came of the protest. The clerk had helped organise the initial protest largely because he was not concerned about reprisals. He had boasted that the personnel manager 'knew about him' and would not fire him. In many ways his efforts on behalf of the RDP workers can be seen as a calculated risk. He was well qualified for a clerical position, but had been working for two seasons in RDP. By organising seasonal workers, he demonstrated to the management that it was to their advantage to keep him away from the less articulate seasonal workers. For them, his promotion emphasised the occupational importance of schooling. They, in spite of their longstanding complaints against the factory management, had stopped work twice in a two-month period and in each case returned to work in order to avoid being branded as 'trouble-makers' and thus jeopardising their chance of permanent employment. In both cases the original protest was severely modified between initiation and execution. In the first instance a 'demonstration' became a petition, and in the second a plan for a work stoppage resulted in the discovery that the clerk was no longer one of them and they were without an English-speaking leader.

Within the union, variations in leadership effectiveness and in the issues raised with management are functions of the personal economic options available to the leaders and to the members. A high proportion of union activists are mechanics. The shortage of trained mechanics in the North, where there are few technical schools, gives them more options than less highly trained men had. Thus mechanics are less tied to patrons or to a particular employer. They may act to advance their individual economic position by investing in the informal economy or may use their present job as a base for further schooling and/or more lucrative employment elsewhere. Two of the mechanics working in one department of NTC not included in the sample discussed above were using their income and skills to pursue these strategies. An Ibo mechanic was saving his money to buy a taxi which a fellow Ibo would drive during working hours. A second man had already applied for a position at a textile factory which was due to begin operation the following year in Zaria, and at the same time he had an application in for admission to Lagos Polytechnic. Men who follow such options tend not to be active in the union because they perceive their economic advancement to lie elsewhere. There remained a small number of mechanics who elected to remain with NTC and to maximise their position within the company. These men formed a core of union activists. As they were aware of the management tactic of separating articulate union men from the rest of the labour force by promotion to the senior staff, it would be difficult to determine the extent to which union activism was a calculated manoeuvre on the part of the mechanics to secure their own advancement. It remains true, nonetheless, that all of the younger NTC foremen had been at one time very active members of the union.

The way in which mechanics' skill-based security enables them to assume active union leadership can be seen through a contrast between two NTC union branch presidents, Christopher Ogbadu and David Gundu. A former mechanic, Christopher Ogbadu was foreman in 1971. He came originally from southern Zaria Province, had attended technical college, and was hired by NTC soon after his graduation. He was active in the union at the time of the 1964 general strike. Under his leadership, the union opposed favouritism in hiring and supported the preferential hiring of Re-drying Plant workers for permanent positions. He felt that national sentiments had to replace ethnic loyalties if Nigeria were to achieve economic and political development and consistently refused to join his ethnic association in spite of constant pressure to do so. Instead, he participated in the Nigerian Trade Union Congress, a nationally-based central labour organisation. Outside the factory Christopher Ogbadu's social network cut across tribal lines to include other men in similar economic positions, but he also invested heavily in one junior brother's business and the university education of another.

Christopher Ogbadu's personal economic position and the influence he exerted on the union stand in marked contrast to that of a later union branch president, David Gundu, a man from Tiv Division of Benue Plateau State. Under David Gundu's leadership the NTC union became a vehicle for consolidating the Tiv position within the factory and at the same time for consolidating, within the Zaria Tiv association, the position of those Tiv who worked at NTC. He and at least two other men were simultaneously on the executive committees of both organisations. The nature of Tiv patron-client relations, as discussed above, obviously required the patrons' access to both management and workers. The NTC union under David Gundu was weak. Although non-Tivs agreed that David Gundu was a 'good man', they also argued that he ran the union 'by the book' and allowed himself to be persuaded by management in negotiations. He sought re-election subsequent to this study being completed, but was unsuccessful. Ethnically based hiring practices had obviously not been a union issue under his leadership. Neither was preferential employment for Re-drying Plant workers. With perhaps a degree of exaggeration, the position of the Tiv patrons could best be described as one of working the system for the benefit of the group of Tiv with whom they had a special relationship. In the circumstances, this attitude makes sense for men whose immediate economic security depended on their continued employment at NTC.

The union president at the time of the field study held a clerical position in the company and, according to accounts of workers and my own observation, rarely entered the factory. It is perhaps instructive that, largely as a result of his family connections with the federal government, more officials in the state and national government attended his wedding than did NTC workers. Shortly after I left the field, he left NTC to open a chain of dry-cleaning plants in the capital cities of the North.

The economic benefits of employment at NTC and the lack of alternative sources of income in Zaria, both of which fostered the maintenance of an ethnically-based patronage system in the factory, shaped worker response to the Adebo award and the introduction of a third shift. Workers took no action which would jeopardise their immediate job or chances for promotion. The same considerations influenced the union leadership in its choice of issues for negotiation with management and its action in specific cases. Only one leader, Christopher Ogbadu, spoke strongly against favouritism in employment and promotion and could be said to have acted consistently to promote the class interests of the workers as a whole. For virtually all workers, especially those lacking technical qualifications, the possibility of economic gains must be carefully balanced against possible alternative sources of income should they lose their job. As long as economic security remains bound to schooling and patronage in Zaria working class solidarity cannot develop. Industrial unions become then not an expression of a class interest, but rather another institution within which conflicting interests can be pursued.

NOTES

1. Such as those found in E. J. Berg and J. Butler, 'Trade Unions', in J. S. Coleman and C. G. Rosberg (eds.), *Political Parties and National Integration in Tropical Africa*, University of California Press, 1964.
2. For a discussion of workers' behaviour in Kano, see P. Lubeck, this volume. A background description to the events that led to the setting up of the Adebo wage commission is provided in the Editors' introduction to Part Three. The situation in Lagos is analysed by Adrian Peace in this volume, and in his chapter 'Industrial Protest in Nigeria', in Emanuel de Kadt and G. P. Williams (eds.), *Sociology and Development*, Tavistock Publications, 1974. Comments on the effects of the Adebo awards on the industrial situation in Zaria are made below.
3. The distinction between the formal and informal economy is developed in K. Hart, 'Informal Income Opportunities and Urban Employment in Ghana', *Journal of Modern African Studies*, 11(1), 1973, pp. 61–89.

4. The critical importance of customer relationships in the informal economy is discussed in greater detail in D. Remy, 'Social Networks and Patron-Client Relations in the Ibadan Cloth Market', unpublished manuscript, 1967, and in D. Remy Weeks, 'Adaptive Strategies of Men and Women in Zaria, Nigeria: Industrial Workers and their Wives', unpublished Ph.D. dissertation, University of Michigan, 1973, pp. 79–104.

5. Remy and J. Weeks, 'Income, Occupation and Inequality in a Non-Industrial Town', in K. Wohlmuth (ed.), *Employment in Emerging Societies*, Praeger, 1973.

6. Peace, 'Industrial Protest'.

7. For greater elaboration see G. P. Williams, 'Political Consciousness among the Ibadan Poor', in Emanuel de Kadt and G. P. Williams (eds.), *Sociology and Development*, and Remy and Weeks, 'Income, Occupation and Inequality'.

8. The data used in the following analysis was collected in Zaria in 1969–71. Personal and employment histories were obtained from the NTC personnel department files of a random sample of one hundred employees. I also observed work place interaction on the factory floor for four to five hours daily over a six-month period. I later interviewed a sample of twenty-four production workers in their homes. During the field work period I lived in a predominantly Hausa occupationally heterogeneous section of the city.

9. E. Wolf, 'Kinship, Friendship and Patron-Client Relations', in M. Banton (ed.), *The Social Anthropology of Complex Societies*, Tavistock Publications, 1966, p. 17.

10. *Ibid.*, p. 18.

11. *Ibid.*

12. Forty ethnic groups were represented in the sample of one hundred workers.

13. Wolf, 'Kinship . . .', p. 17; G. Foster, 'The Dyadic Contract: A Model for the Social Structure of a Mexican Peasant Village', *American Anthropologist*, 61, May 1961, pp. 1173–92.

14. Wolf, 'Kinship . . .', p. 17.

15. J. F. Weeks, 'The Impact of Economic Forces and Institutional Factors on Urban Real Wages in Nigeria', *Nigerian Journal of Economic and Social Studies*, 13, Nov. 1971, pp. 313–39.

16. P. Kilby, 'Industrial Relations and Wage Determination: Failure of the Anglo-Saxon Model', *Journal of the Developing Areas*, 1(4), July 1967, pp. 489–520.

17. A. J. Peace, 'Industrial Protest', and P. Lubeck, this volume.

The Internal Dynamics
of Trade Unions
in Ghana

꧁꧂

UKANDI G. DAMACHI

This paper seeks to analyse the internal dynamics of the Ghanaian trade unions from the following perspectives: (a) the structure of the Ghanaian labour movement, (b) union leadership, (c) union decision-making process, and (d) the worker's perception of his union and industrial relations. While several studies have been made of the trade union movement in Ghana,[1] our study attempts to evaluate the structure and performance of the unions from the point of view of the members and leaders of the labour movement itself.

The material used in this paper was collected during a three-month field trip to Ghana early in 1972. The method of data-collecting included interviews with general secretaries of each of the 17 national unions in the country, and with a sample of 85 workers, 20 of whom were non-union members and the remaining 65 were union members. Seventeen of the 65 union members were also union officials, either shop stewards, regional or branch secretaries, or industrial relations officers. The selection of the respondents was based on the degree of literacy for the following reasons: first, union leaders complained of the great difference of attitudes displayed by literate and illiterate union members, and the difficulty they faced in organising both together. It was therefore necessary to test whether there was any marked difference in the way illiterate and literate union members perceived their unions. Second, given the rate at which literacy is progressing in the country, it could be expected that more and more union members will be literate in the future. Hence, our sample will help us not only to distinguish significant attitudinal differences between literate and illiterate union members, but to predict future trends of union attitudes and activities. For these reasons, 50 per cent of the 85 workers selected were primary or high school graduates, about 15 per cent were primary or high school drop-outs, and about 35 per cent were totally illiterate. We also relied on the Trades Union Congress (TUC) archival materials for information.

The structure of the labour movement

The Trades Union Congress is at present the sole legal union federation. Since the *coup* of 24 February 1966, the TUC has been able to organise, make decisions, and elect its officers in relative freedom, although the government has occasionally sought to exert some influence, and on one occasion has banned the organisation completely.

· The constitution of the TUC pledges that the congress will uphold the dignity of labour by maintaining a genuine workers' movement free from external control and resolutely defend and uphold the democratic foundations upon which the future of Ghana must be built. It will also strive for the achievement of respect for the dignity and rights of the individual.[2]

The TUC consists of 17 national unions with a combined membership of over 700,000. The national unions are responsible to their members on whose wishes they base their working programmes. The basic unit of organisation of a national union is the local branch. Every member of a union belongs to a branch and may attend its meeting, put forward suggestions about terms and conditions of employment, discuss the work and policy of the union, and take part in the election of branch officers. The branch takes action on certain matters considered to be entirely, or mainly, of local interest but refers wider issues to the union's national or regional bodies.

In most of the unions, organisation is based primarily on the place of work, and the governing body consists of elected officials, including a general secretary, an assistant general secretary, a national chairman and his assistant, two trustees, and a treasurer, usually elected on an annual or quadrennial conference of delegates from the branches. The above officials form the national executive committee which is the highest authority between conferences and carries out policy decisions made by delegates.

Membership dues

The main source of revenue for the trade unions and the TUC is membership dues which is 20 new pesewas (i.e. nearly 20 U.S. cents or 4 English pence) per member per month. These dues are deducted at source and distributed as follows: branch union 20 per cent, national union 50 per cent and TUC 30 per cent. A national union pays its staff from its share. With the same amount, it also provides legal assistance to its rank and file members in time of trouble, as well as social benefits at retirement. The 30 per cent paid to the TUC goes to meet the salaries and wages of the secretary general and his staff as well as the cost of seminars and training facilities.

Composition of the Trades Union Congress

The TUC is constituted by: (a) the congress of delegates, (b) the executive board, (c) the secretary general, (d) the specialised departments. The supreme authority of the TUC is, however, the Quadrennial Congress of Delegates, which is attended by accredited delegates of the national unions and members of the executive board. Representation of the national unions at the quadrennial congress is based on numerical strength, so that unions with a membership up to 20,000 elect five delegates, while each 5,000 members over this number is represented by an additional delegate.

The Congress of Delegates meets every four years to discuss matters of general interest to trade unionists and employees. At each congress an executive board is elected to represent the TUC during the ensuing years. The executive board is composed of a chairman, the secretary general of the TUC and the chairmen and general secretaries of the national unions. The board is responsible for carrying out congress decisions and for providing educational and advisory services. It also gives assistance in collective bargaining to national unions which request such assistance.

The executive board is also empowered to mediate in inter-union disputes, to administer the funds of the TUC and to make grants to trade union organisations abroad. It has power to enter into any transactions, to intervene in disputes between national unions and employers (if such disputes affect large groups), and to endeavour to bring about solutions to such disputes in accordance with the interests of the workers affected.

The secretary general, assisted by the heads of the various departments, is responsible for the day-to-day administration of the TUC. To extend the administrative facilities to the rank and file members in the rural areas, various branch unions of the national unions form *district councils* to help promote the social and economic interests of the workers and to secure a united front on questions or matters affecting or likely to affect their interests. The district council also serves as a forum whereby the workers can participate fully in social and community services in their localities. Every council has the following committees: (a) education, (b) social welfare, (c) organisational and (d) negotiating.

In the absence of the executive board, the *working committee* administers the affairs of the TUC. The membership of this committee consists of the secretary general, the chairman, four general secretaries, and four chairmen from the national unions. The representation of the general secretaries and chairmen rotates every three months.

The basic stated objectives of the TUC are to promote the interests of its affiliated organisations and to improve the economic and social conditions of the workers. It works towards the achievement of these objectives mainly through collective bargaining. Now that the structure, composition and aims of the TUC and its affiliated national unions have been described, we turn to consider the characteristics of the union leaders.

Union leadership

The mean age of the union leaders was 41 years, an interesting finding which invalidates the popularly held view that union leaders in most developing countries are young, between 23 and 35 years old. On the contrary, in Ghana the youngest leader was 30 years old and the oldest was 55 years.

All of the 17 general secretaries but one had been rank and file members and had indeed moved through the ranks to their present positions. The only leader who did not go through the ranks was the general secretary of the Health Services Workers' Union who came into his position from the Ministry of Health as a purchasing agent. As a matter of fact, his candidacy for the position of the general secretary was initiated by the Minister of Health. He happened to be the youngest of the union leaders. This is an interesting situation; where members are imposed by a ruling party or a government, they are usually young, educated to some degree, and anxious to move up the social scale. This used to be the pattern during the early stages of trade unionism, when union leaders regarded trade unions as a stepping stone to political careers. But when the members are allowed to elect freely their own leaders, they do so on the basis of union commitment, experience in union activities and leadership ability. This is the present situation in Ghana, for the union leaders are people who have been through the ranks, starting as ordinary workers or artisans, and eventually working their way up. Of the seventeen leaders, ten of them have been unionists for twenty years or more, six over ten years and one for about five years.

The leaders' fathers' occupations varied from unskilled labourer, railway worker, and farmer to an accountant, the only one not of low status. This finding also contradicts the popularly held hypothesis that union leaders in developing countries are young, educated and uncommitted to the unions which they are supposed to represent. Indeed children from elitist families, by virtue of their fathers' occupations and higher educational achievements, tend to aspire to the higher echelons of white-collar occupations rather than to the blue-collar jobs. They do not have to look for a stepping stone in the form of the labour unions, for their elitist positions offer them enough opportunity to improve their status in society.[3]

All the union leaders had a certain amount of education. Six of them were high school graduates, and two of these graduates also had 'Advanced General Certificates of Education'. The remaining eleven were primary school graduates. But all seventeen union leaders had broadened their education through self-learning and training courses in labour and industrial relations, leadership and union organisation. Within Ghana the Nkrumah Ideological School often used to be the starting point for union leadership training during the Nkrumah era. Nowadays, the Labour College runs seminars on all aspects of labour organisation. Countries which have provided and are still providing facilities for the training of Ghana labour leaders are the USA, Britain, West Germany, and the USSR. Until its dissolution the International Confederation of Free Trade Union (ICFTU) Labour College in Kampala used to be another useful place for union education and leadership training.

The leaders resorted to self-learning because all but three of them came from illiterate backgrounds. In several cases, leaders interviewed complained that they had had to drop out of school because of their parents' lack of money. The three with literate parents completed high school—a point which demonstrates the better financial situation of their parents who, because of educational achievement, had better-paying jobs and therefore were able to send their children to school. Also, their literate background was another motivating factor for the children to continue in school. Given their limited education, did the union leaders find it difficult to unionise their workers?

Fifteen of the seventeen union leaders reported that they did not find it difficult to unionise the workers because the workers had come to understand the whole concept of trade unionism. To the urban worker, his union had replaced the head of his family or village chief in the rural area. (The village chief or the head of the family normally mediates or arbitrates among the villagers in time of trouble or feud.) It was now evident to the workers, they asserted, that only by joining the labour movement would they be able to improve their lot socially and economically.

The fifteen union leaders who claimed to have no difficulty in unionising the workers stated that some of the workers who were unwilling to join any union based their reluctance on the belief that the unions had failed to provide substantial benefits for their rank and file members. These workers wanted to be more convinced before they would become members. The workers who held this attitude were generally in African or Ghanaian-owned enterprises.

In order to cross-check this response twenty workers in these firms were interviewed. Sixteen of them were either children, relatives, or 'referrals' by the friends of the employers. These businesses were run on a paternalistic and ascriptive basis—a point which explains the workers' negative union attitude. Two of these twenty workers based their negative union attitude partly on the paternalistic nature of the management in these enterprises, and partly because they were not prepared to pay dues to unions which they considered had achieved very little for the rank and file. Twelve of the respondents used to be unionists before joining the Ghanaian-owned companies. These were very anxious to see their enterprises unionised because they complained of the ascriptive nature of promotions, poor working conditions, authoritarian management, and so on. They preferred to belong to a union because they thought they would be better protected. This group indicated that they would go back to unionised enterprises if they could get employment in any of them. They left their previous unionised jobs for those non-unionised ones because they thought there were better prospects in them, an expectation that was not always fulfilled.

Thirteen of the fifteen union leaders claiming to have no difficulty in unionising workers reported slight checks to membership drives each time the government passed an anti-union bill.[4] The initial reaction to such a bill was membership exodus, but this reaction was only temporary, for the unionists soon realised that without their unions, their job interests (wages, conditions of work, etc.) could not be properly represented before their employers. Such an experience usually made them reactivate their union membership. On the other hand, the remaining two union leaders reported that each time an anti-union bill was passed, the unionists became more convinced that they had to fight for survival. The general secretary of the Agricultural Workers' Union succinctly described this situation to us in 1972 in this way:

When Busia abolished the TUC, the unionists continued to pay their dues by hand. When they were asked to reregister, they refused because they claimed they had been trade unionists all along. Besides, in 1967, the registration of the members was done fast. The unionists jointly passed a resolution in Takoradi that if management did not deduct dues for their unions, they would strike. These are clear indications that they understand what trade unionism is all about, and what it is doing for them. The unionists cannot be misled by outside influence now. It is only when we default in the discharge of our duties that they have reasons to question our stewardship.

The two union leaders who experienced difficulty in unionising the workers blamed it on class snobbery between the literate and illiterate unionists. They complained that 85 per cent of the rank and file members were illiterate. The result was that the illiterate unionists who were not fluent in English usually felt snubbed by their better-educated fellow unionists. The literate unionists insisted on speaking conventional English while the illiterate preferred 'pidgin English'. This preference normally resulted in conflict, with the illiterate unionists angrily withdrawing their membership. To prevent this, the union leaders concerned usually endeavoured to organise them apart. But this in itself undermined the spirit of brotherhood which should exist among all unionists. These leaders pointed out that the key difference between the literate and illiterate unionists was that whereas the literate unionists believed trade unionism represented their interests, the illiterate ones saw it as a means of shielding them from management's disciplinary rod. A constant difficulty for these two leaders was how to unite these two viewpoints.

One can tentatively conclude that the union leaders in Ghana do not have much difficulty in unionising their members. Nevertheless, they experience some difficulties each time anti-labour legislation is passed by the government. For example, when the NLC government passed the Civil Service (Amendment) Regulations, 1967 (Decree 134) removing the compulsory membership clause from the Civil Service Act, 1960, union members had the legal option of deciding to terminate their membership. Those who chose to remain union members were asked to fill option forms authorising their dues to be deducted: that is, they were to 'contract in'. This 'contracting in' process halved the union membership from an all-time peak of 700,000 to about 300,000.[5] As a result of this mass departure of the union members, the unions' financial strength was also greatly weakened.

The trade unions experienced similar difficulties when the Busia Government enacted the Industrial Relations Act, 1971, which expanded the 'contracting in' system. The act further dissipated the union membership already reduced by the NLC decree number 134. For example, the Educational and Teachers' Workers' Union reported a fall in membership from 16,000 in 1969–71 to 7,000. Similarly, the Agricultural Workers' Union dropped from 83,000 to 80,000; while other unions reported similar drops in membership.

These reductions in union membership coupled with the non-compulsory check-off system introduced by the Industrial Relations Act, 1971, also helped to compound the already difficult financial situation of the unions. Although some unions had to increase their dues from 20 to 40 pesewas per month, they continued to face financial difficulties because of their small paying memberships. Consequently, this financial weakness of the unions helped to add to the union administrative bottlenecks and to prevent the unions from implementing most of their social programmes, e.g., co-operatives, credit unions, and so on. The unfortunate thing is that union leaders did not make a serious effort to recruit members.

This inability on the part of the union leaders to canvass for members could be traced to the Nkrumah days when membership was compulsory and union leaders were consequently nothing but 'collectors of dues'. They relied on Nkrumah's Convention People's Party (CPP) which was then in power to penalise any member who was unwilling to pay. With that privilege of compulsory membership gone, the union leaders now complain of lack of transport facilities to go to the villages and canvass for members. Such a complaint is baseless: there are many 'mammy-wagons' to take them to any part of the country. Instead, they prefer the Mercedes-Benz because of its prestige value.

The union decision-making process

To understand the decision-making process, we must first review membership participation in union activities. Participation is conceived as consisting of:

(1) monthly meetings by all branches at district level: these meetings were heavily attended at the time of the research. The author attended some of these meetings in Takoradi, Tarkwa, Kumasi, Accra and Ho and found that union members were enthusiastic about attending them. Attendance at these meetings was up to 90 to 95 per cent of the registered membership in those districts.

(2) Working Committee meetings: union members took turns serving on them. These committees, as noted earlier, dealt with the problems of education for the rank and file members, social welfare, organisation, and negotiations. The purpose of these committees was to involve the members in the decision-making process of their unions and to expose them to the sort of problems their leaders and officers usually faced in the day-to-day union administration.

(3) Seminars and weekend courses: the union leaders believed that the success of trade unionism in Ghana depended on how well informed rank and file members were about union functions, role and activities. These seminars and courses were geared towards educating the union members in labour and industrial relations. These were well attended by the union members. A random sampling of opinion of participants in Takoradi soon after one of these seminars revealed that about 90 per cent of the participants wanted more of such seminars. Such interest is due to the fact that union members

realised that their only chance to rise in the ranks was to be well informed and educated in labour and industrial relations. Education was then considered the key to progress even with the labour unions.

(4) Social activities such as dances, visits, and games: the unions were wont to organise dances and games to promote the spirit of 'brotherhood' among the union members. Most of the national unions had their own bands and soccer teams. Inter-union soccer matches took place quite often, and union members and their families were enthusiastic spectators. These soccer matches helped to induce union members' allegiance to their union and created a healthy competition among the unions.

(5) Monthly meetings of the branch executives to exchange ideas and review labour problems affecting their branch unions.

(6) The bi-annual meetings of the National Executive Council to co-ordinate the union activities.

Given these avenues, it seems union members have ample chance of participating in the decision-making process. In principle, important decisions concerning a national union are made by its delegates' conference. In its absence the National Executive Council of that union which has full representation of all the branches makes final decisions. The decisions normally to be made relate to issues raised by the branches. In the case of grievances, decisions are in principle made first on a branch level, and when that fails the branch refers the case to the regional office. If the grievance is still unresolved, it is then referred to the National Executive. However, before a branch decides whether to make a decision locally or to refer it to the higher union executive, it is first supposed to contact the branch members. The branch members decide in a simple majority vote whether the issue in question should be resolved locally, regionally or nationally.

Diagrammatically, the theoretical procedure for decision-making is thus:

DIAGRAM I

Triangular Decision-Making Process during a Deadlock

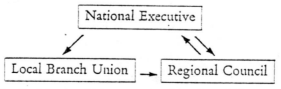

Theoretically the decision-making process is based on full participation and co-operation by the rank and file. As demonstrated in the diagram, when the local branch of a union fails to reach a decision on a problem, it passes it to the

National Executive where a decision has to be made. When the National Executive reaches a decision, it informs the regional council.

In reality, however, the local branch union and the regional council only transmit information to the National Executive. They do not indeed participate in the actual decision-making process; their own form of participation is to act as transmission belts for the processing of information.

Union leaders interviewed disagreed with the above analysis, for they insisted that the decision-making procedure, as diagrammatically shown above, was participatory. We decided to test their concept of participation. This question was put to the 17 union leaders: What do you do when suggestions made by you as a union boss are challenged by some of your union officers? Five of the 17 indicated that they would discard the suggestion. However, they stressed that they would research into it and present it again in a revised form some time in the future. If there were still objections to the revised version of the suggestion, they would recommend a vote on it based on a simple majority.

On the other hand, six of the 17 union leaders stated that if union officers disagreed with any of their suggestions, they would refer the matter to the National Executive Council. At the council, there would be a hearing followed by a vote based on simple majority to decide the issue in dispute. However, these six union leaders asserted that their reaction then would depend on the outcome of the vote. If the vote was against the suggestion and if they felt strongly about the suggestion in question, they would resign their leadership positions. Three of these six union leaders had been long-standing union leaders who considered losing an important vote to be a demonstration of lack of confidence in them by their colleagues. Instead of continuing in office after such a vote, they preferred to resign their offices. The remaining six union leaders stated that their reaction would be guided by the importance they attached to the issue in dispute. If they considered it important, they would first refer it to the National Secretariat for an open debate and subsequently a vote. If they were dissatisfied with the outcome of the vote at this level, they would then refer it to the National Executive Council, which could make binding decisions. Any decision at this level was deemed final. So the difference between this group of six union leaders and the first group of six is that the first group jumped one level of the decision-making process. The first group decided they would refer the dispute straight to the National Executive Council, which made final and binding decisions, rather than first referring it to the National Secretariat. However, the second group of six leaders reported that they would adopt whatever decision was reached by the National Executive Council. Their chief characteristic was to persevere and fight to the end when challenged.

On the whole, the union leaders have good intentions about decision-making, for they want to involve the rank and file in its process. But such good intentions are not reflected in the actual decision-making process, especially when there are union elections. The author was present when national elections were held in Ghana in February–March 1972. Robert Michell's 'iron law of oligarchy' was very much the rule at these elections, at which the seventeen national general secretaries and their officers were mostly returned unopposed. It seemed, to say the least, unlikely that the union executives were all so popular among the rank and file as to merit instant election. Although the TUC constitution guaranteed the practice of democracy, the democratic aspect of the constitution was never applied because of certain loopholes.

Elections were carried out by delegations. The branch unions delegated branch officers to vote for the general secretary and ordinary branch union members to vote for the branch officers. But the general secretary controlled all the power channels within the unions. The branch officers who were delegated to vote for the position of the general secretary sometimes owed their own positions to him. Consequently, if any branch officer-delegate failed to vote for an incumbent general secretary, he faced the danger of losing his executive position in the branch. So a general secretary and his team of union officers could guarantee their re-election by allowing only delegates who they were sure would vote for them to participate in an election. There was no control at the branch level because practically all the delegates were appointed rather than elected, as the constitution required.

The 'iron law of oligarchy' not only operated at the national union level: it was also found at the TUC level. The secretary general of the TUC was the boss of the National Executive Council which consisted of the seventeen national general secretaries. All of them worked as a team for their mutual survival. The secretary general was elected at the quadrennial conference of delegates. He owed his election very much to the national general secretaries who controlled the voting of their delegates to the conference. But once elected, the secretary general became more powerful than any general secretary. He had the constitutional right to overrule any national general secretary. Accordingly, the general secretaries also owed their positions to him, for he could subvert them and cost them their leadership position if desired. Since the secretary general and national general secretaries relied on each other for their mutual survival, they worked together even at elections to maintain their symbiotic relationship.

There were occasions when the 'iron law of oligarchy' did not operate. These occurred when there were internal conflicts within the labour movement, and when the movement was influenced by ideology and politics.[5] These two conditions tended to favour democracy within the TUC. An example of internal conflict within the trade union movement was the leadership struggle in the Industrial Commercial Workers' Union (ICWU). Teivi, the national chairman of this union, failed to be re-elected. As a result, he broke away to form a splinter group called the Manufacturing and Commercial Allied Workers' Union (MACAWU). There was then a bitter contest between Teivi and Edwin Ejah, the national general secretary of ICWU, for the rank and file members.

Whenever there was such a conflict, the democratic nature of the constitution was then applied to the letter of the law because any attempt to subvert the constitutional democratic process by any contesting candidate was liable to be used as evidence against him. The rank and file benefited enormously from such a contest, for it was the only time that they had the opportunity of experiencing how democratic trade unionism operates.

During such conflicts, therefore, branch officers and the rank and file are free to vote for the candidate they deem fit to lead them, while an incumbent general secretary would find it difficult to rig the elections. Such was the case during the ICWU leadership conflict: Ejah won the contest at last not because he was an incumbent but because of his leadership record which convinced the rank and file to vote overwhelmingly for him against Teivi.

We have also postulated that the 'iron law of oligarchy' does not obtain when the union movement is influenced by ideology and politics. Such was the case in 1972 when there was a leadership struggle at the TUC level between Issifu and Tettegah. Tettegah was supposed to be an 'Nkrumahite', and accordingly it was believed that he would continue to practise Nkrumah's ideology and policies. Issifu, on the other hand, was considered to belong to the new politics in Ghana, that of the military rule by the National Redemption Council. The two contesting candidates campaigned vigorously among the rank and file members. Each candidate professed to adhere strictly to the democratic constitution of the TUC.

Unfortunately, the election for the secretary general of the TUC was reduced from the national level to an executive level. The NRC government, afraid that Tettegah might win the contest if a national election by conference delegates were held, advised the seventeen union leaders to elect an acting secretary general to run the TUC for the time being because the government needed time to reorganise itself. Even at this juncture, the result of the election for an acting secretary general was very close—Issifu won by one vote. Here again, however, many of those in the TUC executive exercised their right to vote for the candidate of their choice despite the NRC government influence on them. The NRC government had hoped that Issifu, its favoured candidate, would gain an early victory over Tettegah. But in fact Issifu barely pulled through.

Where, however, internal conflict or ideological divisions do not obtain, the leadership of the Ghanaian labour movement closes ranks and successfully resists challenges from the rank and file.

Workers' perceptions

To understand adequately how a worker views his union, it is vital to note his salient characteristics and the influences that shape his outlook. Of the 85 workers selected, 50 per cent were literate: that is, either primary or high school graduates. Fifteen per cent were functional illiterates (high school and primary school dropouts) and the remaining 35 per cent were completely illiterate. The 50 per cent who were functional illiterates and completely illiterate were attending adult education schools and literacy seminars organised by the labour college to improve their education.

Since most of the industrial estates are located in urban centres, it is therefore not surprising that 75 per cent of the unionists interviewed were found in urban areas. For the sake of convenience, let us call the 75 per cent found in the city 'urbanised unionists' and the other 25 per cent 'rural unionists'. Twenty per cent of the 'urbanised unionists' reported that they would be prepared to return to settle in the rural areas if there were prospects for better employment, in other words more money. On the other hand, only 5 per cent of the 'urbanised unionists' indicated interest in going back to the rural sector for the sake of helping to improve the lot of the villagers. This group claimed that it had skills which could be of value to 'village development', but it regretted the fact that there were so few rural development programmes. The interesting thing about this group was that it consisted of newly-arrived urban migrants who had not lived in the city for more than five years—a point which contributed to their acute attachment to the rural areas. The remaining 50 per cent of the 'urbanised unionists' indicated no interest whatsoever in the rural style of living. As a result, they were not prepared to go back to the rural area even if there were prospects for better jobs. The reason given for this negative attitude to the rural sector was that there were no amenities in the rural areas; but the major reason for refusing to go was due to the fact that this group was used to an urban style of living. The majority of this group had lived in the city for over five years. Although none had any intention of going back to the rural sector to settle or work, they visited the rural areas at least once a year, especially during the 'New Yam Festival', when the first yams of the year are harvested.

With regard to worker consciousness, 65 per cent of the workers interviewed stated that they exchanged frequent visits with co-workers outside union meetings and business hours. This group also participated in the social activities organised by the branch unions. Thirty per cent of the respondents reported that their only form of social participation was attendance at union meetings. Workers in this category stated that they did not particularly care for socials organised by fellow workers even though they had a few friends among them. To them such an occasion was purely 'functional', that is, to help promote union solidarity and present a united front. The remaining interviewees (the remaining 5 per cent) claimed to have no interest in associating with co-unionists outside business hours. Not surprisingly, one outstanding aspect of Ghana trade unions is the united front they present, particularly when they are threatened.

As regards what trade unionism has done for the Ghanaian worker, all the interviewees agreed that the unions had achieved many socio-economic benefits for their members. They stressed that, for the first time, workers were now sure of regular wages and fringe benefits gained mostly through collective agreements. A taxi driver stressed the advantages of being a unionist thus:

> It is only now I fully realise what my union means to me, for since the dissolution of the TUC and the restriction on union activities [the TUC was dissolved in 1971] I have not been able to drive my taxi again. Why? Because the government refused to renew my licence simply because I am not educated. Now I do not know whom to report to.

The workers' faith in their leaders was greatly increased during the Busia regime, for the union leaders staked their careers in the interest of the union members. This display of boldness and determination had a profound impression on the rank and file. It seems fair to say that the days when union leaders used to visualise labour unions as a springboard to political power, or when they used to be political activists serving the interest of their parties, are gone. Ghanaian union leadership is now responsible and committed to the ideas of free trade unionism.

NOTES

1. See, for example, Lester N. Trachtman, 'The Labor Movement in Ghana: a Study of Political Unionism', *Economic Development and Cultural Change*, 11(1), 1962, pp. 183–200; Douglas Rimmer, 'The New Industrial Relations in Ghana', *Industrial and Labor Relations Review*, 14(2), 1961, pp. 206–26 and Jon Kraus, 'The Political Economy of Trade Union–Government Relations in Ghana . . .', Paper presented to the Toronto Conference, April 1973.
2. Ghana TUC, *Constitution, Rules and By-laws of the Trades Union Congress*, Accra, n.d.

3. This point is discussed in Abdel Rahman E. Ali Taha, *The Sudanese Labor Movement: a Study of Labor Unionism in a Developing Society*, Ph.D. dissertation, University of California, Los Angeles, 1970, pp. 190–1.

4. For example, the Busia Government passed the Industrial Relations Act, 1971, which was considered to be anti-union. For details see Ukandi G. Damachi, *The Role of Trade Unions in the Development Process: with a Case Study of Ghana*, Praeger, 1974.

5. *Ibid.*, p. 103.

6. Theoretical support for the above assertion is found in the theory of pluralism expounded by Seymour Lipset, Martin A. Trow and James S. Coleman in their 'Union Democracy in Secondary Organisations', in *American Social Patterns*, William Peterson (ed.), Doubleday, 1956.

PART THREE

Contemporary Working Class
Action

Introduction

Governments in post-colonial Africa of all political persuasions tend to regard trade unions as junior partners in the process of economic development. Where unions have refused to accept such a status, governmental suspicion and hostility have increased in the belief that unions would provide a focus for political opposition or that unrestricted unions would adversely affect economic growth and the expansion of employment. Any distinction between permissible economic activities by the unions and illegitimate political activities, misleading in any case in an underdeveloped society, broke down almost totally after independence. With the government being the major employer and the unions being strategically located in the centres of political activity, even economically-inspired union actions have had clear and visible political consequences. Where, further, governments are weakly-based, yet at least rhetorically committed to the task of economic development, any economic setbacks occasioned by union activities will redound upon the government's popularity and support.

The rulers of post-colonial African states are thus likely to view trade unionism, above all, as a political problem, and see a solution in terms of union subordination to a government-defined 'national purpose'. In seeking to enforce their conception of the labour movements' proper role, governments have utilised both rewards and penalties.[1] Rewards may be as blatant as the co-opting of pliant union leaders into posts offering high remuneration and prestige in political and parastatal bodies, or as subtle as an informal bargain in which union leaders surrender a certain degree of autonomy (e.g., the right to strike; the right to elect top leaders) in exchange for a legislated closed or union shop. Penalties for the infraction of any rules by trade unionists are stipulated in the burgeoning legislation on trade disputes and union organisation. Even a country like Nigeria, which had a tradition of free trade unionism (as defined in

ILO principles), has effectively abandoned its commitment to unregulated bargaining by decrees, passed in 1968 and 1969, severely restricting strikes and introducing an Industrial Arbitration Tribunal in an attempt to regulate wage levels. Though passed initially as an emergency provision during the civil war, the Nigerian leadership shows little inclination to abandon such control five years after the end of the war.[2] Legislative restrictions on unions have frequently been supplemented by harsher measures—by, for example, detaining trouble-some union leaders under preventive detention laws or surreptitiously ousting them from office.

The economic justifications governments have provided to trammel labour organisations include charges that the unions' ability to raise real wages faster than GNP aggravates inflation, exacerbates balance of payments difficulties, limits the potential rate of economic growth by reducing savings, and creates massive urban unemployment by widening the urban-rural income differential. In addition, strike action and worker indiscipline retard productivity and dis-courage foreign investment. The validity of at least some of these charges is subject to doubt. It is too easily assumed, as one writer points out, that the wage earners take no part in the saving process, that unions seek and succeed in obtain-ing higher wages irrespective of the economic condition of the country, that the quality of labour (and its productivity) is unaffected by an increase in income, and so on.[3] It is also frequently difficult, as the protagonists to one heated debate on Nigerian wage determination show,[4] to isolate 'the union factor' in the alteration of wage levels.

But whatever the merits of the various arguments are, it is clear that African governments believe that a case against untrammelled unionism is unassailable. We have then to consider how successful African governments have been in moulding the goals and actions of the unions; firstly, in terms of holding back wage demands and secondly, in terms of defusing the capacity of the unions to act as loci for a political opposition. One general assessment is that 'in country after country, even where the "take-over" has been maximal, unions have continued (frequently covertly) to function to protect the interests of the workers.'[5] The authors of this assessment contend that the lower-level leader-ship of a union continues to agitate for workers' demands even when its head-quarters has been captured by the state. The validity of this assertion for all African countries is difficult to gauge, given the paucity of studies on grass roots unionism presently available. But fragmentary evidence from various parts of Africa suggests that 'economism', or organised action by workers to extract short-range economic gains from employers, is difficult to curb.

A study of the well-remunerated Zambian mineworkers has aptly illustrated the difficulties of restricting economism. Until 1969 the Zambian Government had relied primarily upon exhortation to constrain the consumptionist orientation of the mineworkers. The prime feature of its 'development labour policy' was to transform the Mineworkers' Union from an 'input structure', specialising in the articulation of workers' demands, to an 'output structure', devoted to regulating and controlling the behaviour of its members. In practice, however, the union (as of mid-1969) failed to obtain the workers' support for the development labour policy. On the contrary, the government was confronted with 'less willingness to work hard, greater insubordination, and increased propensities to strike'.[6] It reacted, as Bates indicates in the postscript to his Zambian study, by imposing more direct public intervention into labour relations and union administration.

Grass roots militancy has also persisted in other African countries, as some of the contributions to this volume reveal. Even in the thoroughly repressive environment of South Africa and Namibia, workers have informally organised strikes to protest their many grievances. The joint study by Dekker, Hemson, Kane-Berman, Lever and Schlemmer demonstrates that the African workers have developed solidarity and their own informal leadership in a situation where they possess negligible rights to organise, bargain collectively with employers, or strike. The achievement of limited bargaining rights and of substantial wage increases stemmed essentially from the actions of black workers themselves, despite subsequent heart-wrenching revelations by certain South African industrialists that increased wages were long overdue, and the almost touching arrogance of the British liberal newspaper, *The Guardian*, which, in the course of its campaign on behalf of African workers, adopted a distinct tone of self-congratulation. Whether the emergent collective consciousness seen in the recent South African events will develop in an explicitly radical direction remains to be seen. The authors of our study on Southern Africa rightly point out that 'labour power' is one of the few points of leverage against the regime of the Nationalist party. In their view a reformist or revolutionary scenario in the exercise of labour power are both possible outcomes, but they adopt an open-ended and intermediate position on the ground that it is premature to foreclose predictions on possible future developments. Collective labour action by black workers could, with prescient action, be contained within the constraints of an institutionalised bargaining system. Equally, however, the pattern of the events they describe could recur in outbursts of popular hostility with political issues coming to the forefront as working class solidarity and retaliatory measures by the government intensify.

Other studies in Part Three examine militant working class action in Tanzania, Ghana and Nigeria. In Tanzania, M. A. Bienefeld argues that the widespread wildcat strike activity of 1971-72 reveals an enhanced political consciousness on the part of workers rather than simply a narrow 'economist' mentality. In Ghana, Richard Jeffries contends that the 1961 general strike and subsequent worker protest was precipitated by, but transcended, the workers' wage-related grievances. In Nigeria, grass roots militancy continued even after the promulgation of restrictive labour decrees in 1968–69 made almost all strikes illegal. There was a wave of wildcat strikes—often unofficially sanctioned by middle-level union leaders—in 1970–71; these strikes, as Adrian Peace and Paul Lubeck (in his article in Part Two) both relate, occurred as workers sought to persuade employers to grant a cost of living award, though they had longer-term political implications as well.

Evidence such as that just presented suggests the need for revising certain generalisations about unionised labour contained in Berg and Butler's seminal article entitled 'Trade Unions'. Here they argued that 'almost everywhere' after independence 'labour organisations were taken over by governing parties. This process differs in degree of control: the levers of control are manipulated more gently and discreetly in the Ivory Coast than Guinea, for example. But the result is the same: the labour movement, if not completely subordinated to the party, is at least pliable and responsive to party pressures'.[7] At a later point, the authors expanded upon these remarks by asserting that 'it is only on party sufferance that they [the unions] are given a role to play, and they are constrained to be "reasonable" and "responsible" organs which emphasise productivity and hard work'.[8] A major conceptual problem with this formulation arises from the conception of 'unions' and even 'labour movements' (not to mention 'governing parties') as homogeneous entities reacting in a single way. The authors recognise, of course, that a 'labour movement' consists of various layers—from national federations at the top to the rank and file at the bottom—but they do not acknowledge the different orientations and interests of these layers in their analysis. While the federations and sometimes the headquarters of large national unions have tended to be 'pliable and responsive' to a government's wishes, other headquarters of unions, house unions, and union branches have not. A more tenable generalisation than that offered by Berg and Butler is that individual unions (often including the top leadership) are usually more responsive to the pressures of their members than to those of the ruling elite. Unions (though not federations) have revealed their orientation by cautiously giving precedence to consumptionist aims and individual and collective grievance handling rather than to productionism and workers' discipline.[9]

One reason why some unions have clung to traditional union goals in the face of governmental displeasure is that the union leadership has, (as we argued in the Introduction to Part Two), a continued dependence upon lower-level leaders and ordinary members for financial and personal support. Governments can, of course, always insulate the top leaders from membership pressures by controlling their appointment and making dues-paying by all workers mandatory. But the usual consequence of such moves is to destroy the effectiveness of unions as mechanisms for channelling and resolving tensions and grievances arising from the work process. Workers will regard unions as parastatal bodies as they do in Tanzania, and may well express their dissatisfaction through wildcat strikes, absenteeism and lower productivity.

If union leaders respond in some measure to the aspirations of members, what accounts for the usually militant economism of the latter? This orientation can only be understood within the broad context of the inequitable distribution of rewards in many poor countries. Consumptionism on the part of workers is undoubtedly stimulated by the contradiction between the political class's command that unions restrain wage and related demands in the public interest and its practice of self-enrichment and conspicuous consumption. Writers of a liberal persuasion have often assumed that the new elites are committed, above all, to rapid economic development and social justice.[10] Yet the more usual situation is that foreseen by Davies[11] wherein the government, 'backed by a growing bureaucratic and commercial class, will deny increases in wages and services while at the same time swelling the power, privileges and earnings of the dominant economic groups.' One would expect this growing contradiction to create hostility among manual workers, prompting them to demand reform within the *status quo* or perhaps even fundamental changes.

Have workers' spokesmen gone beyond merely defensive actions (wage demands, grievance-handling) to demand basic changes in the distribution of wealth, power and property rights? Are there any indications that workers in any part of Africa are making the transition from 'trade union' to revolutionary consciousness? According to Lenin's formulation this transition occurs when the limited economic aims of working people are superseded by a recognition of the 'irreconcilable antagonism of their interests to the whole of the modern political and social system'.[12] Workers, perceiving that they are exploited, organise and act politically to destroy the established order and to construct something better in its place.

Studies of that rather hackneyed topic, 'the political role of trade unions', too frequently fail to distinguish between three modes of political activity involving unions. The first mode, and the one least consequential for social change, is the action of union leaders as *individuals*, seeking to promote their own personal ambitions. Where workers have developed only a 'trade-union consciousness' (the normal situation), they expect unions to concern themselves merely with the members' short-run economic interests and not to constitute part of a social movement dedicated to transformational change. This lack of political consciousness *qua* workers (itself possibly the result of the absence of a socialist vanguard) allows top union leaders to take advantage of any opportunities to advance themselves or their political patrons within the existing political order. Hence, the prestige, publicity and patronage (union jobs, scholarships, funds) that attach to top union offices are sometimes committed by labour leaders in political factional struggles which have little if any connection with the basic concerns of workers.[13]

A second mode of political activity involves the operation of unions (or of informal workers' organisations) as a *unit* in the political arena, seeking to influence the content of a government's policies or legislation. 'Economism', though limited in aim to the extraction of economic benefits, does not restrict working class action solely to the economic sphere. As Lenin noted in *What is to be Done?*, this limited aim would often require labour organisations to apply political pressure in order to win concessions. In Africa, unions to be effective must necessarily employ pressure group activities, as the locus of decisions affecting the workers' economic status is usually more in the political than the economic sphere. The state, in most parts of Africa, determines the structure of collective bargaining, plays a large part in regulating the terms and conditions of employment through participation in industrial relations machinery and legislation on minimum wages and fringe benefits, and finally, adopts major economic policies affecting inflation, taxes and foreign exchange controls. Furthermore, since the large industrial enterprises are often either wholly or partially publicly owned or subject to state supervision, workers clearly must direct their efforts towards the governmental machinery in order to obtain gains. But the involvement of unions in political action does not necessarily mean that the workers have abandoned economism.

The final mode of political action also involves trade unionism as a *unit*, but this time as a labour *movement* dedicated to a transformation of the social order. Certain writers on the 'political role of labour'[14] contended that 'political unionism' predominated in Africa; that is, that labour movements gave precedence to transformational goals and actions over limited economic goals. In retrospect, such generalisations seem more a product of a fear of communist agitation generated by the Cold War than of empirical research. Economism has been the prevalent orientation in all African countries, though attention to short-run economic reforms has not precluded radical political action by labour movements in some states. Even egoistically motivated industrial action on the part of workers may have significant and progressive political consequences. In the words of one astute writer:

the 'egoistic' oppositional action of urban wage-earners (and peripheral semi-employed) can debouch on to a genuine critique of the power system of post-colonial clientage—if the confrontation is sufficiently *sharp* and *sustained* and if it is relayed by groups with a wider social vision and programme (revolutionary intellectuals).[15]

In Africa general strikes and urban riotings, the aims of which went briefly beyond demands for limited economic concessions, have recently occurred in the Sudan, Congo–Brazzaville, Ghana, Nigeria and Ethiopia.[16] All these manifestations of worker protest produced or contributed to political crises, acting as flash points of inchoate but generalised dissatisfaction with the realities of political independence.

The studies of post-colonial African countries in Part Three of this book all show how the attempt to redress immediate worker grievances soon took on the character of a critique of the political and social order. In the discussion of the Sekondi–Takoradi strike of 1961, for example, Richard Jeffries argues that while workers may have had a strong aspiration to bourgeois status, they also resented elite wealth, corruption and authoritarianism. He sees the strike as essentially reformist in character, but argues that the skilled workers were able to pose as the spokesmen of the poor common people and were indeed strategically placed to act as an intermediate group between the urban elite and middle class on the one hand, and the common people on the other. Jeffries views the outcome of the link with the urban masses as a form of urban populism, one which has severe limitations as a mode of transformational politics, but that nonetheless represented an important source of dissent on a non-party basis, an 'unusual and important phenomenon in the political life' of Ghana.

In Nigeria, the first major confrontation by the unions with the political leadership occurred in 1964, when the unions came out in a general strike, involving some 750,000 workers. The strike at first represented the claims of a group which did not necessarily articulate a mass populist will against the government, but rather sought to get its own share of the benefits of economic growth. As the strike progressed, however, it began to raise possibilities of a more fundamental order. The government lost any credibility it still retained as to its preparedness to concede to democratic pressures, while workers no longer simply begged for their share of the cake, but rather were questioning the nature of the political system itself.[17] The Nigerian political system in fact suffered grievous damage with the succession of coups and counter-coups in 1966, followed by the horrific three-year civil war. With the collapse of Biafra in January 1970, the deep sense of relief that pervaded Nigeria was accompanied by a set of demands by wage-earners and others that the programme of economic and social reconstruction promised by the military leadership be translated into action. The establishment of a Wage and Salaries Commission in July 1970, under the chairmanship of Chief Adebo, was seen by the Federal Government both as a means to assuage discontent and to reorient the supply of consumption goods and services from the constraints of a war economy.[18]

The commission took written evidence from about six hundred trade unions and staff associations and oral evidence from many other individuals and organisations—one of the most significant attempts at consultation that Nigeria had witnessed for many years. The commission awarded a backdated interim increase in wages and salaries in December 1970, and in its second report in August 1971, raised levels of remuneration further—in total about a 30 per cent increase from April 1970. The question of the applicability of the Adebo recommendations to workers in the private sector was one which produced strong resistance from expatriate firms and a vacillating policy by the Federal Government. Wage determination in Nigeria had always been marked by a strong 'demonstration effect', as private sector employees sought to alter the wages in accordance with a government-worker award. The ambivalent attitude of the government was seen by the workers both as an attempt to cheat them of the just reward and a knuckling under to expatriate pressures. An explosive industrial situation resulted with a large number of wildcat actions taking place in defiance of a wartime decree, still in force, prohibiting incitement to strike. Adrian Peace, writing about the industrial situation below, presents a closely observed portrait of the workers on the Ikeja industrial estate in Lagos. As with the 1964 strike, action undertaken by the workers galvanised a wider dissatisfaction. As Peace writes:

> ... workers pointed to specific instances of social and political injustice in the actions of the ruling elites, most notably in the manipulation of the wage award and the continuation of the government decree against industrial action. But these were viewed as specific grievances illustrative of a much wider and ever-increasing range of social injustices perpetuated by the ruling groups against the masses.

Nigeria, as is well known, pursues an overtly capitalist road of development, its development strategy, as we suggested in our opening essay, being critically dependent on foreign capital and expertise to modernise the country. As such, the industrial disturbances surrounding the Adebo Commission revealed, as Peace indeed argues, the central contradiction inherent in Nigeria's neo-colonial status—that between the externally-based interests controlling the resources of industrial production and the internally-rooted bases of political authority. But, theoretically at any rate, no such contradiction inheres in a socialist road to development, where a country attempts to break with foreign capital and to focus development on the mobilisation of local resources to meet local needs.

M. A. Bienefeld, in his contribution on Tanzania, recognises the crucial distinction between these two modes of development and feels that in the earliest years of independence the socialist alternative was too easily abandoned. Only in 1967 had an alternative set of policies been devised, whereby union co-operation and worker participation in development was to be obtained as a *quid pro quo* for narrowing wage differentials, discouraging the growth of an elite and taking control of the major sectors of the economy. An initial enthusiasm for these 'Arusha' policies was followed, Bienefeld asserts, by a sense of disillusionment that day-to-day working relationships had changed little. In February 1970 President Nyerere, conscious of the sense of grievance, introduced Workers' Councils in an attempt, as he put it, to change workers from a factor of production to the purpose of production. Workers' Councils have always held an important place in Marxist theory. In the view of the prominent Italian Marxist, Gramsci, the 'factory council' was 'the model of the proletarian state' since this institution allowed the proletariat 'to educate itself, gather experience and require a responsible awareness of the duties incumbent upon classes that hold the power of the state.'[19] The operation of the Tanzanian Workers' Councils is a matter of some controversy. One serious limitation is that, unlike in Algeria, where workers' self-management emerged as a result of revolutionary action from below,[20] workers' participation in Tanzania was imposed from above by means of a Presidential decree. In a recent study, Henry Mapolu concludes that management continues very much to be the prerogative of the managers.

> It is difficult to say that there is 'control' of managers by the workers in their act of 'participation'. Perhaps for a long time to come workers' councils will continue to be, as the National Development Corporation says, 'one of the major incentives—above all other techniques' in controlling the workers.[21]

Bienefeld, on the other hand, suggests that pressures from below might modify and vitalise the Workers' Councils. He regards it as a hopeful sign that recent strikes in Tanzania have been directed against unsympathetic management (including African management) and the lack of consultation at the workplace.

Whether workers are in a country that pursues a capitalist path of development (as Nigeria), or one like Tanzania which is groping its way toward a socialist path, workers are treated as a group whose self-interest must somehow be restrained. The economic justifications for this attitude on the part of African governments have already been stated. But certain left-wing theorists have also argued that the structural position of wage and salary earners in African countries means that they assume the status of a labour aristocracy. The interests of unionised workers are thought to be congruent, rather than opposed, to those of the ruling group. Variants of this view have been expounded by Frantz Fanon, and by Giovanni Arrighi and John Saul.[22] The last two writers separate African wage-earners into two strata: the unskilled and temporarily employed workers ('semi-proletarianised peasants') at the bottom, and the smaller upper stratum of skilled and semi-skilled workers who earn three to five times more than those in the lower stratum. The authors then argue that the upper stratum of semi-permanent workers has interests congruent with those of the bureaucratic 'elites' and 'sub-elites'; these three groups together constitute a 'labour aristo-cracy', the hegemonic class wedded to the neo-colonial social order. Hence, the only actual or potential opposition stratum is the proletarianised peasantry. Several of our authors refer to this 'labour aristocracy' thesis—Adrian Peace and Richard Jeffries in particular providing extensive critiques to which John Saul responds in the last contribution to Part Three of this book. The essence of the critique of the labour aristocracy thesis as applied to Africa, rests firstly, on a questioning on empirical grounds of the view that income differentials between urban households of manual wage-earners and rural households are as large as is often supposed. The extra costs of urban life (food, rent, transportation and taxation) as well as the continuing recognition of social ties and obligations by the wage-earner suggest that the gross income comparisons often made between the two groups are misleading. Secondly, as Jeffries and Peace forcefully argue, observations of protests by wage-earners (at least in the cases of Sekondi and Ikeja) show a strong degree of communal popular support of wage-earner demands. John Saul replies in these terms:

> The more privileged and better organised workers have been encouraged to identify upwards—to become partners . . . in the jostling for surpluses among the internationally and domestically powerful—rather than to identify downwards with the ever more 'wretched of the earth' the urban marginals and the average inhabitants of the untransformed rural areas.

He does concede that in the cases that Peace and Jeffries researched, the possibility was raised that all strata of the working class could identify *downwards* and change their basic orientation from co-optation to revolutionary challenge. However, Saul continues to have doubts as to how serious a long-term challenge such initiatives presage, and warns us against adopting a form of 'proletarian messian-ism'.

The long-term possibilities that workers may indeed open out a challenge to incumbent leaderships accounts in part for the latter's restrictive labour policies propounded in the name of equity between rural and urban areas and of econo-mic development, Where, as in Tanzania, such exhortations are coupled with

effective policies to limit the opportunities for ruling groups to gain a disproportionate share of wealth, the possibilities that the wage-earners will subordinate
their interests to the national interest, are greater. It may well be that, regardless
of whether a capitalist or socialist strategy is pursued, industrialisation can only
take place at the expense of the workers and other underlying classes. This, at any
rate, seems to be the experience of all presently industrialised countries. But even
if labour-repressive policies guaranteed economic growth—which they do not
in the context of the present structure of the world economy—there still remains
an ethical question: should workers acquiesce in their exploitation in the belief
that all will benefit from their sacrifice in the future? And will they?

NOTES

1. See E. J. Berg and J. Butler, 'Trade Unions' in *Political Parties and National Integration in Tropical Africa*, J. S. Coleman and C. G. Rosberg (eds), University of California Press, 1964, pp. 366–9.
2. For the provisions of the decrees on labour, see A. Akpala, 'Labour Policy and Practices in Nigeria', *Journal of Industrial Relations*, 13(3), 1971, pp. 274–90.
3. F. I. Ojow, 'Labour Organisations in Economic Development: a Survey of Some Views', *Eastern Africa Economic Review*, 2 (1), 1970, pp. 23–36.
4. The major protagonists to this debate are Bill Warren, Peter Kilby, Elliot J. Berg, John Weeks and Robin Cohen. A discussion of wage determination in Nigeria and a full set of references to the literature is provided in R. Cohen, *Labour and Politics in Nigeria*, Heinemann Educational Books, 1974, pp. 180–212, 214.
5. W. H. Friedland and D. Nelkin, 'African Labor in the Post-Independence Period', paper presented to the African Studies Association (USA) Conference, 1967, p. 4.
6. R. H. Bates, *Unions, Parties, and Political Development: a Study of the Mineworkers in Zambia*, Yale University Press, 1971, p. 56.
7. Berg and Butler, 'Trade Unions', p. 366.
8. *Ibid.*, p. 370.
9. R. Sandbrook, *Proletarians and African Capitalism: The Kenyan Case 1962–70*, Cambridge University Press, 1975, chs 7 and 8.
10. C. Kerr *et al.*, *Industrialism and Industrial Man*, 2nd edn, Oxford University Press, 1964, pp. 60–1; Bates, *Union, Parties . . .*, p. 27.
11. I. Davies, *African Trade Unions*, Penguin, 1966, p. 222.
12. V. I. Lenin, *What is to be Done?*, International Publishers, 1929, p. 32.

13. C. Allen, 'African Trade Unionism in Microcosm: The Gambian Labour Movement, 1939–67', in *African Perspectives*, C. H. Allen and R. W. Johnson (eds). Cambridge University Press, 1970, pp. 393–6, 412–24; R. Gerritson, 'The Evolution of the Ghana Trade Union Congress . . .', *Transactions of the Ghana Historical Society*, 1972; G. Pfefferman, *Industrial Labor in the Republic of Senegal*, Praeger, 1968, p. 85; R. Sandbrook, 'Patrons, Clients and Unions; The Labor Movement and Political Conflict in Kenya', *Journal of Commonwealth Political Studies*, 16, 1972, pp. 3–27.

14. B. H. Millen, *The Political Role of Labor in Developing Countries*, Brookings Institute, 1963, p. 9.

15. R. Murray, 'Militarism in Africa', *New Left Review*, 38, 1966, p. 46.

16. On the Sudan see A.-R. Taha, *The Sudanese Labor Movement: A Study of Labor Unionism in a Developing Society*, Ph.D. dissertation, University of California, Los Angeles, 1970, pp. 92, 105–9, 119–22. On Congo–Brazzaville see W. H. Friedland, 'Paradoxes of African Trade Unionism', *Africa Report*, 10, 1965, p. 10, and P. Waterman, 'Towards an Understanding of African Trade Unionism', *Présence Africaine*, 70, 1970, pp. 10–11. On Ghana, see St Clair Drake and L. A. Lacy, 'Government Versus the Unions', in *Politics in Africa: Seven Cases*, G. Carter (ed.), Harcourt, Brace and World, 1966, and Jeffries' chapter in this book. On Nigeria see E. R. Braundy and A. Lettieri, 'The General Strike in Nigeria', *International Socialist Journal*, 1 (5–6), 1964, pp. 598–609 and R. Melson, 'Nigerian Politics and the General Strike of 1964', in *Protest and Power in Black Africa*, R. I. Rotberg and A. A. Mazrui (eds), Oxford University Press, 1970. On Ethiopia, see document released by the Pan-African Trade Union Information Centre, Kinshasa, 1974, on the Confederation of Ethiopian Labor Unions.

17. R. Cohen, *Labour and Politics in Nigeria*, pp. 164–8.

18. *First Report of the Wages and Salaries Commission*, Ministry of Information, Lagos, 1970, p. 11.

19. Quoted by J. Merrington, 'Theory and Practice in Gramsci's Marxism', *The Socialist Register*, 1968, Merlin Press, 1968.

20. I. Clegg, *Workers' Self-Management in Algeria*, Allen Lane, 1971.

21. H. Mapolu, 'The Organisation and Participation of Workers in Tanzania', Economic Research Bureau Paper, 72.1, University of Dar es Salaam, 1972, p. 32.

22. F. Fanon, *The Wretched of the Earth*, Penguin, 1967, p. 86; G. Arrighi and J. Saul, *Essays on the Political Economy of Africa*, Monthly Review Press, 1973, pp. 44–102, 105–51.

Case Studies in African Labour Action in South Africa and Namibia (South West Africa)

L. DOUWES DEKKER, D. HEMSON, J. S. KANE-BERMAN, J. LEVER and L. SCHLEMMER[1]

It has been widely argued that in a political system as tightly controlled by a dominant minority as in South and South West Africa, one of the few points of leverage at the disposal of the dominated majority lies in the use of what here can be roughly termed 'labour power'.[2] Within this broad argument there are several radically different positions which can be discerned. One influential form of this thesis suggests that, through mechanisms never precisely specified, the increased participation of African workers in the South African industrial process will necessarily result in some significant shift in political power.[3] Implicit in this argument is a rather crude economic determinism, in which the enlarged productive and consumer strength of black workers is conceived to call forth a modified white attitude towards blacks, resulting in some more or less mutually agreeable compromise over the issue of political rights. Here then the South African industrial system is seen as an overriding motor of relatively harmonious socio-political change, undermining white fears for their material position and at the same time accommodating black aspirations towards improved status. In radical opposition to this argument is the position which asserts the irreconcilable antagonism of the interests of whites and blacks *within the present system*, and the necessity for a revolutionary transformation of the whole society through, for example, a 'strategy of insurrection, guerilla warfare and armed invasion'.[4] From this, an explicitly class-based, dialectic perspective, systematic theory specifies the black proletariat as one revolutionary element within the total system, exerting its labour power through collective action and merging the economic struggle with the wider political struggle through tactics such as the general strike. Finally, one can sketch a position more or less intermediate to the two. Here the analysis of African labour power can be directed towards the multitude of collective labour activities of the black majority which could provide the momentum for change—of a reformist or revolutionary kind—in a whole variety of spheres. Whatever the general evaluations to be made, they would be more open-ended—and less theoretically coherent—than in the previous two cases.

By and large this last is the perspective adopted by the present authors. We feel that it is premature to foreclose predictions on possible future developments. Recent events make it clear that widespread processes of worker awareness and action are changing the situation of the past ten years or so, in which the black urban masses responded relatively quiescently to the events around them. Leadership groups and worker strategies are still in the process of crystallisation: the process itself points to increased activity among black workers and the possible re-appearance of African assertion as a major factor within the system. On the other hand, the ability of the white-controlled system to channel, even suppress, these processes, remains evident. The discussion which follows is an attempt to assess the present position in the light of available evidence, and to provide a description of recent events and trends. In presenting case studies of African industrial action in this region, we attempt to describe and evaluate the problems and possibilities facing collective African labour action in particular situations.

Before presenting the individual studies, some remarks must be included in order to provide the context for an understanding of the single cases. These remarks will apply only to South Africa; they are, however, of relevance to Namibia, governed as it is by the South African regime which seeks to implement the policy of apartheid or separate development which was formulated for South Africa. Where necessary, divergencies between South and South West Africa will be made clear in the individual study itself. The following remarks take the form of a consideration, at a very general level, of some of the major constraints, internal and external, facing attempts by Africans to organise and to exert their labour power.

Constraints on African labour organisation
A low-wage, low-skill, low-status labour force

Despite a hundred years of involvement in the South African industrial system, the African labour force remains remarkably little differentiated across the categories of wage, skill and status. Average monthly cash incomes for Africans in 1969–70 in manufacturing, construction, central government employment and mining were R52, R49, R52 and R19 respectively. (The average wage for whites in these sectors varied from R293 to R341 per month.)[5] Further, figures from a recent survey covering 188,233 African workers in the private sector indicate that the African wage structure displayed relatively little dispersion of the mass of workers around the mean wages cited above:[6]

	R40 a month or less	Between R40 and R60 a month	Between R60 and R80 a month	Over R80 a month
%	32	47	14	7
N	59,404	89,069	25,552	14,208

From calculations of the bare minimum needed to cover essentials of urban household expenditure (the so-called Poverty Datum Line), it was estimated that between 60 per cent to 75 per cent of urban African households received an income which would not put them above this minimum.[7] Such poverty is a significant obstacle to the creation of viable workers' organisations, even in the minimal sense that African workers find difficulty in paying union subscriptions.

On the other hand, the existence of low wages, coupled with falling or static real income in an inflationary situation, appears a classic setting for outbursts of worker discontent, and this factor does indeed seem to have been one underlying cause of recent labour unrest in South Africa. Like most other industrial countries, South Africa has been suffering from comparatively high rates of inflation in recent years, a rate which has been calculated to have reached 9.1 per cent in 1972.[8] With respect to skill levels, the same survey cited above revealed at the same time that out of the 188,233 Africans included in the survey, 60 per cent fell into the two lowest grades of skill (covering labourers who require little or no training and education). A further 27 per cent occupied semiskilled jobs of the simplest and most routine type.

Along with the low-wage, low-skill character of the African labour force has gone the tendency of employers to treat African workers as relatively uniform and undifferentiated. Further, even where African workers did acquire the skills which would have entitled them to skilled status, the recognition of this status by employers has often been withheld, and the frequent phenomenon has arisen of Africans performing quite highly skilled work but receiving the status, and often the pay, of their unskilled colleagues.[9] Employer practice, government policy and white labour protectionist strategies have combined to help lock the African worker into his low-skill, low-status role.

Marginal urban status and the constriction of a free labour market

Of immense, if often intangible, consequence for the organisation of the African worker in South Africa is the ever-tighter network of laws imposed on him by a government seeking to implement its declared policy of apartheid or separate development. The main thrust of the policy at present is the creation of the legislative framework (through such laws as the Bantu Labour Act and Regulations issued under its authority, the Physical Planning Act, the Urban Areas Act and the Bantu Affairs Administration Act) whereby most, and perhaps all, Africans in the 'white' areas of the Republic are to be assigned official domicile in one of the African homelands and permitted to work outside such homelands on a contract or migrant basis alone. Such 'guest workers', as the official euphemism has it, already number some 1.3 million, and are recruited through an extensive system of labour bureaux in the homelands, and *only* through these bureaux. Once in the 'white' industrial centres, such migrants are housed on a single basis in the growing number of barrack-like hostels springing up around South African cities.[10] The future of several million Africans who have a qualified right (under Section 10 of the Urban Areas Act) to remain in the urban areas must be seen in the light of the declared intention of the policy to create more and more contract, as opposed to settled urbanised, Africans. Africans qualifying under Section 10 are permitted a free choice of available jobs going in the urban areas for which they are registered, and receive preference for such jobs above migrant work-seekers. Perhaps most secure in status is the African worker who lives in a homeland but crosses every day into the 'white' area to undertake work in one of the recognised border area industries, since in theory all he stands to lose by collective industrial action is his job, rather than, as could happen, his whole urban residential and household tenure. But such border area workers do not, as yet, make up a sizable proportion of the urban African workforce.[11]

It is impossible to assess precisely the impact of this marginal urban status on the ability and willingness of the African worker to undertake labour organisation. On the face of it, and as several writers have suggested,[12] the rightless homeland migrant living in one or other hostel, and the Section 10 African with his problematic urban status, do not offer the most favourable field for stable unionisation. Nor, as will be shown, is it government policy that it should be so. On the other hand, resentment against the contract system and pass laws is a major potential source of African collective action in South and South West Africa today; and as the section on South West Africa indicates, provides grounds for industrial-cum-political action among migrant workers. Such action is, however, not likely to be undertaken within the framework of orthodox trade union institutions.

Exclusion of Africans from the industrial relations system

The cornerstone of the South African industrial relations system is the Industrial Conciliation Act, which bestows statutory recognition on trade unions, affords them recourse to conciliation and arbitration machinery at their request, and provides for the setting up of statutory collective bargaining institutions termed industrial councils. From this system, Africans are explicitly excluded. Trade unions organised by and for Africans are not illegal; they are however assigned to an institutional vacuum. Joint employer/employee industrial councils lay down wage rates and other working conditions for over one million workers, the majority of whom are Africans; but no Africans are at present allowed to sit on the councils. Complementary to the industrial councils is the Wage Board, a government body empowered to lay down minimum wage rates in occupations not covered by industrial council agreements. African workers may give evidence before this Board at its sittings. But it is widely agreed that the Wage Board has failed to effect any marked rise in African wages, much though it may have done to eliminate the lowest gross inter-firm and regional discrepancies in the wages paid to the lowest grades of workers.[13] Space prohibits a full elucidation of the whole effect of the existing complex of industrial legislation; suffice it to say that discriminatory provisions of greater or lesser impact are also embodied in measures such as the Unemployment Insurance Act, the Mines and Works Act, the Factories Act and the Shops and Offices Act. And where the law does not explicitly discriminate, administrative action frequently achieves the same effect.

Restrictions imposed on Africans due to the separate industrial relations system designed for them

Excluded from the established legal system of industrial relations for the most part, the African workers are expected to have their interests served in terms of the 1953 Bantu Labour (Settlement of Disputes) Act. This act has recently been amended (see Conclusion), but until 1973 operated as follows: firstly, strikes by Africans were prohibited, thereby severely circumscribing in law at least the role of African trade unions. African labour interests were the province of the Central Bantu Labour Board, consisting of appointed white officials, together with a series of regional boards. These boards were charged, first and foremost, with the settlement of work disputes, and the aim of officials appeared generally to have been to get the workers involved in a dispute with management back to work with as little fuss as possible; the prosecution of Africans involved in a work stoppage having been usually resorted to only when workers proved more than usually obdurate.[14] Officials of the Bantu Labour Board were also given places on industrial councils, where they were directed to represent the interests of the African workers in the industry concerned. The act recognised a limited form of African labour representation in the form of 'works committees', consisting of elected employee representatives. The functioning of the works committees system, in the wake of the recent labour unrest, was conceded even by the government to have been a failure. Few were established in terms of the act, and employers by and large did not encourage their formation. Slightly more successful were non-statutory committees set up by employers.

Neutralisation of the politicisation of African trade unions

From its earliest days, African trade unionism and worker action in South Africa acted as a vehicle for the articulation of both economic and political grievances. In the 1920s, the Industrial and Commercial Workers' Union under Clements Kadalie gained a wide following among the incipient black proletariat, and functioned, as a recent study suggests, as trade union, political pressure group and mass movement.[15] With the fragmentation and ultimate disappearance of the ICU after 1929, small trade unions arose among blacks, gaining much of their organisational drive from the activities of white and black radical opponents of the white government.[16] Indeed, fear of the potential force for violent change to be exerted by an African mass labour movement under strong communist influence was claimed to be one of the main reasons for the passing of the Supression of Communism Act in 1950. Executive action in terms of the Act did not however immediately remove the radical activist influence over a section of African trade unions, which after 1954 made up the main affiliated membership of the South African Congress of Trade Unions (SACTU). In the sequence of events leading up to the Sharpeville shootings, the banning of the African National Congress and the Pan African Congress, and the subsequent decision of the Congress Alliance leadership to switch to violent tactics, SACTU itself occupied a central role, and many of its leadership personnel were simultaneously involved in trade union activity, the work of the underground Communist Party and the sabotage campaign of the military wing of the Congress Alliance, Umkonto we Sizwe.[17] With the smashing of this underground network by 1964, SACTU itself and most of its affiliated unions ceased to function in all but name inside the Republic.

Side by side with SACTU had arisen a body of African trade unionists, most successfully represented perhaps in the African 'parallel' union of the Garment Workers' Union of South Africa, the National Union of Clothing Workers, who eschewed the political commitments of the SACTU leaders, and who argued in favour of a 'bread and butter politics' approach of reform within the existing legal system. Such an approach is probably the only one which has enabled, and will enable, present African trade unionists to avoid state repression in terms of the Suppression of Communism Act. The point to be made here is that, given intensive police surveillance and government antagonism to African trade unions, African unionists are as a matter of organisational survival forced to accept a role which restricts the function of a trade union to economic and work-place activities. At present, African unionists in office bitterly resist the importation of a politically activist orientation which they consider to be ill-conceived and under present circumstances at least detrimental to the immediate interests of their membership. A recent, and not very successful, attempt to politicise African trade unionism resulted in the banning of the two leaders most closely involved (see the next section). African trade union leaders, aware of their high visibility for the organs of state security, are thus for the moment not likely to take the lead in movements which place a broad political interpretation on the role of African labour action.

Antagonism or indifference of the registered trade union movement
towards African labour organisation

Traditionally, white labour has shared the general prejudices regarding Africans which have permeated white society as a whole, and has added to those its own sectional fears of the competition of black labour for its jobs. With some over-simplification, two broad strands can be discerned. The first consists either of an outright rejection of, or a lack of concern for, the possibility of the organisation of African workers, a position taken up at the moment with some internal differences of opinion by the Confederation of Labour, an all-white co-ordinating body with affiliates mainly in the public and mining sectors. This body has generally taken up the stance that it represents the interest of white workers only, and recently refused to reconsider its position despite urgings from more moderate elements within its ranks. The other stand is represented by the Trade Union Council of South Africa (TUCSA), the other major co-ordinating body with an affiliated membership of both white, and Coloured and Indian workers.

The leadership of TUCSA has campaigned for the admittance of Africans into existing trade unions and as the latest step in its campaign asked for, and obtained, a mandate from the overwhelming majority of its affiliated unions in favour of asking the government to allow Africans into registered trade unions. It is, however, widely accepted that there is no chance of TUCSA's aim being achieved as long as the present government is in power. Nor would it necessarily be in the interests of African workers if it were. Several unions dominated by white artisans inside and outside TUCSA seek the unionisation of Africans on grounds basically of self-interest: they wish to control the growing work-force of blacks moving into their industries in the interests of their present membership. These artisan unions have stated that they would bring Africans into their unions on restricted voting rights which would retain control of unions in white hands.[18] This policy indicates the severe limitations which even relatively 'liberal' white unionists would impose on the expression of African workers interests. The point is further supported by the failure of most white-dominated unions to make any effort to exploit the possibilities for African labour organisation which exist even under the present restrictive conditions: such unions are not interested in fostering for example non-recognised 'parallel' unions, since such unions would not be under the direct control of the registered union itself. Again, despite their nominal adherence to TUCSA's non-racial union policy, Coloured unionists within that organisation have sometimes acted in direct contradiction to the spirit of the policy in the face of African competition for jobs performed by their members.[19] Some exceptions do exist to the pattern outlined above, but most of the unions affiliated to TUCSA do not comprise a force on which African workers can rely for wholehearted backing.

Employer resistance to effective African trade unionism

In a recent article it has been remarked that South African employers as a class have generally opposed barriers on African geographical and occupational mobility, since these have hindered the most efficient exploitation of existing labour resources: they have not, however, opposed the denial of African trade union rights or the differential wage structure for Africans doing the same work as whites.[20] On the whole, this would appear to be an accurate assessment of the situation. In the main, South African employers appear to think that by expanding company welfare and personnel policies, and possibly through greater interest in the newly-amended works committee system, they can stand firm against African trade unionism.

Briefly, then, these can be considered the major constraints with which any

African labour organisation and collective action in South Africa must come to terms. They go some way to explaining why sub-Saharan Africa's largest and oldest industrial proletariat is at the same time perhaps the least organised. Before turning to a more detailed consideration of African labour action in particular circumstances it would ideally be useful to refer to the limited survey evidence which is available on the attitudes and orientations of urban African workers.[21] Regrettably space precludes anything but a few brief remarks in the notes: we pass instead to our three case studies—(a) labour organisation on the Rand, (b) labour unrest in Natal and (c) Namibia.

African labour organisation on the Rand

From the point of view of the hundreds of thousands of African workers employed in or around the Witwatersrand (the major industrial centre in South Africa), only marginal importance can be attached to the role of the handful of African trade unions active in the area. And yet, since these, until recent months, were the only African trade unions in the whole of South Africa, some discussion of their problems and prospects merits attention. Mention was made earlier of the decline of unions grouped under the umbrella of SACTU; as a consequence of this situation African unionism in the Republic faced near extinction. One union, however, the National Union of Clothing Workers (a non-SACTU union), did maintain a viable existence throughout this troubled period. In addition, since 1962, attempts have been made to revive existing African unions and to promote new ones on the Rand. The purpose of this section is to discuss the position of, firstly, the National Union of Clothing Workers; and, secondly, the renewed interest in trade unions which is now manifest among African workers on the Rand.

The National Union of Clothing Workers

With a paid-up membership of 18,000 African employees in the clothing industry in the Transvaal, the National Union of Clothing Workers provides an example of one possible mode of adaptation of African unions to the restrictive conditions under which they may function: namely, the position of the union as a 'parallel' body to that of a recognised union which is sympathetic to the idea of African unionism. The NUCW originated in the decision of the leadership of the Garment Workers' Union of South Africa, a mixed union of whites, Coloured and Indian clothing workers, to organise African women in the clothing industry who, because of a loophole in the Industrial Conciliation Act, were allowed to belong to recognised trade unions. When this loophole was closed with the passing of the Bantu Labour (Settlement of Disputes) Act in 1953, African members of the GWU were formed into a separate body, the National Union of Clothing Workers. The former GWU African organiser, Mrs Lucy Mvubelo, was elected General Secretary.

The NUCW cannot be registered in terms of the Industrial Conciliation Act and thus may not participate in the official decision-making process of the Industrial Council for the Clothing Industry in the Transvaal. Nevertheless, employers afford a degree of recognition to the work of the NUCW, and work through some 300 shop stewards who belong to the union. The union is able to help members to find work, to assist them with such matters as unemployment benefit applications, and administers a burial fund. Difficulties in the way of collecting subscriptions (the check-off is illegal for African unions) have been partially overcome by the device of an administration fee for the burial fund. The union is now so established in the industry that when, for example, employers are faced with work-disputes, the Industrial Council requests the NUCW officials to assist in settling the matter.

Notwithstanding this relatively favoured situation in comparison with other African unions, the NUCW faces a number of problems which illustrate the disadvantaged position of the parallel African union. For one thing, the union operates from offices in the Garment Workers' Union building in Johannesburg which is in a 'white' group area. This location has made it difficult to hold annual general meetings of the membership. More important, however, is the lack of official status of the NUCW within the whole institutional complex of an industrial council. In South Africa these bodies perform many of the services for union members which might elsewhere fall within the ambit of the union. For example, it is the Industrial Council, directed by its executive body on which sit employers and representatives of the registered union, which runs such services as technical training schemes, sick pay, medical benefit, provident fund membership, as well as processing under-payment claims and investigating grievances raised under the ruling industrial council agreement for the industry. (It is to the credit of the GWU that it has seen to it that these benefits are extended to NUCW members.) And of course the agreement itself is negotiated in the absence of NUCW representation. What can be achieved is close and continuing contact on a non-official administrative level between officials of the GWU and the NCUW, and greater use of NUCW officials in the administrative activities of the council. There is room to doubt that the GWU has done quite as much as it could have to exploit the full potential of this situation. The relationship between the GWU and NUCW tends to be that of the 'mother' and 'daughter' union, in part due to an understandable caution on the part of the GWU leadership, in part due to the continuing reliance on the recognised union by the leaders of the NUCW. There are some signs that this is changing, that the NUCW is now more insistent on its status as a 'sister' union.

The relative success of the NUCW is evidence of the need filled by African parallel unions which emphasise their functions of improving the material conditions of the membership. But even here the role of the NUCW is sharply constrained by its unofficial status, and by the cautious approach which union officials are obliged to assume in fulfilling their functions. Recent events in the Transvaal clothing industry illustrate both the strengths and the weaknesses in the position of the NUCW. In March and April of 1973 widespread work-stoppages occurred among African workers (together with a smaller number of Coloured workers) in the industry, provoked by expectations regarding a promised cost of living increase to be awarded by employers. In a three-week period some 21 work-stoppages embracing some 4,608 black garment workers occurred in clothing factories, mainly the larger undertakings, on and around the Reef. It seems clear that workers were spurred by the example of earlier strikes in Natal (see next section) and also on a more restricted scale on the Rand, to organise work-floor stoppages in support of their demands over the disputed cost of living increase. In half the cases, the stoppages occurred after the early morning tea-break, and workers would refuse to return to work, after having discussed their grievances together inside the factory. Only in two cases did the stoppages last more than 5 hours; usually intervention on the part of either or both GWU and NUCW officials, and the announcement of concessions by employers over the cost of living award, were sufficient to get the workers back to work. The existence of an established union such as the NUCW enjoying the confidence of the workers was undoubtedly one reason for the speed in which the disputes were settled. It is also true that the NUCW had not been able to take the lead in pressing the workers' demands, and thus was confined to an intermediary rather than a leadership role—a position which in part was a function of the NUCW's unofficial status as a parallel African union. Finally, it is to be noted that the ability of the NUCW's officials to act as intermediaries depended to a considerable extent on the discretion used by Department of Labour officials who were present at nine out of the 21 disputes. In several cases these officials, following the spirit of government policy, pointedly excluded the NUCW's spokesman from the negotiations between workers and employers.[22]

Emerging worker awareness among Africans

In 1962 the Trade Union Council of South Africa, having decided at its annual conference to accept the affiliation of African unions, established an African Affairs Section, charged with the work of organising African workers. Five small African unions were established by the section, in the face of considerable difficulties. Regarding the external environment of these unions, little help was given by the registered trade unions affiliated to TUCSA. It was the experience of the African Affairs Section personnel that the officials of recognised unions would promise to help, for instance at the level of the industrial council of the industry concerned, but that nothing came of such promises. TUCSA affiliates were contacted by that organisation's sub-committee on the organisation of unorganised workers, but no response was forthcoming. Internally, and for reasons which it is difficult to assess, little response was obtained from among African workers themselves to the idea that they could further their interests by trade union activity. One reason for this state of affairs was probably the introduction of a wider scale than previously of company personnel policies aimed at providing greater security and status.

In 1968, at a time of acute crisis within the ranks of TUCSA itself over the issue of African unionisation, brought about by attacks by the Minister of Labour on the policy, the African Affairs Section was closed down and its personnel dismissed. Internal divisions within TUCSA finally forced the organisation to end the affiliation of African unions, and since this time TUCSA itself has not attempted to organise African trade unions.[23]

In 1970 the Urban Training Project was founded by a group of people, both white and black, who had been involved in the attempts of the African Affairs Section to organise African workers. Again, for reasons which are difficult to pinpoint, the Urban Training Project appears to be making a greater impact in propagating worker awareness of the value of unions than did its African Affairs predecessor. One reason for this new awareness possibly lies in the stirrings of a 'black consciousness' movement in the Republic which emphasises the need for independent black organisations, as opposed to the mixed white and black bodies which have functioned, but with little success from the point of view of real improvements for blacks, over the past years.

The aims of the founders of the Urban Training Project was to establish an educational body which would publicise the existing rights of African workers under the present labour legislation, and which would assist Africans who wished to form a trade union or workers' organisation of any sort. The Urban Training Project is not a trade union in itself, nor a co-ordinating body in the sense that TUCSA and the Confederation of Labour are. Instead, the project aims to foster independent African unions by lending secretarial, organisational and other trade union training where possible. Workers in the laundry and dry cleaning, the chemical and the transport industries have received help in establishing unions. Shop steward courses and seminars on labour legislation have been provided for interested workers.

Within its first year of operation, the executive of the Urban Training Project was faced with an issue which forced it to define its stance regarding its trade union educational activity, and the potential for politicisation to which the existence of African unions can give rise.[24] In brief, the situation arose in which one of the organisers for the project, Mr Drake Koka, was active in the foundation of the Black Peoples' Convention, a body with strong 'black power' overtones and a militant political stance. A unanimous decision of the project's executive (containing both black and white members) decided that Mr Koka's activites were incompatible with his work as organiser for the project, and he was finally dismissed after indicating his unwillingness to forego his political involvements. Mr Koka subsequently announced the formation of the Sales and Allied Workers' Union, which was intended to act as a general union to which all black workers could belong. This union never really got off the ground, but Koka's activities, in which he was joined by another African unionist who had worked for TUCSA's African Affairs Section, appear to have led to his recently being banned in terms of the Suppression of Communism Act. The incident reflected both the dangers inherent in black militancy and the fact that militants do not command a great deal of support from among African trade unionists, if partly for tactical reasons.

African awareness of the constraints of the system within which they function when organising themselves is reflected in the decision by the project to give particular attention in 1973 to the idea of 'workers' committees' and the possibilities which this form of organisation hold out for African labour action. The idea of the workers' committee is to establish independent workers' organisations on a factory-wide basis before negotiations are entered into with employers. It can be argued that the idea of a workers' committee is only marginally different from that of a trade union but in the present political climate it appears that African workers themselves are aware of the prudence of drawing a distinction between the two, and attempting to exploit the little leeway which the present system gives them.[25]

In June 1972 an event occurred which appears to have given considerable stimulus to African awareness of the possibilities of joint labour action. African bus drivers employed by the Public Utility Transport Corporation (PUTCO) on the Reef went on strike to back their wage demands. An offer from the employers of 2 per cent was rejected. Three hundred of the drivers were jailed in Johannesburg, some of them after they had gone to the jail where their colleagues were being detained and demanded that they also be arrested. The PUTCO drivers thereupon formed a Drivers' Committee charged with collecting money for the defence of the arrested men. The Attorney-General subsequently declined to prosecute the men on the charge of striking, and the drivers received a pay increase of 33½ per cent from the employers.[26]

One result of the PUTCO strike was that the PUTCO Drivers' Committee was converted, after advice had been gained from members of the Urban Training Project, into a new union for African transport workers, the Transport Workers and Allied Union. (It is perhaps significant that the members of the Drivers' Committee, in discussing their proposed constitution, rejected the term 'Black' in the title of the union.) The new union is open to all African drivers, conductors and related workers in the transport industry. The executive committee consists of workers in the employ both of PUTCO and the Johannesburg City Council.

The PUTCO strike, together with strikes and other collective action among Durban dockworkers both in 1969 and 1972, proved to be forerunners of a widespread movement among urban African industrial workers in the Republic, a movement directed in the first instance against the depressed living standards of black workers and the unresponsive structure of South African industrial relations. In December 1972 and February 1973 strikes occurred among African municipal bus drivers in Pretoria and Johannesburg; in the former city the stoppage resulted in the arrest of 57 drivers and the conviction of 13 for participating in an illegal strike. A number of drivers involved lost their jobs as a consequence.[27] In Cape Town over 2,000 stevedores staged a work-to-rule campaign during October and November 1972, after a dispute over changed conditions of employment.[28] After the widely publicised Natal strikes in early 1973, sporadic work-stoppages occurred on the Rand in the clothing industry, newspaper and milk delivery services and engineering concerns. While lacking the widespread nature of the Natal strikes, the events on the Rand indicated a renewed willingness on the part of black workers to resort to collective action in support of their demands.

Labour unrest in Natal

In January and February 1973 South African secondary industry experienced its first-ever outbreak of large-scale labour action on the part of its African work-force when some 60,000 or so black workers took strike action in the industries of the Durban–Pinetown–Hammarsdale complex. Possibly 150 firms in all, covering the whole spectrum of secondary industry, were affected by the strike.

Indications that labour unrest was likely among the African work-force in the area had not been altogether lacking before the strikes occurred. On the docks, traditional centre of labour militancy in Durban, worker discontent had been smouldering in the wake of strikes in 1969 and 1972 among the large number of migrant workers employed as stevedores there.[29] More specifically, officials of two registered trade unions, the Garment Workers' Industrial Union of Natal and the Textile Workers' Industrial Union had received several intimations of worker discontent. Where the officials felt that management might be responsive, an attempt was made to convey the feelings of the workers. The Textile Union, for example, warned the manager of cotton mills belonging to the Frame Group three months before the strikes that workers were becoming impatient and had asked the union to take up their complaints. This warning had no effect, apart from increasing hostility between management and the union. At another textile plant in Pinetown the manager said he was 'too busy' to discuss the demands of African workers, two days before a strike broke out at the plant. In all cases where management had been warned by the Textile Union of potential labour trouble, the approaches were snubbed. In the circumstances, as a registered union for whom African workers were officially beyond its province, the union was unable to push the matter further, fearing that subsequent labour unrest would be blamed on it, and that it would be called upon to reveal its sources of information.

Starting in the middle of January with two isolated strikes in Durban[30] the strikes snowballed towards the end of January into what threatened at one time to develop into a general strike. The first factories to be affected were those with the worst conditions, but once the step had been taken by one group of African workers, the strikes spread by force of example. Whole streets would be affected: in Gillitts Road in the industrial complex in Pinetown, for example, the strike started at the lowest paying factory on the street, Consolidated Wool-washing and Processing Mills, but then spread back and forth along the street, engulfing in the process a firm such as Smith and Nephew where wages were considerably higher than in other textile firms. Picketing and incitement to strike is illegal in South Africa but much the same effect was gained by the presence of thousands of workers pouring out of factories and moving en masse down past neighbouring concerns chanting the old war cry of the Zulu armies, 'Usuthu'. Social conditions of the mass of African workers helped communicate the mood of the strikers. In some cases, for example, the congregation of migrant workers from different firms in single quarter hostels and compounds undoubtedly served to facilitate the exchange of information;[31] a situation also served by the packed and gregarious circumstances of the public transportation on which African workers find their way to and from work. African beer halls also served as venues for discussion among workers regarding strike action. Paradoxically, the absence of trade union institutions and of recognised worker leadership also contributed to the remarkable inter-firm, inter-industry solidarity manifest among the strikers. Lacking the directness which trade union involvement could have bestowed, it proved remarkably easy to pull out workers from widely unrelated enterprises. It was sufficient that African workers recognised their common plight in low wages and their inferior status throughout industry as a whole. Lacking leadership recognised by management, and unwilling for fear of victimisation to push forward spokesmen who could have undertaken negotiation before strikes proved necessary, African workers had little other way of making their demands known than by mass strike activity.

By and large, the following pattern can be suggested for those factories whose work-forces were among the leaders in the ripple of strikes which ensued:

(a) Low wages, below R10 a week, for many or most of the African work-force;

(b) Poor labour relations with, for example, a distant and impersonal management; opposition to communication with workers through the efforts of sympathetic officials of registered unions; and the absence of possible management/worker linkages of a direct type, such as the works' committee;

(c) An oppressive personnel and labour control policy signalled by high turn-over, frequent recourse to dismissal, and victimisation of potential spokesmen or leaders.[32]

No company in the region was without one of these conditions, and the strikes caused even factories with a more enlightened management (such as Dunlops in Durban) to collapse once the example had been set by other workers.

A further factor which appears to have played a role in the strikes was the fact that the work-force of the area was largely Zulu-speaking, and did not exhibit the very mixed ethnic conditions of, for example, the work-force on the Reef. It is perhaps the combination of the ethnic homogeneity and the consciousness of a common interest arising from the industrial and wage situation which accounts in some part for the solidarity displayed in the course of the strikes.

Because most of the strikes centred on Durban, observers have sought the cause of them in the level of wages in the area. However, the low wages paid to Africans in Durban do not answer the question why it should have been this area and not another which was affected. A useful comparison here can be made by drawing a line between those workers earning R10 and more a week, and those earning less. The R10 line is of significance in that it was (in the form of the slogan '£I a day') the desirable wage level popularised by SACTU in the late 1950s. More tangible however is the fact that workers who earn *less* than R10.50 a week do not qualify for benefits under the Unemployment Insurance Act, and are thus highly vulnerable to loss of income from illness or redundancy. It is evident that judged by this standard, Durban is by no means the worst paying area in South Africa. While 20 per cent of the African workers in the Durban–Pinetown complex earn less than R10 a week, the figure in Bloemfontein is 85 per cent, in East London 48 per cent, in the Vaal Triangle 42 per cent and on the Rand 20 per cent.[33]

Thus wages by themselves fail to explain why the strikes broke out in the Durban region and not elsewhere. Nevertheless, wages, and more particularly the falling real income due to inflation and particularly food price rises, provided the focus around which worker discontent in the area mounted. It has been calculated that the level of the Poverty Datum Line had risen in the Durban area from R61.74 in 1966 to R83 at present. Increased publicity to figures such as these has undoubtedly broken through to the awareness of the African industrial worker. (In one factory visited in the course of the strike, African workers waved a pamphlet summarising the views of Professor H. L. Watts of the University of Natal, who has conducted research on the PDL, in support of their demands.) In January, at a time when workers had exhausted their holiday pay, they faced increased expenditure on school uniforms and books for their children, and a rise of 16 per cent in rail fares to and from work.

The strikes brought some immediate relief to workers. Increases ranging from R1 a week to R2 a week were awarded in the textile industry. Several thousand municipal workers received R2 a week extra, and in one large motor assembly plant an escalating increase of R4.50 was introduced. Voluntary increases were also granted by managers not affected by strikes seeking to ward off labour unrest.

A feature of the strikes was the relative absence of officials from the registered trade union movement. J. A. Grobbelaar, general secretary of TUCSA, did advise one of the two concerns whose African workers were the first to go on strike in mid-January. But having neither the resources nor the prestige for mediation among African workers, TUCSA was unable to play any prominent role. The most active trade union intervention was undertaken by the two TUCSA affiliates (by no means typical of TUCSA affiliates in general on this score) who before the strikes had had sufficient contact with African workers to realise that labour unrest was sooner or later inevitable. Officials of these two unions, the Garment Workers' Industrial Union and the Textile Union, undertook the job of negotiating between African workers and management in a number of firms. Apart from this, the role of the registered trade unions was peripheral or non-existent. This anomalous situation, where the recognised trade union movement sat largely on the sidelines while large-scale industrial action was undertaken by the major part of the work-force, was due in part to the indifference of many unions to the interests of African workers in the plants in which they are operative, and in part due to the fear of warnings from the Department of Labour should sympathetic union officials have acted on behalf of workers who were not members of their own union. And to indicate the uncertainty of the authorities' attitude towards third-party intervention in the strikes was the presence of the security police: one of the writers was followed by two cars containing security policemen when he visited strike-bound factories.

Similarly impotent were the officials of the industrial councils in the industries where these institutions were functioning. Officials made few attempts at mediation, and frequently sided openly with management. In one major case, that of the Industrial Council for the Textile Manufacturing Industry, the attitude of Council officials arose from the employer orientation of the body. The Secretariat of the Council is operated by the Natal Employers' Association, and workers complain that the institution does not cater properly for their interests.

The only statutory recognised organ through which Africans could have expressed their grievances were works' committees functioning in the Durban area. There were, according to information supplied to the writers by the Secretary of Labour, three such committees in the Durban area in 1970 (in a region where several thousand would have been necessary to cover the African work-force). In 1973, the situation had not changed: only three works' committees constituted in terms of the Act, existed. More numerous were works' committees not established in accordance with the provision of the Act: there were around twenty of these committees in the area. For the most part, however, these unofficial committees were tightly controlled by management and in most cases were not allowed to discuss the subject of wages. During the strikes the works' committees proved to be entirely ineffective as channels of communication and as negotiating agents. When the workers had come out on strike the elected representatives faded away. At one factory, workers shouted: 'We want money first, then we will talk about committees.'

For the most part, caught completely unawares by the intensity of feeling revealed by the strikes, employers in the area desperately cast around for the appropriate response. Consultations were held as far as ministerial level with the Department of Labour. Employer associations, such as the Durban Chamber of Commerce and the Natal Employers' Association in general were anxious not to let workers think that they had gained a position of strength by striking. Members of the Durban Chamber of Commerce were told to grant wage increases but not to negotiate with workers. Similar in tone was the advice contained in a ten-point plan to employers: Do not attempt to bargain as this will 'only encourage the Bantu to escalate his demands.'[34] Many managers were totally nonplussed by the situation, and some admitted to the writers that they were frankly terrified by the sea of black faces whose thoughts were suddenly revealed to be completely unknown to their employers. Most employers remained aloof from the workers, called in the police and waited for the savings of workers to dry up and draw them back to work. Others tried to address the strikers, but were shouted down; in one case a more successful attempt at communication was made when the managing director of a concern moved among the workers, talking with small groups at a time.

It is difficult to assess what the long-term impact of the strikes on management will be. The Natal Employers' Association adopted a particularly anti-worker stance and urged a 'take-it-or-leave-it' approach on employers. The Director of the Association has thrown doubt on the validity of the PDL at meetings with employers in an attempt to evade the issue that African wages are poverty wages. One strong current of thought among management which has emerged is firmly against an attempt to move wages up to the PDL, and instead recommends wages between R12 to R15 a week. Further, it is evident that some employers took advantage of the strike to rid themselves of older workers and 'agitators', and even to dismiss workers who were then offered re-engagement at lower rates than before the strike.

Central to the strike situation were the police who appeared automatically at disputes. The press, and in particular the normally critical English-language newspapers, were profuse in their praise of the 'low-profile' presence of the police during the strikes. No workers were arrested for being on strike as such, though striking by Africans was illegal. In fact, the police had little choice. In a 'leaderless' situation such as that in and around Durban the only alternative to arresting selected 'agitators' was to put the whole labour force of 60,000 workers on strike in jail. There can be no doubt however that the deployment of police even at completely peaceful strikes served to enforce settlements in an atmosphere of state power. At one factory, for example, the police officer reported to the manager and asked: 'What do you want us to do?' When it was apparent that the strikes were spreading widely, police contingents were flown to Durban from Pretoria, and were deployed at strikes dressed in para-military combat uniform, causing workers to fear they had provoked the state into calling out the army.

Since the Durban strikers were, according to government policy, all either actually or potentially 'citizens' of the future 'state' of Kwa-Zulu, the official home of Zulus, it is of interest to note that the homeland authorities themselves appear to have played only a minimal role in the January and February strikes. Discontented dock-workers in Durban had appealed to the homeland authorities in the previous year, but had been unable to secure the intervention of the Zulu chief executive counsellor, Gatsha Buthelezi. During the strikes themselves the Paramount Chief of the Zulus acted as mediator between some of the strikers and the employers, but this appears to have been done against the wishes of the Kwa-Zulu executive under Buthelezi. A more active role was, however, undertaken by Buthelezi and one of his executive council colleagues, Mr Barney Dladla, at a strike at the Alusef aluminium smelter on the north coast of Natal in March. Dladla himself visited the strikers and supported their demands, while Buthelezi threatened to withhold Zulu labour from the plant should wages not be increased.[35] (Buthelezi was warned by a South African Cabinet Minister, Senator Owen Horwood, not to meddle in matters outside Kwa-Zulu.) While severely limited in their ability to intervene on behalf of Zulu workers' interests, Buthelezi and his counsellors do appear to have gained added stature among urban workers by their efforts.

In Durban itself the strikes are reported greatly to have increased the interest of black workers in the possibilities of organisation and collective action. The work of Central Administration Services, a body similar to the Urban Training Project on the Rand, under the aegis of the Natal Garment Workers' Industrial Union and the Textile Workers' Industrial Union, has benefited considerably from heightened awareness among urban black workers.[36] One concrete result has been the formation, in June 1973, of the Metal and Allied Workers' Union for black workers in the engineering industry in Natal.[37]

Namibia (South West Africa): the Ovambo strike and its aftermath

In the years following the granting of the mandate for South West Africa in 1920, employers in the territory formed recruiting agencies for black labour. For the most part this black labour lay dispersed to the north of the territory having been driven off the central high plateau during the German colonisation to make way for white occupation. In 1943 these agencies were amalgamated into the South West Africa Native Labour Association, SWANLA, along the lines of the well-tried monopsonistic gold-mines recruiting system throughout southern Africa. The contract labour system which was established became known as 'omtete uokaholo'—'to queue up for the identity disc'—to black workers. Recruited in the African reserves for work in the southern or 'white' part of the territory, black workers were presented with service contracts and identity permits, while labels bearing the name and address of their prospective employers were hung around their necks. They were then sent south by train to work for periods of twelve to eighteen months before being returned to the reserves.[38]

At present, there are at any one time around 43,000 African contract workers in the southern territory; some 11,000 in farming, 13,000 in mining, 14,000 in government service, commerce and industry, 3,000 in fishing and under 3,000 in domestic service. Of these, some 40,000 are workers from the country's single largest ethnic group, the Ovambo.[39] Namibia's economy is heavily dependent on these workers, but their indispensable contribution to its development has brought them minimal gain. The economy is characterised by high levels of consumption among whites, by its marked export orientation, by the large gap between gross domestic product and gross national income, and by extreme disparities in per capita income between the southern commercialised sector and the reserves to the north. Something like one-third of GDP accrues to foreigners, while the gap between black and white per capita income is much larger than it is in the Republic.

As in South Africa, the workings of the contract system in Namibia served several purposes at once. From the point of view of employers, it rationalised the supply of labour by the creation of a single recruiting system, which eliminated a free and competitive labour market by providing only one channel though which men could sell their labour. Employers were therefore able to keep wages very low. The restricted stay of the contract worker limited employer and local authority responsibility for ensuring decent living conditions for the labourforce. Contract workers could also be conveniently conceived as merely 'supplementing' the income which they were supposed to be able to make from their land in the reserves. The system reconciled the twin policy objectives of meeting the white-controlled economy's demand for labour while at the same time keeping to a minimum the number of non-employed Africans in the 'white' areas. Again, as in South Africa, the practical outcome of the policy for the black contract worker was that his sojourn in the 'white' area was typically spent (outside the farms) in large, all-male compounds. In Katutura, the black township outside the capital city of Windhoek, the compound there housed 6,000 men; in Walvis Bay, centre of the fishing industry, the compound accommodated 7,400 workers. Women were not allowed in the compounds. It was indeed extremely difficult for any women from the reserves to gain the right to leave them to live in the 'white' areas.

It was these same compounds, inevitably perhaps, which were to prove the centres of the strike which broke out in December 1971. The first reported signs of unrest were in the municipal compound in Walvis Bay,[40] where workers had been expressing dissatisfaction for some weeks, and had reportedly written letters to workers elsewhere urging them to strike.[41] The men, through an elected committee, demanded an end to the contract system, failing which they wanted to be repatriated. They drew attention to an earlier remark by a government official to the effect that the workers freely accepted the contract system because they allowed themselves to be recruited voluntarily. Accordingly, they now wished to show that they rejected the system and were therefore freely handing in their contracts. The men were effectively on strike: police moved into the town, and about a thousand men were repatriated to Ovambo.[42]

Discontent also appears to have been endemic at the compound in Katutura. In June 1971 riot police had moved into the compound in search of illegal residents, and over 500 men had been arrested. In November, compound inmates had rioted against the proposed erection of guard towers. News of the threatened strike in Walvis Bay was widely reported in the Namibian press on Sunday, 12 December, and a mass meeting in Katatura that day resulted in a strike by 5,500 men the following day—the first major walk-out of the great strike. Government officials, the headmen brought from Ovambo, tried to persude the men to return to work, pending possible discussions on reform of the contract system scheduled for February. The men, now sealed off in the compound by police, refused; they were then repatriated at their own request.

Within a week some 12,000 workers at a dozen centres were on strike, and by mid-January the number was about 13,500 at different centres. Nearly all the strikers were repatriated. The South West economy was severely affected; white office workers and schoolboys struggled to maintain emergency services, and employers made largely fruitless attempts to recruit other contract labour from places as far away as Lesotho and the North Western Cape.

The strike appeared to take the authorities by surprise, although during the course of the preceding year warning of black dissatisfaction had been issued by African leaders. The leaders of the two Lutheran Churches, which have a very large following among the Ovambos, had strongly condemned the system in an open letter to the Prime Minister of South Africa in mid-1971. The warning deserved serious attention, for the Lutheran Church in Ovambo is perhaps the one organisation in close touch with the feelings and aspirations of the Ovambo people. (It is in fact largely due to the work of the Lutheran missionary in Ovambo, Rauha Voipio, that we have even the limited authentic information on Ovambo feeling that we do. From her research, and from the few written statements of strikers themselves, it is possible to gain an idea of the Ovambos' attitude toward the contract system.)[43]

The Ovambos' word for contract is *odalate*, a corruption of the Afrikaans word *draad*, meaning wire. Ovambo workers talked in terms of being handcuffed by the contracts, whose terms were established unilaterally by the employers' agency, SWANLA. Workers entered into contracts because they had no other means of earning money. The wages themselves were so low as to be a major source of grievance. The Ovamvos objected to being recruited by SWANLA instead of being allowed freely to seek employment themselves, and were resentful of the pass laws which strictly controlled movement outside the reserve. In particular, they objected to the fact that they were compulsorily repatriated to Ovambo when their contracts expired instead of being allowed to stay in the 'white' areas to look for new work.

These were the grievances articulated by repatriated strikers who elected a strike committee and held a meeting of 3,500 men in Ovambo on 10 January 1972. Workers at the meeting described the contract as a form of slavery because blacks were 'bought' by SWANLA and forced to live in 'jail-like' compounds.[44] The meeting approved a delegation to represent the strikers at negotiations on the contract system between government employers and the Ovambo authorities at the rail-head outside Ovambo, Grootfontein, on 19 and 20 January. Just what occurred at Grootfontein is not entirely clear, but it appears that minor concessions were hammered out between white employers and the South African Department of Bantu Development, and that the revised contract terms were then submitted to the homeland leaders (and one representative of the strikers) for approval. The approval was evidently obtained, and a revised contract system was introduced.[45]

Despite the approval which had been obtained from the official African representatives, it is clear that the revised contract system differed little in essentials from the previous one.[46] The Ovambos had gone on strike in order to gain the right of freedom of movement (for themselves and their families) and a free labour market. But the government could never allow this since it ran contrary to the essentials of apartheid and the contract labour system. What the strikers obtained was the abolition of SWANLA, whose recruiting functions were henceforth to be undertaken jointly by the (white) South West administration, the Department of Bantu Administration, and the homeland government (still largely run by white officials). It is arguable that this was a retrogressive step from the Ovambo point of view, since the Ovambo authorities would themselves now have to shoulder the burden of administering a system largely unchanged from SWANLA times, and apparently just as unpopular. The major concessions to the strikers were that contract workers could renew their contracts with the same employer at the place of work instead of automatically being repatriated to their homeland at expiration. They were also apparently given to understand that they could terminate their contracts by giving in their notice and then looking for other jobs in the same area without being first compulsorily repatriated, as happened under SWANLA. However, conditions were laid down before a worker could legitimately give notice to end the contract; any failure to meet these conditions meant that a worker would be viewed as being illegally in the area concerned, and liable to summary repatriation. Should the worker succeed in meeting these conditions, then under the Employment Bureaux Regulations of 30 March 1972 he was required to register at an employment bureau within 72 hours of becoming unemployed. These legal provisions notwithstanding, when the contract system was revised (and apparently relaxed) many workers were under the impression that they could go south on contract and that if they were not satisfied with their jobs, leave them, and freely seek better jobs.[47] Employers, and farmers in particular, were seriously affected as workers attempted to do this. Desertions from farms have been widespread as Africans have moved to the towns in search of better-paid jobs in commerce, industry, and the public sector.[48]

However, it was far from the intention of the revised system to allow such a state of affairs and controls were consequently made much more rigorous,[49] especially controls of 'deserters'—workers who were alleged to have broken contract—and police action resulted in quite large numbers of Ovambos being expelled from the 'white' areas. In addition, it was stipulated that in the event of desertion by an Ovambo contract worker, the Ovambo Legislative Council would refund to the employer the recruiting costs and then recover the money from the deserter.[50] The functions of SWANLA were also in effect revived by the formation of employers' associations after the strike with the purpose of combining to offer uniform wage rates to recruited workers. In February 1972 for example, a committee of the principal employers in Windhoek was formed to eliminate wage competition in commerce. Similarly, farmers formed an association in March to handle recruiting and ensure uniformity of wage rates. Despite all the attempts to restore in effect the pre-strike system, it was reported in March 1973 that the contract system was by no means operating efficiently.[51] Farmers in particular were suffering a serious shortage of labour.

On 20 March 1973 a secret meeting of the SWA and SA Administration and employers was held in Windhoek to tighten controls even further. In future deserters and vagrants are to be blacklisted by both white authorities and homeland governments. The implication is presumably that they will be permanently deprived of employment opportunities. The meeting also establised an all-white advisory and co-ordinating committee to eliminate bottlenecks and problems in the labour system.

Nevertheless, the strike did partially achieve one objective: some wage rates were revised. According to official sources, black wages have risen by between 66 per cent and 100 per cent since the strike.[52] Other sources have found wages as low as R4.50 a month for shepherds, and between R6 and R8.50 a month on farms. In the hotel industry they range between R15 and R30 a month, while the average of domestic servants in Windhoek was found by Voipio to be R22.17 a month. Unskilled construction workers get R7 to R22 a week in cash, and unskilled railway workers R6.50 a week. The USA-owned Tsumeb mine pays a minimum of about R17.60 a week.[53]

No African trade unions exist in Namibia; though they are not illegal, their formation is hardly encouraged by the authorities. The successful organisation of the strike thus relied to a great extent on an appeal to grievances which were recognised and shared by Ovambos throughout the territory.

As a result of the strike and the revised contract system, the homeland government, the Ovambo Legislative Council, is in an invidious position. Early in 1972, during the strike, there were reports from Ovambo that the kraals ('compounds') of Ovambo headmen in the area were being attacked, and rumours of widespread violence were also received from the homeland. The exact extent of this unrest was however never allowed to reach the outside world, as police were sent to the territory, emergency regulations providing for detention without trial were promulgated for Ovambo and non-officials barred from access. Hundreds of people were detained under the regulations, and some eighty people charged with offences ranging from murder and arson to robbery, assault and the possession of dangerous weapons. In the circumstances, it is impossible to say with certainty what the origin and extent of the unrest was: it may well be, as Ruaha Voipio and other church authorities have subsequently stated, that it arose from attempts by the Ovambo Legislative Council to fulfil its side of the Grootfontein agreement and enforce the 'hated system' of contract labour. Coming hard on the heels of the strike action and the meetings of strikers inside Ovambo itself, it is hard to resist the conclusion that the widespread discontent articulated in the course of the strike had spilled over into the homeland itself. It can be suggested that the strike had the effect of politicising the strikers and, once arrived back in the territory, labour discontent generalised to the political level. Given the highly political context of the oppressive labour regime under which the Ovambos existed, this was perhaps inevitable. At any rate, these events have called into question both the legitimacy and effectiveness of the Ovambo Legislative Council (which consists of twenty-two traditional tribal leaders and twenty commoners, all designated by the tribal authorities). The South African authorities in the past have relied heavily, in their justification for the policy of separate development, on the claim that the Ovambos at least supported the system. These recent events suggest that this can no more be taken to be the case and that an open expression of popular wishes would find many, if not the majority of, Ovambos opposed to continued South African control of the mandated territory. The head of the Ovambo strike committee,

Johannes Nangatuuala, has formed a political party, the Democratic Co-operative Development Party in Ovambo which advocates a unitary constitution for Namibia and rejects the creation of separate independent states as envisaged by the policy of apartheid. (His party has been prohibited from holding meetings in terms of the emergency regulations.) And, perhaps more indicative of the mood of workers within the territory, a riot broke out in the Katutura contract labour compound in March 1973, fourteen months after the Ovambo strike. Workers in the compound, who appear this time to have consisted not only of Ovambos, but also Kavangos, shouted down a Kavango homeland government representative who had come to support the proposal by the South African Government for a multi-racial advisory council for Namibia. Workers caused damage to the compound estimated at R20,000 and reportedly destroyed records kept on contract workers.

It is clear that the contract system is operating far from smoothly and it seems doubtful whether it will ever work properly again. Since the strike, the situation in Namibia has been complicated by other developments. In the first place, political consciousness appears to have been generally heightened, and partly to have manifested itself in opposition to the Ovambo Legislative Council. Secondly, the greater attention which SWA is receiving from the United Nations both limits options open to the South African Government and appears to increase options open to black Namibians.

Discussion and conclusions

It is as yet too soon to assess whether recent stirrings among the black proletariat of this region presage an enduring and effective movement of blacks to make use of collective labour action to further their position. So often in the past have blacks mustered an impressive show of collective solidarity, only for it to peter out in the face of police repression on the one hand and minor concessions on the other. Certainly some concessions have been wrung from the white oligarchy: wages have risen considerably for relatively large sections of the black labour force (accompanied, it would seem, by reductions in black employment levels in many firms). Many employers have been brought to realise that previous treatment of their black staff left much to be desired, and the numerous conferences, symposia and employer statements of policy testify to a certain crisis of conscience. Finally, the government has revised the twenty-year-old Bantu Labour (Settlement of Disputes) Act; something which seemed inconceivable even a few months before the strikes.[54] The amended Act now grants legal strike rights to some African workers under conditions partly modelled on those enjoyed by the rest of the labour force. (Briefly, Africans may now strike if they are not employed in 'essential' services or by local authorities; if the matter giving rise to the dispute is not covered by a wage determination less than a year old, or by a current industrial council agreement; if the matter has not been referred to the Wage Board for attention; if the dispute has been referred to a 'liaison' (see below) or works committee, where one exists, or to a Bantu Labour Officer where one does not, and where thirty days have elapsed since notice was given of a dispute.) It is to be doubted whether these cumbersome strike provisions will in fact function successfully, or that they will be satisfactory to the workers concerned. They are, after all, modelled on the provisions first introduced for white, Indian and Coloured workers in 1924 in the aftermath of the 1922 strike, when white labour was unable to prevent this emasculation of its strike rights. In addition it is by no means clear at the moment whether urban contract workers fall under these provisions, and other categories of workers such as agricultural and domestic workers definitely do not. The existence of even these limited strike rights does, however, hold out promise for a certain legal shelter for some groups of African workers whose interest in trade union activity seems to be growing. The amended Act also gives greater encouragement to the formation of committees representing workers in individual plants. Most emphasis has however been placed on the new concept of 'liaison' committees, which are joint employer/employee bodies likely to be dominated by the former, though works committees consisting only of workers must be formed if the workers themselves ask for it, and no liaison committee exists. Finally, the Act provides that for the first time Africans may sit on industrial councils to represent African worker interests—though not as an automatic right, and these Africans are designated by Regional Bantu Labour Boards.[55] These are still important changes of principle in legislation which originally was modelled on what even for the National Party were ultra-paternalistic lines. Thus both employers and government now seem more open to the idea of institutionalising black workers' demands, and creating means whereby a more adequate response can be made. At this micro level, the prospect is not altogether inconceivable that change will ramify throughout the system and in its course bring about a degree of incorporation of the urban African worker into industrial relations decision-making at the level of factory, industrial council and so on.

But the short-run gains remain of problematic value and the most significant longer-term effect of recent events would seem to lie not with the adjustments made by whites but in the renewed sense of solidarity among urban black workers. The strikes themselves have acted as a demonstration of grievances which employers were not willing to recognise until the workers themselves took action. For the most part the strikes were of short duration, and hardly at all resolved into a trial of strength between employers and workers. The relative success of the strikes as a demonstration leaves open the question of collective labour activity in circumstances where workers face a choice between complete capitulation to employers and a prolonged trial of strength. The issue thus needs to be raised of the prospect for a more permanent basis for African labour organisation. The survey material referred to earlier (see note 21) suggests that until the strikes at least African workers did not view an important collective goal to be the establishment of the power of African labour in the medium to long run. It is, however, possible that the strikes have changed this position. What would now be necessary would be an investigation into what African workers perceive the costs of such more permanent labour organisation to be. Such costs are likely to include worker perceptions of what resources (time, money, leadership, personnel) are available from within their own ranks, and what the response of employers and the authorities to such attempts to strengthen African labour power might be. On the latter score, workers may consider that attempts to institutionalise labour activity could be to give hostages to fortune. Leadership which in the strikes was effective because it was informal and not visible to employers and the state, may find itself rendered ineffective if it emerges to view in the form of articulate workers' representatives in trade unions and works' committees.

While the lessons of experience have undoubtedly not been lost on black workers, no clear workers' ideology has shown signs of emerging. It may well be, as young militant black intellectuals have claimed, that:

> The classical western elements of trade unionism have had to be modified to accommodate the fact that black worker interests extend beyond the factory; they extend to the ghetto where black workers stay together in hostels under squalid conditions; to the crowded trains and buses that carry workers in and out of town often at the risk of serious accidents; to the absence of amenities for black workers in and around town; to the stringent, irksome and humiliating application of influx control laws that result in a lot of blacks losing their job opportunities. . .[56]

Such a stance places African collective labour action once again squarely within its political context. It is indeed hard to see how such linkage of economic and broader political issues can be avoided in the long run, hazardous for the proponents of this stance as it may be. Here the possibility is raised of a renewed direct connection of African political movements and worker action, propagated by radicals for much of this century. Inevitably then much will depend on events in the political arena, both within and outside South Africa.

On a final very speculative note, we conclude that recent events suggest two possibilities inherent in the situation. On the one hand, greater willingness of government and employers to respond to black workers' interests could result in the creation of linkages across the major line of conflict in South Africa, and steer the colour/class conflict on the level of the urban black worker into a pattern of fairly constrained, institutionalised bargaining, with political issues deferred for some time, or contained within the limits at present set by government policy. Both sides may see something to be gained hereby; in particular urban Africans may obtain real material improvements. On the other hand, the strikes and African assertiveness may prove to have had only minimal influence on improving the lot of the black urban masses, while stimulating the growth of working class solidarity. The pattern exemplified by recent events could continue and intensify. Periodic build-ups of popular grievance and hostility could recur, to be expressed in large-scale strikes and could move political issues to the forefront. Police action may be less restrained if the authorities perceive that strike action is likely to become repetitious, and to contain a challenge to the system. Within these two schematic alternatives would seem to lie the course of African collective labour action for the immediate future.

NOTES

1. Appreciation is expressed by the other contributors to Jeff Lever who collated the material and was the editor of the paper.
2. See, for example, H. Adam, *Modernising Racial Domination*, Berkeley: University of California Press, 1971, pp. 153–5; F. A. Johnstone, 'White Prosperity and White Supremacy in South Africa Today', *African Affairs*, 69(275), 1970, pp. 132–3.
3. See, for example, M. C. O'Dowd, *The Stages of Economic Growth and the Future of South Africa*, Johannesburg, n.d.
4. R. A. and H. J. Simons, *Class and Colour in South Africa, 1850–1950*, Penguin, 1969, p. 625.
5. J. A. Horner, *Black Pay and Productivity in South Africa*, South African Institute of Race Relations, Johannesburg, 1972, p. 3. (£1 = R1.70 approx.)
6. *Wage Survey 1971–1972*, Productivity and Wage Association, Johannesburg, 1971, p. 3.
7. *A Survey of Race Relations in South Africa, 1971*, S.A.I.R.R., 1972, Johannesburg, p. 179.
8. *Rand Daily Mail*, 13 Mar. 1973.
9. See, for example, L. E. Cortis *et al.*, *The Utilisation of Bantu Labour in the*

Building Industry, National Development Fund for the Building Industry, Johannesburg, 1962, p. 79.

10. For an extensive survey of the position of migrant workers, see F. Wilson, *Migrant Labour*, Spro-Cas, Johannesburg, 1972.

11. See *A Survey of Race Relations in South Africa 1973*, S.A.I.R.R., 1973, Johannesburg, p. 279.

12. J. Rex, 'The Plural Society: the South African Case', *Race*, 12 (4), 9971, pp. 408–9; S. Trapido, 'South Africa in a Comparative Study of Industrialisation', *Journal of Development Studies*, 7 (3), 1971, p. 319.

13. See, for example, A. Spandau, 'South African Wage Board Policy: An Alternative Interpretation', *S.A. Journal of Economics*, 40 (4), 1972.

14. See *Annual Reports of Department of Labour*, and statement of Minister of Labour, *Rand Daily Mail*, 7 June 1973.

15. S. W. Johns, 'Trade Union, Political Pressure Group, or Mass Movement? The Industrial and Commercial Workers' Union of Africa', in R. I. Rotberg and A. A. Mazrui (eds), *Protest and Power in Black Africa*, Oxford University Press, 1970.

16. See E. Roux, *Time Longer than Rope*, University of Wisconsin Press, 1964, and R. A. and H. J. Simons, *Class and Colour . . .*

17. E. Feit, *Urban Revolt in South Africa*, Northwestern University Press, 1971, pp. 163–6.

18. J. Lever, 'Bringing in the Black Worker', *New Nation*, November 1972.

19. See, for example, TUCSA, *Special Conference Report 1967*, p. 31.

20. Johnstone, 'White Prosperity . . .', p. 130.

21. *Editors' note:* We very much regret that restrictions on space have made it necessary to delete a section of this paper reporting on survey evidence. Published data can be found in: M. Brandel-Syrier, *Reeftown Elite*, Routledge and Kegan Paul, 1971; M. L. Edelstein, *What do Young Africans Think?*, S.A.I.R.R., Johannesburg, 1972; P. Mayer, *Urban Africans and the Bantustans*, S.A.I.R.R., Johannesburg, 1972; and T. T. Durand, *Swarzman, Stad and Toekoms*, Drakensberg Publications, 1971. In addition one of the co-authors of the paper, L. Schlemmer, conducted a survey in Durban in 1971–72 covering 350 African workers. Referring only to the section of the survey concerning the evaluation of class consciousness, the authors conclude '. . . the results suggest that *two out of three* or slightly more Africans in Durban see themselves as seriously deprived of opportunity and fair wages. . . . Roughly *one out of three* Africans have an orientation which would approximate to what one would expect of "a class for itself"—a consciousness of shared economic and political interests and of the need for solidarity. While *one out of two* Africans (or somewhat more) seem to recognise the

potential economic leverage which overwhelming dependence on them for labour imparts, only *one in ten* would publicly translate this into action.' The authors caution us that the survey was conducted before the wave of strikes in 1972 and suggest that 'during and after the strikes popular attitudes among urban Africans may have changed considerably'. They nonetheless consider that the attitudes they report 'might also mean that labour action might be limited to a temporary manifestation of intense frustration at a given point in time in the sense that the political and economic background, as well as attitudinal factors, discourage a sustained development of worker consciousness'. Clearly this contentious area of debate is of crucial significance for the future development of black working class action in South Africa. *R.S.* and *R.C.*

22. Information from trade union officials and industrial council agents.
23. See TUCSA, *Annual and Special Conference Reports*, 1967/1969.
24. See here also B. A. Khoapa (ed.), *Black Review 1972*, Black Community Programmes, Durban, 1973, pp. 120–5.
25. Workers committees do, however, lack explicit organisational structure; like formal membership records, subscriptions and so forth. The latter have been found effective in engaging greater membership involvement than otherwise was the case.
26. Khoapa, *Black Review . . .*, pp. 114–16.
27. *Rand Daily Mail*, 9 June 1973.
28. *An Assessment of the work-to-rule carried out by Stevedores in Cape Town during October and November 1972*, Economic and Wage Commission, Students' Representative Council, University of Cape Town, 1973.
29. *A Survey of Race Relations in South Africa 1969*, p. 112; also same source for 1972, p. 325.
30. *Financial Gazette*, 19 Jan. 1973.
31. An important factor in the earlier dock-workers dispute, and also in the later brick-workers' strike which sparked off the whole strike wave.
32. Conditions which marked in particular the textile industry, especially hard hit by strikes in January and February.
33. PWA *Wage Survey . . .*
34. *Rand Daily Mail*, 13 Feb. 1973.
35. *Rand Daily Mail*, 29 Mar. 1973.
36. On Central Administration Services, see L. Douwes Dekker, *Management*, June 1973, p. 8.
37. *Rand Daily Mail*, 11 June 1973.
38. *Supplement* to *Financial Mail*, 2 Mar. 1973.
39. *Sunday Times*, 13 Feb. 1972.

40. *Windhoek Advertiser*, 10 Dec. 1971.
41. See generally *South West Africa—a labour repressive society*, NUSAS Press Digest, Feb. 1972.
42. For this and following two paragraphs, see generally J. S. Kane-Berman, *Contract Labour in South West Africa*, S.A.I.R.R., Johannesburg, 1972; *A Survey of Race Relations in South Africa 1972*.
43. Rauha Voipio, *Kontrak—Soos die Owambo dit sien* (Evangelical Lutheran Ovambokavango Church and Evangelical Lutheran Church, 1972); same author, *Die Arbeidsituasie in Suidwes-Afrika*, S.A.I.R.R., Johannesburg, 1973.
44. The minutes of the meeting appear in Kane-Berman, *Contract Labour* . . .
45. *Windhoek Advertiser*, 21 Jan. 1972.
46. Details of the contracts appear in Kane-Berman, *Contract Labour* . . .
47. *Financial Mail*, 25 Aug. 1972.
48. *Financial Mail*, 23 Mar. 1973.
49. *Rand Daily Mail*, 17 Aug. 1972.
50. Labour Enactment for Ovambo, *Government Gazette*, 18 Aug. 1972.
51. *Financial Mail*, 23 Mar. 1973.
52. *Financial Mail*, 25 Aug. 1972.
53. *Financial Mail*, 19 Jan. 1973.
54. *House of Assembly Debates*, June 1973.
55. Provisions of the Bantu Labour Relations Regulation Amendment Bill (A.B. 71–73).
56. Khoapa, *Black Review* . . ., p. 45.

Socialist Development
and the
Workers in Tanzania

M. A. BIENEFELD

This paper discusses the role of Tanzania's labour movement in the drive to development. Since here there can be no useful distinction between economic and political issues, no such distinction is made. At the same time it is considered essential that, in order to interpret particular developments as either leading to genuine progress or as presaging a deepening contradiction, labour's role be discussed within the context of a specific conception of the development problem.

The discussion which follows is based on the conclusion that development strategies relying on foreign private investment will at best produce 'growth without development'.[1] This implies fitful (occasionally sustained) growth in GDP accompanied by: stable or widening income differentials, and often the absolute impoverishment of substantial sectors of the population; a substantial and probably increasing outflow of surplus; production with low local value added content and a related rapid increase in import requirements; distortions in internal factor prices and the inhibition or destruction of domestic productive activity and initiative; the imposition of severe constraints on domestic policy due to the demands of 'financial responsibility' and the great sensitivity of foreign capital to 'the investment climate'; the formation of an administrative/ managerial group whose cultural and economic ties are externally oriented and whose local power is, in the face of the above developments, increasingly based on repression and counterinsurgency. To escape this pathological condition it is ultimately necessary to make a break with foreign capital from private sources and to focus development on the mobilisation of local resources to meet local needs. In this process one must recognise that the 'divorce between production and distribution policies is false and dangerous' and that 'the distribution policies must be built into the very pattern and organisation of production.'[2]

This does not imply autarchy. Trade would and could take place and technology would be assimilated as quickly as possible, but in the context of a nationally controlled economy.

Such an alternative strategy does not in and of itself say very much about the pace of development that could be achieved with its implementation. This would ultimately depend on the size and resource endowment of the nation in question; on the cultural and ideological base on which it was built; on the existing technological base; and on the possibility of effective economic integration on the basis of approximate equality. These factors may merely determine the rate of growth attainable. Alternatively, they may pose the question as to the point in time, or the level of the development of the productive forces, at which such an alternative strategy becomes clearly superior. If one argues that such an alternative must wait, one implies that peripheral capitalism is developing conditions on the basis of which a socialist strategy can later be more advantageously launched. Against this there is the possibility that the passage of time makes such a transition more difficult. It will become clear that this issue is crucial to an assessment of the Tanzanian experience.

After independence 'African Socialism' was the code word for the alternative to colonial and capitalist exploitation. It held a promise of growth, independence and development on a broad front. It was the pledge of those who had been carefully 'entrusted' with the new administrations. Yet for most it was sheer rhetoric. African Socialism was and 'is a relatively empty ideological vessel'.[3] The constraints of the past and the temptations of the present have conspired to keep it drained.

Tanzania, too, is not a socialist country, and yet it would be wrong to conclude that its commitment is purely rhetorical, though this is undoubtedly true of the commitment of individual members of its government. The truth is that though little has been done in the way of 'building socialism', options have been kept open through curbing certain kinds of development. Against enormous odds the question of a socialist alternative has been kept on the agenda.[4]

> Men make their own history, but they do not make it just as they please;
> they do not make it under circumstances chosen by themselves, but under
> circumstances directly encountered, given and transmitted from the past.[5]

For Tanzania it was a bitter legacy. Tanganyika began its independent existence in 1961 with one of the least formally educated populations in Africa; a miniscule industrial sector; a high dependence on trade in a few primary products; a small and exclusive Asian community in control of what local business there was; and close ties to the old colonial power. It was not a propitious beginning.

Socialism was hardly conceivable under these conditions. After all, in the original conception, the dialectic of history would produce the socialist transformation only when the forces of production had been raised to a very high level through capitalist accumulation. Yet Nyerere has been emphatic in denying that a country like Tanzania 'can only become socialist if it first goes through the stage of capitalism',[6] and in this he may well be right, especially in view of the limited accumulation possible under the distorted peripheral capitalism open to such nations. In any case whether socialism is possible in Tanzania 'is not a question of theory but is a practical question. In practice man must prove the truth.'[7] That is the challenge for Tanzania.

While Mao-tse-tung 'proved the truth' of the assertion that the proletariat need not be the dominant revolutionary force in a preindustrial situation, the political position of the wage earners remains of great importance in a situation where the economic, and hence the political, centre of gravity lies emphatically in a distinct 'modern' sector. The labour force, by virtue of its importance to that sector, occupies an important and sensitive position. If it accepts 'junior partner' status, by behaving in the manner of a 'labour aristocracy', then any challenge to the modern sector and its hegemony becomes infinitely more difficult.

Clearly, wage earners have seldom seriously challenged the ruling elites of post-independence Africa. This has been a consequence of the inevitable weakness of movements whose membership has been unstable, unskilled and uneducated, and whose leadership has been careerist and upwardly mobile, though these attributes are no longer as widespread as they once were. The workers' quiescence has been further related to the ability and interest of the modern-sector firms to pay *relatively* high wages, a fact which gains in importance the more precariously the wage earners are suspended above a great mass of dispossessed lumpenproletariat.

The bureaucrats of international capitalism naturally seek to guarantee the continuation of this quiescence—hence the intensive efforts of national and international unions to create 'responsible' (i.e. business) unions in the new nations of Africa.[8] Hence also the occasional outright support of such unions by international firms, often against the vehement opposition of what local expatriate capital there was.[9] As George Orwell's 'Big Brother' had learned:

to keep [the proles] in control was not difficult. . . . [No] attempts were made to indoctrinate them with . . . ideology . . . [for] it was not desirable that the proles should have strong political feelings . . . [Hence] even when they became discontented, as they sometimes did, their discontent led nowhere, because being without general ideas, they could only focus it on petty specific grievances.[10]

Such manipulative quiescence is, however, constantly threatened by the consequences of the orthodox development strategies described. As Nyerere has said,

> . . . the perpetuation of capitalism, and its expansion to include Africans, will be accepted by the masses . . . for a time. . . But, sooner or later, the people will lose their enthusiasm and will look upon the independence Government as simply another new ruler.[11]

When this happens the people may 'sink back into apathy' or they may come to oppose their rulers. In either case, the threat is formidable, for in Nyerere's words 'without political stability African countries will remain the playthings of others'.[12] The cruel dilemma is that the need for unity may make even a progressive leadership eschew all confrontation with conservative sections of the ruling group, and thereby precipitate that much more fundamental split between the mass of the people and their leaders. It is then that the rulers become the 'playthings of others' with a vengeance. Without the support of the masses and hence increasingly without the capacity to mobilise their energies for development, such elites survive by selling off the country's resources, including cheap labour. In return they receive an income, and aid and assistance to avert instability. Usually this requires increasing amounts of repression; direct military rule is the frequent result. In Tanzania, a growing awareness of these developments and their inevitability led to the serious espousal of a socialist alternative. The relationship between this initiative and the labour movement is something whose significance can be appreciated only in its historical context.

In the struggle for independence there had been very close links between Tanganyika's Federation of Labour (TFL) and African National Union (TANU), so much so that Nyerere has spoken of a transfer of funds 'from the political wing to the industrial wing of the same nationalist movement'.[13] However, with the achievement of that unifying objective this harmony quickly broke down. The source of conflict lay in the fact that the new government accepted that it 'had no choice but to accept a major dependency upon Britain and largely continue the policies which the first TANU government had inherited from the colonial regime'.[14] Not surprisingly, the unions soon found themselves in opposition to 'their own' government, with the pace of prospective Africanisation as the major immediate issue. Certainly this was an emotive issue with a racist tinge in reaction to the racist reality that was the colonial legacy. Certainly it was an issue that was used by opportunist scramblers who sought high positions for themselves. But just as certainly it was an issue which contained within it the most fundamental questions of development strategy. It was possibly that consciousness 'which fails *subjectively* to reach its self-appointed goals, while furthering and realising the *objective* aims of society of which it is ignorant and which it did not choose'.[15]

Initially, Nyerere met this demand head-on. In the pre-independence Legislative Council he ridiculed his 'Hon. Friends who have been pushing us to Africanise in six weeks' and who were thus flattering the colonial administration to think that 'they had trained all the people that we needed'. But this, he added, was far from the truth. Though they would work to make 'the composition of the civil service . . . broadly reflect the racial pattern of the territory's population'. this could happen only in the long term, 'and I want to emphasise the phrase "in the long term" '.[16] Of course, this acceptance of the need for a long apprenticeship involved the crucial assumption that this apprenticeship is best served at the feet of the former master and his ilk. But to counter this implicit assumption would have required an ideological clarity which its opponents did not possess.

As an astute and principled politician Nyerere realised that to win on this issue was not the point. He had said often enough that 'if there is opposition we should try to persuade the people rather than to force them', and so in January 1962 he resigned as head of the government in order to 'undertake my new task—that of taking part in the building of a new TANU'. This would be a TANU which would mobilise the people, and bridge the dangerous distance between them and their rulers. By 1963 the government had broadly rationalised its policies, though unfortunately there were few changes in substance.

On the industrial relations front it launched a three-pronged attack on the dissident unions: it laid the legal basis in 1962 for state control of union activity by making strikes effectively illegal and by providing for the registration of all trade unions, subject to their compliance with certain regulations; it established and raised minimum wages for many workers and introduced severance pay, in recognition of 'the increasing dependence on wages as the sole source of livelihood';[17] finally, it clarified its Africanisation policy by introducing formal 'high level manpower planning', though this did little more than specify the length of the apprenticeship that Tanzania would have to serve (18 years), without querying the underlying principles. The ship of state had been launched in a turbulent sea. Now everyone was aboard, the sails were trimmed and the bow pointed. Those who had questioned the direction of the voyage, if only indirectly, had been silenced, but their fears would come to haunt the ship again.

The development strategy that had emerged was presaged in a paper written by Nyerere before independence. This asserted that the early years of independence would bring an extraordinary demand for foreign investment because the task of closing the socio-economic gap between the different races and communities could not wait.[18] But, while one may expect foreign investment to contribute to growth, it is sheer naivety to expect it to contribute to a narrowing of differentials. It was a crucial point of confusion.

It may be of course that, in the circumstances, Tanzania adopted the only feasible policy—that in places 'too small to enable a viable industry to be set up . . . development necessarily had to be carried out along the lines laid down under the colonial administration'.[19] But even in small countries one must ask whether the short-term gains of such a policy are offset by long-term losses. One's answer to this question depends on how one assesses the contribution of private foreign investment; on the importance one attaches to capital *per se* as the prime mover of development; on the extent to which one focuses attention on the productive capacity of manpower, and especially on its cumulative ability to produce capital *if* it can be mobilised. It depends also on one's conception of the effectiveness with which orthodox educational structures, those utilised in the training and upgrading of skilled manpower, do in fact transmit useful skills; and on whether one believes that expertise at the top is more important than mass enthusiasm and commitment, for by planning the former you may forfeit the latter.

Tanzania has squandered much of the enthusiasm of the masses which did exist at independence. The question arises as to whether this could have been avoided by using the call for Africanisation from the trade unions in a progressive way and by channelling it into a policy of decentralised socialism based on citizenship, not on race. Undoubtedly such a policy would have entailed a certain amount of retrenchment in the 'modern'-sector economy. But at the same time it would have allowed its reorganisation, and might have cut imports dramatically while having little effect on exports. But it is idle to speculate further in such an ahistorical manner. The issue is raised only because more recently the government has recognised the need to move in some such direction, while it is not at all clear whether such a move is now more or less difficult than it would have been at that time. In any event such an alternative was not considered by a leadership which did not at that time see the need for such a break; which had been entrusted with power, at least in part, because it had made clear its belief in the possibility of development within the existing structures; and which was working with a civil service staffed by ex-colonial administrators and an army commanded by British officers. The development of neo-colonialism was not left to mere chance, after all.

Whether the socialist alternative was feasible in 1962 will never be known; the fact was that the government embarked on an orthodox path to development. Its 'African Socialism' was little more than a pious wish, sincere though it was. But this lack of substance notwithstanding, the government undoubtedly assumed that it was pursuing an optimal development strategy. Hence it informed the unions that 'the purpose of Trade Unions [is] to ensure for the workers a fair share of the profits of their labour. But a "fair" share must be fair in relation to the whole society', adding ominously that 'Trade Union leaders and their followers, as long as they are true socialists, will not need to be coerced by the government into keeping their demands within the limits imposed by the needs of society as a whole'.[20] Such threats notwithstanding and though strikes dwindled after their legal restriction,[21] the labour movement split into two groups, with one accepting the government's call for unity, and the other continuing in opposition.

An uneasy peace prevailed until January 1964, when Nyerere announced that since titles to citizenship were now clear, 'the time for . . . compromise with . . . principles has now passed' as far as civil service recruitment was concerned. Whereas previously the government had adopted a policy in which 'for both recruitment and promotion we gave Tanganyika citizens of African descent priority over other Tanganyika citizens', this would now end, since the issue of who was and who was not a citizen had been settled and 'we cannot allow the growth of first and second class citizenship'.[22] To the opposition unions this was a provocation. They had been unhappy enough with the original solution, but now they felt that even the ultimate end of producing a civil service whose composition reflected the racial composition of the country was jeopardised. They felt that, with the enormous educational advantages enjoyed by the Asian community due to the racialist educational system of the colonial period, a system of open competition in effect discriminated against the Africans. There was a 'chorus of angry protests from trade union leaders. The railway union promised to resist the policy change "at all costs", [while] the head of the local government union accused Nyerere of taking the country "back to the colonial period" '. Alluding to the heavy emphasis in Nyerere's speech, on the need to maintain the respect of the outside world, he added that 'if Tanganyika is to gain respect outside by neglecting its indigenous citizens, then we don't want that kind of respect'.

The promised confrontation was never to take place. Less than two weeks after Nyerere's announcement, the Tanzanian armed forces mutinied and imprisoned their British officers. One of their major demands was immediate Africanisation of the army. After five days of uncertainty and lawlessness, 'there were reports that trade union leaders had been meeting with the soldiers at Colito Barracks, and that the unions were planning a general strike for the weekend, in alliance with the mutineers'. At the same time there were 'reports of a plot at the town of Morogoro, headquarters of the plantation workers' union'.[23] Nyerere requested British assistance and the mutiny was put down the next day. Within a month the government had disbanded the Tanganyika

Federation of Labour, detained a number of union leaders, appointed one to a diplomatic post, and established the National Union of Tanganyika Workers (NUTA).[24] Later in the year it provided retirement benefits and additional security of employment for wage-earners.

On the whole these moves were a direct extension of the government's 1962 strategy. They completed the process of taking control of the unions, while continuing to seek to demonstrate, through the legislative provision of benefits, that the government did represent the workers' interests. There is no doubt that the peaceful dissolution of the unions was made possible by the rank and file's basic support of the government, and especially of its two most prominent leaders, Nyerere and Kawawa.[25] No doubt, too, their acceptance of governmental tutelage was influenced by the substantial benefits which the government had provided for the wage earner through legislation. At the same time such acquiescence did not imply unqualified support. In 1963 the TFL'S Grand Council had rejected a government proposal to integrate the TFL and the government,[26] and even after the take-over the workers proved restive about certain implications of government policies.

Though the establishment of NUTA eased the problem of the dissident union leaders, it would have had little effect on rank and file grievances where these existed. Nevertheless, a year after its establishment an observer noted that, 'given the amount of dissension in the old TFL and the inability of Government to control it . . . it is striking that the TANU Government now seems well in control of NUTA'.[27] This suggests that the former leaders had been the source of much dissent, in the sense that while their grievances were 'popular' with their members, they did not necessarily originate with them. Superficially, it appeared at this point that the government had successfully integrated the wage-earners into the consensus on national development.

However, new cracks would soon appear in this edifice, for the nation's development strategy was inevitably leading to a wage policy problem, a related problem of elitism, and a final problem of authoritarianism and apathy. At this point:

> The insoluble internal contradictions of the system become revealed with increasing starkness and so confront its supporters with a choice. Either they must consciously ignore insights which become increasingly urgent or else they must suppress their own moral instincts in order to be able to support with a good conscience an economic system that serves only their own interests.[28]

In Tanzania's case the reaction was increasingly to question the basic strategy. At first the response was based on the belief that in Tanzania, 'for a brief period, society's values and attitudes were in flux' and 'that, by example, by leadership and by teaching, but without coercion, Nyerere could lead his people to adopt institutions which would then bolster and reinforce rather than undermine and corrupt the social values which featured in his vision of a just society'.[29] Only slowly did this lead to the view that the formal institutions were less important than the economic base which underpinned them, and it was at this point that socialism ceased to be merely an intention. One could begin to speak of a move towards socialism.

Though labour's reactions were now obscured by the inscrutable face of NUTA, there were signs that this superficial equanimity obscured considerable discontent. A Presidential Commission appointed to investigate the new union confirmed these suspicions. The report indicted the body as inefficient, bureaucratic and irresponsible, in terms difficult to exaggerate. It spoke of 'the trend towards the disaffection of the members, and loss of enthusiasm by junior officials', and urged 'immediate steps . . . to rectify the situation'. Amid the welter of complaints about union officials and their performance, one may find charges that too much time was spent 'on political issues . . . or some other material not related to the real welfare of members', that 'Africanisation should be speeded up, and the few Africans given responsible positions should not be for "window dressing" purposes only', and that 'a number of leaders enter into suspicious relations with employers. Business is conducted in privacy, through telephone or in English, a language which most members do not understand.'[30] Such comments reflect in microcosm the problem with the entire policy, where apathy and suspicion are the natural counterpart of authoritarianism wielded in the name of expertise—an expertise whose primary function is often personal or institutional aggrandisement.

Efforts at ameliorating these conditions 'from above' simply revealed the depth of the contradiction which had produced them. The government attempted to deal, in early 1965, with the 'discontent [which] arose from the ability of the non-African employer to take decisions which vitally affected the wage-earners and in particular the right of an employer to impose summary dismissal.' At the same time it recognised the 'need to improve standards of discipline' especially 'at a time when a number of wage-earners thought Uhuru would mean restrictions on the right of their largely non-African supervisors and employers to impose disciplinary penalties'. The proposed answer was the establishment of workers' committees, which were to review and have the right to veto any dismissals from employement. Thy were 'to give wage-earners a measure of control over decisions which were previously the prerogative of their employers'.[31] But in a poor country the need for increasing production is great, and production was deemed the responsibility of management. Hence the latter's needs were given priority, and 'the workers' committees tended to be instruments of the employers for keeping the workers down'. The National Development Corporation (NDC), ostensibly representing the national interest in the industrial sphere, commented that 'the workers' committee deals mainly with discipline. It does not deal with politics or personnel policy or even with other aspects of management. . . . Experience has proved that a well-used committee can be a useful tool of good management.'[32]

Naturally, a statement that such committees 'can be a useful tool of good management' is highly ambiguous, the ambiguity arising out of the difficulty of defining what is 'good management', which in turn depends on what one expects from the managerial function. Thus, one expects management to make efficient use of factors of production so as to maximise the production of wealth relative to the resources consumed. In this respect, the 'expert' managers perform quite well, though their contribution is dramatically reduced by their own cost.[33] Furthermore, the cultural and socio-economic chasm between them and their employees, and the fact that they are foreign and racially distinct in a postcolonial situation, means that they are forced to rely heavily on authoritarian methods to achieve an acceptable level of efficiency. This virtually excludes the possibility of creating employment in the context of a community where the employment nexus extends beyond the Friday pay packet, and where performance is guided by a sense of involvement and buttressed by the communal pressures of one's peers. However, these excluded alternatives not only raise the question of what is 'good management' at the level of factor efficiency; their importance becomes dominant when one considers the effect on the development effort in a broader sense. Development is *not* about producing more. Development is about creating more productive communities.

It goes without saying that such managerial alternatives are not easily created. They are certainly not created by simply Africanising present posts. They are also not created by concern about conditions at the place of work alone. They are created, if at all, 'from below', by politically educated workers.

In Tanzania the limitations of the orthodox development strategy were gradually recognised. On one hand the defection of African leaders into the mental and socio-economic world of international capitalism indicated that it was increasingly unrealistic to think in terms of Africans, or even citizens, as a group closing the socio-economic gap between themselves and other groups. On the other hand it was realised that the wage earners as a group had at least partially been 'bought' by successive wage increases, seriously worsening the rural-urban imbalance. At the same time foreign investment had fallen far short of the First Five Year Plan's expectations, and it was recognised that this was related to Tanzania's foreign and domestic policies. The government's options were narrowing.

By late 1966 the government was ready to act. By the end of 1967 a more or less coherent alternative set of policies had been formulated and enacted, though these too bore within them contradictions that would eventually force their own resolution.

These new set of policies revolved around the inhibition of widening income differentials, the discouragement of the growth of a self-serving elite, and the seizure of control of major sectors of the economy.[34] Naturally these aims were interrelated. On the income issue there were substantial salary cuts for government leaders and civil servants, the introduction of a national incomes policy designed to keep the rural-urban differential from widening and to relate wage increments to productivity, and the alignment of parastatal and civil service salaries. Though these changes helped to undercut the consolidation of an elite, the adoption of the leadership code of the 'Arusha Declaration' was of special significance here. Under it, government and party leaders were forbidden to accept directorships, receive second salaries, hold shares in a company, or own houses for rental. Finally on the economic front the government acquired controlling shares in many industries, nationalised (with compensation) the banks, and established a Tanzanian Central Bank. Simultaneously the government was at pains to point out that while 'we have rejected the domination of private enterprise . . . we shall continue to welcome private investment in all those areas not reserved for Government in the Arusha Declaration'.

In practice the newly nationalised industries were largely left in the hands of foreign managers, except in cases like the banks where the former owners refused to co-operate. In most enterprises there was thus little obvious change, and worse still, there was often little or no fundamental change. It is by now a commonplace that 'a combination of minority share-holding with a management contract is a frequent occurrence. Such a combination allows for minimum financial risk and maximum effective control'[35] by the managers.

In industrial relations the government proceeded cautiously. It suggested that the report on NUTA was one-sided, though it acknowledged the existence of a problem. It rejected the major recommendation of the report—to make the post of Secretary General elective—and took little corrective action in response to the serious problems exposed. The reason was undoubtedly its awareness that under the new policies control of trade unionism would be of particular importance, and this control would have to be maintained in the face of severe wage restriction.

Thus the government announced that

. . . there is a change in the role of trade unionism brought about by the new policy of Socialism based on Self-Reliance. Under a colonial administration, even for as long as a system of unrestricted capitalism and private enterprise survived under an independent Government, the labor movement was justified in making profits the basis for higher wage claims. But Socialism now means centralised planning for economic and social development with resulting benefits spread equally throughout all sectors of the community: it does not mean freedom for the trade union movement, or any other organisation or institution, to pursue group or sectional interests to the possible detriment of others.[36]

Of course, in essence, this appeal was precisely the same as that which had been launched under the earlier phase of development. Indeed, it was the same appeal that is launched by *all* governments on the assumption that the *status quo* is essentially fair and just. Here, as elsewhere, the workers had to decide whether the claim was rhetoric, or whether it was 'true'.

Undoubtedly the new policies reawakened popular enthusiasm for the government. But for the workers in particular the euphoria soon waned, owing to the negligible changes effected on the day to day working of industry. Once again local control of industry was anticipated in vain, and once again the issues of Africanisation, equality and dignity became foci of frustration. By 1968 NDC's own paper reported that 'even the casual newspaper reader can hardly help noticing that the way in which large enterprises are managed and organised has become a major topic of public interest.'[37]

Early in 1970 the President addressed the issue. A circular was published, arguing that 'given a proper work environment, the majority of workers can become more creative and produce more'; that 'workers are not just a "factor of production"—they ought to be treated as the very purpose of production'; and 'that industrial discipline can be meaningful only when all involved know fully what, why and how production is carried out.' It suggested that workers' councils be established in each enterprise. In view of the earlier difficulties of enforcing a small and well specified encroachment on management's prerogatives with the introduction of workers' committees, this general and necessarily unspecific exhortation was unfortunately doomed to die in a welter of 'good intentions'. After all, conditions on the factory floor had been little affected by intervening events.

To make matters worse, the structure of the councils gave management 'a surprisingly dominant role' and thus raised the question of whether this was 'a genuine way of bringing the workers to the force of decision-making processes'.[38] It was not: but it did stimulate a very revealing debate.

What this debate revealed was the impossibility of meeting such a demand within the existing structure of Tanzanian industry.[39] Thus NDC officials and managers acknowledged the dismal record in integrating Tanzanians into decision-making even at the managerial level. They called on firms to expand career development programmes 'rather than continuing to hope that their workers would be given scholarships', and themselves pointed out the problem with such suggestions, by stating that 'if top management is not enthusiastic nobody else will take it [in-service training] seriously. In short, a management development scheme which is not supported by top management is worse than none at all.' These undoubtedly accurate reflections provided some indication of the negligible extent to which these 'top managers' could effectively 'involve' their workers in the running of the firms.

Nevertheless, many managers recognised that workers' participation was an idea that could not be ignored. They realised that 'it would be the duty of management to take the initiative in order for workers to participate', and the NDC spoke of 'training areas, such as workers' participation'. One official, obviously concerned that this approach might harbour a contradiction, announced that 'in an organised and systematic manoeuvre, the industrial worker will be *subjected* to a proper socialist consciousness, thereby avoiding the danger of creating an elite in socialist Tanzania.' With such 'friends', the idea of workers' councils needed no enemies.

NDC's General Manager was vaguely optimistic because the Tanzanian workers

> come from an agricultural background. They expect therefore to participate; they are eager to learn and expect also their views to be respected. And, since industry is, for the most part, in the hands of the people, it will be easy to secure the identity of interest which was lacking in the private sector.

Unfortunately problems cannot be solved by redefining them as non-problems. Thus, the NDC management concluded that

> although most NDC companies have fulfilled the statutory requirements for the creation of workers' councils and committees, these bodies have, to a marked extent, faced disappointments, frustrations and even doubts as to the real value of the programme.

Significantly, even this level of debate was not achieved until two events had impressed a sense of urgency on those in control. From below the workers had erupted out of their lengthy silence, in response to the *TANU Guidelines*, or *Mwongozo*, provided in early 1971 by the party leadership.

Mwongozo was a further response to the deepening conviction that current development strategies were misconceived, a conviction which grew as the split between leaders and masses became more obvious. Its most poignant manifestation was possibly in those nationalised industries where the gulf between workers and managers, and that between Tanzanians and expatriates, seemed so resistant to change. Furthermore, the broad significance of this division, long accepted because of the expertise fetish of the conventional wisdom, suddenly revealed itself. In Guinea an attempted coup was foiled when the people rallied to the defence of the government; in Uganda a coup was engineered with effortless ease. The contrast could not have been more striking. The acquiescence of the masses was not enough; without their support African nations would 'remain the playthings of others'.

Mwongozo represented a major restatement of the party's view of the development problem. This view is revealed in the following excerpts:

> The greatest aim of the African revolution is to liberate the African. This liberation is not sent from heaven, it is achieved by combating exploitation, colonialism and imperialism. *Nor is liberation brought by specialists or experts.* We who are being humiliated, exploited and oppressed are the experts of this liberation . . .[T]*he necessary expertise will be obtained during the struggle itself.*
>
> . . . Our aim is to build Socialism . . . The Party has already given guidelines of Socialism in rural areas, education for self-reliance, etc. There is still the need to clarify the Party's policies on other matters, such as housing, *workers*, money and loan policies,
>
> Leadership . . . means organising people . . . we have inherited in the government, *industries* and other institutions the habit in which one may gives the orders and the rest just obey them. If you do not involve people in work plans, the result is to make them feel a national institution is not theirs, and consequently *workers adopt the habits of hired employees.*
>
> . . . There must be a deliberate effort to build equality between the leaders and those they lead. For a Tanzanian leader it must be forbidden to be arrogant, extravagant, contemptuous and oppressive. The Tanzanian leader has to be a person who respects people, scorns ostentation and who is not a tyrant.
>
> . . . For people who have been slaves or have been oppressed, exploited and humiliated by colonialism or capitalism, 'development' means 'liberation'. Any action that gives them more control of their own affairs is an action for development, *even if it does not give them better health or more bread.*[10]

In its historical context the significance of these pronouncements is clear. It was clear also to the industrial workers whose discontent now blossomed forth.

In nine months, more than 45,000 man-days were lost through strikes about arrogant and oppressive management.[41] Naturally, there were allegations of irresponsibility and sabotage and suggestions that Clause 15 of *Mwongozo* should be 'revised' or 'clarified'. Nyerere clarified it in November 1971, asserting that

> it was noteworthy that in the various strikes, workers were not demanding wage increases but protesting against the alleged unbecoming behaviour of certain people in the management and administration echelons. This is a clear indication that the workers understand the Guidelines very well. . . .[42]

Nevertheless, the need for uninterrupted production was also clear, and there were many demands that workers use the established machinery to settle their grievances. Thus, Kawawa urged workers to use this machinery while assuring them 'that they had the upper hand in solving their differences with the management'. In a direct reference to expatriate management the vice-president reiterated that

> the Government would not hesitate to expel any manager who continued to mistreat and despise workers. . . . The workers should expose such elements within their midst without fear of reprisals from the management. The Government would always stand by their side.[43]

Unfortunately the 'established machinery' had woefully broken down. NUTA was often totally ignorant of the approach of major strikes, and in some cases its representatives were shouted down amidst demands for government or TANU leaders. In the final analysis the strikes reflected not only conditions on the factory floors, but also the failure of NUTA. It is no coincidence that the secretary-general of NUTA should have been one of the people who placed at the top of his list of reasons why the workers were striking 'that some workers misinterpret Clauses 15 and 28 of the "Mwongozo" of 1971.'[44]

More recently, there have been a number of strikes concerned with wages, following increases in minimum wages and in prices introduced by the government in 1972. Discontent focused on the disturbance of differentials, especially between recently arrived and more senior workers.

The backdrop for these events was the usual rude awakening that follows the haphazard, import-substituting, branch-plant industrialisation which Tanzania had pursued. The symptoms of economic malaise were the following: a rapid rise in recurrent expenditure leading to budget deficits and an increasing dependence on external funds for development expenditure; a dramatic rise in the government debt with debt-servicing charges rising to $12\frac{1}{2}$ per cent from $9\frac{1}{2}$ per cent of the recurrent budget between 1970–71 and 1972–73; and an adverse move in the trade balance with exports increasing by three and imports by 33 per cent between 1966 and 1970.[45] The orthodox way of papering over such gaps was through an increasing inflow of foreign capital and finance, but Tanzania's refusal to countenance the internal consequences of the orthodox development strategy was inimical to this flow of funds. The choice was to 'toe the line' and produce a 'favourable investment climate', or to establish a planned economy, though this would require the mobilisation of the masses.

Unfortunately, the move to mobilise peoples' enthusiasm cannot be made easily from the top. Such an endeavour implies a certain contradiction under any circumstances, but a 'bureaucratic class ill-prepared to exemplify equality or sacrifice in a country like Tanzania, where just these norms serve as the components of a legitimating ideology, will have grave difficulty in eliciting constructive effort and self-denial voluntarily from the mass of the population'.[46] Nevertheless, the top leadership has maintained a degree of popular support and is seen by large sectors of the population as a foil to the oppressive bureaucrats they come into contact with. This raises the possibility that the masses can be mobilised over the heads of the bureaucrats; this is the task addressed by *Mwongozo*.

Paradoxically, among the reasons why the workers of Tanzania may be susceptible to such leadership is the establishment of NUTA, that moribund organisation. Its creation did successfully forestall the development of self-centred 'business' unions adapted to a capitalist economy. The worker was thus freed from the mesmerising spectacle of the perpetual competition for leadership by men who fight with promises for the spoils of office, while the bureaucratism of NUTA combined with the egalitarian inclinations of the government's top leaders, encouraged the workers to transfer their allegiance to the government. Under these circumstances there arose the possibility of resolving that 'antagonism between momentary interest and ultimate goal' which besets the workers' consciousness. Ultimately, 'the . . . victory of the proletariat can only be achieved if this antagonism is inwardly overcome.'[47]

At the same time the creation of a stable labour force with a real commitment to wage employment has been remarkably successful.[48] Whether what has been created is a proletariat is a moot point. What is true is that most wage-earners are dependent on wage employment and that they represent a stable, regular workforce. Furthermore, their ultimate interest in the abolition of capitalist relations is more evident in the neo-colonial situation, as class interest and national interest coincide on the crucial issue of the antagonistic relations between the national interest and the foreign investor. Even so, 'social consciousness lags behind social being. The objective contradictions of the *ancien régime* have to translate themselves into subjective terms, into the ideas, aspirations and passions of men in action.'[49]

Certainly the consciousness now demanded of the worker, if he is to play his historically progressive role, is more difficult to achieve than was the case of the anti-colonial solidarity whose genesis Iliffe describes so well (pp. 49–72) with respect to the early dockworkers.

It is this process which *Mwongozo* has fostered among the workers.

Few things have proved as controversial in Tanzanian towns as Clause 15 of the 'TANU Guidelines' . . . The working people seem to have found in the Clause a trump card to use in their dealings with their leaders and managers.

As regards talk of need for revision of the clause,

this is of course sheer wishful thinking; history cannot be remade. Even if alterations were made to the Clause, the spirit would never change as far as the working people are concerned.[50]

Thus 'armed with the Mwongozo, the workers appear to have gone beyond the economism of wage demands' and 'their strikes have been about and against unsympathetic management, lack of consultation, "commandism" at the work-place'.[51] It is encouraging to note that a number of the strikes concerned African managers, indicating that the workers had transcended purely racist criteria in their actions.

Tanzania's workers are not on the point of becoming a revolutionary vanguard. However, one must bear in mind that radical consciousness does not always develop gradually over time, and that in the past at the point of revolt 'consciousness has lept forward to catch up with being, and to change it'.[52] Nevertheless, the focusing of workers' attention on questions of participation and control, on questions in other words which cannot be easily accommodated within the capitalist mode of production, has pointed the way out of the impasse of capitalist development. Of Tanzania it can be said that 'in view of the great distance that the proletariat has to travel ideologically it would be disastrous to foster any illusions. But it would be no less disastrous to overlook the forces at work within the proletariat which are tending towards the ideological defeat of capitalism.'[53]

Although class consciousness is ultimately based on the rock of its objective conditions, the workers' subjective perception of these conditions is only related to, but not determined by, them. Because the workers' potentially progressive political role depends on their conscious action, the forces that shape that subjective perception of reality take on a vital importance. In Tanzania, Nyerere's leadership has been of monumental importance in just this respect.[54]

Tanzania's policy has evolved in a progressive direction in response to the contradictions which followed inevitably from its early orthodox development strategy. Because a strong leadership has been honestly committed to development on a broad front, these contradictions have been resolved in a progressive direction. Though at each stage the resolution was partial and incomplete, the question of whether more could have been done at any point is impossible to answer. Recent events indicate an awareness of the necessity of further mobilising the masses, if current contradictions are to be progressively resolved. The people have been encouraged to assert themselves. Unfortunately, when they have done so, they have often been put down: some workers have been imprisoned some students expelled or deported, some officials demoted. This has led to some recrimination, but much of this reflects a great confusion about the objective situation. The reason why the masses *must* be mobilised for a further advance towards socialism, is precisely because no faction within the elite has the power to make such a push—especially since it may involve some lag in the eonomy, or external interference of an open or covert nature. The masses, the workers, the students are not being invited to another flag-raising ceremony. They are being invited to struggle for their 'liberation'.

Worker consciousness has certainly been raised by *Mwongozo* and its aftermath. Just as certainly much remains to be done. NUTA has outlived its usefulness in its present deplorable conditions, and the time may have come to turn to more directly representative workers' organisations with a direct role in the councils of the party. Certainly worker creativity is needed in finding and establishing different relationships at the place of work; relationships which place work into the context of a community. These alternatives must be created by the workers, though they should have the full support of the government. Tanzania has reached a point at which it must surrender its aspirations, or it must rely upon its workers and peasants to a degree undreamed of in the heady days of careful, expensive and elitist high level manpower training. It is a faith that is espoused in dire need and it is a faith of which the workers themselves must ultimately 'prove the truth'.

The challenge to struggle was thrown out by *Mwongozo*. It was based on the belief 'that a free and dignified human being can work productively *without* supervision' and it was aimed at 'the worker's emancipation from the inhuman labour conditions applied by colonial and capitalist employers'.

The workers' struggle will be long and difficult, but in Tanzania they do have important allies in the government. Thus, after the spate of strikes that followed *Mwongozo*, causing much disquiet, the chairman of the Permanent Labour Tribunal announced that 'practically in all strikes investigated by us, most of the workers' grievances were found to be true.'[55] Where else could one read that?

NOTES

1. Clearly these points cannot be argued here, nor can they be established 'beyond a shadow of doubt', especially since the debate is one which affects powerful economic and political interests. They are nevertheless stated here for the sake of clarity. Those who totally disagree with these views will not, of course, find the rest of the discussion very rewarding.

2. Mabub ul Haq, 'Employment in the 1970's: A New Perspective', *International Development Review*, 4, 1971. This very interesting paper goes on to say that this fusion is at least partly achieved through an orientation in which one 'treat(s) the pool of labour as given; at any particular time it must be combined with the existing capital stock, irrespective of how low the productivity of labour or capital may be' (p. 33). Underlying this comment is the belief that in any situation people can be employed productively even without infusions of capital. It is, after all, people who create capital and in the context of the developing countries it is essential that this productive potential be harnessed at *all* levels of production.

3. W. H. Friedland, 'Basic Social Trends', in W. H. Friedland and C. G. Rosberg (eds), *African Socialism*, Stanford University Press, 1964, p. 15.

4. J. S. Saul, 'Tanzania: African Socialism in one Country', in G. Arrighi and J. S. Saul (eds), *Essays in the Political Economy of Africa*, Monthly Review Press, 1973.

5. K. Marx, 'The Eighteenth Brumaire', in K. Marx and F. Engels, *Selected Works*, vol. I, Progress Publishers, 1969, p. 398.

6. J. K. Nyerere, *Freedom and Socialism*, Oxford University Press, 1968, p. 17.

7. K. Marx, 'Theses on Feuerbach', *Works*, vol. I, p. 13.

8. The story is a familiar one. It is described in Ioan Davies, *African Trade Unions*, Penguin, 1966; J. Meynaud and A. Salah Bey, *Trade Unionism in Africa*, Methuen, 1967; Jack Woddis, *Africa: The Lion Awakes*, Lawrence and Wishart, 1961. The process itself is described in striking details in R. Radosh, *American Labour and United States Foreign Policy*, Random House, 1969, chs 10–13. Though this relates specifically to 'subversion' in European and Latin American unions, it brilliantly illuminates the motives and the methods used.

9. This process is described in detail for the Kenyan economy by A. H. Amsden, *International Firms and Labour in Kenya, 1945–1970*, Frank Cass, 1971.

10. G. Orwell, *Nineteen Eighty-Four*, Penguin, 1949, pp. 60–1.

11. Nyerere, *Freedom and Socialism*, p. 29.

12. Nyerere, Address at the University of Toronto (2 Oct. 1969).

13. Nyerere, 'The Task Ahead of Our African Trade Unions', in *Labour* (Ghana TUC Journal), June 1961, cited in Davies, *African Trade Unions*, pp. 110–11.

14. R. C. Pratt, 'Groping Forward: The Emergence of an Ideology in Tanzania, 1945–1968', unpublished manuscript, p. 6.

15. G. Lukacs, *History and Class Consciousness*, Merlin Press, 1971, p. 50.

16. Nyerere, Address to Legislative Council, 19 Oct. 1960, in Nyerere, *Freedom and Unity*, Oxford University Press, 1966, pp. 99–102.

17. The quotation is from J. C. Carlin, 'Tanzania Labour Legislation' (mimeo.), University Adult Education Centre, Dar es Salaam, 1965, p. 5. This is an excellent summary of the early development of labour legislation.

18. Nyerere, 'We cannot afford to fail', *Africa Special Report* (Dec. 1959), in *Freedom and Unity*, p. 73.

19. S. Amin, 'Externally Orientated Development—An Assessment of the Decade 1960–70 for the French-speaking Countries of West Africa', *I.D.E.P./Reproduction/202/*Dakar, 1970.

20. Nyerere, 'Ujamaa: The Basis of African Socialism', in *Freedom and Unity*, p. 169.

21. Man days lost through strikes fell from 414,474 in 1962 to 1,862 in 1965. Annual Report of the Labour Division, 1964/65, Ministry of Communications, Transport and Labour, Government Printer, Dar es Salaam, 1969, Section III, Para. 75, p. 13.

22. Nyerere, 'Tanganyika Citizenship', in *Freedom and Unity*, p. 259. The citizenship issue had been clarified on 9 Dec. 1963, with the expiration of the two-year period within which non-citizens had to decide whether they would become citizens.

23. W. E. Smith, *Nyerere of Tanzania*, Gollancz, 1973.

24. Act No. 18 of 1964, National Union of Tanganyika Workers (Establishment) Act (effective 25 Mar. 1964). The official acronym, NUTA, stresses the institution's close ties with TANU.

25. Michael Kamaliza stated that the 'massive support given to TANU and to the Head of State, President Nyerere' had enabled the establishment of NUTA, and had 'made it possible for our President to appoint the Nation's trade union leaders . . .' Kamaliza, 'Tanganyika's View of Labour's Role', *East Africa Journal*, Nov. 1964, p. 13.

26. H. Bienen, 'National Security in Tanzania after the Mutiny', *Transition*, Apr. 1965, in J. S. Saul and L. Cliffe, (eds), *Socialism in Tanzania*, vol. I, East African Publishing House, 1972, p. 221.

27. *Ibid.*, p. 221.

28. Lukacs, *History and Class Consciousness*, p. 66.

29. R. C. Pratt, 'The Cabinet and Presidential Leadership in Tanzania, 1960–1966', in Saul and Cliffe, *Socialism . . .*, vol. I, p. 237.

30. *Report of the Presidential Commission on the National Union of Tanganyika Workers*, Government Printer, Dar es Salaam, 1967, 1 para., 5, 2, para. 27, and 3, paras 3 and 5.

31. Carlin, Legislation, 20. This also provides a good summary of the conditions laid down in the Security of Employment Act, which had established the committees.

32. H. A. Mapolu, 'The Organisation and Participation of Workers in Tanzania', Economic Research Bureau Paper 72.1, Dar es Salaam, 1972, pp. 20–1. The latter citation stems from the 1970 Annual National Development Corporation Managers' Conference.

33. While it has been said that Tanzania accepts that in profit-cum-risk a yield expectation of about 25 per cent will be necessary to attract foreign investment, 'one has to conclude that some foreign firms transfer annually up to 50 per cent of their own investments abroad via more or less devious means'. A. van de Laar, 'Growth and Income Distribution in Tanzania since Independence', *East Africa Journal*, 1968, in Saul and Cliffe, *Socialism*, vol. I, p. 3.

34. For a detailed discussion of these measures, see van de Laar 'Growth and Income Distribution . . .' Consult also Government Paper No. 4 of 1967, 'Wages, Incomes, Rural Development Investment and Price Policy', Dar es Salaam; Government Printer, 1967, on the new incomes policy; 'The Arusha Declaration and TANU's Policy on Socialism and Self-Reliance', TANU, Dar es Salaam, 1967 (also in Nyerere, *Freedom and Socialism*, p. 231). See also J. K. Nyerere, 'Public Ownership in Tanzania', *The Sunday News* (12 Feb. 1967), and 'Socialism is not Racialism', *The Nationalist* (14 Feb. 1967). (These are both reprinted in *Freedom and Socialism*.)

35. van de Laar, 'Growth . . .', p. 110.

36. Government Paper No. 2 of 1967, 'Proposals of the Tanzania Government on the Recommendations of the Presidential Commission of Enquiry into the National Union of Tanganyika Workers (N.U.T.A.)', Dar es Salaam; Government Printer, 1967, para. 81.

37. *Jenga*, no. 3, 1968, p. 9.

38. *Presidential Circular No. 1 of 1970* (10 Feb. 1970). The issue of workers' councils had been raised in *The Nationalist* (9 Oct. 1969), but there had been no further activity on that front. The circular and its implementations are both fully described in an excellent summary paper by Mapolu, E.R.B. Paper 72.1, pp. 22–23.

39. All excerpts from this debate are taken from *Jenga*, 9, 1971, p. 41, and 11, 1972, pp. 38, 12, 10, 11, and the NDC, *Sixth Annual Report* (1971), p. 19.

40. *TANU Guidelines* 1971 (Dar es Salaam: Government Printer, 1971).

41. This approximate figure was computed from a list given by H. A. Mapolu, 'Labour unrest: irresponsibility or workers' revolution?' in *Jenga*, 12, 1972, pp. 20–3.

42. *The Nationalist* (18 Nov. 1971), cited in *ibid.*, pp. 21–2.

43. *Jenga*, 11, 1972, p. 37.

44. *The Daily News* (24 Aug. 1972).

45. The statistics on trade and on the national debt are taken from the same issue of *Jenga* in which Mr Jamal, the Minister of Finance, warned that 'planners must take into account increases in recurrent expenditure occurring in the two years following implementation of a development project'. As it was, Government budget deficits rose from Shs. 103 million in 1968–69, to Shs. 168 million in 1969–70, and Shs. 223 million in 1970–71. See summary of his speech in *Jenga*, 22, 1971, pp. 43–4.

46. J. S. Saul, 'Class and Penetration in Tanzania', in Cliffe and Saul (eds), *Socialism*, vol. I, p. 121.

47. Lukacs, *History and Class Consciousness*, p. 73.

48. M. A. Bienefeld, 'The Wage Earners', vol. 3, M. A. Bienefeld and R. H. Sabot, *The National Urban Mobility, Employment and Income Survey of Tanzania, 1971*, Report to the Ministry of Economic Affairs and Development Planning, Dar es Salaam, 1972.

49. I. Deutscher, *The Unfinished Revolution, Russia 1917–1967*, Oxford University Press, 1967, p. 13.

50. Mapolu, E.R.B. 72.1, p. 20.

51. P. L. Lawrence, 'Socialism, Self-Reliance and Foreign Aid in Tanzania: Some Lessons from the Socialist Experience', I.D.E.P. Seminar Paper, Dar es Salaam, 1972, p. 19.

52. Deutscher, *Unfinished Revolution*, p. 13.

53. Lukacs, *History and Class Consciousness . . .*, p. 80.

54. There has recently been a 'fashionable' reaction away from Nyerere by many leftists. This has been based on a concern that 'the psychology, attitudes and utterances of personalities are increasingly replacing concrete, material conditions as a yardstick'. (I. G. Shivji, 'Tanzania: The Silent Class Struggle', University of East Africa Social Conference Paper, Dar es Salaam, 1970, i.) More recently it has been suggested that 'overplaying the role of an individual declares (an author) incapable of performing class analysis'. (K. F. Hirji, Book Review, Maji Maji, No. 8, Tanu Youth League (University of Dar es Salaam, Dec. 1972), 35.) Apart from the question of what is 'overplaying', this view is quite wrong if it suggests that no great importance should be attached to Nyerere's leadership in a class analysis.

55. *Sunday News* (18 Mar. 1973).

Populist Tendencies
in the Ghanaian
Trade Union Movement[1]

RICHARD D. JEFFRIES

Frantz Fanon's futuristic analysis of political and socio-economic development in the African states has assumed fresh relevance for many scholars in the light of a clear post-Independence tendency to growing elite-mass differentiation and chronic political instability. This accounts for a valuable emphasis articulated by some recent studies on bringing the 'masses' back into the picture as a vital, if often latent, force in both nationalist and post-Independence politics.

However, Fanon did not consider the unionised workers part of the 'masses' in these countries, but rather a sub-section of the middle class, fundamentally allied with the elite.[2] Their politics would, at best, be 'reformist opportunism' and prove largely irrelevant to the growth of a mass revolutionary movement. Essentially this is the view which John Saul and Giovanni Arrighi have developed more systematically as the 'labour aristocracy thesis'.[3] Yet political strikes by unionised workers have provided, in some of these countries, the main exceptions to the general tendency to the elimination of popular movements as a major political force by the ruling African elites. Strike leaders have articulated virulent criticism of elite wealth, corruption, and authoritarianism. Should we dismiss this as mere sloganeering, of little real significance in the causation of such strike actions or in the developing objectives and policies of trade union movements? If not, do such protest actions suggest the possibility of the development of broad-based mass reformist or revolutionary movements under the unionised workers' leadership? Do they attract the support of significant sections of the urban or rural masses?

An examination of trade union politics in Ghana suggests that the role of reformist ideology in labour militancy, and the potential for 'worker' leadership of a broadly-based 'populist' movement, merit more serious consideration than Fanon, or Saul and Arrighi, allow. This paper focuses on the causation and significance of the 1961 'political strike' by the railway and harbour workers of Sekondi–Takoradi and attempts (a) to show that this strike possessed the character of a 'reformist protest' of a variety best described as 'urban populism', (b) to analyse the historical and structural sources of the railway workers' populist political culture, and (c) to consider the typicality or otherwise of railway worker consciousness and the potential significance of a growing subscription to populist ideology among Ghanaian workers.

The 1961 strike

In September 1961 the railway and harbour workers of Sekondi–Takoradi staged a seventeen-day strike against the Nkrumah government's July Budget, a strike in which, according to well-informed commentators, 'the Government saw its very existence implicitly challenged', and which 'drastically altered the entire character of political activity in Ghana'.[4] The strike leaders were consequently imprisoned for periods ranging from five months to four years, and prohibited from further office-holding in the Railway Union. TUC control over the union was made more tight and direct. Of more general significance, the strike lent urgency to a house-cleaning process within the Convention People's Party, on Nkrumah's instructions, to guard against 'bourgeois' elements. Later in the year a one-party state was established.

The seriousness of the government's reaction was partly due to suspicion of a United Party plot to excite such disturbances throughout the country and so bring down Nkrumah.[5] But, as the President appeared to realise in giving the strikers an assurance of future changes in government policy and conduct, United Party subversion, while certainly an important facilitating element in the strike action, did not itself adequately explain the fact, aims, or significance of rank and file mobilisation and solidarity. Some of the strike leaders ('branch' officials in distinction from the national executive, which tried to avoid involvement) were certainly in touch with United Party representatives before and during the strike, and received money which they used to enable the market women to supply food to the strikers. But these branch unionists, and the market women also, had their own aims and grievances, independent of the United Party interest, and mobilised the rank and file around issues which had, and had to have, nothing to do with subversive 'party politics'. For most of the rank and file were still vaguely pro-CPP rather than supporters of an elitist United Party which held little personal or ideological appeal for them, and knew nothing of United Party involvement.

The formal reason given for the strike, and certainly the cause of much resentment, was immediate economic grievances, the particular, sectional nature of which appears, superficially at least, to lend support to the labour aristocracy thesis. The skilled railway and harbour workers objected to the introduction in the July budget of a compulsory savings scheme, which would involve a five per cent deduction from the wages of those earning more than N336 per annum (most skilled workers earned slightly more than this), and a property tax, to be levied on larger than average sized houses (i.e. two rooms and a hall)—that is to say, measures which would hurt many of them but few of the unskilled workers or unemployed directly. Moreover, Ghana's farmers were being required to make even greater sacrifices in the cause of national development, and the skilled workers could not honestly claim to be so economically desperate as to merit exemption from the government's austerity measures. The most reliable statistics available suggest that Ghana's skilled and unskilled workers enjoyed substantially improved living standards by 1961 relative to a decade earlier, and they were accustomed to the regular seasonal rise in food prices which coincided with the strike action.[6] An explanation of the strike in narrowly economic terms would seem, therefore, to imply quite exceptional unreasonableness on the part of the strikers; and it would appear more likely that the militancy of their reaction—the staging of an illegal strike for seventeen days in the face of detention of leaders and threats of military intervention was clearly an intensely militant act—and the enthusiastic support they received from the unskilled workers, market women, and even some of the unemployed in Sekondi–Takoradi, derived rather from the wider significance these economic issues assumed in the context of the politics of the national labour movement, and of widespread popular opposition to the direction of development of the CPP regime. Implicit references to these wider issues were contained in the precise grounds on which the strike leaders criticised the budget.

The property tax, so they argued, would inhibit private building which was much needed in consequence of the CPP regime's failure to provide sufficient low-cost housing, and, if levied on 'family houses', would indirectly hurt the lower-paid workers and unemployed who depended on extended family charity for their accommodation. Implicit in this charge was a protest against party favouritism and corruption in the National Housing Corporation, which had recently taken over the administration of two new housing estates built in Sekondi–Takoradi supposedly for the lower-paid workers, but had allocated them instead to those who could afford to bribe NHC officials, party big-wigs, and even Accra-based MPs and their girlfriends. Secondly, they objected to the compulsory saving scheme on the grounds that, since it was a new and ideally voluntary form of taxation, 'the people's consent should have been obtained.'[7] Implicit in this objection was an expression of lack of confidence in Parliament, and in the leadership of the TUC which had failed to press the rank and file's demand for negotiations with the government on the budget. It is worth noting in this context the history of opposition, sometimes riotous, to 'arbitrary' taxation in the southern coastal towns of Ghana, and the wide significance 'tax protests' had thereby assumed.[8] The symbolic issue in the 1961 strike was a protest against the increasingly oligarchical and authoritarian style of CPP government, and was clearly articulated in the strike leaders' threat that, 'If Parliament did not give way to the demands of the people, they would disband that body by force.'[9]

The issues in the 1961 strike extended beyond immediate economic grievances, therefore, and beyond even trade union affairs narrowly defined: though somewhat paradoxically, the 'new structure' of the Ghana TUC, established by the 1958 Industrial Relations Act, was from the start the central issue for the strike leaders. This involved wider questions concerning the nature of the CPP regime, since it was the railway workers' conception that the TUC, or national labour movement, should, ideally, be especially concerned to check degenerative elitist tendencies in the political system as a whole. As will later be shown, this conception had informed their struggle against the post-1954 leadership of the TUC, in which the 1961 strike was essentially the showdown. Three years earlier, in 1958, the strike leaders had organised a splinter union, the 'Loco-Electrical', with the support of more than half the railway and harbour workers, outside of, and in scarcely veiled opposition to, the 'new structure', but had been compelled to rejoin the mother union and the TUC by a subsequent amendment to the Act. They had objected not to the principle of a single powerful trade union centre, but to the lack of adequate consultation with 'working unionists' involved in the formulation of the 'new structure'—it was the brainchild of 'party careerists', as the railway workers regarded John Tettegah, Joe-fio N. Meyer, and the other TUC leaders, men with little experience or supporting base in the old trade union movement which had developed from the shop-floors of Sekondi–Takoradi—and to the excessive degree of centralisation and party control it entailed.[10] Certainly this seemed likely to frustrate the 'Loco-Electrical' leaders' own political ambitions, and to curtail their autonomous powers and responsibilities as trade union representatives; but it was also, as they argued to the rank and file, a certain recipe for top-level corruption and unresponsiveness to the membership's demands. Even if the TUC leaders succeeded, through their close ties with the party, in securing substantial economic benefits for the workers, which in 1957–61 they undoubtedly did, it was of overriding importance, these railway unionists insisted, to fight to maintain trade union democracy and independence in view of the pattern of growing corruption, oligarchy, and authoritarianism which characterised the CPP regime.

In explaining why the Sekondi–Takoradi railway workers took the lead in 1961, we have therefore to explain more than their relative organisational ability to do so. Certainly, their concentration in the two large industrial installations, at Takoradi Harbour and Sekondi Location Workshops, made for easy communication, in-depth organisation, and a strong sense of power through solidarity; their relatively high educational level ('middle-school') facilitated awareness and articulation of the wider issues; and their relative job security, as skilled workers, made strike action the more easily contemplated. But also, in contrast to, for example, the mineworkers, who were situated in relatively isolated rural locations, the railway workers' residential integration in the urban centre of Sekondi–Takoradi enabled them to maintain close social ties with other socio-economic groups, and afforded them opportunity for first-hand observation of many aspects of CPP rule and identification with the grievances of the 'common people'.

In addition, or rather as a reflection of this structural situation, they had developed during the nationalist-Independence era a union political culture especially sensitive to corruption, elitism, and authoritarianism, and stressing their own vanguard role in protesting such tendencies in government. Others have remarked on the importance of this cultural heritage of the railway workers, but their description of this as one of 'conventional trade union practices', with 'an economist ideology', is seriously misleading.[11] The railway workers' political culture is more accurately described as one of 'urban populism', and the 1961 strike is best conceived as a familiar form of conflict between 'purist' rank-and-file and 'revisionist' leadership within a populist movement.

Railway union 'populism'

'Populism' is here used in the sense defined by Peter Worsley and Edward Shils,[12] as a style of popular participation rather than a systematic ideology. It involved, however, subscription to two cardinal principles: (a) 'the supremacy of the will of the people over every other standard, over the standards of traditional and other institutions, and over the will of other strata—"populism" identifies the will of the people with justice and morality;' (b) 'the desirability of a direct relationship between people and leadership, unmediated (or certainly 'unobstructed') by institutions.'[13] Such styles of popular participation, it is observed, are generally accompanied by a high valuation of the virtues and culture of the uncorrupted, simple folk, and a converse distrust of the wealthy, over-educated, idle, parasitic, and fundamentally corrupt urban elite.[14] The social structure is conceived dualistically in terms of an elite-mass division and opposition. Often, populism is a form or style of nationalism, in which the native elite are seen as the stooges of an external imperialist power. The populist leader is generally a charismatic figure, and often characterised by a 'strong man' image and by acceptance of violence as a legitimate means of effecting political change. On assumption of power, however, the leader is likely to be faced with an especially acute form of the familiar problem of 'institutionalising' a new, and in some ways inevitably disappointing, order. Increasing separation of leadership from rank and file and attempts to defuse the movement and substitute control for orderly development are likely to be seen as a 'revisionist' betrayal, particularly in view of the vagueness and/or diversity of the movement's positive policy aims.

The Sekondi–Takoradi railway workers' brand of nationalism as expressed in their leading role in the 1959 'positive action' strike, and the nature of their subsequent disillusionment with the CPP regime, were very much to this pattern. They were organised, inspired and led on this occasion not by their official union executive but by Pobee Biney, a charismatic rank-and-file leader, nicknamed 'Let Go The Anchor', who held no official position in the main Railway Union (though he was, in 1949–50, president of the Enginemen's Union and vice-president of the Gold Coast TUC).

Biney's leadership was crucial, firstly in the sense that the prior development of the union had been by no means unswervingly in the direction of populist political involvement. Since the Second World War years, when the union had been reorganised on the advice of the Colonial Labour Department, the Union Executive had been dominated by *ex-officio* clerical staff representatives, who generally favoured a policy of peaceful negotiation and separation of trade union affairs from politics. The skilled and semi-skilled workers, who had been responsible for the original establishment of the union and constituted a majority of the total railway labour force, became increasingly dissatisfied with the ineffectiveness, and, as they saw it, political irresponsibility of this policy. On three occasions in 1947–50 the strong man, Pobee Biney, rose to lead them in unconstitutional but successful 'direct actions', which, implicitly at first and then in 1959 explicitly, challenged the legitimacy of the colonial government structure.

In fact, Biney did more than simply act as a spokesman for rank and file discontent. In addition to re-amalgamating the Enginemen's Union with the main Railway Union to attain greater solidarity, he built up a reputation with the whole rank and file for human approachability and bold representation of their grievances, inspired them with something of his own courage and scorn for the colonial authorities, and educated them in a radical Nationalist ideology. By 1950 his substantive leadership and control of the rank and file was so assured he was able to declare and organise a virtually hundred per cent solid political strike without the active support of the official union executive (the union president resigned in fear of government reprisals) and without even calling a mass meeting.

Biney's ideology,[15] expressed in rousing speeches at union mass meetings, and at the nationalist rallies he organised in Sekondi, might best be termed 'African socialist'. He attacked the evils of colonialism on the grounds not only of economic exploitation but also of its destructive effect on the traditional culture and social relations, the sense of brotherhood of the Ghanaian people.[16] The true 'people' he defined as 'the common people', distinct from the elite of lawyers, civil servants, and other collaborators with the colonial regime. He derided the latter's cultural separatism, their 'white African' dress and manners. He was therefore strongly opposed to the United Gold Coast Convention and its leadership of 'lawyers who would not risk their wigs for the sake of the common man', and totally unsympathetic to the view, prevalent among Railway Union and TUC officials in 1949–50, that staging a strike in support of 'positive action' would be to confuse trade unionism with party politics and to misrepresent those workers, mainly clerical staff who favoured the UGCC rather than the CPP.

This did not mean he wished to 'marry' the Ghanaian labour movement to Nkrumah's Convention People's Party. In the first place he was wary of . Nkrumah's Marxist-Leninist ideas and later came to attack the regime's ideologising as 'that Soviet"ism" nonsense which has nothing to teach us about Socialism'. Secondly, Biney's emphasis on the vanguard role of the organised, enlightened workers in leading the Ghanaian people to achieve their independence involved the corollary that they should continue to act thereafter as defenders of the Nationalist Movement's aims, checking degenerative tendencies in the party-become-government. This implication became clearer from his behaviour after the 'positive action' strike and the CPP's accession to a share of government power: and it was the consistency and idealistic aggression with which Biney acted out his ideology, relatively indistinctive in itself perhaps, that earned him a legendary status in Railway Union political culture surpassing that of Nkrumah and infusing and defining the process of railway worker disillusionment with the Nkrumah regime.

Biney was detained towards the end of the 'positive action' strike in January 1950, and, on his release in 1951, was nominated by the CPP for the Assin constituency in the Legislative Assembly elections; but, unlike so many others, he did not proceed to sell out to the Party, or pursue his personal advancement.[17] Rather, he became rapidly dissatisfied with Nkrumah's failure to help revive the TUC (virtually destroyed in consequence of the 1950 strike and government reprisals), with the slow and petty procedures of parliamentary party politics, the discipline expected of back-benchers, and the debilitating effect of all this on party momentum and idealism. His persistent criticism of the government for doing too little for the workers and common people brought him Nkrumah's displeasure, and termination of his Legislative Assembly membership after only two years. He then returned to help reorganise the Railway Union, but his dismissal from the presidency was engineered within the year by CPP loyalists on the Executive Council. He then took various jobs but appears to have spent a great deal of his time in Sekondi bars, loudly voicing his disillusionment with the Nkrumah government's slide into elitism, corruption, and 'nonsensical' ideology. It is said that Nkrumah tried to bribe him with gifts and offers of jobs to restrain his criticism, but, though he accepted some of these, and in the 1960s became a Government Security Officer, he did so 'merely to keep body and soul together', and refused to perform his so-called duties. Throughout this time, including his spell in the Legislative Assembly, he remained in touch with the common people of Sekondi–Takoradi, maintaining a simple house in Sekondi, and dressed always in a cheap traditional cloth and pair of sandals.

This background helps provide insight into the very real idealistic element in the 1961 strike action. The CPP's rejection of one of the few nationalist leaders who had remained faithful to the original ideals of the movement, consistently and courageously speaking up for 'the common people', came to symbolise for many railway workers the failings of the Nkrumah regime. Biney's embodiment and articulation of 'pure' nationalist ideas lent definition and contrast to CPP 'revisionism'. But Biney's influence was also more direct than this. During his presidency of the Railway Union in 1954–55, he had helped organise an attempt to overthrow the incumbent TUC leadership, and had recruited to positions of officialdom in the Railway Union men especially sympathetic to this aim and to his own populist style and ideology of union leadership. These followers were prominent among the middle-level officials who led the 1961 strike. In 1955–61 they had been, in a sense, continuing the struggle in Biney's absence.

Nevertheless, it would be mistaken to attribute excessive independent influence to the personality of Pobee Biney. In the first place, railway worker populism derived encouragement from a tradition of 'common man' political participation in the Fanti coastal towns of Ghana. The majority of skilled railway workers, including Biney himself, originated from Elmina or Cape Coast, where they were members of Asafo companies, semi-military organisations of the commoners as distinct from the elders and chiefs. During the first half of the twentieth century the Asafo companies were frequently and centrally involved in political disputes over the legitimacy of particular chiefs and their policies, and, sometimes implicit in this, over the institutional reforms the colonial government sought to introduce.[18] Stylistically, the Railway Union's borrowing of Asafo cultural elements can be seen in the use of an Asafo gong-gong, an Asafo battle-cry ('Kryo-be'—'Prepare yourself for the coming struggle'), and, more generally, in the military atmosphere of many mass meetings of the union, with speakers trying to outdo each other in bravado. And the traditional legitimacy of 'common man' collective participation in the politics of the Fanti states perhaps helped provide subjective justification for railway worker self-assertion in national politics, similarly rationalised as opposing autocracy on behalf of the people. In the 1961 strike more particularly, the Asafo influence is apparent from St Clair Drake's on-the-spot account: 'Red head-bands and arm-bands were in evidence everywhere; they were symbols worn in former days by Fanti tribal fighting men to mean, "We are ready for War".'[19]

Secondly, the continuing vitality of this cultural heritage, and the influence exerted in turn by Biney's 'spokesman of the People' conception, derived from their correspondence to the rank-and-file's empirical perception of their situation in the national socio-economic and political structures, and the close interdependence of their own interests with those of other sections of the urban masses. A brief consideration of this structural position *vis-à-vis* other urban groups will also help to explain the support the strike received from virtually the entire Sekondi–Takoradi community.

The social structure of Sekondi–Takoradi and the elite-mass gap

St Clair Drake and L. A. Lacy's account of the 1961 strike emphasises the widespread support it received within Sekondi–Takoradi: 'By midweek practically every activity in the port was closed down. Municipal bus drivers had joined the strike, as had the city employees who collected the sewage daily. Market women dispensed free food to the strikers at municipal bus garages and other strategic points . . . There was an air of excitement and pride throughout the city . . . Morale was high . . . The railway workers were heroes.'[20] Interviews conducted in 1971 suggested that even some of the unemployed participated: 'The support we received from all the people here was so tremendous, we realised we could not back down even if we had wanted to. Many who weren't workers, our unemployed brothers and sisters, for instance, came on the demonstrations. People felt it was a burning issue to the community.'

Sekondi–Takoradi, it must be emphasised, was and is, more than any other Ghanaian city, a predominantly working-class community, dominated both numerically and in terms of general ethos by lower-paid manual workers. The

1955 Population and Household Budget Survey estimated that 90 per cent of earnings in Sekondi–Takoradi came from wage-employment, compared with 67 per cent for Accra and 22 per cent for Kumasi.[31] In 1961 the skilled and unskilled workers employed in the Railway and Harbour Administration constituted almost a quarter of the city's total male labour force of 43,000. Another quarter were employed as skilled or unskilled workers by the City Council, the various government departments (e.g. Public Works, Posts and Tele-communications), the shipping companies, or in one of the several manufacturing industries located there. At least twelve per cent were unemployed, and the proportion of elite elements was very small.[22] In so predominantly a working-class community, many of the unemployed looked to their worker fathers or brothers for assistance, and were therefore directly dependent on the workers' financial capacity for the continuance of this social welfare function. Similarly, the market women and small businessmen relied very largely on the trade of the workers, and had an indirect, but clearly perceived, interest in the financial fortunes of the lower-paid workers and in the politics of the TUC. This close economic interdependence was paralleled on the social and cultural levels by the integration of most workers in the main residential centres of Sekondi–Takoradi, and by the numerical predominance of workers in the majority of associations and meeting places.

In addition to such pragmatic considerations, the unionised workers and other groups among the urban masses were united by a common sense of social injustice, and equally important were not significantly divided by socio-economic differentiation among themselves. Saul and Arrighi suggest that 'wage workers in the upper stratum' (i.e. including skilled workers) 'receive incomes 3–5 times those received by wage workers in the lower stratum' (i.e. unskilled workers).[23] This is simply not true of Ghanaian workers, and more particularly of the railway and harbour workers. Skilled workers have received, on average, almost twice as much as unskilled workers; and this differential has generally been considered justified by the skilled workers' education and training, and by the fact that, being relatively job-committed southerners, they normally have wives and children to support in the city unlike most of the northern migrants who provide the majority of the unskilled labour force.[24] In turn, the skilled railway workers have consistently concerned themselves, in their major wage campaigns and strike actions, with raising the wages of unskilled workers rather than merely securing improved conditions of service for themselves. While the skilled workers have been, in a sense, privileged relative to the unskilled and unemployed, this has not been, judging from interviews, the commonsense view of the Sekondi–Takoradi unskilled and unemployed themselves.[25] The difficulty experienced by skilled workers in making ends meet to support a style and standard of living which includes little beyond the basic necessities is obvious to all. The skilled workers' economic and social distance from the middle-class proper—school teachers, middling businessmen, middle-rank executives—has been, and still is, both considerable and highly visible.

Of far more doubtful legitimacy than the unskilled-skilled worker differential, therefore, has been the scale of differentials between these lower-paid workers and the middle and higher executives in government service. Apart from the minor reforms introduced by the Lidbury-Gbedemah award of 1952, the Nkrumah government did nothing to reduce the gross inequalities in the wage and salary structure inherited from the colonial civil service. This was one of Biney's principal charges against the regime. The intensity of resentment at the continuance of such inequalities could not be doubted on the evidence of interviews: e.g.

> It all depends on cheating. There are so many people being paid fat salaries without working. I didn't go to school but I know my trade. If an educated man comes along and he's given more pay than myself I have to challenge the Government and find out what is happening.

Even more infuriating was the excessive wealth and conspicuous consumption of politicians owing their positions, originally at least, to the votes of the common people. In the 1961 strike action the common people of Sekondi-Takoradi looked to the more highly organised and articulate skilled workers to express their resentment at this growing elite-mass gap.

President Nkrumah himself, it should be noted, recognised this. Earlier in the year, when preparing for the necessity of an austerity budget, and considering the likely obstacles to its popular acceptance, he had publicly criticised the 'self-seeking tendencies' of some members of the party 'who by virtue of their functions and positions are tending to form a separate new ruling class.' This was 'working to alienate the support of the masses and to bring the National Assembly into isolation.'[26] On September 29, recognising that the Sekondi-Takoradi strike had revealed widespread disbelief in the effectiveness of such warnings, the President took more drastic action to implement his 'dawn broadcast'. Six ministers were to resign and to surrender part of their property to the state, among them Krobo Edusei, infamous for the gold bed episode. To this degree at least the 1961 strike was successful and its significance appreciated in governing circles.

The growth of an elite-mass gap, governmental corruption and authoritarianism were, however, apparent in other Ghanaian cities, indeed probably more visibly so in Accra and Kumasi than in Sekondi-Takoradi. Why should the people of Sekondi-Takoradi prove especially sensitive to such tendencies and ready to unite in protest against them? Two main reasons might be given.

Firstly, it would seem likely that general structural factors tend to generate strongly anti-elitist and anti-corruption attitudes among Ghanaian workers, and especially skilled manual workers. For they, unlike some clerical and administrative executives, enjoy few opportunities for benefiting from corrupt practices, or gaining promotion through patronage, while suffering directly from managerial and governmental corruption, to which they tend to attribute government's lack of finance for raising wages. Earlier in this paper the similarly pernicious effects of corruption in the National Housing Corporation were noted. Moreover, government employees, and private employees also to the degree that they recognise the impact of government wage policy on their own wage scales, have a direct financial interest in maintaining democratic processes and opposing authoritarianism in government-management; though other factors making for an anti-authoritarian orientation are probably equally important, the literacy of most skilled workers, for example, and their socialisation in democratic values in the unions. Further, the skilled workers' position in the socio-economic structure, between the unskilled and unemployed, on the one hand, and the middle-class proper, on the other, is a highly ambivalent one, involving a strong aspiration to bourgeois status, to which they feel entitled by virtue of education and training, but at the same time intense resentment of the excessive wealth of the elite which is the most obvious cause of their own impoverishment. For these general structural reasons, then, lower-paid manual workers are especially prone to develop critical attitudes to elitism, authoritarianism, and corruption, and the peculiarity of Sekondi–Takoradi among Ghanaian cities consists, from this perspective, simply in its overwhelmingly working-class composition, and the prevalence of a strong proletarian ethos in the community as a whole.

But in 1961 these sources of special disillusionment with the Nkrumah regime were compounded by more particular communal grievances. Although they had played a crucial and courageous role in the nationalist struggle, the people of Sekondi–Takoradi felt they had gained little from Independence compared with Accra, with its fine new roads and plush hotels; and now their major source of livelihood, the harbour at Takoradi, seemed likely to be severely devalued by the government's construction of a new harbour at Tema, some fifteen miles from Accra. What little had been provided them in the way of new facilities, the new housing estates, for example, had been plundered by CPP officials. More important than the objective extent of exploitation, or deprivation, perhaps, was the feeling that their voice was not heard nor were their interests represented in Accra because of a steady diminution in the channels of communication and influence between Sekondi–Takoradi and the central government during the 1950s.

In consequence, there was a pronounced communalistic element in the 1961 strike and the railway and harbour workers' populist consciousness. The despised elite were the 'big men' in, or from, Accra: the 'common people', the people of Sekondi–Takoradi and the Western Region. This sense of communal, and regional, deprivation was still apparent in 1971, as the following remark by a railway worker illustrates: 'We Westerners, especially, the government never minds us, yet we have all these industries, bauxite and gold and things, and we work much harder than all those office-workers in Accra, drawing their fat salaries. If they don't look out, it will be another Biafra.' Such openly communalistic sentiments are atypical and even frowned upon in Railway Union political culture, but the Accra–Secondi–Takoradi dimension has certainly served to intensify the railway and harbour workers' sense of social distance and conflict between the 'big men' and the 'common people'.

The populist element in Bentum's TUC (1966–1971)

It is clear that the populist consciousness of the railway and harbour workers of Secondi–Takoradi, and their ability to attract the support of other sections of the community, derived in part from particular historical and structural factors, and should not be assumed to characterise the consciousness or position of lower-paid manual workers in other Ghanaian cities. Nevertheless, certain general structural factors might be expected to encourage similarly anti-elitist attitudes among other Ghanaian workers, if in less strongly developed form than in Sekondi–Takoradi. And certainly, the development of the Ghanaian trade union movement after the *coup d'état* of February 1966 demonstrated the enthusiasm of lower-paid workers throughout the country, under conditions of seriously declining real wage levels and the elitist policies of ruling regimes for a militantly reformist, populist-style of union leadership. The 1961 strike was of significance here in providing an historical model for this direction o development: in Bentum's re-moulding of the TUC in 1966–71 the '61 strike was accorded the status of an heroic attempt to maintain the genuine principles of Ghanaian trade unionism.

The steadily pursued policy of Benjamin Bentum (Ghana TUC Secretary-General, April 1966 to October 1971) was to democratise the structure of the national labour movement, and assert its independence of government (and of party politics), while seeking to unite the movement around the conception of acting as 'the watchdogs' or 'the eyes and ears of society'. Under his leadership, the Ghana TUC projected itself as a kind of loyal but radical opposition, pressing for egalitarian reforms in the national wage and salary structure, and articulating policy alternatives on virtually the entire range of governmental issues.

It tended to adapt its policy on strike actions, alternatively condoning or condemning them, according to the government's responsiveness on these general issues of socio-economic and political reform.

Under the NLC regime (April 1966 to October 1969), government–TUC conflict, though serious and growing, was contained within the limits of what the NLC considered legitimate and workable. However, the Progress Party government of Dr Busia (headed largely by the old United Party leaders), looked on the TUC leadership of Bentum with undisguised hostility from the start, attempting first to displace Bentum from the TUC Secretary-Generalship, and later to sponsor an alternative trade union centre. This, coupled with the regime's apparent insensitivity to the workers' rapidly declining financial position—it refused to grant any improvement of the minimum wage while approving higher salaries for Ministers and MPs, retirement on full pay for judges, and the construction of luxurious rest-houses in the regions for visiting government officials—resulted in a vast increase in strike actions, and pushed Bentum into ever more radical and vociferous criticism of the regime.[27] By the summer of 1971 several Ministers were voicing the government's intention of ridding itself of Bentum by abolishing the legal status of the TUC: the September budget provided the occasion for a general strike in which the majority of workers throughout the country participated (though, again, the Sekondi-Takoradi workers demonstrated their especial militancy by staying out the longest, for five days).

The Busia government was quite correct in suggesting that the strike was not solely or primarily motivated by opposition to the budget measures themselves. Although the introduction of a compulsory savings scheme, similar in conception and detail to the national development levy of 1961, was extremely unpopular, the need for some such measure, given the country's critical economic situation, was generally acknowledged; and other items—the reduction in the perquisites of higher civil servants, for instance, and the allocation of extra finance to rural development—invested the budget as a whole with an equitable and purposeful character which the majority of worker-interviewees recognised and appreciated. The general reaction to the budget was one of somewhat reluctant preparedness to sacrifice until, one week after the budget announcement, the TUC leadership declared its opposition on the grounds that it had not been consulted in its formulation. As this implied, the real issue was, or became, that of the general structure and state of relations between the PP government and the TUC, and more particularly, the government's intention, now openly admitted and well known to the union rank and file, to bring in legislation to abolish the TUC. Most workers interviewed during the general strike conceived its purpose quite clearly as a major political and ideological confrontation between the PP government and the TUC, in which it was necessary to express their opposition to Progress Party 'hypocrisy and false aristocracy' ('hypocrisy' being a reference to the increasingly authoritarian character of a regime which claimed to represent a democratic ideal), and their determination to stand by Bentum's attempt to 'speak up for us poor people and tell those big men what sacrifices they should be making'.

In the first week of October the government did in fact abolish the TUC and confiscate its funds, effectively quashing further resistance. The solidarity and enthusiasm for Bentum's leadership displayed by the unions in the face of such suppression was, however, impressive. All the member unions of the TUC, with the single exception of the National Seamen's Union, declared their intention to join in re-organising another trade union centre with Bentum as leader; and the alternative PP-allied centre, the Confederation of Labour, made no significant inroads among the rank-and-file. Towards the end of the year there was much talk among opposition politicians, in the Western and Central Regions especially, of forming a Labour Party, with Bentum prominent in its leadership, which could expect the support of the workers and the urban lower strata more generally. What might have developed must remain hypothetical in view of the effective pre-empting of the situation by the military *coup d'état* of January 1972 and the severe restrictions since maintained by the NRC on both trade union and party political activities. What is clear, however, is that Bentum's militant reformist style of TUC leadership had been extremely popular not only with the unionised workers themselves but also with large sections of the non-unionised urban masses who looked to it for expression of radical criticism of government in the absence of an effective representative opposition party.

Conclusions

From this brief analysis of radical trends in the development of the Ghanaian labour movement it is at least apparent that Fanon's view of the unionised workers in African societies as fundamentally allied with the ruling elite seriously underestimates the factors making for elite-labour conflict, and misrepresents the nature of relations, socio-economic and attitudinal, between the workers and the rest of the urban masses. In some instances at least large sections of the urban masses, and especially those with close social and economic ties with the unionised workers, tend to look to the latter as their spokesmen rather than as a purely self-interested labour aristocracy. To what degree this tendency to worker-mass identification of interests is general in Africa, or is becoming so, it is impossible to say in the present state of research. It is clearly more pronounced in predominantly working-class areas such as Sekondi–Takoradi or Ikeja in Lagos (see Adrian Peace's contribution to this volume), but the evidence from Ghana suggests that this might become a more general phenomenon under certain conditions. In conclusion, therefore, it will be useful to review briefly the structural conditions which might be said to have encouraged the growth of a radical populist orientation in the Ghanaian labour movement as a whole (though actual developments were dependent on the policies of particular regimes, and the initiative and quality of union leadership), and to consider the principal factors affecting the potential significance of such an orientation.

The essence of the populist perspective, as the term is somewhat loosely used here, is the tendency to conceive society in terms of an immense and unjust elite-mass gap, rather than in terms of a relatively continuous and legitimate ladder of socio-economic stratification, or competitive sets of patron-client networks. It has been argued that most of the lower paid manual workers, skilled and unskilled, who constitute the backbone of the Ghanaian trade union movement are relatively uninvolved in patronage networks, at least not to their own benefit. Moreover, post-Independence development in Ghana has in fact resulted in a large proportionate increase in the share of national wealth going to the top elite, and a considerable increase in the comfortable bourgeoisie of middle-ranking civil servants, businessmen, teachers, etc.; but the main proletariat of skilled and semi-skilled workers has suffered, in common with the unskilled workers, relative impoverishment of a degree which has virtually wiped out any difference between average rural real incomes and those of the lower paid urban workers.[28]

By 1970 the differential ratio of the lowest paid to the highest paid in government service was 1:39 (a fact much publicised by the TUC and well known to the rank-and-file), and the failure of wages to keep step with inflation meant that all but the most senior of skilled workers were living on, or just below, the poverty datum line.[29] Certainly the skilled workers are privileged relative to the unemployed, and they tend still to hold bourgeois aspirations for themselves and/or their children. But their economic and social distance from the middle class proper is considerable, being able to afford only occasional forays into the 'smart clothes, beer-bar' world of the latter, and, with the abolition of free secondary school education, they can hardly be said to have even one foot on the steeply rising embourgeoisement ladder.

This situation in the socio-economic and political structures is a highly ambivalent one, involving a strong aspiration to bourgeois status, but, at the same time, real resentment of elite wealth, corruption and authoritarianism. With their relatively high level of education and organisation, the skilled workers understandably pose as the spokesmen of the poor, common people, and they are indeed most accurately placed as an intermediate and potentially mediating group between the urban elite and middle class, on the one hand, and the common people on the other. To this situation, populist ideology has clear, if somewhat intermittent, relevance. In Ghana, as in several of the Latin-American countries, urban populism might well be the response of unionised workers to a stagnant economic situation, urbanisation without industrialisation, and intense frustration of their social mobility aspirations.

At the same time severe limitations as to the likely development and significance of such populist tendencies must be recognised. It would be wrong to imply commitment on the part of Ghana's workers to any systematic or revolutionary programme beyond maintaining trade union independence and the right to voice public criticism of government, especially on the issues of corruption and reform of the socio-economic structure; or to suggest that their trade union activity is, or is likely to be, consistently controlled or moderated by concern for the people as a whole, the rural populace and urban subproletariat, rather than their own interests. Since these other groups well realise this, and the government is able to play off, even create, conflicts of interest between them, and since the process of alignment is liable to be frequently interrupted, or preempted, by *coups d'état*, the development of a broad-based populist movement must appear unlikely, though by no means impossible.

Nevertheless, in so far as rank and file populist attitudes provide an important and powerful basis of support, and even ideological dynamic, for the attempt to develop an independent, reformist trade union movement, articulating dissenting views on general policy matters on a non-party basis, it is an unusual and important phenomenon in the political life of the country. In serving at least to raise the level of political debate and the pressure on government to redistribute national wealth, it perhaps deserves more serious and sympathetic consideration than Fanon or his followers allow.

NOTES

1. This paper is based on research carried out in Ghana in April to December 1971, financed by the SOAS Scholarships Committee and the University of London Central Research Fund.
2. Frantz Fanon, *The Wretched of the Earth*, MacGibbon and Kee, 1965, p. 98.
3. Giovanni Arrighi and John S. Saul, 'Socialism and Economic Development in Tropical Africa', *The Journal of Modern African Studies*, 6(2), 1968, pp. 141–69; Arrighi and Saul, 'Nationalism and Revolution in Sub-Saharan Africa', in Ralph Miliband and John Saville, *The Socialist Register*, Merlin

Press, 1969, pp. 137–88. For a lucid presentation of the main points of the
labour aristocracy thesis, see Adrian Peace's contribution to this volume.

4. St Clair Drake and L. A. Lacy, 'Government Versus the Unions: the
Sekondi-Takoradi Strike, 1961', in G. Carter (ed.), *Politics in Africa: 7 cases*,
Harcourt, Brace and World, Inc., 1966, p. 68. The majority of unionised
workers in Sekondi-Takoradi participated in the strike at one stage or
another, but the skilled railway and harbour workers gave the lead and
stayed out by far the longest.

5. For the Nkrumah government's interpretation, see *The Statement by the
Government on the Recent Conspiracy*, Government Printer, Accra, 1961.

6. This generalisation is based on W. B. Birmingham's 'Index of real wages of
the unskilled labourer in Accra, 1939–59', in *Economic Bulletin*, Legon,
Ghana, 4 (3), Mar. 1960, p. 2, and its extension into the 'sixties by Killick in
Birmingham, Neustadt, and Omaboe (eds), *A Study of Contemporary Ghana*,
Allen and Unwin, 1966, vol. 1, p. 141. Throughout this period the wage rates
for skilled workers in the railway administration have maintained a fairly
steady relation to those for unskilled labourers, and differences in the price
indices for Accra and Sekondi-Takoradi appear to have been relatively
negligible.

7. Interviews with the strike leaders. In clarification of the point about the
Housing Tax, many of the unemployed, and some of the lower-paid
workers, did (and still do) pay little or no rent for accommodation in the
houses of richer relatives. If these houses were to be subject to taxation, so it
was argued, their owners would be inclined to demand rents of such dependants, or even to eject them and let rooms instead to tenants who could
afford high rents.

8. The most notable instances of violent opposition were the October 1931 tax
riots in Sekondi and Cape Coast.

9. Drake and Lacy, 'Government Versus the Unions', p. 99.

10. Bulletin of the Joint Council of Railway Unions, 8 Sept. 1958, R.U.A.

11. Lacy, 'Government Versus the Unions', p. 115.

12. Peter Worsley, 'The Concept of Populism', in G. Ionescu and E. Gellner
(eds), *Populism, its meanings and national characteristics*, Weidenfeld and
Nicholson, 1970, pp. 212–50.

13. *Ibid.*, pp. 243–4.

14. Some of the literature on Populism emphasises its specifically rural location
and orientation, and would deny applicability of the term to urban movements, conceiving the people as the urban as well as rural lower strata. This
seems to the present writer, as indeed to many of the contributors to the
1967 LSE Conference on Populism, unnecessarily specific. In this particular

case, for instance, the traditional society and culture were urban, that of the Fante coastal towns.

15. This interpretation of Biney's ideology is based primarily on oral sources, and therefore presents the way his ideology was generally understood and/or has been remembered. Phrases in quotation marks are frequent sayings attributed to him, translated from the Fante.

16. Biney's concern for the traditional culture did not extent to support for the continued political authority of the chiefs, whom he characterised as 'our little gods of times past, now become messenger-boys of the Colonial Government'.

17. The interpretation of Biney's career presented here is that current among the railway workers, rather than an attempt at historical objectivity. While this legend does appear to correspond closely to the historical reality on all empirical points, alternative interpretations obviously are possible on such matters, as, for example, the reason for Biney's dismissal from the Legislative Assembly and the Railway Union Presidency. Party and trade union officials claimed at the time that this was because of his excessive drinking and rude demeanour. It might be noted that Biney's drinking exploits were not necessarily a disability in the eyes of the railway workers, who rather applauded them as a 'strong man' trait; also, that Biney's downfall did coincide closely in time with the expulsion from party and trade union hierarchies of two of Biney's close and political ideological associates, Turkson Ocran and Anthony Woode, for alleged communism.

18. Ansu Datta, 'The Fante Asafo: a Re-examination', in *Africa*, 42 (4), Oct. 1972, p. 365.

19. Drake and Lacy, 'Government Versus the Unions', p. 98.

20. *Ibid.*

21. *Sekondi-Takoradi: Survey of Population and Household Budgets, 1955*, Government Printer, Accra, 1956, p. 11.

22. 1960 Population Census of Ghana, Government Printer, Accra, 1961.

23. Giovanni Arrighi and John S. Saul, 'Nationalism and Revolution in Sub-Saharan Africa', p. 135.

24. On the relatively high job commitment of Ghanaian skilled workers see Margaret Peil, *The Ghanaian Factory Worker: Industrial Man in Africa*, Cambridge University Press, 1972, pp. 101–3. Takoradi skilled workers appear to be more committed than those in other Ghanaian cities, however, with 68 per cent of those surveyed by Peil having been in their job for longer than five years.

25. This brief and, unfortunately, simplistic summary of prevalent attitudes is based on open-ended interviews with a sample of 90 railway workers, and

informal conversations with several hundred workers and unemployed primarily in Sekondi-Takoradi but also in Accra and Kumasi, in May to November 1972.

26. Dawn Broadcast, *Evening News*, 3 Apr. 1961, p. 2.

27. In 1970 the Ministry of Labour handled 55 strikes, involving the loss of 132,708 man-days, more than double the figure for 1968 (Government Press Release, 6 June 1971).

28. D. Rimmer, 'Wage Politics in West Africa' mimeograph, University of Birmingham, 1970, pp. 33–5. K. Edusei, *Distribution of Money Incomes In Ghana*, Legon Institute of Social and Economic Statistics, 1971. *The Report of the Commission on the Structure and Remuneration of the Public Services in Ghana* (Ministry of Information, Accra, 1967) calculated a 40 per cent decline in the real income of the minimum wage-earner in 1960–66, and estimated that rural and urban workers earned approximately equivalent real wages. On the basis of the Ghana Economic Survey (Accra, Central Bureau of Statistics, annual), a further decline of some 20 per cent might be calculated for 1966–71.

29. Poverty Datum Line at May 1970 equalled approximately NC. 36 per month. Average skilled worker income in the railways was approximately NC. 38. Average unskilled worker income NC. 26. (£1 Sterling equalled NC 2.40).

The Lagos Proletariat:
Labour Aristocrats or Populist
Militants?

ADRIAN PEACE

To enter a discussion on the nature of 'social class' in the African context is to move into treacherous territory. The somewhat elementary position adopted here can be stated briefly: the Nigerian working class are those wage-earners who stand in a consistently subordinate relationship in the industrial mode of production, whose surplus product is appropriated by those who own the means of production, whether the latter be indigenous to Nigerian society or external to it, and who on the basis of this relationship can identify a common opposition to their own economic interests and act accordingly. Quite explicitly, then, I am concerned here with social action on a class basis undertaken by factory workers in Lagos as a segment of the Nigerian working class: my experience does not extend to government and public corporation workers though I suspect that much of the analysis presented here does in fact also apply to those in the state sector.[1]

Clearly, however, while I am here concerned specifically with a sector of the Lagos proletariat, the particular as much as the generalisable characteristics of this stratum can only emerge within the context of more broadly-based theoretical statements synthesising a diversity of sociological studies of a comparative nature. Sociological theories are of value only if our understanding of particular events, social processes and institutions is thereby heightened. One such statement is the 'labour aristocracy thesis' concerning the African working class. As a general thesis, it should stand up to examination in the light of the experience of the Lagos proletariat, but, as I will try to show, it does not—indeed cannot—do so. In my view, the labour aristocracy thesis, widely accepted as it is, represents a serious barrier to an accurate understanding of the present (and probably future) responses of Lagos wage-earners to their class position. A markedly different perspective is outlined in this paper: if this has any wider application its value can only be judged by others with experience and opinions quite different from my own.

The labour aristocracy thesis

As with most sociological theories concerned with the economic development and underdevelopment of sub-Saharan Africa, the labour aristocracy thesis has somewhat diverse and eclectic roots: it thus brings strange bedfellows together. Historically, the first commentators were the colonial administrators themselves, who feared the development of exceptional rural-urban divisions where early wage-earners could force up their wage rates by collective action (a by no means unimportant consideration for this paper). Contemporaneously, perhaps the greatest influence is found in the writings of Frantz Fanon, most notably in *The Wretched of the Earth*. But the most systematic academic contribution is the work of Giovanni Arrighi and John Saul, who in an early article entitled 'Socialism and Economic Development in Tropical Africa' initially set down views they have subsequently elaborated at greater length.[2]

Arrighi and Saul's central concern is with the dominant patterns of extraction of economic surplus produced within the new African nation-states following political independence. They argue correctly that economic surplus produced by the peasantry, rather than being reinvested to the benefit of the mass of the people, is for the most part repatriated by overseas companies or consumed wastefully by indigenous elites. Such established processes in their turn militate against increased productivity generated by a discontented and hostile peasant class.[3] For present purposes, attention is to be focused on one particular area of surplus consumption, for it is here that Arrighi and Saul identify a source of class conflict crucial to their overall thesis. The roots of such conflict are to be found in the colonial period, but the outcome is of the greatest importance for the present time:

> The higher wages and salaries [established during the colonial period] foster the stabilisation of the better-paid section of the labour force whose high incomes justify the severance of ties with the traditional economy. Stabilisation, in turn, promotes specialisation, greater bargaining power, and further increases in the incomes of this small section of the labour force, which represents the proletariat proper of tropical Africa. These workers enjoy incomes three or more times higher than those of unskilled labourers and together with the elites and sub-elites in bureaucratic employment in the civil service and expatriate concerns, constitute what we call the labour aristocracy of tropical Africa. It is the discretionary consumption of this

class which absorbs a significant proportion of the surplus produced in the money economy.[4]

Here, then, Arrighi and Saul identify in Africa a critical deviation from the classic theory of increasing class conflict between ruling class and proletariat as economic development proceeds apace. Far from bourgeoisie and proletariat being forced into increasingly irreconcilable camps, their economic interests and political ideologies become increasingly complementary over time to a point at which they are virtually indistinguishable. Since Arrighi and Saul concentrate almost exclusively on the peasant-produced surplus, the only inevitable major polarisation occurs with the peasantry on the one hand and the forces of elite, sub-elite, and wage-earners—'the proletariat proper'—on the other. In contrast to the Marxist model of increasing exploitation *within one mode* of production, the dominant pattern of class exploitation occurs *between two modes* of production.

Such complementarity of elite, sub-elite and wage-earners' politico-economic interests has not emerged in an entirely uniform fashion. The economic superiority of the elite and sub-elite is firmly rooted in the colonial situation when the functional indispensability of the early African middle class ensured a high economic return relative to the peasantry and the forerunners of the modern labour force. Though some measure of economic superiority over the peasantry was achieved by wage-earners during the colonial period, their inferior standing relative to elite and sub-elite was substantially corrected by the advent of international capitalist oligopolies into the manufacturing arena immediately before political decolonisation. After independence, such enterprises moved to break out of the 'vicious circle [of] 'high [labour] turnover—low productivity—low wages—high turnover' [which militated against] the development of a semi-skilled, relatively highly paid labour force'[5] by paying sufficiently high wages to stabilise its composition: this strategy in its turn began a 'spiral process' involving both expatriate companies and African governments equally concerned to make permanent their respective labour forces and win over skilled workers from one sector to another.

While acknowledging some differentiation between elite, sub-elite and wage-earning class, nevertheless Arrighi and Saul feel justified in treating them as an entity. They do, however, point to one further division within the wage-earning class which is of considerable importance here:

> . . . the wage-earning class is polarised into two strata. Wage workers in the lower stratum are only marginally or partially proletarianised as, over their life cycle, they derive the bulk of the means of subsistence for their families from outside the wage economy. Wage workers in the upper stratum, generally a very small minority, receive incomes sufficiently high (say 3–5

times those received by wage workers in the lower stratum) to justify a total break of their links with the peasantry. This is a type of 'optional proletarianisation' which has little in common with processes of 'proletarianisation' resulting from the steady impoverishment of the peasantry.[6]

Only the 'upper stratum', characterised by their complete reliance on their urban-industrial experience, are to be included in the labour aristocracy. Though one may question the notion that the 'lower stratum' constitute a 'marginally or partially proletarianised' class—in my view once a worker enters the factory floor then he is 'proletarianised', though he does not, for example, necessarily act similarly to his West European counterpart—nevertheless one may accept this distinction here.

More important in this context is the separation of distinct courses of political action for the two sub-groups within the wage-earning class as a whole. Arrighi and Saul maintain that the close identification of the permanently employed 'upper stratum' with the elite and sub-elite remains valid: but 'this lower stratum, consisting of workers and unemployed who retain strong links with the peasantry, has in fact interests which are antagonistic to the present order'.[7] Notwithstanding the fact that to date, members of the urban lumpenproletariat have proved the most politically promiscuous of all socio-economic strata in Africa, constantly at the beck and call of the highest bidder, Arrighi and Saul suggest that Fanon's view of the lumpenproletariat as the urban spearhead of a peasant-dominated revolutionary movement has considerable relevance.[8] Such antagonism is not, however, a part of the elite-proletariat relationship where only minor differences have emerged. For example, 'where wage restraint began to be demanded of those junior partners to the "aristocracy" its imposition was made difficult by the unambiguously privileged position of its other members, the politicians and the salariat'.[9] Yet such differences are of slight importance alongside the overriding consensus and filiation.

Before moving to a critique of the Arrighi-Saul position by setting it against the Nigerian experience, one can point to certain merits. First, the existence of economic classes with distinct socio-political interests is granted rather than regarded as problematic. Second, the major problem is identified in terms of the sources, mode of extraction, pattern of expropriation and manner of consumption of the economic surplus. Third, certain socio-political processes general to a fairly wide range of African states, such as the general absence of labour radicality and the occasional embryonic peasant rebellion, can be accommodated, though not adequately explained, in terms of the labour aristocracy thesis. But there are very considerable limitations to which I now turn.

There are three possible interpretations by which the African wage-earning class is viewed as exceptional among the urban masses—as an economic elite, a status elite, and as a political elite. Arrighi and Saul concentrate on the first and last, as outlined above, while a number of sociologists have added the second.[10] It is noteworthy that Lagos is a most convenient location for testing the labour aristocracy thesis in the West African context. Here is one of the longest established wage-earning forces and one of the first to be organised under the umbrella of colonial rule. And currently, minimum wage-rates in the Lagos area stand at £13 per month while in the Western State where the vast majority of the population are farmers (by no means the poorest occupational category in Nigeria) the average income is probably no more than £35 per annum. It is, however, precisely such concentration on objectively measurable criteria such as differential wage-rates which imposes the greatest restraint on the explanatory value of the labour aristocracy hypothesis. Economic return is most certainly of considerable significance, but one needs to go further, looking at other characteristics of the wage-earning population, such as how they respond to their class situation and why they do so.

The nature of the Lagos proletariat
An economic elite?

At first sight, urban wage-earners' minimum income rates throughout the colonial and post-colonial periods appear to have given this class of employees substantial economic benefits over other urban and rural strata. The 1971 minimum wage of £13 per month represented a return several times higher than the average for the population of Western Nigeria as a whole. Further, successive commissions of inquiry into wages and salaries have, in recognition of rises in the cost of living, adjusted the minimum wage rate over time.

But throughout, this has quite emphatically been a *minimum* wage rate calculated to cover the subsistence level of *the individual workers*. No account has been taken of the costs for maintenance of workers' wives and children in a society where, in the past more than at present, wage-earners frequently had two domestic units. Nor did it allow of any unforeseen hazards facing the wage-earner or his family. Because Nigeria, like any other colony, had to be self-supporting, the most profitable extraction of the surplus product of the peasant population partly depended on the cheap construction of a suitable infra-structure, an integral element in which were exceptionally low wage-rates for the small labour force.[11]

Against a background of continuing labour surplus, successive wage commissions had to do no more than periodically raise wage rates in acknowledgement of (though not correspondence with) rises in the cost of living: increases in real wages were considered unnecessary. Throughout the colonial period, the emphasis was on eradicating even the potential for the emergence of rural-urban differentials which might afford the wage-earning class a higher standard of living and improved life-chances by comparison with the peasant class. Rare occasions of labour shortage which allowed concerted industrial action against prevailing wage-rates, such as the Lagos strike of 1897, achieved little more than strengthening the resolve of the administration not to allow similar conditions to recur.[12] Particularly in Nigeria, this was facilitated by the absence of other employers of wage labour whose interests conflicted with those of the administration. In contrast, in certain East African territories, the different labour market demands of the white planter population encouraged wages above subsistence level: in Kenya for example the legal minimum wage acknowledged the requirements of the worker, his family, and their 'obligatory and socially desirable expenditure' such as taxes and school fees.[13] In Nigeria, only on occasions did members of wage commissions consider such generous notions as 'need' and 'minimum living standard' worthy of note: invariably the government did not.

Not only did substantial qualitatively different standards of living for wage-earners fail to emerge during the colonial period: post-independence developments have reinforced government-stipulated wage rates as being the minimal payments necessary to keep unskilled labour in the wage-earning sector rather than returning to the land or entering into the lowest and most unstable reaches of trading. Two examples of official concern will suffice to illustrate this feature. The Morgan Commission of 1964 estimated the minimum cost of living for a young unskilled labourer entering wage employment for the first time, and sufficient to meet the requirements of himself, a wife and a child, at £202 per annum in the Lagos area. In the commission's own words, this minimum cost of living by comparison with prevailing wage levels confirmed that 'most workers are living under conditions of penury'.[14] Despite this, Morgan further acknowledged that implementation of these wage rates would bring economic ruin and so cut the zonal rate for Lagos to £144. Though under pressure from a general strike, the federal government reduced this further to £110 per annum. Seven years later, notwithstanding an equally sympathetic wage commission under Chief Adebo, and despite extreme inflation generated and compounded by the civil war, the attempt to alleviate '*intolerable suffering at or near the bottom of* the wage and salary levels' by raising the minimum daily rate from 7s. 6d. to 10s. was eradicated by inflation in the course of a few months as the prices of foodstuffs and accommodation soared uncontrollably to a new peak.[15]

The central point, then, is that wage and salary rates tell us little if anything unless complemented by data on the cost and standard of living in African urban areas. On the economic plane alone there are clearly very considerable limitations on the value of the labour aristocracy thesis of Arrighi and Saul when applied to the Nigerian case. Since economic standing and political interest-expression of the wage-earning class are intimately related in the thesis, the latter too requires critical examination. Before this, however, I wish to consider briefly the possibility of viewing the workers as a status elite in the urban arena for two reasons. First, status considerations can assuredly (if not to the same degree as economic ones) drive a wedge between wage-earners and other urban groups and the peasantry and thereby influence their political alliances in the national arena. Second, status relationships are of considerable importance for the view outlined below that the Lagos wage-earning class is best seen as a political reference group for the urban masses in general.

A status elite?

A most frequently observed development in African urban status systems involves the acquisition by Africans of Western cultural elements exhibited by the white colonial elite and the educated indigenous elite of the present. Such a search for 'civilised' or 'Westernised' status attributes appears to seep down to the lower reaches of the hierarchy, involves a rejection of rural culture and the creation of a cultural bond between the national elite and members of the employed class.[16] Where the ruling elites have the means whereby such status attributes can be dispensed to the masses, the potential for an appeal to common interests on a political basis is at least present. Of all proponents of the labour aristocracy view, Fanon is most explicit on the importance of this bond between national elite and wage-earning class. He writes of the latter: 'Their way of thinking is already marked in many points by the comparatively well-to-do class, distinguished by technological advances, that they spring from. Here "modern ideas" reign.'[17] A number of sociologists with Fanonist inclinations have laid considerable emphasis on this cultural symbiosis between the two classes.

Such an emphasis on acquiring the artifacts of 'civilised' status cannot, however, be so emphatically applied to the Lagos proletariat. The majority of workers drawn from the Yoruba of the Western State have an extended history of pre-colonial urbanisation;[18] so the dominant elements of the existing cultural system are as appropriate to the modern urban context such as Lagos as they are to the more established ones such as Ibadan. Unlike the majority of African migrant workers drawn from scattered rural villages with little experience of urban conditions, Yoruba wage-earners enter the Lagos arena with substantial cultural resources on which they can freely draw, so that the customary division between 'modern' urban townsmen and 'traditional' rural farmers is, in Lagos, inapplicable.

Certainly there are some status-enhancing features attached to the role of permanent worker, most notably relative stability and security in both public and private employment. But precisely in these factors lies the rub since these create new obligations. Wage-earners frequently form the focal point of urban networks comprised of kinsmen in less fortunate circumstances who constitute a serious drain on whatever financial surplus permanent workers may accumulate. This development of mutual support systems is too well-known to require further expansion here. But one point is of considerable significance. Because relatively secure wage-earners are relied upon by a host of others in marginal unstable employment and yet move quite outside the 'employed' category, the political activity of the wage-earning class and its success or failure in gaining higher wages by collective action has quite direct repercussions for these same urban dwellers, including those quite outside the dependent capitalist mode of production. Not only do these share the benefit of collective action: they closely empathise with whatever interpretations permanent workers place on the activities of management and government, operating autonomously or in concert. And in such an association of interests those marginal to wage-employment are not alone, as indicated below.

On the other hand, a most significant nexus of deference-entitling properties centre on the role of the private entrepreneur, a role taking multifarious forms but one admired by wage-earners and non-wage-earners alike in Lagos society: it is to this position that the majority of workers aspire. Not only prevailing low wages but the nature of factory employment itself indicate to workers that only marginal socio-economic mobility is possible for most. Highly rewarded skilled posts are few in number in the technologically advanced private companies and these are often filled by older workers with specific technical qualifications gained before entering factory employment. Such skills as can be developed on the shop floor are limited to specific tasks and are not easily transferable. By contrast, the realm of the entrepreneur working and living in the surbuban neighbourhoods and communities around Lagos has far greater potential. Through such occupations as transporting, trading and contracting, illiterate and semi-literate men have achieved considerable economic standing and in many instances political power, often from humble origins. A variety of factors, ranging from sheer entrepreneurial expertise to immense good fortune, figure in their personal histories: but the precise combination of influences rarely detracts from the deference and admiration such individuals receive from all quarters. Further, the business organisation of such men (finding new clients, responding to changes in trade, exploiting new opportunities for trade), requires them to live alongside the class of urban poor from which they have emerged. Spurning the aloofness of well-educated industrial managers, bureaucrats, white-collar salary-earners and teachers who live in the more exclusive suburbs, the successful independent man thus acts as a constant reference point for the young worker living alongside him and associating with him or his kinsmen in neighbourhood and community affairs. In these circumstances, the factory worker views wage employment as a means to the end of entrepreneurial activity; over an extended period of time he hopes to save capital and develop skills which will place him on the lower reaches of the entrepreneurial scale.

So, though wage-earners are differentiated from other urban strata on certain criteria, there are other factors which unite these strata. Furthermore, a crucial link is the fact that the economic activity of the entrepreneurial class depends substantially on the wage and salary structure. Collective action by the proletariat to force wage increments will, if successful, promote further opportunities for the individual entrepreneur. For the present, however, the emphasis is on the important sharing of prestige elements by members of the lower strata of Lagos society. Values and sentiments attached to the wide range of entrepreneurial activity promote unity, not division, between those inside and outside the industrial mode of production.

A political elite?

So one arrives, by a somewhat crude deductive process, at the possibility of the Lagos proletariat as a political elite. But the perspective suggested here is markedly different from the Arrighi-Saul formulation whereby the urban proletariat (or at least their representatives), elite and sub-elite constitute a triumvirate of political power dividing between themselves a peasant-produced surplus. In contrast, it is argued that the Lagos proletariat is best viewed as the locally-based political elite of the urban masses, a reference group in political terms for other urban strata who substantially rely on the prevailing wage structure for satisfaction of their own interests in the urban arena, and, furthermore, look to the wage-earning class for expressions of political protest against a highly inegalitarian society. In this sense the Lagos proletariat may be termed 'populist militants': 'militants' in the sense that they have the organisational capacity and resolve to oppose firmly those actions of the ruling groups which they consider to be most iniquitous, 'populist' in that they thus express through their class actions general grass-roots sentiments of strong antagonism to the existing order. The value of this perspective is best judged by reference to class action by the proletariat as such, but there are certain structural considerations which *prima facie* provide background support.

Consider first the distinctive features of the industrial mode of production. In the Lagos arena, the extreme division between those who own the means of production and those who do not has no parallel in the broader system of socio-economic relationships. This division contrasts strongly with relationships in the entrepreneurial realm. In the case of a trading or transporting business involving several dozen workers headed by a self-made entrepreneur, the distinction between 'owner' and 'employee' is viewed primarily as a division of labour and thus does not encourage the growth of class consciousness among the latter directed against the former. The distinctiveness of modern technological production is reinforced by the concentration of private expatriate companies in large industrial estates within the Lagos metropolitan area, each estate having a labour force several thousand strong.

Second, the life-styles and life-chances of the Lagos proletariat are intimately bound up with the strategies and tactics of the national ruling elites in a formally institutionalised manner. This is obviously true of most lower class Nigerians, but of wage-earners it is accurate to an exceptional degree precisely because of the 'minimum wage level'. State intervention can suddenly and substantially affect the buying and saving power of the workers as a whole. In addition, the relatively recent arrival of large-scale expatriate manufacturing oligopolies has further compounded rather than detracted from this clear dependence on the political class. Though such enterprises do frequently pay higher wages than government, nevertheless, the majority of workers begin on the minimum wage level and remain close to it: and since private enterprises invariably match all-round increments stipulated by state decree, private sector employees expect as of right that they will receive similar benefits. So the link from the shop floor to the corridors of national political power has been reinforced by the advent of the new imperialism.

Third, owing to the density of the wage-earning population in Lagos and the slightly higher wages in acknowledgement of the prevailing cost of living, wage increments have substantial repercussions throughout the breadth of Lagos society. Here the economic interests of the labouring class merge with those of others. Such interdependence was most graphically expressed by an illiterate market woman who, on hearing of nearby workers successfully gaining wage increases, commented: 'So our young men have got more money? It is good for now we shall eat.' With the greater part of low wages being spent on rent and footstuffs, landlords and market women are the major beneficiaries: traders, craftsmen and suppliers of other urban services also share such increments, as higher prices immediately follow general wage and salary awards.

Gains made by the working class are, then, shared by an inestimably wider population.

Fourth, there are important historical precedents whereby the proletariat have merged as the stratum most ready to articulate political grievances felt by the urban masses. Of all socio-economic groups created by the colonial situation, the Lagos wage-earners were most immediately and enduringly cast in the role of concerted opposition. Whereas the colonial administration exhibited deep-felt paternalism towards the peasantry and established at least a working relationship with the African middle class, wage-labourers became Nigeria's awkward class in the eyes of administrators, eager to translate their class experience into political insitutions and actions, most notably trade unions and strikes.[19]

Finally, there is the fact that the wage-earning force is composed of 'our young men', i.e. men characterised by their youth, level of education and high expectations. Particularly the Action Group party's policy of free primary education in the Western Region released finances for the secondary education of favoured sons, thus raising simultaneously educational and aspirational levels among Yoruba youths. In turn this creates certain expectations of workers by the predominantly illiterate population: a higher degree of political sophistication is anticipated in consequence of their ability to read newspapers, understand commentaries in English on the radio, converse and organise freely across tribal divisions, and so on. This collective status ascribed by others contributes substantially to the role of the proletariat proper as a reference group on matters of political import: this role is strikingly confirmed when class action does occur on a broad basis.

The Adebo affair

In July 1970 the Federal Military Government established a Wages and Salaries Review Commission under the chairmanship of Chief S. O. Adebo in recognition of the '*intolerable suffering at or near the bottom of* the wage and salary levels'. Following extensive investigation of the national situation spread over several months, an interim cost of living allowance (cola) of 1s. 7d. per day for daily paid workers and £2 per month for all wage and salary earners then earning less than £500 per annum was awarded by the commission. The cola award was to be backdated some nine months, so that workers could expect to receive a bulk sum of two months' wages where they were on the minimum wage level and of two weeks where they fell just within the maximum limit stipulated.[20]

The Adebo award was made with specific reference to workers in public employment but contained the recommendation that private employers should follow suit. For workers and unions in the latter category, much depended on government approval of the award illustrating from the outset the importance of state influence. But although the government immediately approved all increments for both sectors, shortly afterwards the Federal Commissioner for Labour, Chief Enahoro, excluded from compulsory payment those expatriate companies, which, since 1964 (the time of the last all-round wage and salary award) had granted increases to their workers on the basis of the cost of living.

This qualification followed representations from the Nigerian Employers' Consultative Association (NECA) on behalf of mainly West European expatriate concerns, such as the United Africa Group, which had granted such increments previously, by contrast with Lebanese, Indian and Chinese companies which had not. Under the commissioner's new ruling the crucial question revolved around interpretation of past collective agreements between management and house unions, the characteristic form of trade union organisation in the private manufacturing sector. This proved difficult since managements frequently bargained on one basis (such as level of productivity) while house union leaders bargained on another (such as cost of living.) Both sides began to marshal their respective arguments to present to the Ministry of Labour as the final arbiter on whether the increments had to be paid or not by particular companies. A more detailed analysis is available elsewhere of the subsequent sequence of events on the industrial estate of Ikeja north of Lagos which culminated in strike action.[21] In general outline this pattern was followed elsewhere in Lagos. Here a brief summary must suffice. Elected house union officials aimed at settling the dispute within the bounds of institutionalised procedures on which they customarily relied, an approach necessitated by a government decree forbidding industrial action without prior approval from the Ministry itself, an unlikely prospect in such circumstances. Initially workers agreed to follow the official union line of accommodation within the prevailing system despite having their hopes of back-dated pay and overall increases suddenly dashed. After a week or so of prevariacation by both management and government representatives, however, go-slows and strikes in a few factories quickly escalated into widespread strikes and lockouts on all the major Lagos industrial estates. These involved several thousand workers at roughly the same time.

Such improvised and unco-ordinated action did not, however, involve for most workers a complete rejection of the established industrial dispute procedure: it was rather a temporary measure necessitated by immediate exigencies. Once managements had been 'brought to their knees' by cessation of production, they would be only too ready to return to the bargaining table with union representatives and formulate a just settlement. However, a minority of workers who physically attacked managers and plants made a substantial contribution to revealing a central contradiction inherent in Nigeria's neo-colonial status. This was between, on the one hand, the externally-based interests in and control of the resources of industrial production and, on the other, the internally-rooted bases of political authority—in brief, the interests of the international capital oligopolists versus the interests of the indigenous political class.

In varying degrees managers of industrial plants involved in the dispute feared possible destruction of machines, besides being concerned at the huge losses in production resulting from closure. More generally, since all such plants are capital-intensive and wages and salaries form a comparatively small proportion of running costs, the minimisation of possible sources of persistent disruption is a *sine qua non* for all expatriate managers. While they may justify marginal wage increases as a part of total costs to shareholders and directors in Britain, Italy, Japan, etc., profit losses resulting from extended disputes are more difficult to excuse, especially when these result from protests by poorly rewarded workers demanding only slight improvements. This is not of course to say that such increments are lightly given; but against this background larger, successful companies are responsive to 'reasonable' wage demands.

Herein lies a major source of embarrassment for the state, which employs the majority of urban workers. The government cannot oppose such increments where these are justified on the basis of increased productivity and thus an addition to gross national product. But neither is it able to match such increments within the public sector where considerations of size and nature of work are of a quite different order. The political class is, in effect, faced with an insoluble problem: how to legitimate their rule on the basis of looking to the interests of the masses (and with increasing frequency explaining away lack of material improvement on the grounds of the colonial legacy and contemporary neo-imperialist 'conspiracy'), when in real terms Nigerian workers benefit substantially from continued expatriate influence rather than from broadening state intervention. Increasingly the 'credibility gap' widens.

This crucial conflict of inter-elite interests influenced relationships between Lagos managements and workers. Expatriate managers looked to protection from the government when, literally in some cases, under attack from their employees, and also to a speedy pronouncement from the Mininstry of Labour to resolve the dispute. Neither was forthcoming, giving rise to speculation that the government was taking advantage of ongoing conflict between employers and employees in order to demonstrate to the former that, whatever the source of capital, expatriate interests nevertheless have considerable obligations to honour *vis-à-vis* the political class. Faced with such a noncommittal stance on the government side, the unified opposition which the managerial class had temporarily sustained then collapsed, and certain employers granted

the cola (cost of living) award to their workers. A minority managed to continue somewhat desperate delaying tactics until finally the government announced that in view of the hostile reaction to the Enahoro limitation all
workers would receive both backdated pay and the full cola award. In brief,
then, the conflicts surrounding the Adebo affair suggested that a new working
relationship between the political class and the owners of industry was in the
making. During the course of this realignment in the balance of power, workers
and their leaders successfully tapped divisions between the two, and in particular
exploited the vulnerability of their employers, in order to gain the award.

Even in this necessarily brief account, certain ideas suggested above are
demonstrated with some clarity. The relationship between the political class and
the proletariat can serve as the starting point. In itself, it is significant that in this
highly inflationary situation affecting the urban masses as a whole, government
intervention in the form of the Adebo Commission was specifically directed at
wage and salary earners. At least in part this constituted a recognition of the
potential political repercussions from the wage-earning class should no attempt
be made to alleviate increasingly intolerable economic conditions in the urban
arena.

Further, concerted action emerged quickly in all the industrial estates. The
structural considerations which facilitate such escalation have already been
mentioned: once the 'trigger' mechanism (i.e. the designation of certain categories as special cases) was operated, then the conflict spread rapidly. This case
of grass-roots mobilisation is all the more significant in manufacturing industries
on the estates in view of the nature of the 'national' labour movement. Such
federations as claim a national following have limited influence here and their
representatives are viewed by house union leaders and workers alike with some
distrust in that 'they are like the politicians', 'they fear our rulers too much',
'our managers can buy them off with a few pounds'. By comparison, workers
feel they have considerable control over their own elected officials—'Of course
our leaders are good, we workers can get rid of them if they are not', and 'all
presidents fear [annual] elections, for if they do not do a good job they are out'.
Such views were borne out during the Adebo affair, for, though several thousand
workers were engaged in industrial action, no national labour figures approached
the Ikeja estate on the northern boundaries of the capital, though virtually all
are based in Lagos. By comparison, house union leaders were exceptionally
active, involved in a continuous stream of public meetings, negotiations with
managements, and constant discussions on the shop floor and in their own
homes.

But, throughout, the most salient feature to emerge in direct social action and
expressed attitudes was workers' consistent awareness that collective action was

the only means to achieve their particular goals. Most workers interpreted the situation as a clear coalition between managers and political leaders to cheat them of their due rewards, being unaware of the divisions between the elites described above—alliance at the top thus demanded alliance at the bottom. And though some objected to the use of violence and full strike action, the continuance in force of Decree 53 which banned all incitement to strike (initially a wartime measure) was viewed as a further instance of elite 'conspiracy' to deprive workers of their rights. Thus most workers felt quite justified in joining unofficial industrial action until such time as managements were prepared to negotiate with elected union officials.

Above all, the Adebo affair demonstrates how, in view of the political sophistication of local union leaders and the critical responsiveness of their large followings, the established coalition of national political class and expatriate elite proves vulnerable in a crisis situation. House union leaders are fully aware of the high premium placed on continuous production by the employers running capital-intensive plant, of the ease in passing increased production costs on to the consumer, and of the necessity for long-term planning. It is just such considerations upon which measured judgement by union leaders can capitalise when members are sympathetic to the problems of leadership. And during this crisis period, though there was no overall co-ordination, the relationship between leaders and workers in individual enterprises was crucial to the successful outcome. Most workers appreciated that, since industrial action was proscribed by government decree, their leaders would run the risk of imprisonment if they adopted a more forceful line. So where, as one striker expressed it, 'the workers have the power to oppose by themselves', they felt justified in filling the imposed vacuum by unofficial strike action. Once this power had broken the management, then the previous system of negotiation could be resumed with union presidents and their colleagues reassuming their formal role of workers' spokesmen around the bargaining table. This is the pattern which effectively emerged in time. Once management agreed to pay the award, union leaders advised their followers to return to the shop floor, after which the necessary formalisation of new wage-agreements took place.

Thus far, however, this suggests no more than the fact that the Lagos proletariat have a greater propensity for effective political mobilisation than other groups in protection of their own class interests. That they constitute a reference group in political terms for the urban masses can only be shown by more specific analysis of precisely what interests the proletariat represented at this time, directly or indirectly.

Undeniably specific economic interests were the subject at issue. The proletariat has distinctly circumscribed economic interests of which the Adebo award formed part and parcel. In some ways Lagos workers could be said to be acting in protection of distinct sectional interests on the lines of the labour aristocracy thesis. But such a formulation of sectional interests is exceptionally misleading; it assumes that by pressing for material improvement accruing directly to themselves wage-earners are thereby depriving other groups of the same resources which would fall to them in other circumstances. But as indicated above, wage increments successfully fought for by the proletariat are generally viewed as acting to the benefit of others in the Lagos arena; the amount of money circulating there increases substantially to the advantage of the huge heterogeneous petty bourgeois category. Such resources would not be released were it not for the organisational capacity and propensity for political action exhibited by the working class. Their particular economic interests thus complement those of others beyond the wage-earning sector *per se*.

The nature of identification between wage-earners and non-wage-earners is not, however, limited to this plane. It extends into the more ambiguous and nebulous area of social justice. Though this may constitute the most important joining of interests and sentiments of all, one here encounters a most difficult subject of interpretation. One can refer only to expressed attitudes, and this admittedly is a less certain basis on which to found sociological analysis than direct action.

During the course of the Adebo affair, workers pointed to specific instances of social and political injustice in the actions of the ruling elites, most notably in the manipulation of the wage award and the continuation of the government decree against industrial action. But these were viewed as specific grievances illustrative of a much wider and ever-increasing range of social injustices perpetrated by the ruling groups against the masses—achieving their fullest expression in the huge inequalities of wealth and power within Nigerian society as a whole. Of such extreme inegalitarianism wage-earners are acutely aware by virtue of the national elites being primarily Lagos-based. Perceptions of gross inequality are continually reinforced by day-to-day experience of exceptional conspicuous consumption in an urban arena overwhelmingly characterised by the poverty of the majority.

More particularly, such social injustice includes the gradual elimination of workers' rights to personal improvement and, by implication, those of their children. For the individual the combination of low wages, high cost of living and extended family commitments pre-empt any short term possibility of becoming an entrepreneur or educating offspring through secondary school to university. In that many current members of the national bourgeoisie are themselves of humble origin, widespread deference to their abilities and achievements was apparently common in the past.[22] But those in the lower reaches of Lagos society today consider the former are obstructing rather than encouraging others to gain access to the top; all claims by the elite to be acting 'in the interests of the people' are condemned as so much cant, when tribalism, nepotism and corruption are so manifestly the tactics of many in positions of power.

Such views are not, of course, the preserve of workers alone. Shared antipathy to the *status quo* extends throughout the various strata of the urban poor, and takes a number of forms cross-cutting occupational boundaries. During the Adebo crisis, for example, individual workers on strike with insufficient savings to sustain them for an extended period looked to kinsmen and friends beyond the industrial mode of production for support both in the urban and rural areas. This occurred in only a few cases since opposition to their demands crumbled relatively quickly. In other more extended periods of labour withdrawal I recorded cases of practical sympathy by non-wage-earners in the form of loans and also, in the case of petty traders, extended credit for food purchases. (Historically a most noteworthy expression of such solidarity occurred during the 1964 general strike, when the market women of Lagos, always a most potent political force, gave full support to workers' actions by joining in protest marches.)[23]

For the most part, such identification of socio-economic interests occurs in interpersonal situations of limited significance. But such actions do indicate to workers that, when engaged in political protest, they are simultaneously expressing the sentiments of other less organised, less vocal but equally exploited urban dwellers. A Yoruba worker involved in strike action expressed a commonly held view as follows:

This cola award is our right because Adebo gave it to us all. Now management and government are trying to cheat us. This takes place all the time and always it is the *mekunnu* (common people) who suffer while the big guns take all. All *mekunnu* are with us in times like this for we are all oppressed in the same way. Market women and traders rely on our needs for their incomes. When politicians take all the money we suffer together. There can be no justice at all. But the workers have the power to change things. . . .

And on the other side, from a tailor:

These workers must strike for their cola, otherwise they will starve. Money for all *mekunnu* is short. If workers have no money, they don't buy shirts from me or food from the market. And where there is no money there is no improvement. Now I as a tailor have only one voice and it cannot be heard. The workers are different. They can stand and shout together. They must gain their cola . . . because they are numerous in

Lagos. The politicians always ignore the poor; they like money too much. We all hate these big men and the workers are showing it, that's all!

Conclusion

By contrast with the Arrighi–Saul labour aristocracy hypothesis in which the elite, sub-elite and wage-earning class have primary economic interests in common and develop political alliances accordingly, it is suggested here that the Lagos proletariat has the organisational capacity and class consciousness to wrest wage increments from those competing elites which collectively comprise the contemporary Nigerian ruling class. Such material benefits coincide with those of members of other urban strata, but additionally workers' class action has a populist character in that, in the words of T. S. di Tella, 'it is also supported by non-working-class sectors upholding an anti-*status quo* ideology.'[24] In the view of the present writer, a central weakness in the Arrighi–Saul formulation is the assumption that marginal increments in wages and salaries benefit workers alone when, in effect, such increments have repercussions throughout the urban arena and promote economic and political identification between the labour force and non-wage-earners. Wage-earners also express a sense of generalised social injustice not yet compounded by the development of distinct sectional interests which divide the lower strata among themselves. Therefore, should a radical movement from below emerge, social categories who have no established avenues for political protest—such as traders and the lumpenproletariat—will follow those who have. In Lagos this applies above all to the proletariat.

Furthermore, the unambiguously exceptional case of southern Africa apart, the Arrighi–Saul model fails to give weight to the scale and tactics of exploitation *within* the industrial sector as such. Since, according to their argument, wages and salaries are high, the extent of surplus extraction within the industrial mode of production scarcely merits attention. But the root of widespread political protest is the nature of such exploitation, based as it is on minimum wage and salary levels. The upshot of such processes are crucial in promoting identification *between* workers and the peasant class. For example, during the Adebo strikes, comparisons were frequently drawn between the urban protest movement and earlier rural ones, notably the *agbekoya* peasant uprising in Nigeria's Western State: 'What farmers were doing recently, we are doing now'; 'workers, like farmers, have to get better prices by all means'; 'the farmers' uprising and our strikes are one and the same for the *mekunnu* are all one against the rulers'.[25] Such comments indicate that, far from being in opposition to one another, peasantry and proletariat have a similar socio-economic status, that of producing classes equally exploited by surplus expropriators. For those involved, it appears that the mode and degree of exploitation are of less importance than the fact of exploitation itself, as expressed quite simply in the recurrent expression: 'We are all suffering'.

This is not to reject the labour aristocracy thesis in its entirety: it does appear to have considerable explanatory merit when applied to certain East African states where labour demands were such as to require wage rates allowing Africans above-minimum standards of living. The experience of Tanzania in particular, from where Arrighi and Saul draw the greater part of their illustrative material, is certainly a case in point of substantial rural-urban living standard differentials being rooted in the colonial experience.[26] Further, a case could be made for terming the highly-skilled, well-paid West African industrial workers an aristocracy relative to the urban masses as a whole, but only with very substantial modifications of the thesis such as to make it unrecognisable from its present form. This category (it is no more than that and certainly not a group or class), is extremely small and widely dispersed; its members depend on paper qualifications and highly personal contact with influential managers to gain promotion or better salaries. And because of its size and distribution in a multiplicity of public and privately-owned work places, its political significance is negligible.

But when the labour aristocracy thesis is applied to the majority of unskilled and semi-skilled Lagos wage-earners, its explanatory value is slight indeed. There are obviously economic and status differences within these strata, too, but these are of limited significance; with the possible exception of more educated white-collar workers, such distinctions do not appear to influence trade union membership or propensity to industrial action. The influence of such wage differentials is frequently mitigated by non-work considerations. The more a worker receives, the more pressing become demands from kinsmen and acquaintances both in urban and rural areas. Such intricacies cannot be developed here: the central point remains that, though the great majority of workers have broken their links with the peasantry and become wholly reliant on the industrial urban experience (for Arrighi and Saul the definitive indicators of 'optional proletarianisation'), their relationships with the national elites are characterised by hostility and conflict rather than acknowledgement of congruity of essential interests.

More tellingly perhaps, *if* academic debate *is* to be made relevant to socialist goals of development, serious conceptual or empirical shortcomings in the former ill serve the political strategy by directing attention away from important areas of exploitation. To concentrate on the flow of economic surplus from the peasant economy to the urban-industrial sector rather than explore the exploitative nature of both is, as Gavin Williams puts it, 'a classic example of the "displacement" of the "primary contradiction" between the interests of the exploiting and the exploited categories on to a "derived" contradiction between exploited classes.'[27]

In sum, then, Lagos workers are acting in response to a deeply felt sense of exploitation. Throughout the colonial period and a decade of political independence, the wage-earning class has been forced into a substantial degree of accommodation to the prevailing distribution of scarce resources in their society. From time to time, however, in circumstances of exceptional duress—the general strike of 1964 or the Adebo affair of 1971—the existing framework has been unequal to the pressures imposed on it by the underlying contradictions of a neo-colonial economy.

Such protest is not the monopoly of the proletariat, as illustrated by the *agbekoya* movement of Yoruba cocoa-farmers. But by comparison with the peasantry, the wage-earning class is continually involved in developing and refining those organisations which reflect a growing class consciousness determined by their consistently subordinate relationship to the industrial mode of production. A class-based act such as the one described here is not to be seen as an isolated experience under exceptional circumstances. It is, more importantly, a particularly overt manifestation of on-going socio-political processes. In Nigeria, as elsewhere in Africa, the relative absence of prominent and widespread political activity by the proletariat can be too easily explained in terms of apathy, indifference, the absence of class consciousness, and the like. One is reminded most vividly of a costermonger's salutary comment to Henry Mayhew on mid-nineteenth-century England:

> People fancy that when all's quiet that all's stagnating. Propagandism is going on for all that. It's when all's quiet that the seed's a-growing, Republicans and Socialists are pressing their doctrines.[28]

NOTES

1. The research on which this paper is based was financed by a grant made by the Social Science Research Council (UK) to Dr P. C. Lloyd of the University of Sussex, for the study of social stratification among urban Yoruba. I would like to thank Richard Sandbrook, Robin Cohen, John Saul and other members of the Toronto conference for critical comments on an earlier draft of this paper. Responsibility for the views expressed remains, of course, mine alone.

2. Giovanni Arrighi and John S. Saul, 'Socialism and Economic Development in Tropical Africa', *Journal of Modern African Studies*, 6(2), 1968, pp. 141–69.

3. *Ibid.*, 142.

4. *Ibid.*, 149.

5. Giovanni Arrighi, 'International Corporations, Labor Aristocracies and Economic Development in Tropical Africa', in Robert I. Rhodes, *Imperialism and Underdevelopment: A Reader*, Monthly Review Press, 1970, pp. 220–67.

6. Giovanni Arrighi and John S. Saul, 'Nationalism and Revolution in Sub-Saharan Africa', in Ralph Miliband and John Saville, *The Socialist Register*, Merlin Press, 1969, pp. 137–88.

7. *Ibid.*, p. 169.

8. Frantz Fanon, *The Wretched of the Earth*, Penguin, 1967, ch. 2.

9. Arrighi and Saul, 'Socialism and Economic Development . . .', p. 162.

10. Robin Cohen and David Michael in 'The Revolutionary Potential of the African Lumpenproletariat: A Sceptical View', consider the emergence of a Fanonist tradition. *Bulletin of the Institute of Development Studies*, University of Sussex, July 1973.

11. John F. Weeks, 'Wage Policy and the Colonial Legacy—A Comparative Study', *Journal of Modern African Studies*, 9 (3), 1971, pp. 361–87.

12. A. G. Hopkins, 'The Lagos Strike of 1897: An Exploration in Nigerian Labour History', *Past and Present*, 35, 1966, pp. 135–55.

13. Weeks, 'Wage Policy and the Colonial Legacy . . .', pp. 363–71.

14. *Report of the Commission on the Review of Wages, Salaries and Conditions of Service of Junior Employees of the Federation and in Private Establishments* (The Morgan Report), Federal Government of Nigeria, Lagos, 1964.

15. *First Report of the Wages and Salaries Review Commission* (The Adebo Report 1), Federal Ministry of Information, Lagos, 1971. See also, *Second and Final Report of the Wages and Salaries Review Commission* (The Adebo Report 2), Federal Ministry of Information, Lagos, 1971.

16. J. C. Mitchell, *The Kalela Dance*, Manchester University Press, 1956; A. L. Epstein, *Politics in an Urban African Community*, Manchester University Press, 1958; Valdo Pons, *Stanleyville: an African Community under Belgian Administration*, Oxford University Press, 1969.

17. Fanon, *The Wretched of the Earth*, p. 86.

18. Peter C. Lloyd, *Yoruba Land Law*, Oxford University Press, 1962, ch. 3; P. C. Lloyd, B. Awe and A. L. Mabogunje, *The City of Ibadan*, Cambridge University Press, 1967; A. L. Mabogunje, *Urbanisation in Nigeria*, University of London Press, 1968.

19. Arnold Hughes and Robin Cohen, 'Towards the Emergence of a Nigerian Working Class: the Social Identity of the Lagos Labour Force, 1897–1939'

(Occasional Paper, Faculty of Commerce and Social Science, University of Birmingham, Series D, No. 7, 1971); Wogu Ananaba, *The Trade Union Movement in Nigeria*, C. Hurst, 1969.

20. *The Adebo Report* 1, (1971), p. 14.
21. Adrian Peace, 'Industrial Protest in Nigeria', in Emanuel de Kadt and G. P. Williams, *Sociology and Development*, Tavistock Publications, 1974.
22. Peter C. Lloyd, 'Introduction' and 'Class Consciousness among the Yoruba', and Barbara B. Lloyd, 'Education and Family Life in the Development of Class Consciousness among the Yoruba', in Peter C. Lloyd, *The New Elites of Tropical Africa*, Oxford University Press, 1966.
23. Robert Melson, 'Nigerian Politics and the General Strike of 1964', in R. I. Rotberg and A. A. Mazrui, *Protest and Power in Black Africa*, Oxford University Press, 1970.
24. Torcuato di Tella, 'Populism and Reform in Latin America', in Claudio Veliz, *Obstacles to Change in Latin America*, Oxford University Press, 1965. See also Richard Jeffries' paper in the present volume.
25. Gavin Williams, 'Political Consciousness among the Ibadan Poor', in Emanuel de Kadt and G. P. Williams, *Sociology and Development*. See also the forthcoming volume by C. E. F. Beer, based on his 'The Farmer and the State', Ph.D. thesis, University of Ibadan, 1971.
26. G. K. Helleiner, 'Socialism and Economic Development in Tanzania', *Journal of Development Studies*, 8 (2), 1972, pp. 183–204.
27. Gavin Williams, 'The Political Economy of Colonialism and Neo-Colonialism in Nigeria', unpublished paper.
28. Quoted by E. P. Thompson, *The Making of the English Working Class*, Penguin, 1968, p. 781, from Henry Mayhew, *London Labour and the London Poor*, 1862.

The
'Labour Aristocracy'
Thesis Reconsidered

JOHN S. SAUL

The concept of the 'labour aristocracy' as previously employed in literature to facilitate an understanding of Africa's current class structure and revolutionary dynamics has come in for pointed criticism in preceding chapters, particularly that written by Adrian Peace.[1] Since the theoretical work jointly undertaken by Giovanni Arrighi and myself which made use of this term has been singled out in certain of these criticisms it was felt that some brief comment might be in order here.[2] Not by way of self-justification—indeed, it appears that the term as used in that work may do more to conjure up unintended echoes than to clarify the contemporary situation and for that reason the advisability of its continued use is very much open to doubt—but rather to suggest directions which further analysis might take. However, one point should be made clear at the outset: that such analysis must not be isolated from political considerations. The 'structures of domination' in contemporary Africa are such that only *revolutionary* solutions to the development problem seem promising and viable ones. Therefore the main point of interest concerning the role of the working-class (and concerning the trade unions which claim to institutionalise that class's presence in economic and political arenas) must be the extent to which the role so played either facilitates or cuts against a radical challenge to the *status quo* of underdevelopment and neo-colonial domination.

As originally applied to African reality in our earlier essays the concept 'labour aristocracy' had several seeming virtues. To begin with, it fitted neatly into an overall theoretical model designed to highlight the primacy of the contradiction between international capitalism on the one hand, and any given African territory on the other. One historic function of imperial penetration was to force the proletarianisation of sufficient numbers of the indigenous precapitalist population to staff the lower echelons of the colonial state apparatus and to work the extractive and (later) semi-industrial sectors developed by such penetration. A pattern of *migrant-labour*[3] became the characteristic mechanism by which indigenous societies adapted to these imperial demands for labour-power, any 'push from behind' (such as might be caused by a drying-up of access to the means of production in the rural areas because of over-population and/or expansion of holdings/enclosure by a rural capitalist class) being a much less prominent factor. For those Africans who chose to stay more permanently in the wage sector, full proletarianisation was therefore *voluntary* in a way that it was not for the peasant pitch-forked into the wage system in, say, the classic British case.[4] This was true both for 'educated' elements in the state apparatus and for better-paid workers in sectors where international capitalism could afford to pay a sufficiently high wage to encourage the migrant to sever most of his/her ties with a rural base.[5]

The use of the term 'labour aristocracy' underscored important points, therefore. First, it pinpointed the similarity, historically, between the structural position of the 'elites' (and 'sub-elites') in bureaucratic employment *and* of the wage workers, both supplying their labour-power to service imperial exploitation and both having objective grounds for developing a stance of conscious opposition to that pattern.[6] At the same time, it took cognisance of the extent to which material benefit—sufficient, that is, to encourage 'voluntary proletarianisation'—lay at the heart of the choice of roles within the system by bureaucrat and by the better-paid, more stabilised, worker. In this way it highlighted the irony of the fact that these elements were, of indigenous strata, at once the *most exploited* (in the scientific sense) and among the most 'benefited' by the system (in the absence of a very strong national bourgeoisie and certainly as compared with the great mass of semi-proletarianised or wholly rurally-based agriculturalists). And when this social structure became overlaid, as it was increasingly, by a cultural/ideological pattern premised on the centrality of incremental material benefit, rather than on the possibility of systematic transformation of the exploitative linkages with imperialism or with employer, any class (or even national) interest on the part of these urban elements in the promise of such a transformation was even further blurred.

The institutional implications of this situation can be demonstrated in African practice, of course. Not surprisingly, trade unions have come to encapsulate (quite) precisely the bargaining concerns of these strata in their most narrowly 'consumptionist' definition.[7] The 'more privileged' and better organised workers have been encouraged to identify *upwards*—to become partners (albeit the most junior of partners) in the jostling for surpluses among the internationally and domestically powerful (including most prominently in the latter category the elites and sub-elites themselves)—rather than to identify downwards with the even more 'wretched of the earth', the urban marginals and the average inhabitant of the untransformed rural areas.[8] Faced with explaining both the acquiescence of even the proletariat proper in that 'false decolonisation' which the attaining of formal independence generally signified, and the absence of any subsequent root and branch challenge to the *status quo*, it was tempting to view the labour aristocracy, broadly defined, as being sufficiently favoured to have become the domestic guarantors of the neo-colonial solution. And this temptation became all the more seductive when set in opposition to the crude and and unrealistic 'proletarian messianism' which dotted much of the radical literature on Africa at the time of our writing (1967–68).

Thus the term 'labour aristocracy' helped to capture the reality that the most organised and articulate of those proletarianised by the imperial impact appeared to have been 'processed' in such a way as to facilitate their material and cultural identification with the system of neo-colonial domination. But, as Bertel Ollmann has recently emphasised,[9] concepts are both necessary *and* dangerous in scientific work, dangerous particularly in work directed towards a dialectical analysis of real historical processes. Inevitably they freeze a reality which is in flux, and their use may come seriously to distort analysis when this danger is not borne firmly in mind. And as noted, and despite its utility for many purposes, it now seems that the term 'labour aristocracy' as used in our earlier work is particularly prone to producing such unintended consequences.

In the first place, given the direction of developments in the post-colonial period, use of the term begins seriously to distort the image of the 'elites' and 'sub-elites' and to overemphasise the continuing similarity of their structural position to that of the working-class *per se* (even that of the most strategically situated of this working class). For the elites' self-interest in the *status quo* congeals more quickly (hardening, in effect, their 'relative social autonomy and plasticity'[10]), while, at the same time, their control over the state increasingly grants them a different kind of position in the production process than that of merely proletarianised 'employees' of imperial concerns, whether such concerns be private (corporations) or public ('the colonial state'). After independence, the state becomes, in its own right, an instrument for extracting surpluses on their behalf, and the elite's interest much more that of a dominating class—a 'petty bourgeoisie' or 'bureaucratic bourgeoisie'.[11] Even if certain material benefits continue to encourage the upper echelons of the working-class to play the role of junior partners to these indigenous dominants, the workers nonetheless seem more differentiated from, and potentially mobilisable against, such a petty bourgeoisie than the term 'labour aristocracy', used most broadly, might otherwise imply.[12]

Secondly, even if the term were to be applied more narrowly to skilled, relatively well paid, organised workers, it may still freeze reality in a misleading manner, masking—for the analyst and the radical activist—the contingent nature of such workers' vested interests in the *status quo*. Indeed, certain of the criticisms of Arrighi's and my formulations suggest that, unintentionally, we may have done precisely this. For the capacity of the neo-colonial economic system to deliver payoffs is strictly limited in contemporary Africa; in the absence of structural transformation premised on socialist strategies, crises and/or stagnation are inevitable, and, concomitantly, the co-optation of even the most stabilised sections of the working class is that much more difficult. In such circumstances the extent of false consciousness will be less dramatic and some of the classic strengths of the urban working class more evident (e.g. the insight into the capitalist system which is made possible by the experience of exploitation, direct and unmediated, at the work-place; the spirit of collective activity which can parallel, for the proletariat, the centralisation of production following upon some measure of industrialisation). Then too the upper stratum of the workers will be most likely to identify *downwards*,[13] becoming a leading force within a revolutionary alliance of exploited elements in the society.

To be sure, Arrighi and I did not have any illusions about the long-term development potential of peripheral capitalism in contemporary Africa. However, one implication of Adrian Peace's essay is that it has even less viability in the short-term than we supposed; the bankruptcy of this option, in Nigeria at least, is already providing the objective conditions for the radicalisation of all strata of workers in his view, and in particular of the most stabilised of them.[14] In addition, he argues (much more explicitly) that the term 'labour aristocracy' has indeed encouraged analysts, *by definition* as it were, to underestimate the level of consciousness and revolutionary potential of the proletariat proper in contemporary Africa. As should by now be apparent, the seriousness of such a charge cannot be overstated!

Peace's article (immediately preceding) offers evidence that the Nigerian working class has indeed sloughed off any characteristics which might brand it a 'labour aristocracy'. Much of the evidence (with respect both to their level of consciousness and to their actions) is impressive and does begin to underline the possibility that all strata of the working class will 'go the other way'—from co-optation towards revolutionary challenge—and that the 'downward identification' of the more stabilised, better-paid workers can become their dominant characteristic.[15] At the same time, it must be noted that there are also real ambiguities in his evidence. Some of the indications of downward identification which he cites, for example, seem to be as much proof of the existence of a form of patron–client network (dressed out in kinship terms) between a paid worker and his hangers-on as testimony to the forging of revolutionary solidarity. More important, one may doubt the precise extent of the challenge to the *status quo* which is really represented even by such dramatic stirrings. Thus Peace asserts in his article:

> The relationship between the political class and the proletariat can serve as the starting point [of analysis]. In itself, it is significant that in this highly inflationary situation affecting the urban masses as a whole, government intervention was specifically directed at wage and salary earners. At least in part this constituted a recognition of the potential political repercussions from the wage-earning class should no attempt be made to alleviate increasingly intolerable economic conditions in the urban areas.

Here the 'political elite' seems to be moving, as at various subsequent stages of the 'crisis' described by Peace, to pre-empt too radical a dénouement; an implicit bargaining process was underway, in which the peasantry, for example, was virtually unrepresented! It was, of course, fortunate for international capitalism and the Nigerian ruling class that peripheral capitalism retained enough life to deliver the goods to organised workers However, one wishes Peace had addressed himself more formally to questioning how long this kind of system can continue to do so,[16] and how fundamental a challenge the workers' action really represented under the circumstances. Similarly Jeffries, who seeks in his own essay to paint a picture of proletarian radicalism in Ghana which would stand in sharp contrast to the actions and attitudes of any so-called 'labour aristocracy', succeeds primarily in documenting a kind of 'populist' outburst (as he himself terms it), the basic demands of which were ultimately absorbed, with only minimal disruption, into a quite conventional bargaining process. In these cases, to be sure, the working class does seem poised to move leftwards, and the contingent, open-ended character of its potential roles more clearly revealed. But revolutionary classes must be made of even sterner stuff.

A return to 'proletarian messianism' is no answer, therefore. Certainly there are crucial constraints (some of them quite specific to the current African situation) upon the revolutionary spontaneity of a stratum still small and often *relatively* well-placed to advance its immediate interests. Thus Peter Waterman's identification of a crucial missing link in Nigeria itself—a revolutionary ideology and the revolutionary intellectuals who could make it relevant to the working class—seems a sound complementary emphasis.[17] Similarly, in Tanzania, struggle *within* the petty bourgeoisie and the attempt by the more progressive tendency within that stratum to (among other things) mobilise the workers and maximise the likelihood of their making a positive contribution to the country's move towards socialism has been, if anything, even more important than any pressure for radical solutions arising from the working class itself.[18] Furthermore, the importance of the vast mass of the peasantry must continue to be stressed, not merely with reference to Southern Africa where urban marginals and rural dwellers are so crucial to the liberation struggles, but in independent Africa where a new revolutionary alliance must eventually be formed. There is still much to be learned from Fanon (*pace* Jack Woddis)[19]—all the more so when one considers that the stagnation induced by neo-colonialism will not soon allow for the proletarianisation of vast numbers. Ironically, in most African countries only some form of socialism seems likely to have the economic strength to so 'proletarianise' the peasantry as to provide a fully fledged proletarian input to the African future![20]

But having reinforced these points, we must agree that the essence of Peace's critique does stand up: the African working class should not be *prematurely labelled* (as appears to have been the mistake in referring to it in such an evocative term as 'labour aristocracy'). The role of this class is far from being frozen by history or by any internal logic of the current African socio-economic structure. What is needed instead is to concentrate attention upon *the processes* which are at work in specific African settings. This means identifying, analytically, the objective conditions under which a more conservative or a more radical stance towards the neo-colonial situation is likely to be adopted by the working class (and further working out a prognosis for African political economies which specifies the likelihood of their providing such conditions). It also means identifying, politically, the organisational and ideological steps necessary to facilitate the emergence of those subjective conditions which are equally essential to the historical assertion of a revolutionary proletariat, and its alliance with other progressive elements, in contemporary Africa. For ultimately, adequate 'working definitions', concepts which illuminate processes without denaturing them, will best be forged by those engaged in significant practice.

NOTES

1. References to essays by Peace and others are to their papers as originally presented at the Toronto workshop; I have not had the opportunity to review the final drafts submitted for publication or to take account of any possible revisions in them. Moreover, the present 'note' merely summarises the oral comments which I made in discussion at that workshop.
2. These original papers, cited by Peace and dating from 1967/68, now appear as chapters 1 and 2 in Giovanni Arrighi and John S. Saul, *Essays on the Political Economy of Africa*, Monthly Review Press, 1973.
3. Peace's view that 'once a worker enters a factory floor then he is "proletarianised"' seems a vastly over-simplified way of dealing with the pro-

cesses which continue to define the African labour force; Arrighi's 'Labour Supplies in Historical Perspective: A Study of the Proletarianisation of the African Peasantry in Rhodesia', ch.5 in Arrighi and Saul, *Essays . . .*, provides a more subtle approach to the urban-rural continuum in Africa.

4. This is not to ignore the fact that use of *force* (ranging from the imposition of arbitrary and compulsory taxes to much more direct methods) was the predominant element in the colonial strategy for drawing Africans into the labour market, but merely to suggest that a 'migrant-labour' response, with its range of distinctive corollaries, remained the central one. In parts of Southern Africa where sharp encroachment upon African land rights was a more characteristic companion-policy the situation was somewhat different, and the pace of proletarianisation to that extent stepped up (cf. Arrighi, *ibid.*).

5. Arrighi's 'International Corporations, Labour Aristocracies, and Economic Development in Tropical Africa' (ch. 3 in Arrighi and Saul, *Essays . . .*) is particularly suggestive in exploring the calculations of the multinational corporations which encourage them to behave in this manner.

6. Within such a framework, for example, one could attempt to explain 'the relative social autonomy and plasticity' of this elite (noted by Roger Murray in his 'Second Thoughts on Ghana', *New Left Review*, 42(34) Mar.–Apr. 1967, and the logic of the situation which led Cabral to expect some of these elements to 'commit suicide' (in his famous phrase).

7. This was a tendency all the more likely when it is realised that many of the best organised and articulate African trade unions have been, historically, those representing civil servants—the 'bureaucratic bourgeoisie' on the rise, as it were.

8. Nor was it surprising in such circumstances that the encroachment upon trade union autonomy which has been so prominent a feature in independent Africa generally could be interpreted as much more a political counter in a fairly narrowly circumscribed power game than part of any discernible effort to hold the line on wages and further squeeze the working class.

9. Cf. Bertel Ollman, *Alienation: Marx's Conception of Man in Capitalist Society*, Cambridge University Press, 1971, especially Part I.

10. See footnote 6, above.

11. These elements often spill over into the middle levels of the private sector in their activities, of course—and they remain firmly subordinated to imperial interests as well!

12. In addition, such aspects of the assertion of government control over the trade unions as do in fact represent growing class conflict can also be more easily appreciated; cf. footnote 8.

13. Such 'downward identification' would be not only with peasants, but with other, less stabilised, members of the urban work force. One additional weakness of the original concept probably was the tendency which it had to *dichotomise* too schematically that work force as between 'labour aristocrats' and semi-proletarianised elements, rather than merely to emphasise the placing of all workers—whatever the differences between them—*on a continuum* between urban and rural settings and identifications. To approach the situation in the latter manner will, in future, make it easier to analyse *the processes* which affect the emergence of class solidarity—or the reverse.

14. Much of this is implicit; unfortunately Peace does not present clearly the nature of the broader contradictions within the Nigerian political economy, some appreciation of which seems, nonetheless, to premise his argument.

15. It may be that part of the difference in emphasis reflects the differential pace of emergence of contradictions basic to neo-colonial development as between West Africa on the one hand and East and Central Africa (where Arrighi and I carried out our first-hand empirical research) on the other; perhaps it is significant that Sharon Stichter's paper on Kenya given at the Toronto conference argues strongly that the Kenyan organised worker still basically reflects material/cultural attributes of the 'labour aristocracy' syndrome—a term she herself uses to describe them. See Sharon Stichter, 'Trade Unions and the Mau Mau Rebellion in Kenya', Paper to the Toronto Conference, April 1973 (not reproduced in this volume).

16. For example, an assessment of the extent to which it was merely the availability of oil revenues which helped ensure such breathing space in the specific case of Nigeria would have been illuminating.

17. Peter Waterman, 'Communist Theory in the Nigerian Trade Union Movement', *Politics and Society*, 3(2) Spring 1973. A version of this paper was also presented to the Toronto conference.

18. On this subject see Bienefeld's contribution and my own 'African Socialism in One Country: Tanzania' in Arrighi and Saul, *Essays . . .*, ch. 6; for an alternative formulation see Henry Mapolu, 'The Organisation and Participation of Workers in Tanzania', Economics Research Bureau Paper 72.1 (Dar es Salaam: Economic Research Bureau, University of Dar es Salaam, 1972).

19. Cf. Jack Woddis, *New Theories of Revolution*, International Publishers, New York, 1972, ch. 2.

20. I am well aware that this formulation raises a whole host of further, quite basic, questions which simply cannot be dealt with in the space available.

Conclusion

ROBIN COHEN AND RICHARD SANDBROOK

The workers, now that they have their 'independence', do not know where to go from there. For the day after independence is declared the trade unions realise that if their demands were to be expressed they would scandalise the rest of the nation: for the workers are in fact the most favoured section of the population, and represent the most comfortably off fraction of the people . . .

FRANTZ FANON, *The Wretched of the Earth.*

Fanon's trenchant criticism of Africa's supposedly selfish and over-privileged unions and workers has helped to crystallise a left wing orthodoxy concerning the structural position of the better-off wage and salary earners in under-developed countries. It is an orthodoxy that is by no means antithetical to the views of many development economists or indeed African governments, of either a left or right wing political persuasion.

It is nevertheless a viewpoint that has been challenged by several contributions to this volume. Historically, the depiction of workers as a 'favoured section' of the population could hardly be further from the truth. Workers were badly paid and often brutalised by the agents of colonialism and white domination. Nor was wage labour either attractive or 'comfortable', except insofar as the colonial administrations required a small salariat to act in a service capacity to maintain the *pax colonica.* But work on the docks, in the mines, on the railways and on public works was an altogether less enjoyable prospect. It was in these arenas that the first attempts at self-expression and the creation of new organisations em-bodying a corporate workers' identity, emerged.

The contributions to the historical section of this book (Part One) lay emphasis on three major issues. First, the work relationship was a more important determinant of an African worker's social role than has frequently been portrayed. Despite simultaneous attachments to ethnic loyalties, the worker was able, at a very early stage of involvement in wage employment, to conceptualise the character of his exploitation, organise to defend his position and strike to advance or protect his interests. Strike action in particular was undertaken without the help of external influences, but instead was conditioned by the perceived injustices of the day-to-day working conditions and employment relationship. Second, in several cases there does appear to be a growth of a reasonably homogeneous corporate identity which approximates a class consciousness. For a newly emergent proletariat with strong ties to their rural backgrounds this may, at first sight, appear to be a surprising phenomenon. But, even in the comparative experience of industrialised nations, such a development is not unknown. In the United States, Finland and France, researchers have found a greater class consciousness among workers uprooted from an agrarian background than those from an industrial background.[1] Third, worker organisations, though short-lived and sporadic, on occasions managed successfully to mobilise a wide range of workers, from different ethnic backgrounds and with different levels of skill, for a limited tactical end.

While the description of workers' expressions of resentment and resistance to incorporation into a world capitalist market provide an essential corrective to much elite-based African history, we must recognise the severe and deep-seated limitations to these early manifestations of worker consciousness. The degree of consciousness among African workers was never sufficiently intense for the working class to become the 'general representatives' of their societies. As Marx wrote of the classes in nineteenth-century Germany:

> . . . there is lacking the generosity of spirit which identifies itself if only for a moment, with the popular mind, that genius which pushes material force to political power, that revolutionary daring which throws as its adversary the defiant phrase, *I am nothing, and I should be everything.*[2]

The stuff of which African worker protests in the pre-World War Two period was made was usually far more prosaic. Strike action was often localised, and union organisation effective only as long as the grievances which galvanised a sense of dissatisfaction persisted. In Kenya, Stichter reminds us that Asian workers remained apart from struggles by African workers whose racial bonds were congruent with their occupational solidarity. In Dar es Salaam, Iliffe argues that group consciousness among dockworkers can only be linked with a more generalised class consciousness at a much later stage. In the Rhodesias, Turner shows how the separation of the industrial work force from other urban elements meant that effective protest remained confined to the industrial situation. Yet against these examples must be set the rail strike of 1947–48 in French West Africa, described by Allen. Here an obdurate management and colonial administration provoked a display of worker solidarity and popular support that lifted an industrial dispute into the realm of an overt attack on French colonial rule.

One danger present in analysing the long-term significance of such events is the temptation to see them as part of an incremental chain, a logical progression to a more-and-more expansive and pervasive consciousness. A more sophisticated version of the same view is the notion of 'dual consciousness', whereby a surface manifestation of acquiescence by workers is paralleled by a cumulative growth in *latent* consciousness of exploitation, which only needs a 'trigger' to bring it to the surface. As Mann points out in his work on the Western working class, other contradictory processes are at work, including the possibilities either of heavy defeat (which may lead to apathy) or of economistic gains, which may act in a like manner on workers' attitudes.[3] In the African situation, one of the most important mediating factors was the growth of a nationalist movement. African workers and trade unions clearly had interests in harmony with the leaders of the nationalist parties—the colonial state and foreign capital provided a common enemy. On the other hand, there were clear divisions of long-term interests between the nationalist parties and the unions and between different layers in the labour movements. The period of colonial dyarchy meant that the African politicians derived their power more from the legitimacy accorded to them by the colonial authorities, than that won in the streets of the capital cities. Workers in the government services were now confronted by new incumbents occupying the offices of their old enemy, the colonial state. Large foreign firms, on the other hand, appeared in a more benevolent light—they offered more favourable conditions of work and were often prepared to make wage concessions in advance of the government itself. Such alliances between unions and parties as were contracted during the nationalist struggle were superficial and intermittent, and operated at a federated or national union level with little reference to rank and file opinion. Where the politicians were able to reach grass-roots opinion, they did so, for the most part, through the activation of ethnic politics and patron-client networks.

Union support, during the period of the 'transfer of power' became marginal or irrelevant to the practice of government, even if nationalist ideologies were linked with notions of African Socialism or some brand of welfare capitalism. With the coming of political independence, two interrelated tendencies were apparent. First, there was a progressive atrophy of local and mass support for the parties as economic and political power crystallised in the hands of a small group of power wielders. Second, the corporate interests of the wage and salary earners remained or emerged as an intact force, unable to be fully accommodated in the system of rewards established by the independence leadership. In our Introduction to Part Two, we argued that trade unions continue to act as the main institutions for advancing the interests of the wage and salary earners. The militancy that is often displayed by the union leaderships is a testament to the general responsiveness of the top and particularly middle level leaderships to the demands of the rank and file. But one should not be misled into thinking that militant trade unions in Africa are manifestations of the collective will of the workers embodied in a vigorous union democracy. On the contrary, leadership insecurity and factionalism are more potent explanations for the continuing militancy of union officials. Nor, of course, have unions always been effective in providing organisational support for previously unorganised workers. The contributions by Remy and Lubeck show how workers had to rely on their own resources and internally-generated leadership in a moment of industrial crisis.

Despite such failures of union activities as these, however, there are many instances of unions elsewhere in Africa which have continued to function as separate islands of political and economic activity, and which are not directly or completely subordinated to the whims and directions of the independence leadership. Hand-in-hand with the organisational integrity of the unions was a movement, in most, if not all, African countries, by the ruling classes towards an identification with the metropolitan interests they once purported to oppose. As Fanon cynically wrote, the 'innermost vocation [of the nationalist bourgeoisie] seems to be to keep in the running and to be part of the racket'.[4] While few radical authors would dispute that Fanon has given an accurate characterisation of the leadership of those countries in Africa that are actively pursuing a capitalist road to development, the Editors and several contributors to this volume do not believe that workers can convincingly be portrayed as active collaborators in 'the racket'.

One should perhaps first point out an obvious exception to Fanon's dictum in the form of workers living in the white dominated countries of South Africa, Namibia and Rhodesia. Any action undertaken here by black workers could hardly be represented as an act emanating from an over-privileged section of the population. The ratio of white to black wages had until 1970 been consistently worsening for black workers, despite an increasing imbalance within the black wage-earning sector between those who worked in manufacturing and service industries and those employed in the even more poorly remunerated mining and agricultural work forces. In Southern Africa, a labour aristocracy of *white* workers certainly exists—one that has indeed helped to vote the Nationalist Party into power and keep it there, obtaining, in exchange, job protection and disproportionately high rates of remuneration. In the face of this 'oppressor worker class', as Sam Mhlongo describes it,[5] any hopes of proletarian unity are chimerical and there is little doubt that radical action undertaken by black workers will have to form part of a wider racial struggle for black liberation.

A vision of the workers as one element in a partnership to maintain the neo-colonial order would also seem inappropriate to those few countries in Africa—Guinea, Tanzania, Algeria, Guinée-Bissau, possibly Mozambique—where the leadership is itself publicly committed to a socialist path. In these cases the workers' struggle takes on different forms. There is no doubt a continuation of economistic-style demands, but also a qualitative shift to other kinds of demands, moving frequently from governmental consultation with unions, to workers' participation and finally to workers' control of the industries they are employed in. This, then, is the partnership not of a 'racket', but one which, in theory, demands co-operation in the building of a socialist state. In practice, of course, both the trade unions and the governments concerned have been operating under serious constraints and have succeeded in only a limited way in securing the mobilisation of the population as a whole, particularly those living in rural areas.

It is the assumed disjunction of interest between the peasantry and working class that has provided the underpinning to the theory of a labour aristocracy as applied to other African states. This debate has gained our attention earlier and that of our contributors to Part Three, so there is little need to restate the basic points of contention here. It does, however, seem worthwhile to comment briefly on the capacity of the working class to co-operate with other dispossessed segments in the population. The potential of the working class to identify 'downwards', as John Saul calls it, is a matter that will ultimately be tested by real struggles in the real world. There is little doubt that alliances of a kind between market women, lumpen elements, the unemployed, small craftsmen etc., and wage-earners have been forged in the past, as the cases described by Jeffries and Peace demonstrate. But the word 'alliances' suggests a concrete programme and a set of worked out reciprocal trade-offs between the parties to the agreement. This is rarely the case. In only a few instances that we know of—the Sudan, Ethiopia, one section of the Nigerian labour movement—have the trade unions attempted to systematise a broader social programme directed away from immediate grievances and wage demands to such issues as cheaper transport, low-cost housing, social welfare programmes, inequitable tax systems, and so on.

Some might argue that such public posturings are contrived to act as public relations exercises, designed precisely to counteract the image and reality of the egotistical wage-earner. Such a view would be too cynical. Unions are often operating in societies where the avenues and opportunities for the expression of public dissent have increasingly been blocked off by repressive governments.

Workers continue to live in poly-class locales—among their extended kin and relatives with whom they are still involved in bonds of loyalty and obligation. It is from this central datum that the idea of workers as spokesmen, or foci of dissent, springs. The persistence of such ties must lead one to question any depiction of the workers that draws firm parameters between *their* interests and those of a wider urban populace.

At this stage it cannot firmly be asserted that workers will assume a permanent and leading radical role in their societies. Such manifestations that could superficially point in this direction have all indicated that a counter-ideology to that of the ruling classes remains at the level of a loosely-held populist sentiment. Moreover, workers have generally failed to make their own struggles relevant to the vast masses outside the urban areas, and have failed to sustain a radical political alternative once the dust has settled on their immediate sources of grievances. What can be said with certainty is that workers and trade unions are not as totally impotent as some writers imagined, nor, on the other hand, do their demands 'scandalise' many non-wage-earners in the urban areas. Workers in dependent capitalist African societies may not know fully 'where to go'; but they do know where their rulers are going and they have shown that they are not prepared to acquiesce passively in their own exploitation.

NOTES

1. J. C. Leggett, *Class, Race and Labor*, Oxford University Press, 1968; E. Allardt and S. Rokkan, *Mass Politics*, The Free Press, 1968; R. F. Hamilton, *Affluence and the French Workers in the Fourth Republic*, Princeton University Press, 1967. Studies cited by M. Mann, *Consciousness and Action Among the Western Working Class*, Macmillan, 1973, who also notes instances where a rural background produces a deferential and conservative working class.
2. Cited in T. B. Bottomore and M. Rubel, *Karl Marx: Selected Writings in Sociology and Social Philosophy*, Watts and Co., 1956, p. 180.
3. M. Mann, *op. cit.*, pp. 45–7.
4. F. Fanon, *The Wretched of the Earth*, MacGibbon and Kee, 1965, p. 122.
5. S. Mhlongo, 'Black Workers' Strikes in South Africa', *New Left Review*, 83, 1973, p. 49.

Select Bibliography

This bibliography contains all the major secondary sources used by the Editors and contributors to this volume, as well as some additional items of interest. Readers are referred to the notes at the end of each chapter for specialised references and citations.

ADAM, H. *Modernising Racial Domination*, University of California Press, 1971.

AKPALA, A. 'Labour Policies and Practices in Nigeria', *Journal of Industrial Relations*, 13(3), 1971, pp. 274–90.

AKPAN, M. B. 'The African Policy of the Liberian Settlers 1841–1932: A Study in the Native Policy of a Non-Colonial Power in Africa', Ph.D. thesis, Ibadan, 1968.

ALLEN, C. 'African Trade Unionism in Microcosm: The Gambian Labour Movement, 1939–67', in *African Perspectives*, eds. C. H. Allen and R. W. Johnson, Cambridge University Press, 1970.

— 'Unions, Incomes and Development', in *Developmental Trends in Kenya*, Proceedings of a Seminar, Centre of African Studies, University of Edinburgh, 1972, pp. 61–92.

ALLEN, V. L. *Power in Trade Unions: A Study of Their Organization in Great Britain*, Longman, 1954.

— 'The Meaning of the Working Class in Africa', *Journal of Modern African Studies*, 10(2), 1972, pp. 169–89.

AMSDEN, A. H. *International Firms and Labour in Kenya: 1945–1970*, Frank Cass and Co., 1971.

ANANABA, W. *The Trade Union Movement in Nigeria*, C. Hurst, 1969.

ARRIGHI, G. 'International Corporations, Labour Aristocracies and Economic Development in Tropical Africa' in *Imperialism and Underdevelopment*, ed. R. I. Rhodes, Monthly Review Press, 1970.

ARRIGHI, G. and SAUL, J. S. 'Nationalism and Revolution in Sub-Saharan Africa', *The Socialist Register, 1969*, Merlin Press, 1969.

— *Essays on the Political Economy of Africa*, Monthly Review Press, 1973.

BALLARD, J. 'The Porto Novo Incidents of 1923: Politics in the Colonial Era', *Odu*, 2(1), pp. 52–75.

BARBASH, J. *American Unions: Structure, Government and Politics*, Random House, 1967.

BATES, R. H. *Unions, Parties and Political Development: A Study of Mineworkers in Zambia*, Yale University Press, 1971.

BELING, W. A. (ed.) *The Role of Labor in African Nation Building*, Praeger, 1968.

BERG, E. J. 'French West Africa' in *Labor and Economic Development*, ed. W. Galenson, Wiley, 1959.

— 'Backward-Sloping Supply Functions in Dual Economies: the African Case', *The Quarterly Journal of Economics*, 25, 1961.

— 'The Development of a Labour Force in Sub-Saharan Africa', *Economic Development and Cultural Change*, 13, 1965, pp. 394–412.

— 'Urban Real Wages and the Nigerian Trade Union Movement, 1939–1960: A Comment', *Economic Development and Cultural Change*, 17, 1969, pp. 604–17.

BERG, E. J. and BUTLER, J. 'Trade Unions' in *Political Parties and National Integration in Tropical Africa*, eds. J. S. Coleman and C. G. Rosberg, University of California Press, 1964.

BRAUNDI, E. R. and LETTIERI, A. 'The General Strike in Nigeria', *International Socialist Journal*, 1(5–6), 1964, pp. 598–609.

BYL, A. and WHITE, J. 'The End of Backward-Sloping Labour Supply Functions in Dual Economies', *Cahiers Economiques et Sociaux*, 4(2), 1966, pp. 33–42.

CLAYTON, A. and SAVAGE, D. C. *Government and Labour in Kenya: 1895–1963*, Frank Cass and Co., 1974.

CLEGG, I. *Workers' Self-Management in Algeria*, Allen Lane, 1971.

COHEN, R. 'Further Comment on the Kilby/Weeks Debate', *Journal of Developing Areas*, 5, 1971, pp. 155–64.

— 'Class in Africa: Analytical Problems and Perspectives', *The Socialist Register, 1972*, Merlin Press, 1972.

— *Labour and Politics in Nigeria*, Heinemann Educational Books, 1974.

CONWAY, H. E. 'Labour Protest Activity in Sierra Leone', *Labour History*, 15, 1968, pp. 49–63.

COWEN, E. A. *Evolution of Trade Unionism in Ghana*, Ghana TUC, n.d.

DAVIDSON, B. *Which Way Africa?* Penguin, 1964.

DAVIES, I. *African Trade Unions*, Penguin, 1966.

DENZER, LARAY. *Selected Papers of I.T.A. Wallace-Johnson*, Frank Cass and Co., forthcoming.

DEYRUP, F. J. 'Organized Labour and Government in Under-developed Countries: Sources of Conflict', *Industrial and Labor Relations Review*, 12, 1958, pp. 104–12.

DRAKE, ST CLAIR and LACY, L. A. 'Government Versus the Unions: The Sekondi-Takoradi Strike of 1961', in *Politics in Africa: Seven Cases*, ed. G. Carter, Harcourt, Brace and World, 1966.

EPSTEIN, A. L. *Politics in an Urban African Community*, Manchester University Press, 1958.

FANON, F. *The Wretched of the Earth*, Penguin, 1967.

FAWZI, S. ed din. *The Labour Movement in the Sudan 1946–1955*, Oxford University Press, 1959.

FIRST, R. *Power in Africa*, Pantheon, 1970. (UK edition published under the title *The Barrel of the Gun*.)

FRIEDLAND, W. H. 'Paradoxes of African Trade Unionism: Organizational Chaos and Political Potential', *Africa Report*, 10, 1965, pp. 6–13.

— 'Co-operation, Conflict and Conscription: TANU–TFL Relations, 1956–64' in *Transition in African Politics*, eds. J. Butler and A. A. Castagno, Praeger, 1967.

— *Vuta Kamba: The Development of Trade Unions in Tanganyika*, Stanford University Press, 1969.

— 'African Trade Union Studies: Analysis of Two Decades', paper to African Studies Association, Philadelphia, 8–11 November 1972.

FRIEDLAND, W. H. and NELKIN, D. 'African Labor in the Post-Independence Period', paper presented to the African Studies Association Conference, 1967.

GERRITSEN, R. 'The Evolution of the Ghana Trades Union Congress under the Convention Peoples' Party: Toward a Reinterpretation', *Transactions of the Ghana Historical Society*, 1972.

GOLDSTEIN, J. *The Government of British Trade Unions*, Allen and Unwin, 1952.

GOODMAN, S. H. 'Trade Unions and Political Parties: the Case of East Africa', *Economic Development and Cultural Change*, 17(3) ,1969, pp. 338–45.

GRILLO, R. D. 'The Tribal Factor in an East African Trade Union' in *Tradition and Transition in East Africa*, ed. P. H. Gulliver, University of California Press, 1969.

— *African Railwaymen: Solidarity and Opposition in an East African Labour Force*, Cambridge University Press, 1974.

GUTKIND, P. C. W. 'The Emergent African Urban Proletariat', occasional paper Centre for Developing-Area Studies, McGill University, No. 8, 1974.

HART, K. 'Informal Income Opportunities and Urban Employment in Ghana', *Journal of Modern African Studies*, 11(1), 1973, pp. 61–89

HELLEINER, G. K. 'Socialism and Economic Development in Tanzania', *Journal of Development Studies*, 8(2), 1972, pp. 183–204.

HENDERSON, I. 'Wage Earners and Political Protest in Colonial Africa: the Case of the Copperbelt', *African Affairs*, 72 (288), 1973, pp. 288–99.

HILL, P. *The Gold Coast Cocoa Farmer*, Oxford University Press, 1956.

HINCHCLIFFE, K. 'Labour Aristocracy—a Northern Nigerian Case Study', *Journal of Modern African Studies*, 12(1), 1974, pp. 57–67.

HOPKINS, A. G. 'The Lagos Strike of 1897: An Exploration in Nigerian Labour History', *Past and Present*, 35, 1966.

HUGHES, A. and COHEN, R. 'Towards the Emergence of a Nigerian Working Class: The Social Identity of the Lagos Labour Force 1897–1939', occasional paper, Faculty of Commerce and Social Science, University of Birmingham. Series D, 7, 1971.

INTERNATIONAL LABOUR OFFICE. *African Labour Survey*, Geneva, 1962.

IONESCU, G. and GELLNER, E. (eds) *Populism: its Meaning and National Characteristics*, Weidenfeld and Nicholson, 1970.

JOHNS, S. W. 'Trade Union, Political Pressure Group or Mass Movement? The Industrial and Commercial Workers' Union of Africa' in *Protest and Power in Black Africa*, eds. R. I. Rotberg and A. A. Mazrui, Oxford University Press, 1970.

KADALIE, C. *My Life and the ICU*, Frank Cass and Co., 1970. (Edited and with an Introduction by S. Trapido.)

KERR, C., DUNLOP, J. T., HARBISON, F. H. and MYERS, C. A. *Industrialism and Industrial Man*, 2nd edn., Oxford University Press, 1964.

KILBY, P. 'African Labour Productivity Reconsidered', *Economic Journal*, 71, 1961, pp. 273–91.

— 'Industrial Relations and Wage Determination: Failure of the Anglo-Saxon Model', *Journal of Developing Areas*, 1, 1967, pp. 489–520.

— 'A Reply to John F. Weeks' Comment' *Journal of Developing Areas*, 3, 1968, pp. 19–26.

KING, K. 'The Nationalism of Harry Thuku: a Study in the Beginnings of African Politics in Kenya', *Transafrican Journal of History*, 1, 1971, pp. 39–59.

LEDDA, R. 'Social Classes and Political Struggle', *International Socialist Journal*, 4(2), 1967, pp. 560–80.

LENIN, V. I. *What is to be Done?* International Publishers, 1929.

LIPSET, S. M. 'The Political Process in Trade Unions: A Theoretical Statement' in *Freedom & Control in Modern Society*, eds. M. Berger, C. Page and T. Abel, Van Nostrand, 1954.

LUKACS, G. *History and Class Consciousness*, Merlin Press, 1971.

LYND, G. (pseud.) *The Politics of African Trade Unionism*, Praeger, 1968.

MAGRATH, C. P. 'Democracy in Overalls: The Futile Quest for Union Democracy', *Industrial and Labor Relations Review*, 12, 1959, pp. 503–25.

MAPOLU, H. 'The Organization and Participation of Workers in Tanzania', Economic Research Bureau Paper 72.1, University of Dar es Salaam, 1972.

MAYER, P. *Townsmen or Tribesmen*, Oxford University Press, 1961.

MELSON, R. 'Nigerian Politics and the General Strike of 1964' in *Protest and Power in Black Africa*, eds. R. I. Rotberg and A. A. Mazrui, Oxford University Press, 1970.

MERRINGTON, J. 'Theory and Practice in Gramsci's Marxism', *The Socialist Register, 1968*, Merlin Press, 1968.

MEYNAUD, J. and SALAH BEY, A. *Trade Unionism in Africa*, Methuen, 1967.

MILLEN, B. H. *The Political Role of Labor in Developing Countries*, Brookings Institute, 1963.

MORGENTHAU, R. S. *Political Parties in French-Speaking West Africa*, The Clarendon Press, 1967.

MURRAY, R. 'Militarism in Africa', *New Left Review*, 38, 1966, pp. 35–58.

NOVEMBER, A. *L'Evolution du mouvement syndicale en Afrique occidentale*, Mouton, 1965.

NYERERE, J. K. *Freedom and Socialism*, Oxford University Press, 1968.

OJOW, F. I. 'Labour Organizations in Economic Development: A Survey of Some Views', *Eastern African Economic Review*, 2(1), 1970, pp. 23–36.

ORDE BROWNE, G. ST J. *The African Labourer*, Frank Cass and Co., 1967.

ORR, C. A. 'Trade Unionism in Colonial Africa', *Journal of Modern African Studies*, 4(1), 1966, pp. 65–81.

OUSMANE, S. *God's Bits of Wood*, Heinemann Educational Books, 1970.

PEACE, A. J. 'Industrial Protest at Ikeja, Nigeria' in *Sociology and Development*, eds. Emanuel de Kadt and G. P. Williams, Tavistock Publications, 1974.

PEIL, M. *The Ghanaian Factory Worker: Industrial Man in Africa*, Cambridge University Press, 1972.

PFEFFERMAN, G. 'Trade Unions and Politics in French West Africa during the Fourth Republic', *African Affairs*, 66, 1967.

— *Industrial Labor in the Republic of the Senegal*, Praeger, 1968.

PORTER, D. 'Workers' Self-Management: Algeria's Experiment in Radical Democracy', paper presented to the African Studies Association, Los Angeles, 16–19 October 1968.

POUPART, R. *Première esquisse de l'évolution du syndicalisme au Congo*, Brussels, Institut de Sociologie Solray, 1960.

RIMMER, D. 'The New Industrial Relations in Ghana', *Industrial and Labor Relations Review*, 14 (2), 1961, pp. 206–26.

— 'Wage Politics in West Africa', occasional paper, Faculty of Commerce and Social Science, University of Birmingham, 1970.

ROBERTS, B. C. *Labor in the Tropical Countries of the Commonwealth*, Duke University Press, 1964.

ROPER, J. *Labour Problems in West Africa*, Penguin, 1958.

ROSS, A. M. *Trade Union Wage Policy*, University of California Press, 1948.

ROUX, E. *Time Longer than Rope*, University of Wisconsin Press, 1964.

SANDBROOK, R. 'The State and the Development of Trade Unionism' in *Development Administration*, eds. G. Hyden, R. Jackson and J. Okumu, Oxford University Press, 1970.

— 'Patrons, Clients and Unions: The Labour Movement and Political Conflict in Kenya', *Journal of Commonwealth Political Studies*, 16, 1972, pp. 3–27.

— 'The Working Class in the Future of the Third World', *World Politics*, 15(3), 1973.

— *Proletarians and African Capitalism: The Kenyan Case 1962–70*, Cambridge University Press, 1975.

SAUL, J. S. and CLIFFE, L. (eds) *Socialism in Tanzania*, East African Publishing House, 2 vols, 1972.

SCOTT, R. *The Development of Trade Unions in Uganda*, East African Publishing House, 1966.

— 'Trade Unions and Ethnicity in Uganda', *Mawazo*, 1(3), 1968, pp. 42–52.

SEIDMAN, J. 'The Labor Union as an Organisation' in *Industrial Conflict*, ed. A. Kornhauser *et al.* McGraw-Hill, 1954.

SIMONS, R. A. and SIMONS, H. J. *Class and Colour in South Africa 1850–1950*, Penguin, 1969.

SINGH, M. *History of Kenya's Trade Union Movement to 1952*, East African Publishing House, 1969.

SMOCK, D. R. *Conflict and Control in an African Trade Union*, Hoover Institution Press, 1969.

STICHTER, S. 'Trade Unions and the Nationalist Movement in Colonial Kenya', paper presented to the African Studies Association Conference, Philadelphia, 8–11 November 1972.

TAFT, P. *The Structure and Government of Labor Unions*, Harvard University Press, 1966.

TAHA, A.-R. 'The Sudanese Labor Movement: A Study of Labor Unionism in a Developing Society', Ph.D. dissertation, University of California, Los Angeles, 1970.

TANZANIA, Republic of. *Report of the Presidential Commission on the National Union of Tanganyika Workers*, Dar es Salaam, Government Printer, 1967.

— *Proposals of the Tanzanian Government on the Recommendations of the Presiden-*

tial *Commission of Enquiry into the National Union of Tanganyika Workers*, sessional paper 2, Dar es Salaam, Government Printer, 1967.

THOMAS, R. W. 'Forced Labour in British West Africa: The Case of the Northern Territories of the Gold Coast, 1906–27', *Journal of African History*, 14(1), 1973, pp. 79–103.

THOMPSON, E. P. *The Making of the English Working Class*, Penguin, 1968.

THUKU, H. and KING, K. *Harry Thuku: an Autobiography*, Oxford University Press, 1970.

TRAPIDO, S. 'South Africa in a Comparative Study of Industrialization', *Journal of Development Studies*, 7(3), 1971, pp. 309–20.

UNITED STATES GOVERNMENT, *Report of the International Commission of Inquiry into the Existence of Slavery and Forced Labour in the Republic of Liberia*, Washington, Printing Office, 1931.

WARMINGTON, W. A. *A West African Trade Union*, Oxford University Press, 1960.

WARREN, W. M. 'Urban Real Wages and the Nigerian Trade Union Movement, 1939–60', *Economic Development and Cultural Change*, 15(1), 1966, pp. 21–26.

— 'Urban Real Wages and the Nigerian Trade Union Movement, 1939–60: Rejoinder', *Economic Development and Cultural Change*, 17, 1969, pp. 618–33.

WATERMAN, P. 'Towards an Understanding of African Trade Unionism', *Présence Africaine*, 76, 1970.

— 'Communist Theory in the Nigerian Trade Union Movement', *Politics and Society*, 3(2), 1973.

WEEKS, J. F. 'A Comment on Peter Kilby: Industrial Relations and Wage Determination', *Journal of Developing Areas*, 3, 1968, pp. 7–17.

— 'Further Comment on the Kilby/Weeks Debate: An Empirical Rejoinder', *Journal of Developing Areas*, 5, 1971, pp. 165–74.

— 'The Impact of Economic Conditions and Institutional Forces on Urban Wages in Nigeria', *Nigerian Journal of Economic and Social Studies*, 13(3), 1971, pp. 313–39.

WHITELAW, W. E. 'Nairobi Household Survey: Some Preliminary Results', Institute for Development Studies, University of Nairobi, staff paper no. 117, 1971.

WODDIS, J. *Africa: the Lion Awakes*, Lawrence and Wishart, 1959.

ZELNICKER, S. 'Changing Patterns of Trade Unionism: the Zambian Case, 1948–1964', Ph.D. dissertation, University of California, 1970.

Index

abusa, 13
Acra, 185, 270–3 *passim*
Action Group Party (Nigeria), 291
Adebo Wages and Salaries Review Commission, 142, 150–2, 171, 202, 286, 291, 294–6; on corruption and income inequities, 151
African Labour Union (Tanzania), 55–6
African National Congress (ANC, South Africa), 212
African Railway Workers' Trade Union (ARWTU, Northern Rhodesia), 74, 77, 79–86 *passim*; amalgamation with RRAEA, 86–7, 90–1; *see also* Railway African Workers' Union
African Socialism, 240, 313
African Teachers' Union (Kenya), 38
African Workers' Federation (AWF, Kenya), 41–4; alliance with Kenya African Union (KAU), 43
agbekoya: peasant uprising (Nigeria), 298, 300
Agege, 163
Algeria, 315; workers' self-management in, 203
Allen, C. H., 17, 18, 74, 313
Allen, V. L., 134
alternation, theory of, 15–16
Americo-Liberians, and slave labour, 13
ankofone, 13

Ansprenger, Franz, 102
apartheid, 4, 208, 210, 229, 232
aro, 13
Arrighi, Giovanni, 140–2 *passim*, 204, 261, 270, 282–5 *passim*, 298–9, 303, 306; *see also* dependency theory, and labour aristocracy thesis
Arusha Declaration, 203, 249
asafo: cultural influence on Ghanaian railway workers, 268–9
Aujoulat, Dr., 100
'Autonomy', as demand by French West African unions, 103

Bantu Labour (Settlement of Disputes Act), 211; amendment, 232–3
Barthes, Governor-General, 105, 106, 108
Bates, R. H., 197
Béchard, Paul, 108
Bentum, Benjamin, 273–5
Berg, Elliot, 15; and Jeffrey Butler, 18, 74, 99, 118–20 *passim*, 198
Biafra, 201
Bienefeld, M. A., 203
Biney, Pobee, 266–9; ideology of, 267–8
Black Peoples' Convention (South Africa), 219
Busia, Dr. K. A., 183, 184, 191, 274
Buthelezi, Gatsa, 226

'cadre unique': demand by French West African workers, 105–6

Cape Coast, 268

Cape Town: strikes in, 220

Central Bantu Labour Board (South Africa), 211–12

Cissoko, Fily Dabe, 108

class consciousness, forms of, 7–8

Comrie, William, 78

Confédération Française des Travailleurs Chrétiens (CFTC), 100–1, 109

Confédération Générale du Travail (CGT), 100–1, 109

Confédération Générale du Travail 'Africaine' (CGTA), 101–2; formation of, 103–4, 110–17

Confederation of Labour (Ghana), 275

Congo-Brazzaville, 201

Congress Alliance (*Umkonto we Sizwe*, South Africa), 212

Convention People's Party (CPP, Ghana), 185, 262, 264, 267, 268

Conway, H. E., 74

Cordell, E. A., 81

Cornut-Gentille, Bernard, 103, 110

Dar es Salaam, 16, 312; as a port, 51

Davies, Ioan, 199

Democratic Cooperative Development Party (Namibia), 232; see also Ovambo

dependency, Arrighi's theory of, 140, 141; relations between national and international unions, 135, 145

desertion, as protest to labour recruitment, 26

Dia, Mamadou, 110

Diallo, Abdoulaye, 116

Diallo, Seydou, 101

Diallo, Yacine, 108

di Tella, T. S., 298

Dladla, Barney, 226

Dockworkers' and Stevedores' Union (Dar es Salaam), 65–9

Drake, St Clair, 269

'dual consciousness', of workers, 313

Durban, Chamber of Commerce, 224; textiles strike in, 221–6

'economism', as union orientation, 196, 199, 200

Edusei, Krobo, 271

Ejah, Edwin, 189

Elmina, 268

Enahoro, Chief A., 292

Epstein, A. L., 77

Ethiopia, 201, 315

ethnicity, as cleavage in unions, 133–4

Everard, H. B., 90

factionalism, intra-union, 133–4

Fanon, Frantz, 1, 204, 261, 275, 277, 282, 284, 287, 308, 311, 314

Ferrey, Maître André, 107

Fiah, Erika, 67

Finland, 312

Force Ouvrière (FO), 101

France, 312

French Cameroons, 18

French Communist Party (PCF), 100, 109

French West Africa (AOF), 5, 17, 18, 313

Friedland, W. H., 49

Garment Workers' Union (GWU, South Africa), 215, 216, 217

Garvey, Marcus, 67

Ghana, 5, 178, 198, 201, 261, 307; wage employment in, 130

God's Bit of Wood, see under Sembene Ousmane

Gold Coast, 18

Gramsci, Antonio, 203

Griffin, Sir Arthur, 83

Grobbelaar, J. A., 223

Grootfontein, 229

'growth without development', 239

Guardian (London), 197

Guèye, Abbas, 100

Guèye, Abdoulaye, 112

Guèye, Bassirou, 101

Guèye, Lamine, 106, 108, 111

Guinea, 18, 198, 252, 315

Guinée-Bissau, 315

Hamilton, G., 65–7 *passim*, 69

Hatchell, G. W., 63; tribunal award, 64, 65

Hoffman, Judge H. J., 88–9; tribunal award, 89
Horwood, Senator Owen, 226
Houphouët-Boigny, Félix, 110, 112

Ibadan, 163, 164, 287
Ibbotson, Percy, 84
Igala, patronage system in NTC (Zaria), 167–8
Ikeja, 276
Iliffe, John, 16, 17, 312
Indigenisation of Industries Decree (Nigeria), 142
Industrial Commercial Workers' Union (ICWU, Ghana), 189
Industrial Conciliation Act (South Africa), 211, 216
Industrial Relations Act (Ghana, 1958), 264; (1971), 184
internal colonialism, 4
international capitalism, 248, 303, 304, 307; and unions in Africa, 241
Intersyndicale Ouvrière, 100
Issifu, A. M., 100
Ivory Coast, 198

Jeffries, Richard, 198, 201, 204, 307, 315
Johannesburg, 216, 220
Johnson, R. W., 110

Kadalie, Clements, 212
Kaduna, 141, 146
Kamba, millenarian movement among the, 26
Kano, 139, 163; as industrial centre, 140; Hausa capitalists in, 140–2; Islam and union demands in, 158; strike committees in, 140, 150, 153–4, 159
Katilungu, Lawrence, 85, 120
Katutura, 227–8; see also Windhoek
Kavango, labour riot by the, 232
Kawawa, Rashidi, 246, 253
Kenya, 5, 14, 16, 18, 312; African occupational structure, 38–9; Masters and Servants Ordinance (1910), 26; proletarianisation in, 22–7; race and class in, 36; wage employment in, 130

Kenya African Civil Service Association, 38
Kenya African Union (KAU), 43
Kenya Federation of Labour, 19
Kenyatta, Jomo, 43
Kerr, Clark, 1
Kibachia, Chege, 41–3 passim
Kikuyu, Barbers' Association, 40; opposition to taxation and land appropriation, 25
kipande, 30
Koka, Drake, 219
Konkola, Dixon, 80–1, 85–92 passim
Kumasi, 185, 270, 271
Kwa-Zulu, 225–6

labour aristocracy, 2, 3, 241: thesis, 142, 261, 275; critique of, 204, 281–5, 287, 296, 298–300; merits of, 284; reconsidered, 303–8
Lacy, L. A., 269
Lagos, 4, 163; private entrepreneurs in, 288–9; proletariat in, 281–300
Lenin, V. I., 5, 6, 7; on labour aristocracy, 3; on unions and revolutionary consciousness, 199, 200; on workers, 1
Leopold, King of Belgium, 13
Lesotho, 228
Liberia, 13; see also Americo-Liberians
Lugard, Lord, 14
lumpenproletariat, 241, 284

Macharia, Mwangi, 43
Mann, M., 313
Manufacturing and Commercial Allied Workers' Union (MACAWU, Ghana), 189
Mao Tse-tung, 1, 241
Mapolu, Henry, 203
Marx, Karl, 1, 7, 50, 312
marxist, analysis of labour, 5–7 passim
Mathu, Eliud, 41, 42
Meyer, Joe-fio N., 264
Mhlongo, Sam, 314
Michels, Robert, 132, 188
millenarian movements, as opposition to wage labour, 25–6; see also Mumbo cult and Kamba

Mombasa, 31; early strikes in, 33–4; urban work force, 35; urbanisation and strikes, 36–8

Morgan Commission (Nigeria), 286

Morgenthau, Ruth Schachter, 110

Mortimore, Edward, 102

Mozambique, 315

Mtonga, T. M., 88, 89

multinational corporate capitalism, 140, 141; *see also* international capitalism

Mumbo, cult of, 25–6

Municipal African Staff Association, 38

Mvubelo, Lucy, 216

Mwongozo, 251–6 *passim*; *see also* TANU Guidelines

Nairobi, African Taxi Drivers' Union, 40; early African strikes in, 34; urban work force in, 35

Namibia, 2, 4, 197, 207, 210; economy, 227; contract labour in, 227–32; *see also* Ovambo, *omtete uokaholo* and South West Africa

Nangatuuala, Johannes, 232

Natal, 14, 217, 220, 221; Employers' Association, 224–5; Garment Workers' Industrial Union, 221, 223

National Development Corporation (NDC, Tanzania), 248; and workers' councils, 251

National Housing Corporation (Ghana), corruption in, 263, 272

National Liberation Council (NCL, Ghana), 184

National Redemption Council (NRC, Ghana), 189

National Union of Clothing Workers (NUCW, South Africa), 215–17

National Union of Tanganyika Workers (NUTA), 135; establishment of, 246; discontent in, 247; government reaction to report on, 249–56; workers' attitude to, 253

Nationalist Party (South Africa), 223, 314

N'Gom, Jacques, 101

Nigeria, 5, 18, 162, 195, 198, 201, 307; Industrial Arbitration Tribunal in, 196;

wage employment in, 130; workers and social injustice in, 296–8

Nigerian Elements Progressive Union (NEPU), 143, 146, 158

Nigerian Employers' Consultative Association (NECA), 142, 292

Nigerian Tobacco Company (NTC, Zaria), 164–76 *passim*; patron–client relations in, 165–8; union ineffectiveness, 173–4

Nigerian Trade Union Congress (NTUC), 143

Nigerian Workers' Council, 143

Nkomo, Joshua, 85–92 *passim*

Nkrumah, Kwame, 185, 189, 262, 267, 268, 271

Northern Peoples' Congress (NPC, Nigeria), 143, 146

Northern Rhodesia; government support for unions, 91–2

Northey, Governor: labour policy in Kenya, 28

November, Andras, 103

Nyerere, Julius K., 203, 246, 255–6; early views on development, 243–4; on Africanisation, 243, 245; on capitalism in Africa, 242; on Socialism, 241; on workers and TANU Guidelines, 253

occupational status, as cleavage in unions, 133

odalate, 228; *see also* Namibia, contract labour in

Ollman, Bertel, 305

omtete uokaholo, 226–7; *see also* Namibia, contract labour in

Orwell, George, 241

Ousmane, Sembene, 102, 106, 107; *see also God's Bits of Wood*

Ovambo, 226–32 *passim*; *see also* Namibia

Painters' Union (Kenya), 40

Pan African Congress (PAC), 212

Parti Démocratique du Guinée (PDG), 112–13, 116

Peace, Adrian, 74, 163, 202, 204, 303, 306–8 *passim*, 315

peripheral capitalism, 3, 5, 6, 21, 22, 306, 307

Pfefferman, Guy, 102, 103

Pinetown, strikes in, 221

populism, among urban workers, 265–9, 273–7, 289

Pretoria, strikes in, 220

Progress Party (PP, Ghana), relations with TUC, 274–5

'proletarian messianism', 305, 307

Public Utility Transport Corporation (PUTCO, South Africa), 219, 220

Railway African Staff Association (Kenya), 38

Railway African Workers' Union (RAWU, the Rhodesias), 73, 91, 93

Railway Union (Ghana), 261, 266

Rassemblement Démocratique Africain (RDA), 100

Rhodesian Railways Act (1949), 79

Rhodesian Railways African Employees' Association (RRAEA, Southern Rhodesia), 74, 78–9; amalgamation with ARWTU, 85–7, 90–1; *see also* Railway African Workers' Union and Rhodesian Railways African Workers' Union

Rhodesian Railways African Workers' Union, 87

Rhodesias, the, 14, 73, 312

Sarr, Ibrahima, 105, 106, 109

Saul, John, 204, 261, 270, 282–5 *passim*, 298–9, 315; *see also* labour aristocracy thesis

Section Française de l'Internationale Ouvrière (SFIO), 102, 108

Sekondi-Takoradi, 4, 107, 185, 201, 263, 265, 271; communal grievances in, 272; social structure of, 269–72, 275

Senegal, 17

Senghor, Leopold, 106, 108, 111, 112

Shanin, Teodor, 7

Shils, Edward, 265

Sichalwe, John, 79–81 *passim*, 85

Soumah, David, 110, 115

South Africa, 2, 4, 14, 15, 197, 207, 210; African unions in politics in, 212–13;

constraints on African labour, 208–15; exploitation of black workers in, 3; future of black workers' organisation in, 233–5; wage employment in, 130

South African Congress of Trade Unions (SACTU), 212, 213, 215

South West Africa, *see under* Namibia

South West Africa Native Labour Association (SWANLA), 226, 229

Southern Africa, 308; white labour aristocracy in, 314

Stichter, Sharon, 15, 16, 312

Sudan, 201, 315

Suppression of Communism Act (1950, South Africa), 212, 213

Sykes, Wahid Abdul, 65–7 *passim*

Takoradi, *see under* Sekondi-Takoradi

Tandau, A. C. A., 49

Tanganyika African National Union (TANU), 130, 242–3; *Guidelines*, 251–256 *passim*, *see also Mwongozo*; relations with TFL, 242–5

Tanganyika Federation of Labour (TFL), 49, 69; dissolution, 245–6; relations with TANU, 242–5

Tanzania, 5, 6, 197, 199, 203, 204, 299, 307, 315; government and union relations, 244–5; socialism in, 240–1; soldiers' mutiny, as demand for Africanisation, 245; wage employment in, 130; workers' committees in, 203, 247–8

Tarkwa, 185

Teivi, A. K., 189

'téléguidage', as union control by parties, 18, 99; critique of, 117–18

Tema, 272

Tettegah, John, 189, 264

Thiaw, Abdoulaye, 112

Thika, Native Drivers' Association, 40; strikes in, 32–3

Thompson, E. P., 17, 50, 159

Thuku, Harry, 30

Tiv, 167–8, 175; *see also* patron–client relations in NTC (Zaria)

Touré, Sekou, 104, 110; as union secretary,

Touré, Sekou—*contd.*
101; and demand for 'autonomy',
114–115; as popular union leader,
116
Trade Union Congress (TUC, Ghana);
abolition by Busia government, 183; and
the CPP, 264–5, NLC, 274, PP, 274–5;
ideology and politics, 188; National
Executive Council, 186–8; organisational structure, 179–81; under Bentum,
273–5; union leadership and decision
making, 181–8; workers' perception of
unions and leaders, 190–1
Trade Union Council of South Africa
(TUCSA), 213, 214, 218
trade unions, and revolutionary consciousness, 199; relations with post-colonial
governments, 195
tribalism, *see under* ethnicity
Tudun Wada, 163
Turner, Arthur, 16, 17, 312

Uganda, 24, 252
union democracy, 132
Union Général des Travailleurs d'Afrique
Noire (UGTAN), 101
United Gold Coast Convention (UGCC),
267

United Labour Congress (ULC, Nigeria),
140, 143
United Party (Ghana), 262
United States of America, 312

Voipio, Rauha, 228, 231

Walvis Bay, 227–8
Waterman, Peter, 307
Welensky, Roy, 80
West, Dr E. M. B., 79, 84
What is to be Done?; *see under* Lenin
Williams, Gavin, 300
Wilson, Mr Justice, 60
Windhoek, 227, 230, 231; *see also* Katu-
tura
Witwatersrand, 215
Woddis, Jack, 308
Wolf, Eric, 165, 167
Worsley, Peter, 265
Wretched of the Earth; *see under* Fanon

Zambia, 5, 196; Mineworkers' Union,
197; wage employment in, 130
Zaria, 163, 164, 168, 170, 171, 176;
patron-client relations in, 165; *see also*
NTC
Zuccarelli, François, 103
Zukas, Simon ber, 85